COVERING
THE BODY

COVERING THE BODY

The Kennedy
Assassination,
the Media, and
the Shaping of
Collective
Memory

BARBIE ZELIZER

The University of Chicago Press / Chicago and London

Barbie Zelizer, a former reporter for the Reuters News Agency and the London *Financial Times*, is assistant professor of rhetoric and communication at Temple University.

The University of Chicago Press, Chicago 60637
The University of Chicago Press, Ltd., London
© 1992 by The University of Chicago
All rights reserved. Published 1992
Printed in the United States of America

01 00 99 98 97 96 95 94 93 92   5 4 3 2 1

ISBN (cloth): 0-226-97970-9
ISBN (paper): 0-226-97971-7

Parts of chapter 3 are adapted from "Achieving Journalistic Authority through Narrative," *Critical Studies in Mass Communication* 7, no. 4 (December 1990): 366–76, and are reprinted by permission of the Speech Communication Association. Some of the material in chapters 8 and 11 appeared in an article, "De l'Exercice illégal de l'histoire: Amateurs, journalistes, historiens et l'assassinat de J. F. Kennedy," *Hermes* no. 8/9, "Frontières en Mouvement" (Spring 1991). Paris, CNRS Press.

Library of Congress Cataloging-in-Publication Data

Zelizer, Barbie.
    Covering the body : the Kennedy assassination, the media, and the shaping of collective memory / Barbie Zelizer.
       p.   cm.
    Originally presented as the author's thesis (Ph.D.)—Annenberg School for Communication, University of Pennsylvania, 1990.
    Includes bibliographical references (p.   ) and index.
    ISBN 0-226-97970-9. — ISBN 0-226-97971-7 (pbk.)
    1. Kennedy, John F. (John Fitzgerald), 1917–1963—Assassination.
  2. Journalism—United States—History—20th century. I. Title.
E842.9.Z45 1992
364.1'524—dc20
                                            92-5478
                                            CIP

Contents

          Authority   189

          Epilogue: Beyond Journalistic Authority to the
          Shaping of Collective Memory   201

          Notes   215
          Bibliography   267
          Index   291

Preface and Acknowledgments

This did not begin as a book about Kennedy or Kennedy's death. It began as an exploration of journalistic authority. As a reporter, I had often wondered about the ways in which half-jumbled wisps of conversation became full-blown news stories that were told with a knowing and certain voice. As I made my way out of journalism and into academia, I carried that curiosity with me, making it the topic of my doctoral dissertation and, in turn, the focus of this book. It was, in the words of the fairy tale, a case of the emperor's new clothes. The ability of journalists to set themselves up as all-knowing observers of the real world was everywhere, but it was nowhere to be seen.

So I set out to uncover it, not realizing that the story of the media and the death of John F. Kennedy was in many ways bigger than the tale I hoped to capture. Along the way, I encountered numerous individuals whose concern for the story I used as data was longstanding, sincere, and well-founded. They influenced the nuances of my telling this particular tale in untold ways. The arrival of Oliver Stone's movie, *JFK*, in December of 1991 introduced yet another unexpected turn. It had me sitting frantically as this book went to galleys with my *TV Guide* in one hand, laptop computer in the other, gauging the surge of interest in the assassination story. That effort resulted in the epilogue, which addresses directly the turns introduced to the assassination story by Oliver Stone's film. While requiring me to refocus some of the issues I had been discussing, all of these developments helped legitimate my own examination of journalistic authority and collective memory.

Covering the Body owes its existence to many people. At the University of Pennsylvania, Larry Gross was not only helpful but instrumental in shaping both the study and the manuscript that resulted. I remain deeply indebted to him for his everpresent support, critical eye, humor, and friendship. Other teachers at Penn, Roger Abrahams, Charles Bosk, Carolyn Marvin, and Joseph Turow, offered encouragement, intellectual breadth, and criticism. Charles Bosk played a critical role in convincing me to examine the Kennedy assassination, and Roger Abrahams injected me with regular doses of inspiration. During various stages of the writing of this book, John Goldsmith, Kathleen Hall Jamieson, Phyllis Kaniss, John Nerone, Michael Schudson, Eviatar Zerubavel, and Yael Zerubavel provided insightful commentary. For giving technical assistance and helping me procure documents related to the assassination, I thank John Massi and Adele Chatelain at the Annenberg School for Communication, Jim Cedrone of the Kennedy Library, the Vanderbilt Television Archives, Andrew and Linda Winiarczyk of the Last Hurrah Bookshop, KTRK-TV of Houston, and Gilbert Cates Productions, Inc. The Annenberg School for Communication provided much-needed funding.

Fellow students at the Annenberg School—particularly Victor Caldarola, Colleen Davis, Amy Jordan, Pamela Sankar, Marsha Siefert, Lois Silverman, and Diane Zimmerman Umble—proved to be true friends and tactful critics. The Department of Rhetoric and Communication at Temple University, and particularly Tricia Jones, gave essential support, while Sari Thomas and Marsha Witten offered helpful suggestions about parts of the manuscript. John Tryneski of the University of Chicago Press supported the project with enthusiasm, and Janice Fisher edited with a flourish. For helping me maintain a life outside of the academy, I particularly thank Ellen and Perry Berman and Anita Spiegel and Bill Lautenberger. Debbie Graham and Sharin Zar extended their talents to provide emergency childcare.

And in the end it comes to family. My father, Cody Zelizer, died while this manuscript was in progress, and my youngest child, Gideon, was born. They gave this project a perspective that made it both more and less important than it might otherwise have been. My sister Judy Shifrin creatively translated the book's central theme into artwork that now thematizes my study. I am also thankful for three very special people who experienced the direct effect of this book on their daily lives, and not always in enjoyable ways—my mother, Dorothy Zelizer, and my two older children, Noa and Jonathan. They lent their support, their hugs, and their drawings and poems even when they weren't sure of this project's final destination. But above all, this book owes its existence to the one person who understood its scope in some ways better than myself—my husband, Michael Glick. In serving as reader, anchor, courier, critic, and friend, he deserves much more than a note of acknowledgment. I dedicate this book to him.

ONE

Introduction: Narrative, Collective
Memory, and Journalistic Authority

Common sense is quite wrong in thinking that the past is fixed, immutable, invariable, as against the ever-changing flux of the present. On the contrary, at least within our own consciousness, the past is malleable and flexible, constantly changing as our recollection reinterprets and reexplains what has happened.[1]

This is the story of the assassination of John F. Kennedy as American journalists have retold it both to the public and to themselves. For most adult Americans, the memory of the events of 22 November 1963 is ineradicable and penetrating. For American journalists, the day had an added significance. Those assigned to "cover the body"— the journalistic term for following the president wherever he went— were simply doing their job, patrolling a journalistic beat. Yet for those on assignment in Dallas that day, the term took on morbid overtones. "Covering the body" became a code name for covering Kennedy's corpse, a literal indicator for events that even today rattle the memories of most Americans.

The positioning of journalists and the U.S. media within those memories is the topic of this book. What made them into credible, authoritative, and preferred spokespersons of the assassination story is a tale with many turns and nuances. It derives from a popular regard for journalists that assumes their straightforward promotion as authoritative and credible observers of the "real world." Yet from discussions about Watergate to recollections of the Spanish-American War or the 1937 Hindenburg disaster, journalism is cluttered with practices that should cause people to question reporters' right to tell the news. Few people consider what advantages make the media better equipped to offer a "preferred" version of reality. The boundaries of their cultural authority have therefore remained unexplored, largely because few people have bothered to question them.

Through an examination of journalists' narratives about the Kennedy assassination, this study explores how journalists have established themselves as the story's authoritative spokespersons. Journalists have made the assassination story as much a tale about themselves as about the thirty-fifth president of the United States, thus strengthening their position as cultural authorities concerning events of the "real world."

What Is Cultural Authority?

Understanding how the media have established themselves as authoritative spokespersons for the assassination story depends on a more general understanding of the workings of cultural authority. Among academics, the particular set of qualities that invests certain people with more authority than others has long generated debates about domination, power, and expertise. This book assumes that authority acts as a source of codified knowledge, guiding individuals in appropriate standards of action. Emile Durkheim's notion of collective representations, as a means by which people structure collective ways of understanding the world, suggests that authority is engendered by individuals who give it meaning through representational form.[2] Folklorists, anthropologists, and sociologists have all drawn upon this view to regard authority as a ritual act binding members of communities together. Victor Turner sees rituals as moments for individuals to question authority and consolidate themselves into communities.[3] Roger Abrahams regards cultural performances of all sorts as a means of internal group authentication.[4] Anthony Giddens presents a nonlinear view of the workings of authority, maintaining that notions about authority are codified, then fed back to their codifiers, who codify them yet again.[5]

The assumption here is that authority creates community among people who share like notions about it. Such a premise posits the workings of authority within the realm of communicative practice. James Carey supports a cultural, or ritual, view of communication as "the sacred ceremony which draws persons together in fellowship and commonality . . . through sharing, participation, association, fellowship and the possession of a common faith."[6] Periods of marked intensification give community members a way to question and ratify basic notions about authority. Authority thereby becomes a construct of community, functioning as the stuff that keeps communities together. This book adopts such a view of cultural authority to explore how—and why—groups like journalists would be interested in putting forward their own versions of public events.

In other words, authority is important not only for its effect on publics but also for its effect on communicators. Cultural authority helps journalists use their interpretations of public events to shape themselves into authoritative communities. This is particularly relevant when so many groups—journalists, politicians, historians—use constructions of reality to mold external events into preferred forms. As an implicit feature of public discourse, then, the workings of authority have made it possible for those who have retold the assassination story to shape the American public's memories of that event.

The Interplay of Authority and Memory

Much of what we remember as the assassination story has emerged at different points in the tale's retelling, because authority is shaped at many points in time. Patterns of authority are worked out in collective memory, where they take on specific preferred forms that are determined by their retellers. In G. H. Mead's view, collective memory helps people use the past to give meaning to the present and to exercise the full spread of power across time and space.[7] Using memory as an "instrument of reconfiguration" rather than retrieval has been most effectively discussed by Maurice Halbwachs.[8] According to Halbwachs, collective memory constitutes memories of a shared past by those who experienced it and whose conscious and strategic efforts have kept it alive. Collective memory reflects a group's codified knowledge over time about what is important, preferred, and appropriate.

In recent years, the issue of collective memory has drawn attention in various academic quarters. In geography, Ralph Lowenthal discussed the workings of memory in public domains.[9] In history and criticism, Barbara Kruger and Phil Mariani brought together a collection of essays that addressed the interrelationship between history and memory.[10] In cultural studies, the Birmingham Center for Contemporary Cultural Studies issued its well-received book, *Making Histories*.[11] George Lipsitz wrote *Time Passages*, a book that addressed the workings of popular memory and popular culture from an American studies perspective.[12] Another collection of essays, *Collective Remembering*, brought together research from social psychology, anthropology, communication, folklore, and sociology.[13] Pierre Nora's meticulous tracing of France's national memory addressed many of the same issues from a French perspective, while Michael Kammen explored the interplay of tradition and collective memory from an American point of view.[14] And in 1989 the journals *Communication, Representations,* and *Journal of American History* all devoted special issues to the idea of social, or collective, memory.[15]

While these efforts regard memory as an implicitly social activity, they also see it as not necessarily consensual. As communication scholars John Nerone and Ellen Wartella maintain, contest is positioned at the heart of all communicative practice invested in retelling the past.[16] Considerations of collective memory are fundamentally interested in the contest surrounding the authoritative view of the events such memories represent.

Collective memory is important for discussions of cultural authority because it allows for the emergence of patterns of authority over time. As the vessel of codified knowledge across time and space, collective memory reflects a reshaping of the practices through which people construct themselves as cultural authorities. In the case of the Kennedy assassination, this suggests that different groups, bearing their own agendas, have promoted different, and possibly competitive, versions of the events of President Kennedy's death since it occurred.

The Kennedy Assassination: A Critical Incident in Collective Memory

Critical incidents are what Claude Lévi-Strauss once called "hot moments," moments or events through which a society or culture assesses its significance.[17] Coining the term in a discussion of decision-making processes in media organizations, George Gerbner allowed that critical incidents give members of organizations a way to defuse challenges to recognized authority.[18] When employed discursively, the term *critical incidents* refers to those moments by means of which people air, challenge, and negotiate their own standards of action. In this view, collective memories pivot on discussions of some kind of critical incident. For journalists, critical incidents suggest a way of attending to moments that are important to the continued well-being of the journalistic community. Critical incidents uphold the importance of discourse and narrative in shaping the community over time.

The Kennedy assassination can be seen as a critical incident for the U.S. media. It was a turning point in the evolution of American journalistic practice not only because it called for the rapid relay of information during a time of crisis, but also because it legitimated televised journalism as a mediator of national public experience.[19] The immediate demand for journalistic expertise and eyewitness testimony that characterized this event caused the public to rely on journalists for its clarification. Journalists went beyond familiar practices to cover the events of President Kennedy's death, improvising within the configuration of different circumstances and new technologies to meet ongoing demands for information. Ever since, journalists have used the event as a benchmark in their discussions of appropriate journalistic practice.[20] In other words, the Kennedy assassination has evolved into a critical incident against which journalists test their own standards of action. They use it to discuss, challenge, and negotiate the boundaries of appropriate journalistic practice.

Central to retellings of the events of Kennedy's death are pictorial repetitions of such key images as the shootings of Kennedy and of Lee Harvey Oswald, Caroline Kennedy and her mother kneeling beside the president's coffin, John-John Kennedy's respectful salute, the eternal flame, and the riderless horse. These moments—captured by the media in various forms—have been replayed as markers of the nation's collective memory each time the story of Kennedy's death is recounted. Narrative brings these images together in meaningful ways, lending unity, temporal and spatial sequencing, and form. Narratives that persist today bear collective authority.[21] Equally important, they have lent stature to the people who inscribed them in collective consciousness. As Ulric Neisser observed in his discussion of "flashbulb memories": "Memories become flashbulbs primarily through the significance that is attached to them afterwards: Later that day, the next day, and in subsequent months and years. What requires explanation is the long endurance (of the memory)."[22] Remembering the assassination, and shaping how the public remembers it, have thus come to be regarded by American journalists as strategic accomplishments.

The Workings of Journalistic Authority

The strategic nature of journalists' memories of the Kennedy assassination, however, has not been readily explored in studies of journalism. Rather than promote considerations of what the event meant to journalists, scholars have tended to approach the coverage of Kennedy's death as what might be considered a study in transmission. They have considered how many people knew what, how long it took them to learn it, and from whom they learned it. The first such study was a collection edited by Bradley Greenberg and Edwin Parker in 1965;[23] a similar perspective has been adopted in other studies of the assassination coverage.[24]

Toward an Alternative View of Journalism

In large part the focus on transmission of the story has derived from two prevalent notions about journalistic practice. These concern the stature of journalism as a profession, and the relevance of authority for an understanding of news-making practices.

Examining journalism as a profession has generally yielded an unclear picture. Academics have tended to use the notion of "profession" to organize reporters conceptually into communities with requisite bodies of codified knowledge.[25] Defined as an ideological orientation toward work that is realized via skill, autonomy, training and education, testing of competence, organization, codes of conduct, licensing and service orientation, the profession is seen as giving journalists a sense of community.[26] Yet unlike classically defined professions such as medicine or law, journalism has not required the trappings of professionalism: many journalists do not readily read journalism textbooks, attend journalism schools, or enroll in training programs.[27] Codes of journalistic behavior are not written down, codes of ethics remain largely nonexistent, and most journalists routinely reject licensing procedures.[28] Journalists are also indifferent to professional associations, and the largest professional association—the Society of Professional Journalists/Sigma Delta Chi—claims as members only 17 percent of American journalists.[29] Journalists act as members of a professional collective in only a limited sense. As one researcher has suggested, "the modern journalist is *of* a profession but not *in* one . . . the institutional forms of professionalism likely will always elude the journalist."[30]

Prevailing views of journalistic authority yield a similarly unclear picture. Largely compounding the error discussed by Carey, communication researchers have envisioned authority as an act of transmission, or an effect on others. Journalistic authority has been alternately seen as an effect on audiences, on organizational actors, or on wide-ranging sociocultural systems. The first view conceptualizes journalistic authority as a one-on-one correlation between "what journalists say" and "what audiences believe," with journalistic authority—or "credibility"—becoming a function of the belief it induces in audiences.[31] The second view, which dominates in organizational studies, regards journalistic authority as a set of strategies by which participants compete for power within news organizations.[32] Derived from Warren Breed's classic study of social control in the newsroom,[33] it sees journalists engaged in strategic behavior to gain power over others—managing time, imposing predictable frames for organizing resources, mitigating interpersonal conflict, routinizing or engaging in purposive behavior.[34] The final view regards journalistic authority as a social construction in order to address larger sociocultural questions of power and domination.[35] "Authority" is taken as a marker for the power behind the construction of news, and emphasis is on the cooptation of external political or economic issues of power within news discourse.[36] Each view relies on notions of linearity, influence, and effect in conceptualizing journalistic authority.

Both the emphasis on professional communities and the view of authority in terms of effect have made it difficult to consider collective aspects of journalistic practice. By echoing what Carey called a "transmission" view of communication, existing views of journalistic authority emphasize its perceived effect on others and tailor its exploration to notions of influence. We are led to understand the assassination story through its effect on audiences, while losing any consideration of authority's function as collective knowledge or as a guide for journalistic practice, particularly through assassination retellings.

Similarly, viewing journalists as members of a professional community overlooks the less formal ways in which journalists develop a sense of their own collectivity. Rather than look at reporters as "unsuccessful professionals,"[37] for instance, we might ask how journalists actively shape themselves into a community. The existence of such a collectivity is hinted at in Robert Park's notions about news as a form of knowledge;[38] in Dean O'Brien's examination of journalistic pseudo-environments;[39] and in Michael Schudson's consideration of the ways in which knowledge is shaped by and among journalists.[40] More generally, sociological studies of news organizations maintain that most reporters possess a distinct sense of their own collectivity; their high degree of specialization and expertise favors horizontal management over vertical, collegial authority over hierarchical.[41] While reporters are rarely informed of rules or boundaries of action by their superiors, their internalization of a collective sense of appropriateness suggests an extended degree of "creative autonomy"[42] and the existence of a shared collective or institutional frame that exists beyond specific news organizations. In other words, journalists actively engage in cultural discussion and argumentation and accomplish work by discussing with other reporters the issues that are important to them. Professions, then, may not be the most effective context for envisioning journalistic collectivity, and models which view journalists solely as members of a profession may offer a restrictive view of journalistic practice, professionalism, and communities—and, hence, authority.

These points suggest that journalists generate a sense of their own collectivity in less formalized ways than those offered by professional codes and in less linear ways than those offered by notions of effect.

This brings us to a working definition of *journalistic authority*. Conceptualized as "the ability of journalists to promote themselves as authoritative and credible spokespersons of 'real-life' events," journalistic authority is seen as the specific case of cultural authority by which journalists determine their right to present authoritative versions of the world. Journalistic authority is situated in journalistic practice, where reporters have long had access to technological, narrative, and institutional circumstances that support their ready circulation of preferred versions of "real-life" activities. Much journalistic practice constitutes "undercover work" of a sort: journalists present events through explanatory frames that construct reality but do not reveal the secrets, sources, or methods of such a process.[43] Audiences tend to protest this only when they dislike what is being portrayed. Because the selection, formation, and presentation of events ultimately hinge on how journalists decide to construct the news in one way and not another, acting appropriately "as journalists" depends on reporters' ability to make use of codes of collective knowledge. Sandwiched between the audience and the event being reported, reporters are able to construct what they see as preferred and strategically important through some assumption of authority for the stories they tell. As the following chapters will show, such an assumption is instrumental in helping reporters put forward their own versions of the assassination tale.

Journalists as an Interpretive Community

The idea of the interpretive community has drawn interest in areas beyond studies of the media. Dell Hymes sees the "speech community" as a group united by its shared interpretations of reality.[44] Stanley Fish defines interpretive communities as those which produce texts and "determine the shape of what is read."[45] Scholarship in anthropology and folklore holds that interpretive communities display patterns of authority and communication in their dealings with each other.[46] All of these notions bear some relation to the concept proposed by Robert Bellah and his colleagues of "communities of memory"—groups that use shared interpretations over time. "In order not to forget [their] past, [communities become] involved in retelling constitutive narratives."[47]

What does this imply for journalists retelling the story of the assassination? Most studies of journalistic practice have tended to understate the role of narrative in shaping journalistic collectivity.[48] Narrative practices are infrequently mentioned in academic studies of the media, despite the fact that narrative strategies, distinctions between fact and fiction, stylistic determinants, and issues of presentation all concern journalists in their renditions of public events, like those surrounding Kennedy's death. How journalists have ascribed to themselves the power of interpretation, the ways in which certain interpretations have carried across news organizations, and how reporters have marginalized other groups with alternative versions of the same events are revealed by their patterns of retelling. These patterns suggest that journalists function as an interpretive community, a group that authenticates itself through its narratives and collective memories.

The constitution of journalists as an interpretive community means that they circulate knowledge among themselves through channels other than the textbooks, training courses, and credentialing procedures stressed by formalized codes of professionalism. It also suggests that journalists collectively legitimate their actions in ways that have little to do with the effect of their news-relays on audiences. This does not mean that other professional communities, such as those of doctors or lawyers, do not do the same. Nor does it mean that the journalistic community is not concerned with professionalism; rather, the journalistic community activates its concern through its discourse about itself, and through the collective memories on which it is based.

Examining journalists as an interpretive community thus suggests an alternative analytical focus on journalists and journalistic practice. Commonly held distinctions among reporters—such as differentiations between beat reporters and generalists, columnists and copy writers, anchorpersons and health correspondents—are seen here as less central to their collectivity than more general dimensions of the community itself. Dimensions such as the individual, organization/ institution, or structure of the profession all suggest potentially different motivations for journalists seeking to establish themselves as cultural authorities. As this book will show, such dimensions of community have figured in assassination retellings particularly because they have helped the media accomplish the aim of collective legitimation.

This study considers the journalistic community not only as a profession, following sociological models, but also as an interpretive community that uses narratives and collective memories to keep itself together. Through narrative, the role of the individual, the organization/institution, and the structure of the profession become key factors in delineating the hows and whys of journalistic practice. Through shared narrative lore, reporters are able to espouse collective values and notions that help them maintain themselves as an authoritative interpretive community. This perspective addresses the ways in which journalists use credibility, power, or authority for themselves, with significant implications for audiences, organizations, and larger sociocultural questions of power.

Toward a Cultural View of the Kennedy Assassination

The idea that communication activities have cultural functions for groups engaging in them raises several questions about journalists' retellings of the assassination of John F. Kennedy. How is narrative used to legitimate journalists' right to present the event? What did the assassination mean to the journalists who covered it? Which aspects of the story were important? How were they constructed as important over time? How did journalists use narratives about their coverage to consolidate themselves into an authoritative interpretive community? These questions and others make up part of what Turner, Carey, and others would call the "cultural" dimensions of the assassination story.

Implicit here is a recognition of the dependence of journalistic authority on the acquiescence of audiences. The employment of narrative to legitimate journalists' versions of public events becomes most effective when audiences do not exercise their right to question it. The emphasis on the cultural dimensions of the story thus rests, firstly, with the audiences who have allowed it to flourish.

By tracing how the media have treated the assassination story in narrative, and by exploring how they have manipulated it in ways that are critical to their own self-legitimation, this study examines the role of the assassination story in marking journalistic community. Recalling Giddens, Durkheim, and Halbwachs, it examines how journalists have used narrative practice as a means of collectively representing shared codes of knowledge, which they then feed back into the community to set themselves up as cultural authorities. How their narratives have changed over time and space, and the ways in which collective memory has generated a shared body of knowledge, are seen as part of the establishment of journalistic authority.

Journalistic authority is posited here as an "ideal type." Other sociological studies—Eviatar Zerubavel's research on time or Erving Goffman's discussion of forms of talk—have adopted a similar approach.[49] Although this methodology does not aim to provide an all-inclusive or conclusive picture of the theoretical construct being examined, it does provide a clearer picture of the major patterns by which the construct emerges. By examining discursive patterns that give a fuller sense of the construct, this study offers a theoretically unified yet empirically eclectic perspective on the workings of journalistic authority.

The study also uses what Barney Glaser and Anselm Strauss call a "strategically-chosen example" to detect the presence of journalistic authority.[50] While the selection of the Kennedy assassination as a strategic example depends on its appropriateness as described above, assassination retellings may exemplify the traits of retellings of other critical incidents as well. In other words, the patterns of authority through which the assassination story has been retold can serve as a prototype for studying the media's retellings of other events.

Organization of the Book

The analysis in this study is based on systematic examination of the published public discourse by which journalists have recollected their part in covering Kennedy's death. The study employed diachronic textual analysis of narratives taken from the printed press, professional and trade reviews, television retrospectives, film documentaries, and books that have appeared since 1963.

Discourse about the role of the media in covering the assassination was explored through contemporaneous citations found in various public affairs indexes.[51] Narratives were examined for a nearly thirty-year period in both mediated and professional discourse. Mediated discourse, in which journalists discussed the assassination with the general public, included mass-mediated accounts of original assassination coverage and discussions about such coverage.[52] Professional discourse, in which journalists discussed assassination coverage among themselves, was found in the trade press, published speeches, and professional journalism reviews, such as the *Columbia Journalism Review, Washington Journalism Review, Editor and Publisher, Broadcasting,* and *The Quill.* The proceedings of various professional associations—such as the Society of Professional Journalists/Sigma Delta Chi, American Society of Newspaper Editors, and National Association of Broadcasters—were also surveyed.[53] These arenas were extended when appropriate by examining instructional discourse, found in textbooks, how-to manuals, and other published guidelines for new journalists. The focus, however, remained on journalistic discourse in and about the media.

The book is organized into four sections. Part 1, "Contextualizing Assassination Tales" (chapters 2 and 3), presents the general background against which the media were able to tell the assassination story. It situates the events of the assassination against the cultural

and historical context, including the state of journalistic professionalism, the emergence of television news, shifting boundaries of cultural authority, and the self-reflexivity of sixties-era narratives. Each
feature is discussed in conjunction with journalists' ability to promote
themselves as authoritative spokespersons for the events of Kennedy's
death, in order to show why the assassination story emerged as a
critical incident for American journalists. This section also explores
the centrality of strategies of rhetorical legitimation in journalistic
practice.

Part 2, "Telling Assassination Tales" (chapters 4–6), relays the original narrative corpus of the assassination story, from which the media
have worked their retellings over time. It examines the accounts of
reporters covering Kennedy's death as the journalists set them forth
at the time and compares them with journalists' initial reconstructions of the same stories in the weeks immediately following the
assassination, both in the media and in professional forums. This
section traces how the assassination story evolved from this body of
narratives into a critical incident for American journalists. It shows
how journalists made narrative adjustments to reconsider and recast
the story even at the time of the assassination.

Part 3, "Promoting Assassination Tales" (chapters 7 and 8), examines larger shifts in boundaries of cultural authority, which have had
bearing on the ability of journalists to promote themselves as part of
the assassination story. It explores how official assassination memories were de-authorized and the record of Kennedy's death made accessible to nonofficial retellers seeking to reconsider its events. This
section shows how the media have promoted themselves over other
sources—particularly historians and independent critics—in attempting to retell the assassination story. Issues about the authority of official documents, technology, and the workings of collective memory
are involved in journalists' attempts to promote themselves as the
assassination's preferred retellers.

Part 4, "Recollecting Assassination Tales" (chapters 9–11), explores
how the media have perpetuated themselves in collective memory as
part of the assassination story. It considers how journalists have
kept their narratives alive by embedding them within independent
memory systems that focus on three dimensions of the journalistic community—the individual, the organization/institution, and the
structure of the profession. Journalists have employed these different
memory systems to perpetuate their versions of the assassination narrative and their role as its authoritative retellers.

Contextualizing, telling, promoting, and recollecting—these mechanisms emerged as central in establishing and perpetuating journalists as authoritative spokespersons for the story of Kennedy's death. By examining how these mechanisms have been employed, this study tracks the canonization by the media of a central moment in American history.

Part One: Contextualizing Assassination Tales

TWO

Before the Assassination

The Kennedy assassination took place at the intersection of several culturally significant circumstances that affected how journalists would constitute, recollect, interpret, challenge, and perpetuate its story. Images of these circumstances were themselves molded not by remote historians sifting through documents but by participant-observers whose actions and views were part of the decade's concerns and problems. These views modulated assassination retellings and helped make the event a critical incident for the American media.

Professionalism, Cultural Authority, and the Self-Reflexivity of Sixties-Era Narratives

Journalists' retellings of the Kennedy assassination were part of an extended body of literature that looked back at major events of the time. Self-reflexive narratives, punctuated with questions about cultural authority and the relevance of history in everyday life, cast the sixties as a time of social, cultural, and political transformation.[1] Morris Dickstein said the era had provided a "point of departure for every kind of social argument," encouraging everyone to become "an interested party."[2] Social and cultural enterprises were lent a historical cast. As one chronicler, Todd Gitlin, later claimed, "it seemed especially true that History with a capital H had come down to earth, either interfering with life or making it possible; and that within History, or threaded through it, people were living with a supercharged density: lives were bound up within one another, making claims on one another, drawing one another into the common project."[3]

Individuals contended that their everyday lives had been infused with history and historical relevance. "We nurtured a daring premise," said one. "We were of historical moment, critical, unprecedented, containing within ourselves the fullness of time."[4] History was not only viewed as accessible, but was woven into the missions by which both individuals and groups claimed to be seeking to authenticate themselves.

The Event as Cornerstone of Sixties-Era Narratives

Chronicles of the sixties looked at the decade through events. Events helped mark public time, demarcating "before" and "after" periods and generating the era's signature of upheaval, social invention, and change.

Yet which events were recast depended on larger social, cultural, and political agendas. Some writers, such as Norman Mailer, maintained that the sixties began with the 1960 presidential elections, and Mailer's celebrated article about the 1960 party conventions, "Superman Comes to the Supermarket," reflected upon the arrival of the hero with "a dozen faces."[5] Others held that the election was the beginning of a "historical free fall (assassinations, riots, Viet Nam, Watergate, oil embargoes, hostages in Iran, the economic rise of the Pacific Rim nations, on and on—glasnost, China) that has created an utterly new world and left America searching for its place therein."[6]

Writers framed the decade as an amusement park, full of barely controlled chaos and recklessness, and with theaters of activity on every corner. The assassinations of John F. Kennedy, Malcolm X, Martin Luther King, and Robert Kennedy raised serious questions about the quality of American leadership, ushering in what the editor of one magazine called "two decades of 'accidental' presidencies."[7] The Vietnam War instilled doubts about the authority and justification of the U.S. presence abroad, while the civil rights movement generated large-scale activism on the home front. Publication of the Pentagon Papers and the beginnings of the Watergate scandal displayed illegalities within the private spaces of government. Student activism and the culture of protest, marked by the free speech movement, university protests, and the Kent State University shootings, showed the disjunctions that were splitting the nation's college population.

The Kennedy assassination was often cast as a prototype for the events that followed. It was, said one writer, "the day the world changed," a rite of passage to what was called the end of innocence.[8] The assassination symbolized a "rupture in the collective experience of the American people."[9] Many chroniclers felt that Kennedy's death generated doubts about existing boundaries of cultural authority. "The whole country was trapped in a lie," recalled activist Casey Hayden. "We were told about equality but we discovered it didn't exist. We were the only truth-tellers, as far as we could see."[10] Said another critic: "We came to doubt the legitimacy and authority of the doctor pounding our chest, and of the cop pounding the beat."[11]

Doubting external authority, chroniclers began to cast themselves as cultural, social, and political arbiters instead. "Where the critic of the fifties would appeal to . . . tradition, the critic of the sixties was more likely to seal an argument with personal testimony," said Dickstein.[12] Writers adopted, in Fredric Jameson's terms, a "reified, political language of power, domination, authority and antiauthoritarianism."[13] Their narratives about everyday life increasingly focused on power—questioning it, negotiating it, defying it, and ultimately creating new forms by which it could be realized. As they upgraded the values of immediacy, confrontation, and personal witness, and legitimated a subjective view of events, these writers saw the sixties as a chipping away of consensus. Whether such a consensus had ever existed became less important than the fact that it was invoked in recollections of the era.

One particular group for whom this invoking of consensus had relevance was the up-and-coming professionals. Despite larger questions about legitimating authority, there flourished among the middle class a cadre of professionals who developed a "track for running faster and stretching farther."[14] Their actions too were shaped by concerns about history and their place in it. Large-scale public events were held responsible for rattling the foundations of a variety of professions—writing, art, medicine—in a way that made its members rethink boundaries of appropriate practice. Questions about power and authority became direct challenges to their changing self-images as professionals, and they increasingly began to address ongoing questions about cultural authority.

Journalistic Professionalism and Cultural Authority

The media were not immune to these circumstances of change. In looking back, journalists claimed that the sixties had been a time of professional experimentation and personal involvement. *Esquire* magazine maintained that "no longer were there observers, only participants. This was especially true of journalists. They were part of the problem, part of the solution, and always part of the story."[15]

Journalists' heightened participation in events gave rise to new forms of writing, reporting, and presenting news. Some journalists embraced a subjective perspective in their writing, facilitated by circumstances that demanded their presence. Others took on a pseudo-historical cast in writing about everyday life. Still others experimented on the fringe with "new journalism," or with a broad spectrum of underground writing.[16] In the center, other journalists left the staid establishments of the "newspapers of record" and ventured into less secure territories of newer media establishments.[17] As David Halberstam noted, it was a time when "the old order was being challenged and changed in every sense, racially, morally, culturally, spiritually, and it was a rich time for journalists. For a while there was a genuine struggle over who would define news, the people in positions of power or the people in the streets. It was as if . . . every element of the existing structure of authority was on the defensive."[18] All of this meant that more general concerns about the shifting boundaries of cultural authority presented journalists with specific professional challenges, new practices, and alternative ways of legitimating themselves.

Journalism and the Kennedy Administration

One arena of interest to the media during the sixties was the Kennedy administration. In their narratives, journalists highlighted those dimensions of Kennedy's presidency which they contended had elevated journalism's status.

Presidential Attentions

The administration of John F. Kennedy displayed remarkable attention to the problems of American journalists. All but one of Kennedy's news conferences were "on the record."[19] Hallmark decisions for which he would be known and remembered as president—deciding to debate Richard M. Nixon, warning the Russians about missiles on their way to Cuba, or assuming responsibility for the Bay of Pigs invasion—were interpreted as having been taken with, if not motivated by, some regard for the media. One account of Kennedy's fastidious media behavior even held that journalists were "there to help him arrange reality, to make style become substance, to define power as the contriving of appearances."[20]

Hints of the president's attentiveness to the media were found already in Kennedy's campaign for the presidency. Press Secretary Pierre Salinger maintained that Kennedy had directed his staff to make the 1960 presidential campaign as convenient as possible for the media to cover.[21] Kennedy handed journalists transcripts of remarks made on the campaign trail within minutes of having made them. These "instant transcripts," explained Salinger, eliminated the time-consuming chore of reporters having to verify remarks with his office.[22] What Salinger did not say was that the transcripts also gave journalists the feeling that the president was attending to their needs. This tension between catering to journalists and manipulating them permeated accounts of the Kennedy administration.

During the administration's early years, Kennedy's attentiveness to the media was well received by the press corps. Journalists tended to be complimentary in their dispatches about him and at times displayed a certain suspension of critical judgment. In 1961 Arthur Krock wrote in the *New York Times* that "press requests are being fielded to the President in greater numbers than previously. . . . And Mr. Kennedy's evaluations of the merit of such questions is fair and generous."[23] Hugh Sidey of *Time* saw the administration this way: "Has there ever been a more succulent time for a young reporter? I doubt it. . . . It was a golden time for scribes. He talked to us, listened to us, honored us, ridiculed us, got angry at us, played with us, laughed with us, corrected us, and all the time lifted our trade to new heights of respect and importance."[24] Reporters perpetuated Kennedy's reputation for culture and integrity; Kennedy, for them, appeared to symbolize all that was well with America. Later, reporter Tom Wicker maintained that the press of the Kennedy era, "if it did not cover up for him, or knowingly look the other way, did not put him or the White House in his time under as close and searching scrutiny as it should have."[25]

A number of other factors dissuaded the media from being too critical of the president. He was thought to be polished and eloquent, energetic and witty. He was both Harvard-educated and a war hero. His rhetorical style, youth, and promises of a "new frontier" were interpreted as appealing, different, and refreshing. In Wicker's view, this encouraged the press to "give Kennedy more of a free ride than any of his successors have had. One [factor] was . . . the man's wit, charm, youth, good looks, and general style, as well as a feeling among reporters that he probably liked us more than he liked politicians, and that he may have been more nearly one of *us* than one of *them*. . . . Hence, there was at the least an unconscious element of good wishes for Kennedy."[26] Reporters willingly overstated these sides of Kennedy in their dispatches, to the same extent that they understated other points, such as his having Addison's disease and conducting extramarital affairs.[27]

One arena which journalists overlooked was his personal ties with reporters. While Kennedy maintained social relations with certain high-ranking journalists, including Charles Bartlett (who had introduced him to Jacqueline Bouvier), Joseph Alsop, and Benjamin Bradlee, this aspect of his life was ignored in most journalists' writings.

Although *New York Times* correspondent James Reston suggested that the president stop seeing reporters socially, when his suggestions were rejected outright, there was little ado among the media.[28] Correspondent Benjamin Bradlee's 1973 book of reminiscences, *Conversations with Kennedy*, which related how Bradlee and the president had regularly swapped gossip and information about the administration and the press corps, was generally reviewed favorably by the media.[29] One exception was writer Taylor Branch, who lambasted the relationship between Kennedy and Bradlee in *Harper's* magazine. In an article subtitled "The Journalist as Flatterer," Branch called the book "one of the most pathetic memoirs yet written by an American journalist about his President": "The Bradlee who covered Kennedy was hardly the prototypical reporter—cynical and hard, with a knife out for pretense and an eye out for dirt. He was hardly the editor he became under Nixon."[30]

Yet Kennedy's familiarity with journalism endeared him to most reporters. They stressed the fact that in 1945 he had served as a special correspondent for the International News Service and that his wife had been an "inquiring photographer" for the *Washington Times-Herald*.[31] He had won the coveted Pulitzer Prize in 1957 for *Profiles in Courage*.[32] Thus, in a lead article in November 1960, the trade magazine *Editor and Publisher* lamented the loss of "a first-rate reporter," saying that "a President who knows how to write a news-story and a first lady who can snap good news-pictures will be residing in the White House after January 20."[33] "Had he outlived his time in the White House," senior columnist Joseph Kraft later commented, "it is probable that in some way he would have turned to journalism."[34] Gloria Steinem also recalled that his administration was the only time a reporter felt that "something we wrote might be read in the White House."[35] All of this made the journalistic community "a natural constituency for [Kennedy]. He was interested in the same things they were, had gone to the same schools, read the same books and shared the same analytical frame of mind. By and large he was more comfortable with reporters than he was with working politicians."[36] Whether or not this was true mattered less than the fact that journalists recalled it as having been so.

From Affinity to News Management

The perception that Kennedy was more a part of the journalistic community than separate from it would help explain over time the central effect of Kennedy's death on U.S. journalists. Yet the aura of affinity between Kennedy and the media grew weak at times, especially when the president's attempts at image management conflicted with his voiced concerns for an independent press. Decades later, columnist David Broder recalled how the president had successfully converted a portion of the press corps into his own cheering section.[37] *Newsweek* was charged with regularly adjusting its news coverage so as to enhance Kennedy's image, while the *New York Times* was lambasted for suppressing its knowledge of the Bay of Pigs invasion.[38] Concerns with image management were frequently displayed; they included canceling twenty-two White House subscriptions to the *New York Herald-Tribune* because Kennedy was upset by its coverage of his administration;[39] bawling out *Time* reporter Hugh Sidey in front of his editor for providing too low an estimate for a crowd drawn by Kennedy;[40] cooling long-standing relations with then-confidant Bradlee because of a remark the reporter made about the Kennedys;[41] and denying journalists access to his staff because he took offense at their stories.[42] Charles Roberts, who covered Kennedy for *Newsweek,* later maintained that the administration was "intolerant of any criticism. . . . 'You are either for us or against us,' is the way Kenny O'Donnell, the President's appointments secretary, put it to me."[43]

Predictably, such activities somewhat chipped away at journalists' stance of suspended judgment, and accusations of "news management" began to circulate among White House reporters. Following the Cuban missile crisis, Arthur Krock wrote that a policy of "news management not only exists, but in the form of direct and deliberate action has been enforced more cynically and boldly than by any previous administration in a period when the U.S. was not at war."[44] I. F. Stone accused Kennedy of deception and deterioration in standards of leadership, in his newsletter of 26 April 1961: "The President's animus seems to be directed not at the follies exposed in the Cuban fiasco but at the free press for exposing them."[45] Years later, Henry Fairlie complained that both Kennedy's policy of news management and his social flattery of journalists had made it difficult for journalists to be objective about him.[46] All of this suggests that Kennedy's close ties with the press were already beginning to unravel at the time of his death. Yet the larger picture remained one of general support, affinity, and loyalty between much of the media and the administration.

Kennedy as "the Television President"

Whether journalists chose to praise or criticize the Kennedy administration, they recognized that Kennedy had a special regard for television. It earned him the appellation of "the television president." As

Halberstam observed, he and the television "camera were born for each other, he was its first great political superstar."[47]

To an extent, Kennedy's affinity with television was thought to have been orchestrated by members of his family, who had worked earnestly to promote his nomination. Halberstam related the following story:

> In 1959 Sander Vanocur, then a young NBC correspondent, was stationed by the network in Chicago and soon found himself being cultivated by Jack Kennedy's brother-in-law Sargent Shriver . . . one evening there was a party at the Shrivers' home and a ruddy-faced sandy-haired older man walked over to Vanocur and said, "You're Sander Vanocur, aren't you?" Vanocur allowed as how he was. "I'm Joe Kennedy," the man said. "I saw you at Little Rock. You did a good job down there. I kept telling Jack to spend more time and pay more attention to guys like you and less to the print people. I think he's coming around."[48]

As Kennedy grew into his administration and his concept of the presidency, so grew his interest in journalism and his curiosity about television.

That interest was sparked when he was believed to have won the election of 1960 because of his understanding of television. High praise for Kennedy's performance in the "great debates" came from those who watched him on television: people who listened to the debates on radio perceived Nixon to be the winner, while those who saw the debates on television perceived that Kennedy had won.[49] The debates were held responsible for improving Kennedy's sagging second place in the polls.[50] It was assumed that he won the election "largely because of the way he looked and sounded on the TV screens in our living rooms."[51]

Journalists recalled how Kennedy had used his knowledge of the medium to full advantage in the debates: he rested before his televised appearances, applied cosmetics to hide facial blemishes, and allowed himself to be extensively coached beforehand.[52] Don Hewitt, who directed the debates, later maintained that "television had a love affair with Jack Kennedy."[53] The significance of his performance extended well beyond the political campaign: television was "legitimized as the main instrument of political discourse . . . [It was a] triumph not just for Kennedy but for the new medium; within hours no one could recall anything that was said, only what they looked like, what they felt like."[54] After the debates, recalled reporter Edwin Guthman, the age of television journalism was said to have begun.[55]

Kennedy's decision as president to implement regular, live televised news conferences had similar impact. It was regarded by press journalists as "an administration disaster second only to the Bay of Pigs,"[56] but television journalists were overjoyed. They lauded the detailed attention with which he organized his first conference. Observing that "Hollywood could not have done better in preparing a spectacular," one reporter recalled how Kennedy brought down a TV consultant from New York to arrange staging, used white cardboard to dispel facial shadows, and at the last minute resewed the drapes hanging behind the lectern.[57] Kennedy's preparation for each conference was "intensive and elaborate"[58] and was accompanied by a stringent briefing, during which Salinger predicted questions and collected responses from Kennedy staffers. The president then convened a "press conference breakfast" where he practiced answering questions.[59]

The live news conferences provided the right stage for Kennedy. Tom Wicker maintained that they gave the president a "perfect forum for his looks, his wits, his quick brain, his self-confidence. Kennedy gave Americans their first look at a President in action . . . and he may have been better at this art form than at anything else in his Presidency."[60] A frequent participant on behalf of the *New York Times*, James Reston, recalled how the president "overwhelmed you with decimal points or disarmed you with a smile and a wisecrack."[61] It was characteristic of his administration that on 22 October 1962, Kennedy chose to go on the air at 7 P.M. to demand that Russian missiles be removed from Cuba. His message's effect on the nation had much to do with its televised delivery. "By delivering the ultimatum on TV instead of relying on normal diplomatic channels, Kennedy magnified the impact of his actions many times over, signaling to the world that there would be no retreat."[62] These acts, in David Halberstam's words, "helped to make television journalists more powerful as conduits for politicians than print ones."[63]

Kennedy's high regard for television continued throughout his administration. In December 1962, he became the first president to conduct an informal television interview with reporters from the three networks.[64] Benjamin Bradlee, upset over the deviation from routine practice, wrote the following in his journal:

> December 17, 1962. The President went on television live tonight, answering questions from each network's White House correspondent . . . I watched it at home and felt professionally threatened as a man who was trying to make a living by the written word. The program was ex-

ceptionally good, well-paced, colorful, humorous, serious,
and I felt that a written account would have paled by
comparison.[65]

When Bradlee confronted the president with the disturbing effect the
television interviews would have on print journalists, Kennedy re-
torted, "I always said that when we don't have to go through you
bastards [the printed press], we can really get our story over to the
American people."[66] Kennedy allowed cameras to film his efforts to
integrate the University of Alabama;[67] his trips to Paris, Vienna, and
Berlin; and his warnings to the Russians to keep away from Cuban
shores. In another domain, Jacqueline Kennedy took the American
people on a televised tour of the White House.[68] Kennedy thus became a promoter for the journalistic community, and for television
journalists in particular.

Images of Kennedy as president set the stage for memories of Kennedy after his death. It was no surprise when a memorial section of
Newsweek magazine, published the week after Kennedy's assassination, hailed his effect on journalism and television in these words:
"no President had ever been so accessible to the press; no President
ever so anxious for history to be recorded in the making; he even let
TV cameras peek over his shoulder in moments of national crisis."[69]
At a time when the boundaries of cultural authority were changing,
the ties between Kennedy and the press corps defined journalistic
community in a way that was instrumental for journalists seeking to
legitimate themselves. Kennedy's interest highlighted the importance
of journalism by upholding it as a profession and granting legitimacy
to those employed by television. The Kennedy administration thus
gave journalists a way to address larger questions about cultural authority, history, and professionalism.

Both the shifting boundaries of cultural authority and Kennedy's
consistent interest in journalism helped frame the early sixties as
"great years for journalism."[70] Journalists applauded the Kennedys
for providing good copy, and the growth of well-established news
organizations, such as the *New York Times* and *Newsweek*, was seen as
a precursor to a more general expansion of the profession. Observers
felt that journalism's stature as a profession was enhanced. By 1962
journalists "saw their career increasingly as a profession. . . . Which
meant that there were obligations and rights and responsibilities that
went with it. They were better paid, more responsible and more serious. They were not so easily bent, not so easily used."[71] Journalists
felt that they were entering a period of growth and maturation, in

which many assumed that new opportunities for cultural and social legitimation would present themselves.

The Uncertain Legitimacy of Television News

Growth was not shared equally across the media, however. During Kennedy's ascent to the presidency, the stature of television news were still being debated. Television news was considered a bastard child by the journalistic community, dismissed as "a journalistic frivolity, a cumbersome beast unequipped to meet the demands of breaking news on a day-to-day basis."[72] Every press journalist still believed that "his was the more serious, more legitimate medium for news."[73] The superiority of print over television was "a view widely shared by TV newspeople themselves in the sixties. . . . Examples of original reporting on TV were rare then, and the medium was still essentially derivative."[74] Television reporters who had original angles on a story often fed them to wire-service reporters, so as to capture the attention of their New York editors.[75] It was not surprising, then, that a few months before the Kennedy assassination, the International Press Institute rejected a move to admit radio and television newspeople, stating that they did not constitute bona fide journalists.[76]

The Beginnings of Legitimation

Yet already by the early 1960s, interest in television news had begun to blossom. The average American household used television for four to five hours daily by the summer of 1960, and 88 percent of all homes owned television sets.[77] Certain technological advances, particularly the increasingly widespread use of videotape and the employment of communications satellites in 1962, improved the broadcast quality of television news.[78] Networks were able to alter existing formats of news presentation, moving from the "talking head" set-up toward more sophisticated ways of including actual news footage in broadcasts.

Institutional changes also worked to the advantage of television news. Officials within the Federal Communications Commission (FCC) proposed an independent news association devoted only to broadcasting.[79] Newton Minow, the newly appointed FCC chairman, called for an increase in the time devoted to television news to offset what he called the "vast wasteland" of television entertainment programming. In the fall of 1963, the fifteen-minute time slot of television news was expanded to a full half-hour on both CBS and NBC, although ABC retained the shorter format until 1967.[80] To mark the occasion, Kennedy gave interviews to all three networks, and then held a second interview when one network later discovered that its camera had broken.[81] Television networks opened new bureaus to accommodate a growing demand for information.[82]

The legitimation of television news was also linked to the medium's technological attributes. Advocates began to suggest that television might be a better medium than print for transmitting certain kinds of news stories. The new technology was seen as helping cameramen and reporters cover events "that might have been barred to them in the past."[83] Observers pointed to a range of stories at which television excelled; for example, the civil rights movement gained most of its public support through television, with its "leaders . . . masterful at manipulating television, conscious of the way certain images could be used to move the electorate."[84] As David Halberstam later commented, "gradually in the last year of Kennedy's life, [*Time* journalist Hugh] Sidey noticed a change, not so much in Kennedy's feeling about the magazine's fairness as in his estimation of its importance. The equation had changed with the coming of television. In Washington the power of print was slipping and slipping quickly. Television gave greater access, so television got better access."[85] The growing status of television even prompted one member of the print media to call the press "mere 'extras' at JFK's press conferences—shows so obviously staged for television."[86]

Implicit in what journalists saw as television's burgeoning legitimacy was an increasing acceptance of its technological advances. Reporters held television's technological "improvements"—immediacy, visual elements, drama—responsible for making TV news a bona fide journalistic form. Television began to be seen as promoting a "better" form of journalism than that offered by print.

Consolidating Legitimation

This all changed considerably by July 1964, the summer following Kennedy's assassination. By then, television journalism had emerged as a powerful force in American life and politics. Journalists felt that this was displayed at the Republication National Convention in San Francisco's Cow Palace. Seen as "players in the game itself,"[87] journalists were booed by convention delegates and carried off the floor by security guards and police. Significantly, press journalists did not play alone in such a game. Tom Wicker recalled how "those fists raised in anger at the men in the glass-booths—the 'commentators' and the 'anchor men'—bore this message too: The 'press' had become inextricably linked with television in the public mind."[88]

Linking print and television journalists underscored their unification into one professional community. More important, the role of TV reporters as makers of news had made them deserving of careful consideration. As Republican nominee Barry Goldwater later said, "I should have known in San Francisco, that I won the nomination [there] but lost the election."[89] His staff "had not reckoned with television, or how necessary it was to restrain its appetite for drama."[90] Television journalists had become a force to be dealt with.

In looking back, chroniclers contended that events at the Cow Palace reflected significant changes in the legitimacy granted television journalists, who the previous year had been denied membership by an international press organization but were now considered "active players." The uncertain professional beginnings of 1963 had been pushed into definite legitimacy thirteen months later. There had been a clear change in the circumstances by which television journalists—and by implication all journalists—could authenticate themselves.

In part, that clear change was brought about by coverage of Kennedy's assassination. Television, said one critic, "was at the center of the shock. With its indelible images, information, immediacy, repetition and close-ups, it served to define the tragedy for the public."[91] At the end of 1963, a Roper survey maintained that Americans relied for news as much on television as on the printed press.[92] By the late sixties, television had come of age as the preferred medium for news.

The Assassination as Critical Incident

The Kennedy assassination was positioned squarely in the middle of a process by which television was recognized as a legitimate medium of news transmission. Television journalism was said to have grown up in Dallas, "for never before had it faced such a story with so much of the responsibility for telling it."[93] That journalists themselves saw the fates of Kennedy and television as intertwined underscored the quest for legitimation in both arenas. It is significant that figures in the television industry, particularly television journalists, regarded Kennedy as a midwife to their own birth. A special edition of *Broadcasting* magazine, published the week after the assassination, included a section entitled "The Dimension JFK Added to Television." It went as follows:

> From the Great Debates where America first saw this young
> man to the TV close-up of a U.S. President telling the
> American people we were about to blockade Cuba and
> might even go further, he took radio and television off the
> second team and made them peers of the older print me-
> dia. Electronic journalism and its newsmen grew in stature
> by leaps and bounds. . . . The medium needed no further
> assurance of its place in society than the President's exclu-
> sive interviews with CBS's Walter Cronkite and NBC's Chet
> Huntley and David Brinkley.[94]

Members of the journalistic community felt that Kennedy's interest
had engendered the broadcasting industry's growth and had enhanced journalists' professional legitimacy. Such a view was apparent
in eulogies for the president, which were printed in trade publications under titles like "Kennedy Retained Newsman's Outlook."[95]

All of this cast the assassination coverage against a larger backdrop
of legitimating the American media. Holding television news responsible for communicating the tragedy supported larger discourses
about the authority of journalists at the same time as it underscored
the value of television news. The public's exposure to the assassination was made possible by television, and to a large degree TV technology was hailed for providing the nation's memories of the event.

The legitimation of television journalists was construed as having
been gradual but certain. Like other enterprises of the decade, legitimation was seen as assisted by self-reflexive narratives that addressed
the shifting boundaries of cultural authority and definitions of professionalism, changing consensus about what was important, and a
recognition of the increased relevance of history in everyday life.
Chroniclers of the decade therefore adjusted their narratives—about
the sixties, about Kennedy's administration, and about the legitimation of television news—until similar notions figured in all. In telling
and retelling tales of the assassination, journalists invoked a context
that underscored the function of history and historical events for professional legitimation.

This is not to say that all professionals became historians, only that
more direct access to historic events influenced how professionals
determined their boundaries of appropriate practice. Circumstances
made it easier for journalists to borrow from history in their attempts
at self-legitimation. Journalists saw themselves taking on expanded
roles of cultural authority, and acting in new and different ways as
social, political, and ultimately historical arbiters. They perpetuated
memories of the assassination in a way that made sense of ongoing

issues about the time, the profession, and the emerging technologies with which they told their stories.

All of this directly affected the way in which coverage of the Kennedy assassination would be retold by the media. Most reconstructions of the sixties linked narratives about television journalism with narratives about the Kennedy administration, a tie that was torn asunder with the president's assassination. In an ironic twist, Kennedy's death fueled the concerns and energies of the era's observers, offering them a way to debate timely issues of authority, power, connectedness, and historical relevance. His death was used by journalists to legitimate television, so that the medium that had served him best in life continued to serve him in death.

The Kennedy assassination thereby became one stage on which journalists played out their legitimation as professionals. It provided the background for the movement of television journalists from the ranks of outsiders to "central players." In this way, it was able to serve as a critical incident for journalism professionals, through which they would evaluate, challenge, and negotiate consensual notions about what it meant to be a journalist.

THREE

Rhetorical Legitimation and
Journalistic Authority

The ability of journalists to establish themselves as authoritative
spokespersons for the assassination story was predicated on their use
of narrative in deliberate and strategic ways. Journalists' claims to legitimacy were no less rhetorically based than their narrative reconstructions of the activities behind the news. It was thus in narrative
that the media needed to legitimate their claims to the story of Kennedy's death.

Creating a Place for Narrative

The ways in which narrative helps legitimate its tellers—that is, establish them as connected, credible, authoritative spokespersons for a
tale—have long been of interest to theorists of public discourse and
communication. At focus is a concern for the rational and strategic
aims of language.

Aristotle was perhaps first to define rhetoric as invoking the effect
of persuasion, or the wielding of power. As communication scholars
John Lucaites and Celeste Condit said, "The primary goal of rhetorical discourse is what the persuasion achieves. . . . Rhetorical
narratives exist beyond [their] own textuality."[1] Max Weber similarly
regarded narrative as an act of strategic dimension, holding that rational activities like speaking or telling stories constitute attempts to
achieve legitimation.[2] More recently, Jürgen Habermas maintained
that speakers use language to effect various kinds of consensus about
their activity: "Under the functional aspect of reaching understanding, communicative action serves the transmission and renewal of
cultural knowledge; under the aspect of coordinating action, it serves
social integration and the establishment of group solidarity; under the
aspect of socialization, it serves the formation of personal identities."[3]
Habermas contended that speakers often use language and discourse
to achieve aims related to freedom and dependence, in that a speaker's words may uphold or disavow social cohesion, group solidarity,
or legitimation.[4] The ability of communication to support consensus

in realizing these aims determines whether true, or effective, communication has been achieved.

Scholars have also argued that narrative provides an underlying logic for implementing more general communicative rules and conventions. For example, certain notions about narrative as strategic practice suggest its implication in the accomplishment of community and authority.[5] Narrative becomes an effective tool in maintaining collective codes of knowledge, functioning much like a meta-code for speakers, as proposed nearly two decades ago by Roland Barthes. It allows for the effective sharing and transmission of stories within culturally and socially explicit codes of meaning.[6] Within the meta-code of narrative, reality becomes accountable in view of stories told about it. But it becomes accountable only to those who share the codes of knowledge it invokes. These points—the ability of narrative to invoke community, its employment as a strategic act of legitimation, and its function in constructing reality—imply the strategic nature of narrative acts.

It is thus no surprise that narrators might use a broad range of narrative and stylistic devices to uphold their own status and prestige. As Hayden White argued, "once we note the presence of the theme of authority in the text, we also perceive the extent to which the truth claims of the narrative and indeed the very right to narrate hinge upon a certain relationship to authority per se."[7] Questions of narrative have thus come to be regarded as at least partly entwined with questions of authority and legitimation.

Narrative's role in achieving authority becomes especially relevant when considering how particular stories evolve. Scholarship by Hayden White, Hans Kellner, and others has shown that, over time, speakers reposition themselves with regard to original events, thereby reconfiguring their authority.[8] Aims having little to do with narrative activity become differentially embedded in narrative. In White's view, this has made historical inquiry less motivated by "the necessity to establish *that* certain events occurred than by the desire to determine what certain events might *mean* for a given group, society, or culture's conception of its present tasks and future prospects."[9] Which narrators eventually emerge as authoritative voices of a given story is thereby linked with the practices by which they are rhetorically legitimated and the authority through which they are culturally constituted.

Such premises about narrative and rhetorical legitimation are of direct relevance to journalism professionals, whose work has long been characterized as an entanglement of narrative, authority, and rhetorical legitimation.[10] While all professional groups are constituted by formalized bodies of knowledge, much of journalists' professional authority lies not in what they know but in how they represent their knowledge. This means that concrete decisions about practical problems often displace knowledge altogether.[11] What the media do to present news—how they structure a given story—thus becomes as important as what they did in covering it. Narrative, in other words, offers the media an effective way of legitimating themselves as spokespersons for a story.

The issue of journalistic legitimation through narrative is particularly salient in a mass-mediated age, in which media technologies have expanded the range of public forums available to journalists. Over the last half century, media technologies have enlarged the potential for tellers of stories to connect themselves, effectively and authoritatively, to public events.[12] As modern forms of public discourse have offered an increasingly complex mix of content attending to various communicative aims, different problems have become implicated in the achievement of rhetorical legitimation. This is particularly true for mediated public discourse.[13]

Within these parameters, the foundations of cultural authority are embedded within narrative. Journalists used narrative to legitimate their actions as professionals in numerous stories that addressed not only coverage of Kennedy's death but also ongoing discourses about cultural authority, journalistic professionalism, and the legitimation of television news. Through narrative, journalists consolidated themselves into an interpretive community, one held together by its tales, narratives, and rhetoric.

Strategies of Retelling the Assassination

Retelling the story of Kennedy's death gave ample opportunity for the reconstructive work implied by narration, producing a huge body of literature. Nearly 200 books that were published within 36 months of the tragedy have since been joined by over a thousand periodical pieces and books, dozens of television retrospectives, at least twelve newsletters, and numerous bookstores specializing in assassination literature.[14] In the mass media, names of reporters have been thrust forward, often ahead of those of their organizational employers, as emblems of authority for the events of those four November days. Retelling the assassination thus has provided the opportunity to spread tales and gain status for their telling.

The media were not the only ones vying to retell what had happened, especially when conspiracy theories began to gain credibility during the late 1960s. By that time, in Dan Rather's words, "newsmen, police, intelligence agencies examined the evidence,"[15] as also did historians, novelists, and screenplay writers. One indication that the media would not play a subordinate role in retelling the events of that November weekend was found in *Newsweek* correspondent Charles Roberts's early (1967) critique of the work of independent critic Mark Lane. Roberts complained that Lane, who claimed to have provided "the only complete published list of witnesses" to the assassination, failed to include "some 50 Washington correspondents who were on press buses."[16] As early as 1967, then, journalists were interested in promoting themselves as central players in the record of Kennedy's assassination.

For journalists, narratives about Kennedy's death were a way to evaluate and reconsider consensual notions about professional practice and appropriate boundaries of journalistic authority. Journalists had many ways to reference their role in covering the story. Appraisals of Kennedy's administration mentioned covering his assassination.[17] Nostalgic "period" pieces incorporated journalists' personal memories.[18] Articles, books, and documentaries provided investigatory glimpses of the assassination, including fresh perspectives on conspiracy theories. As the narrator of one 1988 TV retrospective remarked, after showing film of Kennedy being hit by bullets, "President and Mrs. Kennedy in the final seconds before that awful moment [pause]. A moment etched forever in our hearts. An hour later NBC correspondents Chet Huntley and Frank McGee relayed the news we had all feared most."[19] The relay of assassination memories ensured that the journalist-as-teller became embedded in the event's retelling, thereby creating a place for journalistic narratives within the assassination story.

Regardless of the medium used, retellings of the assassination were shaped by how journalists decided to narratively reconstruct its events. By definition, narrative accommodated the narrator's inclusion within the assassination story. This meant, first of all, that most assassination narratives bore the name of their authors. Other than editorials bearing the collective mark of the institutions that produced them, very few articles or news items about Kennedy's death remained anonymous. Instead, most efforts at journalistic recollection were identified by an individual reporter's name. One CBS retrospective, for instance, documented the four days of Dallas coverage through the persona of anchorperson Dan Rather. By repeatedly coming back to film clips of Rather, the documentary supported his central presence as its narrator and underscored his part in the network's original coverage from Dallas.[20]

There were many ways to narrate the story of Dallas. The events of November 1963 constituted an imprecise history, which the media readily reshaped. One 1988 NBC TV retrospective, for example, was structured so that reporters could introduce rounds of narration to mediate the original events of the assassination. The documentary positioned Edwin Newman as external narrator; Chet Huntley, David Brinkley, and Frank McGee as internal narrators; and various reporters—such as Bill Ryan and Tom Pettit—as on-site chroniclers of events.[21] Once these positions were briefly identified, the story progressed as if there were no significant difference in the temporal frames that each chronicler occupied. In fact, however, Edwin Newman spoke twenty-five years after events, Frank McGee spoke on the night of the assassination, and Tom Pettit spoke a few moments after Lee Harvey Oswald was shot. The fact that they were all brought together within what appeared to be a single time frame neutralized the differences involved in occupying very different temporal frames. It made the role of external narrators central in a way that suggested a (false) proximity to the events in Dallas, and enhanced the authority of spokespersons who were both temporally and spatially distant from the original events of Kennedy's death.

This particular narrative reconstruction—telling the story (of recollections of the assassination) of the story (of the assassination coverage) through the story (of the journalists who covered it)—accommodated the inclusion of narrators regardless of the part they had originally played in the assassination coverage. It documented the connection of several journalists to the events of the assassination and often created a connection where one was lacking. It also gave journalists a way to legitimate their connection to the story years after the assassination had taken place, and miles away from its original events.[22] The fact that the event's original recording—the television footage or step-by-step prose accounts of Kennedy's shooting—often stayed the same while the narration about it changed with each retrospective or publication allowed journalists to differentially contextualize stories of their coverage. The contexts they chose corresponded to larger discourses, particularly about the legitimacy of television news and the consolidation of journalism as a profession.

Significantly, the perceived need for narrators in assassination retellings referenced a collective code by which journalists agreed to accommodate their own presence in narrative. The place created for narrative within assassination retellings, then, upheld consensus among journalists about the centrality of narrative. Narrative was seen as helpful in consolidating journalists into a community, in facilitating constructions of reality, and in realizing aims of legitimation. In all cases, narrative was invoked as a strategic and rational act.

The media relied upon three main strategies to tell the assassination story and, at the same time, assert their authority in its telling. These strategies—synecdoche, omission, and personalization—were invoked both separately and together to represent the events that took place in Dallas.

Synecdoche

Synecdoche—the narrative strategy by which the part "stands in" for the whole[23]—allowed journalists to borrow the authority accrued from having covered certain events and apply it to events they did not experience. Through synecdoche, journalists retelling the assassination story enlarged the tale to include elements that focused on their part within it.

For example, *New York Times* reporter Tom Wicker used a rifle being withdrawn from a window in the Texas Schoolbook Depository to stand in for witnessing Kennedy's shooting.[24] Another journalist used a bullet being pumped into Oswald's stomach to signify the shooting of Kennedy's presumed killer.[25] In yet another case, a foot sticking into the air from the back of the presidential limousine was used to signify Kennedy's death.[26]

The best illustration of synecdochic retelling came in the media's efforts to turn their assassination coverage from a problematic performance into a professional triumph. Scholarship on the assassination has maintained that journalists provided effective coverage of the events of those several days.[27] In particular, their coverage of the murder of Lee Harvey Oswald and capture of his shooting on live camera, although originally seen as overstepping the boundaries of appropriate journalism, was later viewed as exemplary reporting. Similarly, the media's coverage of Kennedy's funeral made them into masters of ceremonies who were celebrated for their active part in healing the nation.[28] In the context of these two events of the longer assassination weekend, journalistic coverage of Kennedy's assassination has been touted by journalists, scholars, and the public as a triumph of contemporary media history.

Yet closer examination reveals this to be a constructed notion developed after the assassination weekend had passed. Moments of journalistic triumph were unevenly scattered across the assassination weekend. Coverage of the assassination began, in Wicker's words, "when it was all over."[29] The coverage was prompt and comprehensive but fraught with problems: journalists did not see Kennedy shot, sometimes did not hear Kennedy shot, filed reports on the basis of hearsay and rumor, lacked access to recognizable and authoritative sources, and processed faulty information.[30] Proven journalistic methods—such as relying on eyewitness status, seeking out high-ranking sources, and verifying facts—were all unhelpful; the speed with which information could be transmitted outpaced the reporters' ability to gather it. They simply could not keep up, in front of one of the largest audiences in media history.

Journalists' professionalism was further challenged by the active involvement of amateurs and laypersons. The most detailed eyewitness testimony was provided not by the fifty-some journalists in the motorcade but by ordinary bystanders who, unlike the journalists, were not paid to "cover the body" of the president but who did so anyway.[31] Photographic documentation, including the famous Zapruder film, was provided not by the journalists riding in the presidential motorcade but by local merchants, housewives, and businesspeople.[32] Abraham Zapruder, the dressmaker who provided what has been called one of the most studied films in history, initially forgot his motion-picture camera and had to go home to retrieve it before the motorcade's arrival.[33]

While these points will be addressed in detail in later chapters, the overview given here underscores the problematics of covering Kennedy's death. As far as the provision of information is concerned, journalists simply did not make the grade, their coverage reflecting instead a situation of journalistic failure. Journalistic authority thus needed to be constructed not through their actions but through narratives about those actions—that is, journalists had to rhetorically legitimate themselves to offset a basically problematic performance.

Journalists achieved this by telling the assassination story through one larger narrative that had two high points: Oswald's murder and Kennedy's funeral. The way that journalists covered Oswald's murder became a prototype for the coverage of unexpected events. *Broadcasting* magazine called their capture of his shooting a "first in television history."[34] Similarly, in covering Kennedy's funeral, journalists anchored the event in a way designed to help heal the nation.[35] These two dimensions of the assassination story prompted observers to tout the whole coverage as a major triumph. Journalists catered to this perception in their stories about the event. They made the assassination narrative into one long story that extended from Friday, when

Kennedy was shot, until the following Monday, when he was buried. By doing so, they overstated their successes and underplayed their failures. By treating their successful coverage—the funeral and the shooting of Oswald—as if it represented all journalistic performances of the assassination weekend, they turned aside potential criticism.

Rhetorical legitimation through synecdoche was thus facilitated by the sequencing of events during the extended weekend. Using parts of the narrative to signify the whole worked to journalists' advantage. Their lack of eyewitness status in Kennedy's shooting was resolved by their presence both at his funeral and at Oswald's murder. Verifying facts appeared less salient once the facts of Kennedy's death and Oswald's presumed role in it were confirmed. The accessibility of sources seemed less important as nonofficial eyewitnesses, usually bystanders, recounted what had happened. Disjunctions between the rapid pace of information relay—made possible by wire services, radio, and television—and the slower pace of journalists' information gathering became less central by the time of the funeral, where little information gathering was necessary. Within all of these circumstances, the fact that the media had missed the actual shooting of the president was transformed from an independent mishap that cast serious doubts on their professionalism into an incidental part of a larger journalistic triumph. Synecdoche thus not only helped journalists assume responsibility for events that went beyond their personal experience; it also masked some of the problems implied by certain dimensions of their coverage.

Synecdochic retellings were complicated by the variety of media involved. For example, technology was portrayed as central to the accomplishment of journalistic work, and photographs, films, and other media technologies all permitted journalists to reconstruct their role in the assassination in a way that let them take responsibility for the work of others—other journalists and news organizations, as well as nonjournalists, such as Zapruder.

The adoption of one long narrative, however, worked especially to the advantage of television. Within the parameters of the television narrative that extended from the Friday to the Monday, the master assassination narrative took shape. The larger narrative not only told the story of Kennedy's assassination and burial but also conveyed the difficulties, tribulations, and triumphs of television reporters trying to cover those events. Telling the assassination story meant telling the story of its TV coverage.

Synecdoche was also called into the service of groups jockeying for position within the journalistic community. By rearranging their narratives, journalists sought to uphold the primacy of certain reporting channels (television and press) over others (radio), as well as the primacy of one reporting community (national) over another (local). The role of (national) television was used to signify that of the American press corps.

Thus synecdoche served a variety of purposes. It gave the media a credible role in the larger assassination narrative by making them responsible for the story in its entirety. It blurred what was and was not "professional" about journalists' coverage, and helped reporters assume responsibility for events beyond their personal experience. It caused discussions to hinge less on what journalists had actually done and more on the images of journalistic coverage that both journalists and news organizations wanted to perpetuate. It helped shape professional in-fighting, ensuring that national television and the national press were given a central role within the assassination narrative. In short, synecdoche allowed journalists, particularly television journalists, to emerge as authoritative spokespersons for the assassination story, regardless of what they personally had done, seen, or heard.

Omission

A second strategy used in retelling the assassination story was omission. Like synecdoche, it invoked activities of rearrangement, but it also offered a distinct way of adjusting material to fit larger goals of authority. Journalists rearranged the times, people, and places associated with the original events of the assassination. Left out of retellings were the various roles played by radio, local media, and amateurs.

Radio offered the most glaring example of how central aspects of assassination events were omitted from the assassination narrative. Although most television retrospectives employed radio broadcasts as background when discussing television's part in covering the assassination, few identified radio's coverage—whether by medium, network, or individual reporter. Films showed journalists huddled outside Parkland Hospital in Dallas, clutching notepads and pencils, listening to radio journalists paraphrase intermittent wire-service accounts of what had happened.[36] Yet no mention was made of radio's role in this scenario. Books and articles repeated fragments from vaguely referenced "radio broadcasters." In nearly every case, the role of radio has been simply erased from journalistic recollections of the events in Dallas.

Narratives also neutralized the importance of local media, whose assistance in covering the assassination was essential for getting the story out. At the time of the tragedy, local media—particularly in Dallas but elsewhere too—were immediately hailed for their help.[37] One trade publication offered lengthy descriptions of how the local press had "played" the story.[38] Broadcasters in Oregon were congratulated for their sense of responsibility to the public. "Those broadcasters," commented the article, "can be proud to be members of the broadcasting industry."[39] Yet as time passed local media began to go unmentioned in assassination recollections, until contemporary retellings have in effect obliterated their role in covering the story.

In other rearrangements of assassination coverage, particular people have disappeared from the story. For example, reporter Eddie Barker, then local news director of the Dallas CBS affiliate, provided the first unconfirmed report that Kennedy was dead. At the time, *Broadcasting* magazine told what happened: "KRLD-TV newsman Eddie Barker, after having talked to a doctor at the hospital, made the initial report that the President was dead. Walter Cronkite in New York continually referred to this report but emphasized it was not official. Thus, CBS had a beat of several minutes that Mr. Kennedy had died of his wounds."[40] Dan Rather, also at the scene of the assassination, accompanied Barker's dispatch with two unofficial confirmations before Kennedy's death was officially established.[41]

In most current chronicles, however, Barker's role in the story has shrunk to near omission. Today it is mentioned in only the most extensive and detailed accounts. Instead, chronicles tend to follow the line taken by this 1989 recounting: "The eyes of Walter Cronkite swelled with tears when he heard, from a young Dan Rather, that President Kennedy was dead."[42] Another version, penned in 1983, similarly claimed that "thanks to Rather, CBS achieved another 'first'—the news that Kennedy was dead."[43] Yet another, written in 1978, implied that first Rather, then Barker, had received word of Kennedy's death.[44]

Several points suggested in earlier chronicles have been invalidated by these more recent accounts: that CBS News in New York heard the news initially from Barker and only afterward from Rather; that Cronkite's eyes swelled with tears when he received official confirmation of the death, not when he heard it from Rather; and that the "first" of reporting Kennedy's death was accomplished by Barker, not Rather. Most present-day accounts of CBS's coverage of events specifically highlight Dan Rather within the story at the expense of the lesser-known Eddie Barker (who was employed by a CBS affiliate). In

other words, the role of the local reporter has been consistently understated alongside the more extensive accounts accorded his better-
known and more prestigious national counterpart.

Narratives have also displaced the controversy surrounding television's possible facilitation of Lee Harvey Oswald's death. The intrusive presence of journalists in the corridor where Oswald was
shot—the cables and equipment, the crowd of reporters—generated
many official and professional censures of journalistic behavior.[45]
Foremost here was a special session of the American Society of Newspaper Editors that brought together the heads of seventeen news
organizations to discuss what the *Columbia Journalism Review* called
"judgment by television."[46] A section of the report of the first official
investigation of Kennedy's death, the Warren Commission, on "the
activity of newsmen" examined the problematic aspects of journalists' performance in Dallas.[47] Yet today that dimension of journalistic
behavior in Dallas is rarely mentioned. Contemporary versions of the
Oswald story have instead recast it as a professional triumph for the
scoop of having caught the murder on live camera.

Each omission was linked with larger discourses about journalistic
professionalism and legitimation. Understating the role of radio, amateurs, and local media overstated the role of television, journalism
professionals, and national media. The downplaying of television's
culpability in Oswald's death supported emergent definitions about
what it meant to be a professional journalist, particularly in national
television. Omission thus reflected ongoing discourses about the
rightful boundaries of journalistic authority. The narratives that en-
dured emphasized the professionalism of national journalists, particularly television reporters, in covering the story. The media thus
asserted their authoritative status when retelling the assassination
story by omitting features that undermined, shadowed, or contradicted their authority.

Personalization

A third strategy for retelling the assassination was personalization. Reporters recollected the assassination in terms of their own experiences.

Journalists first personalized the story by referring to their familiarity with the events of Dallas, usually their presence there during
the assassination weekend. *Newsweek* reporter Charles Roberts detailed what he saw in an article called "Eyewitness in Dallas."[48] *Time*
correspondent Hugh Sidey authorized his account of the Kennedy
presidency by noting that "I was with him in Dallas, Texas on Novem-

ber 22, 1963. . . . Few correspondents who were there will ever forget that day."[49] In one of his books, Tom Wicker of the *New York Times* noted that his "two years as White House correspondent included coverage of President Kennedy's assassination."[50]

Pictures from the assassination weekend were reproduced with markers encircling reporters' torsos or heads. The article by Roberts reproduced a photograph of the author at the swearing-in of Lyndon B. Johnson aboard Air Force One. In the picture, thick white arrows pointed at the reporter's head, positioned behind that of the vice president.[51] A book by the same author reproduced on its back flap a picture of his Dallas press credentials.[52]

Television retrospectives began by setting out the November 1963 presence of their narrators, specifying exactly where in Dallas they had been. Reporter Steve Bell, who had been a national correspondent at the time, recollected the scene on the occasion of the twenty-fifth anniversary of Kennedy's death, in a report on the evening news in Philadelphia: "In Omaha, Nebraska, this young reporter and his wife had just been told by the doctor that our first child would be born any day now. Then the President was dead, and I was sent to Dallas to cover the aftermath."[53] The program then documented not only what had happened when Kennedy was shot but what else Bell had done in Dallas. It included footage of Bell's original televised coverage.

Setting up the journalist's presence in Dallas was central to legitimating the journalist as an authoritative spokesperson for the assassination story. When presence was impossible, journalists documented their efforts to be present. "At the time the shots were fired, I was an hour and a half out of Honolulu," wrote Kennedy's press secretary, Pierre Salinger, who then turned around the air carrier on which he was traveling and flew back to Washington.[54] Twenty-five years after the event, when television reporter Edwin Newman was called upon to narrate NBC's six-and-one-half-hour reconstruction of events, he began by noting that "I myself, having been told that I would be going to Dallas, went instead to Washington on a plane NBC had chartered."[55] Reporter John Chancellor introduced another television retrospective by talking about his experiences in Berlin at the time that Kennedy was shot.[56] Left unclear in both cases was why their personal experiences gave these particular reporters special authority to speak about the events of Kennedy's death.

In some cases, recalling the assassination story was grounded in the monitoring positions that certain reporters—such as Harrison Salisbury and Walter Cronkite—held at newspaper or network headquarters. In an article entitled "The Editor's View in New York," Salisbury recalled how he had organized assassination coverage for the *New York Times,* with his reconstruction of events reinforcing the important role he played.[57] Indeed, the relevance attached to monitoring the assassination story tended to be underscored in assassination tales from the outset. Marya Mannes wrote in December 1963: "I listened to the familiar voices of those men who we are highly privileged as a people to have as interpreters of events: Edward Morgan and Howard K. Smith, Walter Cronkite and Eric Sevareid and Charles Collingwood, Chet Huntley and David Brinkley, Marvin Kalb and Robert Pierpoint."[58] Few of the reporters Mannes mentioned were in Dallas. Most were anchorpersons or correspondents who monitored and commented upon the assassination story from afar.[59]

Personalization thus allowed media institutions to invoke the experiences of certain journalists as legitimate reconstructions of the assassination story. But by positioning themselves in the narrative through personal experience, journalists sidestepped the possibility that working from afar might be considered a flawed way to cover the assassination weekend. The fact that personalized narrative was held up by news organizations as a legitimate way to recollect the assassination story reinforced its importance. Wittingly or not, it also set up a credible framework by which to legitimate certain journalists as narrators of the assassination story, regardless of their actual role in covering it.

Rhetorical Legitimation: Cultural Authority through Narrative Adjustment

By setting up narratives in which they emerged as authoritative spokespersons for the assassination story, the media established their own rhetorical legitimation. While narrative did not constitute the complete process by which journalists would emerge as the story's preferred spokespeople, it nonetheless laid the groundwork for their authority. Since journalists' retellings of the story of Kennedy's death accommodated narrators in a variety of forms, retellings of the story became largely dependent on the presence of journalists. Narrative thereby set in motion a somewhat circular process of legitimating journalists as authoritative spokespersons. Over time, the assassination story came to be told mainly by journalists who were sufficiently authoritative to speak for its events. But by the same token, journalists became increasingly legitimated as spokespersons for the story through their presence in it.

The narrative strategies by which journalists retold the assassination story set up an extensive network that allowed them to rhetorically reconstruct their part in covering it. Personalization highlighted the importance of the reporter within the larger context of the president's death. Omission absented certain journalists, practices, and news organizations from those recollections. And synecdoche contextualized journalists' statements within larger discourses about the legitimation of television journalism and the journalistic profession. The precise ways in which the media used these strategies will be addressed in later chapters, but it is fitting to note here that the strategies were predicated on a self-referential discourse that in many cases advanced a false authority for the events of that weekend.

The centrality of narrative was predicated on the acceptance and recognition of narrative adjustment as a legitimate way of retelling the assassination. This acceptance erased barriers that in other circumstances might have obstructed the legitimation of journalists. The media's attempts to legitimate themselves appear to have been fertilized by the peculiar reality-based claims of assassination narratives and by the large spatial and temporal spans through which they were disseminated. This in turn encouraged the adjustment of narratives in accordance with even larger agendas—about journalistic professionalism, cultural authority, and television journalism. Within these cycles of rhetorical legitimation, journalists functioned as an interpretive community through their retellings.

Significantly, the acceptance of narrative adjustment as a mode of retelling the assassination stemmed in no small part from the chaos surrounding the events of Kennedy's death. Audiences existed, however briefly, in circumstances of confusion, void, and uncertainty. The media's ability to step into those circumstances and emerge as authoritative spokespersons was thus in part derived from the public's suspension of judgment. The overwhelming need for cohesion and community that the events of the assassination created—not only for journalists but also for the public—helped journalists flourish as cultural authorities through the narratives they told.

Part Two: Telling Assassination Tales

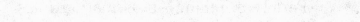

FOUR

"Covering the Body" by Telling
the Assassination

This numbed grief must be made articulate.
Editorial, *The Reporter* [1]

21 November 1963 was a routine day for the fifty-odd journalists who traveled with John F. Kennedy on a campaign trip to Dallas. They were expected to "cover the body," a journalistic assignment holding them responsible for monitoring the president's activities. It was not a particularly exciting beat, because journalists who covered the body simply followed the president wherever he went. But the assignment could become extremely important if the unpredictable were to happen. In such a circumstance, "covering the body" would make it possible for journalists and news organizations to keep up with the news. It gave news organizations a way of routinizing the unexpected. [2]

On 22 November 1963, however, "covering the body" took on a literal connotation, as Kennedy's assassination threw the boundaries of appropriate journalistic practice into question. Journalists were expected to "cover" Kennedy's dead body. What they could and could not do—or did and did not do—in covering the assassination story rattled formalized notions about what it meant to be a professional journalist. It is possible to see what happened to those notions by tracing the narratives through which the media recounted their part in the assassination story at the time of Kennedy's death.

Over the decades since Kennedy was assassinated, the media have transformed their accounts about his death into one long narrative memorializing the slain president. Journalists' memories extend over what appear to be four continuous days of grief and mourning. They begin with the arrival of the Kennedys in Dallas, extend through the president's motorcade and death, and conclude with his state funeral. Stories of this four-day period have come to constitute the master narrative by which the particulars of Kennedy's death have been told. Through it, the media have assumed responsibility for many of the smaller events that made up the assassination story, regardless of what they themselves saw, heard, or did.

Yet at the time of the assassination, journalists faced tasks that were far more discrete. Their coverage called for behavior that lay outside the bounds of formalized journalistic standards. The tragedy fell into what Gaye Tuchman has called the "what a story" category, the story that sidesteps routinized expectations, has no steadfast rules of coverage, and calls for strategies of improvisation and redefinition.[3] Herbert Gans has similarly discussed the "gee whiz" story, a classification which includes stories that do not fit into commonplace categories.[4] The assassination story thus called for the media to do whatever they could—through improvisation, trained instinct, or sheer good fortune—to acquire information. This presented a quandary, for while journalists did not possess standard guidelines for covering such a story, what journalists did, or said they did, had much to do with how they viewed themselves as professionals. Motivating their actions were fundamental notions about professionalism, journalistic practice, and the media technologies that assisted and hindered them in formulating authoritative stories. Their need to formulate such stories with few formal guidelines thus made the establishment of their authority all the more critical.

"Covering the Body": The Story as Corpus

Although they provided prompt and comprehensive coverage of Kennedy's assassination, journalists covering the event faced difficult and unanticipated circumstances. Most journalists did not see the event, and in some cases did not hear it; incorporated hearsay, rumor, and faulty information into their chronicles; and failed to seek out recognizable and authoritative sources. Journalistic methods upon which most reporters had come to rely—such as eyewitness status, access to sources, and fact verification—proved unhelpful and yielded an incomplete version of the story. The speed with which information was transmitted exceeded journalists' ability to gather it, and their inability to keep up was apparent to one of the largest viewing audiences in media history.

When Kennedy was assassinated, news editors quickly labeled the event "the biggest story of their lifetime."[5] Within twenty-four hours more than 300 media representatives had arrived in Dallas.[6] Because of the story's numerous unpredictable and potentially unmanageable angles, news organizations assigned individual journalists to seemingly finite "mini-events" within the more generalized assassination

story. Yet their assignments did not always match events as they occurred. The assassination remained a "breaking story" throughout.
The coverage of Lee Harvey Oswald's transfer, for example, became
coverage of his murder. Covering the succession story meant witnessing Lyndon Johnson's swearing-in amid the cramped conditions
aboard Air Force One. Those assigned to write the follow-up on Kennedy's shooting wrote instead about the killing of Officer Tippit and
about confusing medical briefings in Parkland Hospital. Although
the state funeral provided one forum in which the story's different
threads were temporarily brought together, journalists approached
the larger assassination story through units that seemed manageable
to them. This meant that they concentrated on independent and often
isolated moments of coverage that were later brought together in
larger narratives, where it was possible to recall, reconsider, and rethink the hows and whys of journalistic practice.

Moments of Coverage

While intended here as an analytical tool, reducing the assassination
story to discrete moments of coverage in effect reflected the task orientation of journalists covering the story. Journalists concentrated on
the immediate tasks to which they had been assigned.[7] Their accounts
generally focused on five moments of coverage: Kennedy's shooting;
the hospital; Johnson's swearing-in; the follow-up to Kennedy's shooting, including the murder of Lee Harvey Oswald; and Kennedy's
funeral. The following pages summarize how journalists recounted
those moments at the time of the assassination.

The Shooting

Although more than fifty Washington correspondents were in the
president's entourage, at the moment of Kennedy's assassination
most were corralled inside two press buses and a pool car taking them
to downtown Dallas. As a result, covering the assassination began, in
one reporter's view, "when the central fact of it was over."[8] By the
time a few reporters broke loose of the entourage,[9] the president's car
had already sped off to Parkland Hospital. Consequently, reporting
on the assassination was reconstructive and derivative from the beginning. Most reporters simply missed the initial event.

Typical reports of the shooting, taken respectively from radio, television, and the print media, went as follows:

It appears as though something has happened in the motorcade route. Something, I repeat, has happened in the
motorcade route. Parkland Hospital—there has been a
shooting. Parkland Hospital has been advised to stand by
for a severe gunshot wound. The official party, as I can
see it, turning around, going to the emergency room at
Parkland Hospital.[10]

At about 12:32, the motorcade turns a corner into a park-
way. The crowds are thinner . . . three shots are heard, like
toy explosions. [NBC cameraman Dave] Weigman jumps
from his car, running toward the President with his camera
running. People scream, lie down grabbing their children.
I leave the motorcade and run after police, who appear to
be chasing somebody. The motorcade moves on fast.[11]

As our press bus eased at motorcade speed down an in-
cline toward an underpass, there was a little confusion in
the sparse crowds that at that point had been standing at
the curb to see the President of the United States pass. As
we came out of the underpass, I saw a motorcycle police-
man drive over the curb, across an open area, a few feet
up a railroad bank, dismount, and start scrambling up
the bank.[12]

In each case the perspective was partial; no account confirmed that
the president had been hit. Accounts began through the uncertain
perspective of the bystander and sometimes incorporated innuendo,
rumor, and half-truth alongside verifiable fact. It took time before
journalists definitively knew what had happened. Afterward some
reporters maintained that they "were not aware that anything serious
had occurred until . . . two or three minutes later."[13]

For journalists who wanted to uphold their status as preferred observers, this situation posed obvious difficulties. While the assignment of "covering the body" gave them generous boundaries—of
proximity and access—in which to play out their authoritative presence in the story, the fact that they missed the event raised professional problems. Furthermore, because news organizations hungered
for a continual stream of information, the disjunctions felt by reporters sent to "cover the body" were magnified.

When Kennedy was shot, Jack Bell of the Associated Press was in
the pool car in the presidential motorcade. The *New York Times* published his account the next day, prefacing it with the observation that
he had "witnessed the shooting from the fourth car" in the procession.[14] The claim was doubtful, especially when Bell himself authorized the event through what he had *heard*, not what he had *seen:*

"There was a loud bang as though a giant firecracker had exploded in the caverns between the tall buildings we were just leaving behind us. In quick succession there were two other loud reports. The ominous sounds of these dismissed from the minds of us riding in the reporters' pool car the fleeting idea that some Texan was adding a bit of noise to the cheering welcome. . . . The man in front of me screamed, 'My God, they're shooting at the President.' "[15] As Bell looked back at the building from where he thought the shots had come, he said he "saw no significant signs of activity."[16] His narrative suggested that he also did not believe what he did see; when the pool car pulled up at Parkland Hospital, he jumped out and looked in the back seat of the presidential limousine: "For an instant I stopped and stared into the back seat. There, face down, stretched out at full length, lay the President, motionless. His natty business suit seemed hardly rumpled. But there was blood on the floor. 'Is he dead?' I asked a Secret Service man. 'I don't know,' he said, 'but I don't think so.' "[17] Even faced with firsthand evidence of an action that others contended had blown half of the president's head away, Bell needed confirmation.

Ironically, the Associated Press's eyewitness account for the assassination came from a staff photographer. Photographing the motorcade, James Altgens telephoned his Dallas editor with the news that Kennedy had been shot. "I saw it," he said. "There was blood on his face. Mrs. Kennedy jumped up and grabbed him and cried 'oh no!' The motorcade raced onto the freeway."[18] The Associated Press ran that account in full. Altgens's photograph of a Secret Service agent climbing over the back of Kennedy's limousine was transmitted twenty-five minutes after the shooting.[19] Two weeks later, *Editor and Publisher* published a profile of Altgens entitled "Lone 'Pro' on Scene Where JFK Was Shot." Tracing his career as a professional photographer, the article hailed the fact that Altgens's photographs remained exclusives "for 24 hours—until some amateur film turned up."[20]

During the shooting, Merriman Smith of United Press International (UPI) was seated in the same pool car as Bell. Like Bell, he did not see the event but did hear the shots. Over the pool car's radiophone, he reported that "three shots were fired at President Kennedy's motorcade in downtown Dallas."[21] Seeing but not knowing, hearing but not seeing, neither seeing nor hearing: such were the foundations on which journalists built their accounts of the event. As William Manchester later said of Smith: "Smith was not as astute a reporter as he seemed. Despite extensive experience with weapons, he had thought the sounds in the plaza were three shots from an automatic weapon, and in a subsequent message he identified them as bursts. But his speed was remarkable."[22] Initial reports of the assassination, while rapidly transmitted, thus displayed partial knowledge.

The lack of complete information was exacerbated by the virtual paralysis of the machinery of government information. Unlike the death of Roosevelt, which was "announced by a simultaneous phone call to three wire services from the White House,"[23] this death found official channels of information relay temporarily blocked, confused, or simply unavailable. Journalists initially had three choices: to exclude problematic information, to include it, or to qualify its inclusion by admitting that it had not been verified. As Wilbur Schramm later said, reporters on the Dallas story were "up against one of the classical problems of journalism: What constitutes evidence? When does a report have enough support to justify passing it along?"[24] Reporters lacked the time, the sources, and the circumstances to satisfactorily resolve such issues.

Information about the shooting was strung together in bits and pieces. Reporters needed to establish first that shots had been fired, then that the shots had wounded the president, whether the wound had been fatal, the truth of rumors of his death, and finally that he had died. With each step in that sequence, the certainty among journalists about what had happened grew. But each step also generated new questions, uncertainties, and inaccuracies. Accomplishing professional goals of coverage in an accurate, fact-based, and verifiable fashion was virtually impossible.

The main thrust of coverage was to inform the public quickly. Approximately sixty-one minutes elapsed while journalists worked their way down the initial story's sequence. First reports reached the wires just four minutes after the shots were fired.[25] Six minutes later, at 12:40 P.M., Walter Cronkite broke into CBS's "As the World Turns" to announce—in UPI's words—that "in Dallas Texas, three shots were fired at President Kennedy's motorcade. The first reports say that the President was seriously wounded."[26] Radio brought intermittent and fragmentary updates, mostly reworded wire-service accounts, such as this one: "We interrupt this program to bring you a special bulletin from ABC Radio. Three shots were fired at President Kennedy's motorcade today in downtown Dallas, Texas . . . State and local police have sealed off the area at Hyannis Port, where the Kennedys live. No one permitted to get near that area."[27] Before Kennedy was officially pronounced dead, more than half of the nation had heard news of the assassination attempt.[28]

These accounts do not suggest that journalists knew much more than their dispatches revealed. As William Manchester later re-counted, during that first hour "the ratio between the public and its true informants was roughly 38,000,000 : 1. The Cronkites and Hunt-leys were as out of touch as their demoralized listeners; the best they could do was pass along details."[29] Filmed footage showed journalists huddling in groups outside Parkland Hospital, clutching notepads and pencils. Many listened to radio, whose reporters, relatively un-encumbered by equipment, transmitted the paraphrased accounts of wire services. Television followed suit.

As the story edged on, reporters shared tasks by crossing the boundaries often imposed by news organization or medium. Local news staffers helped national organizations flesh out details.[30] *New York Times* reporter Tom Wicker maintained that "nobody thought about an exclusive; it didn't seem important."[31] Cooperation, as a standard of action, was "greater than it ever had been in the indus-try's history."[32] Although there were tales of rivalry and competition typical of everyday journalistic practice, it is significant that journal-ists' retellings of their coverage emphasized cooperation. Such an emphasis underscored the ritual aspects of telling the assassination tale, in which relaying the story temporarily became a collective goal, to be realized through shared knowledge. It thus made sense that the assassination story would come to be invoked by journalists inter-ested in setting up common boundaries and a collective frame for establishing authority.

The Hospital

An impromptu press conference at Parkland Hospital gave journalists their first chance to acquire information through institutional relay, less than an hour after the president was shot.[33] The conference, held by acting press secretary Malcolm Kilduff, confirmed that the presi-dent was dead. It led into a medical briefing, attended by surgeon Malcolm Perry and neurologist Kemp Clark, which generated one of the major sources of confusion over the exact nature of Kennedy's head wound and was called "the most tempestuous hour in the his-tory of American journalism. . . . The scene was bedlam. Several cor-respondents were hysterical. A question would be asked, and the doctor would be halfway through his answer when another reporter broke in with an entirely different question. Misquotations were inevitable. . . . Medical briefings were supposed to quash misunder-standings. The one at Parkland did exactly the opposite."[34] When re-porters asked Perry if it was possible that one bullet could have struck the president from the front, the doctor replied affirmatively. *Time* reporter Hugh Sidey, realizing the implications, cried, "Doctor, do you realize what you're doing? You're confusing us." But reporters quickly transmitted his answer to the public, and the next morning Americans across the country were already "convinced that a rifleman had fired from the top of the underpass."[35] This in turn gave rise to one of the major controversies over the nature of Kennedy's head wound.[36]

Soon after, transport of the presidential coffin from the hospital to Air Force One gave some journalists what would be their closest and most authoritative sightings of the president. In the *New York Times*, Tom Wicker's account of the activity around the bronze coffin was laced with the intricate detail of eyewitness reporting: "Mrs. Kennedy walked beside [the coffin]. Her face was sorrowful. She looked steadily at the floor. She still wore the raspberry-colored suit in which she had greeted welcoming crowds in Fort Worth and Dallas. But she had taken off the matching pillbox hat she wore earlier in the day, and her dark hair was windblown and tangled."[37] His account focused largely on the appearance and actions of the widow. Ten days later, his account of the same event was more distanced: "They brought the body out in a bronze coffin. A number of White House staff people—stunned, silent, stumbling along as if dazed—walked with it. Mrs. Kennedy walked by the coffin, her hand on it, her head down, her hat gone, her dress and stockings spattered. She got into the hearse with the coffin. The staff men crowded into cars and followed."[38] In the second account, Wicker reported Jacqueline Kennedy's actions alongside those of the White House staff, suggesting that he had taken a metaphoric step backward to include them in the picture. By this time, the journalist was sufficiently distanced from the widow's grief to report her activities around the casket as part of a larger discourse about the continuity of government and government machinery. Significantly, the casket's removal was, in Tom Wicker's words, "just about the only incident that I got with my own eyes that entire afternoon."[39]

The events at Parkland Hospital slightly offset the jarring confusion of the first hour that followed Kennedy's shooting. Journalists were able to activate the institutional channels through which they usually obtained their information. Transport of the president's coffin reinforced the eyewitness status of those journalists who witnessed it. Journalists' presence at Parkland Hospital provided details that helped journalists legitimate themselves as spokespersons for the story. For that reason, details from the hospital—stories of journalists milling about outside, the medical briefing, the transport of the body—filled audio, prose, photographic, and filmed assassination accounts. This was not because the hospital constituted a central part of the larger assassination narrative. Rather, it was because it signaled a return to order until more authoritative filmed and photographic records of the actual shooting would become available. Coverage of journalists' presence at the hospital offered a way for them to maintain their authority as professionals, and thus to credential their coverage of the story. In other words, emphasizing this particular moment of coverage helped journalists lend credence to their presence within the larger assassination narrative.

The Swearing-In

Following the shooting, coverage of the assassination branched in three separate directions—the swearing-in, the investigative follow-up to Kennedy's murder, and the national mourning for the president.[40] In one arena of coverage, journalists were assigned to what William Manchester later suggested was the "other story"—Lyndon Johnson's succession as president.[41] Confused communiqués between Kennedy's staff, Attorney General Robert Kennedy in Washington, and the president-elect resulted in a hasty decision to inaugurate Johnson at the airport before Air Force One was airborne. Johnson agreed for reporters to be present as eyewitnesses.[42]

This made the swearing-in one of the few times during the assassination weekend when journalists played an officially recognized role as eyewitnesses. Three journalists agreed to serve as the press pool. Merriman Smith of UPI said, "Jiggs Fauver [of the White House transportation office] . . . grabbed me and said Kilduff wanted a pool of three men immediately to fly back to Washington on Air Force One, the Presidential Aircraft. . . . Down the stairs I ran and into the driveway, only to discover Kilduff had just pulled out in our telephone car. Charles Roberts [of *Newsweek*], Sid Davis [of Westinghouse Broadcasting] and I implored a police officer to take us to the airport in his squad car."[43] Davis went aboard the plane to cover the swearing-in but did not return to Washington.[44] He instead supplied pool coverage of the event to a busload of reporters who arrived as the plane took off. Said one reporter, "I shall not soon forget the picture in my mind, that man [Davis] standing on the trunk of a white car, his figure etched against the blue, blue Texas sky, all of us massed around him at his knees as he told us of what had happened in that crowded compartment in Air Force One."[45] Thus was Johnson's swearing-in chronicled. Special importance was accorded the role of White House photographer Cecil Stoughton, who produced the official photograph of the event. *Editor and Publisher* said that the shot of Johnson raising his hand "may become one of our most historic photographs." [46]

But the uncertainty and hasty arrangements surrounding Johnson's swearing-in resulted in coverage that was spotty and uneven. The *New York Times* complained that "no accurate listing of those present could be obtained." [47] The thirty-four words that made Johnson president were recounted verbatim, with little attempt to enclose them within a larger narrative. Accounts, scripted like descriptions of photographic poses, stiffly recorded who stood next to whom and what color clothes each person wore.

The fact that reporters witnessed the swearing-in was nonetheless important for establishing professional credibility. It gave journalists a professional presence within the larger assassination story, and that presence was highly regarded by other members of the press corps. Charles Roberts was interviewed on the "Huntley-Brinkley Report" the night of the assassination about his experiences in witnessing the swearing-in. [48] Roberts also used his attendance at the swearing-in and the plane ride home to credential his writing of a 1967 book about the assassination. [49]

The Follow-Up

A much larger group of journalists set to work unraveling some of the assassination's threads. Their follow-up work began Friday night, when Dallas police attempted to hold a midnight photo opportunity with Kennedy's accused killer, Lee Harvey Oswald. More than 100 persons filled the halls of the police station, whose conditions were "not too much unlike Grand Central Station at rush hour." [50] The police's attempts to deal with the mounting pressure for information were met with a growing influx of reporters. In one view, the resulting situation was near chaos: "Cameramen stood on the tables to take pictures and others pushed forward to get close-ups. . . . After Oswald had been in the room only a few minutes, Chief Curry intervened and directed that Oswald be taken back to jail because, he testified, the 'newsmen tried to overrun him.'" [51] Oswald was to be transferred from the city to the county jail on Sunday morning. Armed with details of the transfer, the press corps arrived in groups. By 10 A.M., an estimated fifty journalists were in attendance in the basement of the city jail, including still photographers, television camera people, and reporters from all media.[52] Conditions for coverage were among the best available to journalists during the assassination weekend.

The transfer began almost immediately. Reporters pushed and shoved to get a word with Oswald. As one participant recalled, "all the newsmen were poking their sound mikes across to him and asking questions, and they were everyone sticking their flashbulbs up and around and over [Oswald] and in his face."[53] The "near-blinding television and motion picture lights which were allowed to shine upon the escort party increased the difficulty of observing unusual movements in the basement."[54] This would later give rise to discussions about whether journalists had facilitated Oswald's death. Tom Pettit of NBC later remembered that

> in that throng it was difficult for any reporter to sort out who was who. But for the television reporters the problem was compounded by the need for simultaneous transmission. What was recorded by microphones and cameras (either film or live) would go on the air without much editing. What transpired in the hallway was broadcast without much opportunity for evaluation. And the television reporter could not move about freely, since his own movement was limited by the length of his microphone cable.[55]

What happened after that became, in the eyes of certain observers, "a first in television history."[56] Jack Ruby stepped out from the group of reporters, drew a gun, and pulled the trigger. Oswald slumped to the floor. The irony that he had been hidden by the very group of journalists trying to record his transfer was momentarily lost as the group shifted its focus to record the murder in sound, voice, still photographs, and live television.

Radio reporters called out the news of Oswald's shooting, with Radio Press International broadcasting the sound of the shot to its subscribers around the world.[57] Ike Pappas, who was then a reporter for WNEW Radio in New York, was one of those present:

> I went forward with my microphone and I said, this is the last time you can talk to Lee Harvey Oswald, ask that question again, and I said "Do you have anything to say in your defense?" Just as I said "defense," I noted out of the corner of my eye, this black streak went right across my front and leaned in and, pop, there was an explosion. And I felt the impact of the air from the explosion of the gun on my body. . . . And then I said to myself, if you never say anything ever again into a microphone, you must say it now.

> This is history. And I heard people shouting in back of me
> "he's been shot." So I said the only thing which I could
> say, which was the story: "Oswald has been shot. A shot
> rang out. Oswald has been shot."[58]

Despite Pappas's immediate presence, he did not himself piece together the information that Oswald had been shot. His relay of the incident was thus in some sense derived from the accounts of reporters around him.

Written accounts dwelled on the incredibility of Oswald having been shot in view of the photographic and television cameras.[59] Still photographs of the homicide pushed editors at the *Dallas Morning News* into publishing a second edition: the photograph on its front page displayed Ruby clearly pointing a gun at Oswald; a photograph taken seconds later, by *Dallas Times-Herald* photographer Bob Jackson, showed Oswald crumpling under the impact of the gunshot.[60] One trade article, entitled "Pictures of Assassination Fall to Amateurs on Street," held that photographic capture of Oswald's death offset the largely amateur photographic recording of Kennedy's shooting— pictures that were "out of focus" and photographers who were "non-professional."[61] Photographic coverage of Oswald's death upheld the professionalism of news photographers whose work, with the exception of Altgens's photograph of the presidential car, had until that point played little part in recording the story.

But the story of Oswald's murder belonged mainly to television. Recounted *Broadcasting* magazine, "For the first time in the history of television, a real-life homicide was carried nationally on live television when millions of NBC-TV viewers saw the November 24 fatal shooting in Dallas of the man accused of assassinating JFK two days earlier."[62] The story played live on NBC. CBS recorded the event on a local camera. Although the network's New York headquarters were not featuring that camera on live feed, they were able to replay immediate coverage from a videotape monitor.[63] ABC, whose cameraperson had already moved on to the county jail, had to compensate with unfilmed accounts of the story.[64]

The presence of journalists was quickly made an integral part of the story of Oswald's murder. A caption under the photograph of Oswald sinking to the floor read, "Dallas detectives struggle with Ruby as newsmen and others watch."[65] Reporters recounted the cries of NBC correspondent Tom Pettit and other reporters on the scene. Replays of Pettit shouting, "He's been shot, he's been shot, Lee Oswald has been shot!" constituted one way to legitimate the journalist as eyewitness. They also referenced the institutional presence of the news organization to which he belonged.

A special section of *Broadcasting* magazine, issued one week after the assassination, carried the following description of Oswald's murder: "Oswald, flanked by detectives, stepped onto a garage ramp in the basement of the Dallas city jail and was taken toward an armored truck that was to take him to the county jail. Suddenly, out of the lower right hand corner of the TV screen, came the back of a man. A shot rang out, and Oswald gasped as he started to fall, clutching his side."[66] A telling feature of this narrative came in its second sentence, which was repeated verbatim in numerous media accounts: "Suddenly, *out of the lower right hand corner of the TV screen*, came the back of a man" (emphasis added). The juxtaposition of reality and televised image, by which Oswald's killer was seen coming out of a corner of the television screen rather than a corner of the basement, paid the ultimate compliment to television's coverage of the event. In the case of Oswald's death, television was featured as offering a reality that seemed momentarily preferable to the real-life situation on which it was based.

Coverage of Oswald's murder thus resolved to some extent the uncertain eyewitness status of reporters, which had characterized their coverage of Kennedy's shooting. The adjunct technologies used by journalists authenticated them as eyewitnesses through various replays of the incident. The event, now witnessed by camera as well as by the human eye, emphasized the media's presence, particularly that of news photographers and television journalists, and brought it into assassination chronicles. Reporters would replay the murder across media with the assistance of tapes, recordings, and photographs. Through technology, their reactions would become embedded in the story's retelling.

The Mourning

Still another arena of coverage took shape in Washington. From Saturday onward, the media began to attend to the growing processions of mourners. The fact that Kennedy's body would lie in state in the Capitol rotunda before the funeral offered journalists a continuous stage of activities connected with the assassination story. Decisions to display those activities reflected far-reaching normative and organizational responses to the assassination story.

Newspapers canceled columns of advertisements in order to make room for extra copy.[67] *Parade* magazine held up distribution of an issue that featured an article about Jacqueline Kennedy in the White House, feeling that it would be insensitive in the aftermath of the assassination.[68] Networks canceled commercials and substituted special coverage for scheduled programming.[69] Making the Kennedy assassination their only story through Monday evening, television cameras focused nonstop on private citizens viewing the presidential coffin. NBC broadcast continuously for nearly forty-two hours.[70] The long and continuous coverage highlighted what many observers called the best of television, which "transported the viewer to the scenes of news."[71] Coverage culminated in Kennedy's funeral on Monday, which by Nielsen estimates constituted the heaviest day of television viewing within the assassination weekend, with 93 percent of TV-equipped households viewing the funeral procession to Arlington National Cemetery.[72]

Central to all moments of coverage within the assassination story was the media's role of offering consolation. Covering the assassination turned journalists into agents of unification and reassurance. The "individual catharsis, the laying of doubts to rest and the reinforcement of American norms" were more the rule than the exception.[73] Communication channels "reassured people that the functions of government were being carried on smoothly, that there was no conspiracy and that there was no further threat."[74] Trade magazines later set aside special sections to laud radio and television's deportment, dignity, and maturity in covering the news.[75] Television broadcaster Edwin Newman said on the night of the assassination:

> We shall hear much in the next few days about the need to bind up the wounds of the nation, and about the need for all Americans to stand together. We may treat those words as empty slogans or as real needs to be genuinely met. Whatever we do, that can be no guarantee that what happened today will not happen again. But what is within our power, we should do. And it is within our power to be more serious about our public life.[76]

James Reston's Washington column the day after the assassination was perhaps first to set out in print the parameters of journalistic consolation. Entitled "Why America Weeps," the column began: "America wept tonight, not alone for its dead young President, but for itself. The grief was general, for somehow the worst in the nation had prevailed over the best. . . . There is however consolation in the fact that while he was not given time to finish anything or even to realize his own potentialities, he has not left the nation in a state of crisis or danger."[77] Celebrated by other journalists as "magnificent . . . its content better than reality," Reston's column was eventually regarded as a landmark piece of assassination coverage.[78] Other news organizations positioned the words of journalists in prominent places. One Colorado newspaper relocated the column of Walter Lippmann to the lead spot on the front page and ran his reaction alongside details of the assassination.[79]

The role of journalists in providing consolation grew with their coverage of the mourning and the funeral. Media presentations were saturated with messages of stability, unity, and continuity. Mourning Kennedy was treated like grieving for a friend. Political questions, such as the possibility of upheaval, threat, or conspiracy, were thrust aside. The mood was one of continuity rather than disruption.

The sounds of mourning resounded long after the funeral concluded at Arlington National Cemetery. The day after Kennedy's burial, the *New York Times* recalled "the tattoo of muffled drums, the hoof beats of the horses, the measured cadence of the honor guards, a tolling of a distant bell, and the sound of bands as they played marches and hymns."[80] Sounds were broadcast with an immediacy that brought listeners from across the world in contact with the event as it unfolded.[81] The silence of journalists who catered to them reinforced their supportive role.

The poignancy of the weekend belonged most of all to television's treatment of the visual image. It was ironic that television's triumph resulted from the fact that the voices of its commentators were silent; as the *New York Times* commented in a bracketed and separate paragraph about television's performance: "And often there was silence."[82] It went on to say that "when the day's history is written, the record of television as a medium will constitute a chapter of honor."[83] *Broadcasting* magazine called television's continuous coverage mature, dignified, expert, and professional.[84] "Touches of pure television," in addition to the filming of Oswald's murder, included Jacqueline Kennedy kneeling in the rotunda with daughter Caroline to kiss the flag on the coffin, son John Jr. saluting the caisson outside St. Matthew's Cathedral, the towering figure of Charles de Gaulle marching beside the tiny frame of Haile Selassie, and the dignity of the riderless horse.[85] In many of those moments, the "good taste of television asserted itself as the cameras veered away to ensure privacy"; in others, the cameras anticipated what the audiences wanted to see.[86]

Consolation, Information, and Authority

The ability of the media to tell the story of the Kennedy assassination was accomplished despite uneven moments of coverage. Some of these moments—such as the funeral and the murder of Oswald—

constituted professional triumphs. Others—notably the actual assassination—were fraught with conduct that failed to meet professional standards. In the latter case, formalized notions of journalistic practice gave way to journalists' ability to respond in whatever way possible to unexpected circumstances. Thus, the lack of access to sources led to an overemphasis on activities at the hospital, even though journalists acted in an unruly fashion at the hospital press conference. Coverage of the swearing-in, hailed for its photographic record rather than its presentation in prose, was terse, uneven, and stilted. The murder of Oswald posed serious questions about the intrusive nature of journalistic practice.

The casting of the assassination coverage as a story of professional triumph was thus not always supported by journalists' activities on the scene. It was, however, embedded in the narratives by which they would later reconstruct their activities. Rhetorical legitimation would be invoked over time as an antidote to what was in many ways a situation of journalistic failure. In retelling their coverage, journalists would successfully emerge as professionals and reinstate their authority for the story of Kennedy's death.

Already by the end of the assassination weekend, the media had begun to refine the story in the direction of a larger narrative. Charles Collingwood of CBS gave the following brushed-up scenario of the Kennedy shooting on Monday evening. By then, he was armed with a still photograph of the incident:

> This was the scene in the big open Lincoln a split second after that shot. The President is slumping to his left. Mrs. Kennedy, half rising, seems to stretch out an encircling arm. Governor Connally, in the seat ahead of the President, is half-turned toward the President. He's either been hit himself or is about to be. At this moment, no one knew how seriously the President had been wounded. But from this moment, events in Dallas moved with dizzying speed.[87]

Collingwood's account differed considerably from the wire-service reports that television correspondents had delivered verbatim just four days earlier. In the later version, the photograph of the shooting provided the focal point of Collingwood's story. His familiarity with its details hid the fact that he himself had not witnessed the event. The photograph legitimated him as an eyewitness—if not of the event, then of its record. The reconstructive work of narration thus bolstered his partial authority for the event. It also embedded the media's role in the story's retelling. As Collingwood said already on the evening of November 25, "in this day of television and radio, the word spread quickly. Work in offices and homes came to a standstill, as people sat transfixed by television and radio sets."[88] Few accounts of the assassination omitted this point.

It is therefore no surprise that what the media later said they did in covering the assassination story often did not match their original activities. The resolution of many problems of coverage through the long weekend—such as the lack of eyewitness status, the need to gain access to high-ranking sources, the pressure to verify facts, and the unmatchable pace of information relay—suggested that the larger context would help journalists recast individual mishaps of coverage as incidental parts of a larger drama.

This explains why already by Monday many journalists had begun to retell the event from the perspective of authoritative chroniclers, their accounts replacing the uncertain words of bystanders with more definite observations. Armed with bystanders' eyewitness accounts, amateur photographs, preliminary reports offered by the police and medical establishment, and later filmed chronicles, journalists began to counter their own problematic authority. Because their retellings contextualized discrete moments of coverage within one coherent narrative, the image of professional journalists would emerge not from single events like the Kennedy shooting but from the master narrative into which they were eventually recast. This made journalists into authoritative spokespersons for the story in its entirety, not just for the discrete moments of coverage they personally saw and heard (or, in the worst of cases, did not see and did not hear). More important, their retellings began to reveal characteristics of the larger discourses into which the story of the assassination would eventually be coopted.

In recounting their part in covering Kennedy's assassination, reporters created boundaries of the event that went beyond the actual moments during which the president was killed. Adopting synecdochic representations of the story, they reconstructed the event as one master narrative, which began Friday morning, when President and Mrs. Kennedy were met with bouquets of red roses at Love Airfield in Dallas, and ended Monday afternoon, when the slain president was laid to rest in Arlington National Cemetery. This stretch of four days entered the collective consciousness and has been perpetuated by reporters as a single story, which sought to lend closure to the events of Kennedy's death. It made the media's presence meaningful not only because of the information they provided but also because of their ability to narrate a gripping public drama and guide the

American people through shock, grief, and reconciliation.[89] Regard for their skills in the provision of information was thus in part determined by regard for their rhetorical talents.

This situation established boundaries by which the media could legitimate themselves as an authoritative interpretive community. To do so, reporters had to overcome many of the problems of providing information that were posed by the assassination story. To compensate for its unroutinized and unpredictable conditions and pressing institutional demands for information, journalists needed to construct themselves as a community that provided more than just information. Thus they recast their role as one of providing both consolation—acting as masters of ceremonies and playing an active part in healing the nation—and information.

The enduring quality of reporters' tales also rested beyond the event, with technology. It is not coincidental that journalists' memories of the assassination paralleled the coverage of the event by television. Professional memories began and ended in direct correspondence with the coverage the medium provided, adopting the four-day time span that lent the event continuity. The ready adoption of television's technological parameters, however, raised serious questions about the degree to which reporters' authority for telling the story was originally justified. The perpetuation over time of the narratives offered by one technology affirmed the extent to which journalists' professionalism depended on the medium of television. Technology, in a sense, stabilized the incomplete nature of professional practice.

The master narrative of Kennedy's death thus told of "covering the body," both literally and figuratively. Its message was one of information, on the one hand, and of solace and consolation, on the other. In such a way, the media sought to lend closure to events that they figured would otherwise remain difficult and incomprehensible. The implicit message of stories about "covering the body" of President Kennedy laid the foundation for reporters to erect a story of journalistic professionalism. Authority for the story was not always grounded in journalistic practice, but rather in narratives about practice, in which journalists gave themselves a central role in the story. Journalists—particularly television journalists—therefore came to use the assassination tale strategically to legitimate themselves as professionals, transforming the narrative as much into a story about American journalists as about the nation's thirty-fifth president.

FIVE

"Covering the Body" by Mediated Assessment

In the weeks immediately after the assassination, journalists made efforts to turn the story into a tale of professional accomplishment. Their narratives in the media stressed the importance of reporters' improvisational and instinctual behavior over their formalized professional routines. Journalists thereby stretched notions of professional journalistic practice to legitimate themselves as authoritative spokespersons for the assassination story.

Journalists set forth two assessments of their assassination coverage: they addressed the limits of their authority through stories of mishap, and they showed how they had overcome such limits through stories of triumph.

Stories of Mishap

Journalists' stories of mishap emerged from the public perception that the assassination story had placed "perhaps the heaviest burden in modern times on the news-gathering capabilities of the American press."[1] The event's disorder, the unevenness of different moments of coverage, reporters' failure to gain access to sources and inability to verify facts—all called for journalists to employ a variety of coping strategies.

To some extent, coping strategies were necessitated by the unusual nature of the event and the unending demand for information that it generated. *New York Times* reporter Tom Wicker heard a car radio blare news of the president's death while he was among those milling about outside Parkland Hospital. "No authority," he said later of the broadcast. "No supporting evidence, but I believed it immediately because in that situation it sounded right and it sounded true."[2] Elsewhere he said that he knew of "no reporter who was there who has a clear and orderly picture of that surrealistic afternoon; it is still a matter of bits and pieces thrown hastily into something like a whole."[3] Nonetheless, journalists were expected to respond instantly to unexpected circumstances, bend established rules and procedures on a hunch, and be correct in doing so. By raising questions about givens of practice and rearranging the significance attached to them, they were able to deal with mishaps and reinstate their authority for the story.

Missing the Scoop

One mishap which appeared in mediated accounts was a tale of missing the journalistic "scoop." This arose from the fact that Kennedy's shooting, the major event of the weekend, was mainly witnessed by amateurs, not professionals. In prose accounts journalists had no choice but to incorporate the words of laypersons who provided pieces of what had happened. Amateurs, such as Abraham Zapruder, Mary Muchmore, and Orville Nix, had recorded the shooting on film and had outpaced the "TV cameras recording the motorcade [which] didn't get usable pictures";[4] still photographic evidence of Kennedy's shooting had been provided by amateur photographers Mary Moorman and David Miller, who captured the moment with Polaroid cameras, in what one trade publication said were distanced, unprofessional, and unfocused images.[5] Professional photographers admitted that they "never had a chance to take a picture," other than the Associated Press shot of the Secret Service agent sprinting onto the back of the Kennedy automobile.[6] Eyewitnesses, such as Jean Hill and Howard Brennan, had given statements about what they had seen and heard.

All of this lay activity challenged journalists' professionalism. In order to make coverage of Kennedy's death a story of professional triumph, it became necessary to lessen the importance of the "scoop" that so many of them had missed by redefining what it meant. Goals moved from generating firsthand information to collecting it secondhand: UPI, for example, "claimed it provided the first film for TV of President Kennedy's assassination when it sold sequences shot by Dallas amateur photographer Mary Muchmore to WNEW-TV New York."[7] Similarly, *Life* was hailed for running Zapruder's sequence as a four-page photographic spread in its 29 November issue. The poor alternative this offered to journalists providing footage themselves was not addressed in either case: in the text accompanying the pictures in *Life*, Zapruder's name was not mentioned, and the sequence was described as a "remarkable and exclusive series of pictures," which displayed the details of Kennedy's death "for the first time."[8]

Professional photographer Richard Stolley recounted how *Life* sent him to engineer purchase of the Zapruder film. He observed that Zapruder "was gentle with us, almost apologetic that it was a middle-aged dressmaker and not one of the world-famous photographers with the Presidential press party who had provided the only filmed account of the President's murder."[9] Bidding over the heads of UPI, the Associated Press, and rival newsmagazines, *Life* paid $150,000 for all rights to the film. The purchase was undoubtedly intended to boost magazine sales, but it also corrected with money what *Life*'s staff had missed in practice. Interestingly, it also highlighted the importance of technology, for *Life* bought the technologically produced *record* of the assassination, not the coverage itself. This extended the practices by which journalists could consider themselves authorities for the assassination, in that buying the record of someone else's efforts of coverage became equated with having covered the event themselves.

Similar attempts surrounded still photography. James Featherston, a reporter for the *Dallas Times-Herald,* told of obtaining a Polaroid photograph of the shooting from a woman bystander, although some reports held that he took it by force.[10] Photographs were sometimes published with no mention of the amateurs who took them, violating the generally accepted rules of acknowledgment.

Discomfort about missing the major scoop of the assassination weekend was reflected in interviews conducted with journalists one year later. They held that most news organizations—which had been lauded for their good taste in refraining from showing explicit photographs or footage of Kennedy's assassination—would have displayed the footage had it been available. Said one researcher: "The American public beyond Dallas did not witness the assassination of the President simply because the television cameras had not been set up in the fateful block and because film of the event was not available until some time later, when its news value had changed to historical value."[11] Missing the footage thus punctured the authority of journalists as professionals.

Yet discomfort was lessened by technology, which made it possible for journalists to turn first-order collection of information into second-order collection of the information gathered by others. In their narratives, journalists adjusted "missing the scoop" into a second-order practice, in which they bought, took, or borrowed the records generated by others. Technology thus helped journalists hold onto their professional image.

Being a Secondhand Witness

Another tale of mishap focused on what has since become a mainstay of on-the-spot journalism, the eyewitness report. Long discussed as a controversial area of the legal system, where its unreliability tends to undermine its value,[12] eyewitness testimony presented a body of data that remains a lingering source of uncertainty about the assassination record.

In covering Kennedy's death, questions of eyewitness testimony—and who was competent and authorized to provide it—were complicated by the large numbers of people who had gathered to watch the presidential motorcade. Journalists mingled with the crowds, and their observations were countered or supported by lay testimony. This called into question the eyewitness report as a specific form of journalistic recordkeeping and had an observable effect on journalistic claims to the role of eyewitness. In the opinion of *Newsweek* correspondent Charles Roberts, journalists were supposed to be "trained professional observers."[13] Yet few journalists actually saw the president being killed. As William Manchester later said, reporters "weren't learning much where they were. . . . They were dependent on the cooperation of colleagues and tolerant passers-by who hopefully would be reliable."[14] "If I learned anything in Dallas that day, besides what it's like to be numbed by shock and grief, it was that eyewitness testimony is the worst kind," Roberts recalled.[15] In his 1967 book on the assassination, Roberts tore apart the authority of the eyewitness report as a genre. The "more that is written about Dallas on the basis of eyewitness recollection, the more my suspicion is confirmed," he said.[16] Tracing his own faulty recall of details associated with the president's car, the grassy knoll, the swearing-in, he described some of the problems surrounding eyewitness testimony:

> To be a witness to the events that followed the final shot was like witnessing the proverbial explosion in a shingle factory and not knowing, at each split second, where to look. I would hesitate to testify under oath to some events I saw peripherally. With hindsight, I now realize that many of the words I frantically took down from the mouths of witnesses during the next few hours were the product of imagination, shock, confusion, or from something much worse—the macabre desire of some bystanders to be identified with a great tragedy, or to pretend greater first-hand knowledge of the event than they actually possess.[17]

While Roberts complained that eyewitness testimony provided incomplete, faulty, subjective data, he nonetheless carefully documented his own eyewitness stature. His book was billed as an "eyewitness reporter's documented point-by-point study."[18] The dustjacket's back flap displayed a picture of his press credentials under the title: "official White House badge which [he] wore during the assassination." The flap also told readers that Roberts "was in the first press bus of the Kennedy motorcade when the shots rang out. He was one of only two reporters who witnessed the swearing-in of Lyndon Johnson aboard Air Force One at Dallas and then accompanied the new President, his wife and Mrs. Kennedy to Washington aboard the plane bearing the body of the slain President."[19]

Roberts's book displayed a picture of Johnson's swearing-in with the caption, "standing behind the President is Charles Roberts, author of this book."[20] The same picture was reproduced in *Newsweek* with a thick white arrow pointing to Roberts, alongside the caption, "The long voyage home: Charles Roberts (arrow) covers LBJ's swearing-in."[21] All of this suggests that while Roberts (or his publisher) was ambivalent about his eyewitness status, he was also careful to document it. The extensive credentialing attested to the importance of eyewitness status for members of the journalistic community.

Roberts was not the only reporter to admit such an ambivalence. Tom Wicker, writing in the *New York Times* the day after the assassination, pointed out that "most reporters in the press buses were too far back to see the shooting. . . . It was noted that the President's car had picked up speed and raced away, but reporters were not aware that anything serious had occurred."[22] Wicker went on to lament the limited vision of most reporters in the motorcade. Yet Wicker's own eyewitness account was systematically circulated as one of the more detailed eyewitness reports of the assassination.[23]

Journalists tried to compensate for the unreliability of eyewitness reports by rearranging pieces of the story, so that the eyewitness account became less central to the overall assassination report. Using techniques of synecdoche, omission, and personalization (described in chapter 3), they downplayed the flaws of the eyewitness report while at the same time underscoring its importance as a method of recordkeeping. Technology helped them do so, providing a stabilizing influence by offering a record of journalistic presence through technological output, such as photographs and films. For example, footage that "witnessed" Oswald's shooting helped underscore reporters' eyewitness status, regardless of what being an eyewitness helped them see. Technology thereby helped journalists uphold their authority as professionals by redefining aspects of journalistic practice. By concentrating on events that featured journalists as eyewitnesses, journalists made secondhand-witness status less of a mishap in the assassination's overall narrative than it might have been.

The role of eyewitness was thus invoked both as a basis for journalistic authority and as a faulty method of journalistic recordkeeping. Journalists' ambivalence about it suggested that they remained unclear about the part it should play and also hinted at why the assassination encouraged the reordering of certain professional practices.

Interfering with Events

The possibility that journalists had interfered with events of the assassination weekend was also aired in the media. This particular mishap entered into tales of covering Oswald's murder, in which journalists publicly considered their responsibilities on two fronts—physical (facilitating Oswald's murder) and legal-ethical (circulating half-truths and prematurely establishing Oswald's guilt).

Physical interference in the events surrounding Oswald's murder was problematic for reporters who publicly questioned whether it was possible for them to have been present without interfering. Because Oswald had been shot at close range by Jack Ruby, who emerged from a group of journalists standing in the basement of the city jail, journalists asked whether they had facilitated Oswald's death. They considered whether journalistic practice was at odds with the procedures for transporting Oswald safely. The sheer number of reporters, cables, and pieces of camera equipment was blamed for cluttering the spaces around Oswald. Marya Mannes penned her complaints at the time in *The Reporter:*

> The clutter of newsmen and their microphones in the basement corridor. The milling and talking, and then those big fat men bringing the thin pasty prisoner, and then the back of a man with a hat, and then Oswald doubled, and then pandemonium, scuffles, shouts and young Tom Truitt and his microphone in and out of the picture trying to find out what happened. Questions seethed through my mind: How in God's name could the police expose a President's assassin to this jumble of people at close range? [24]

It was no coincidence that many journalists' complaints centered on television and its elaborate technology. The newness of television news meant that many reporters were unaccustomed to the equipment that television journalists brought with them.

Another concern among journalists centered on their legal-ethical interference, particularly the adoption of half-truths and the premature establishment of Oswald's guilt. *Newsweek* magazine commented on Oswald's statement that he had not killed anyone by stating, "This was a lie."[25] When the *New York Times* published a banner headline that read "President's Assassin Shot to Death,"[26] one observer lamented the disappearance of the term *alleged*. The facts were insufficient to prove his guilt, contended Richard Tobin in the *Saturday Review*. "Lee Harvey Oswald had not yet legally been indicted, much less convicted, of President Kennedy's assassination. The *New York Times* had no right whatever under American law or the standards of journalistic fair play to call the man the 'President's assassin'. . . . What did the *Times'* own banner line do if not prejudge without trial, jury or legal verdict?"[27] The headline prompted the *Times's* editor Turner Catledge to publish a letter in which he admitted that the paper had erred.[28]

For journalists discussing the assassination story in the media, interference in events ranged from the placement of cables to larger questions about the media's ability to determine reality. Journalists raised questions about whether the physical, ethical, and legal dimensions of their behavior had undercut their professionalism. It was thus no surprise that they used tales of interference to air fundamental questions about appropriate journalistic practice, particularly in conjunction with the budding technology of television.

Succumbing to Technology

Lesser mishaps ranged from minute detail that was incorrectly conveyed to entire stories that never made it to print or broadcast. These included misquotations, inaccuracies, and contradictory reports about the make of the gun, the number of shots, the number of assassins, and the location from which the assassin had fired.[29] Even whether or not Jacqueline Kennedy's skirt had been spattered with blood was discussed.[30]

Many mishaps had to do with technology and the fact that journalists felt that they had not always mastered it. Dallas TV reporter Ron Reiland, "the only reporter" to accompany police to the Texas theater where Oswald had hidden, mishandled the equipment necessary for indoor filming, "suffering one of the hardest scoop losses of the period."[31] NBC's Bill Ryan read verbatim from the Associated Press bulletins held by technicians at his feet and held up photographs of the motorcade because there was "no videotape and no film."[32] A phone patch to NBC correspondent Robert MacNeil at Parkland Hospital failed because of overloaded circuits.[33] It took CBS nearly twenty minutes to join Walter Cronkite's face with his voice, an incident that encouraged network officials later to install a special "flash studio" facilitating simultaneous visual and audio transmission.[34]

One reporter's technological mishap was often another's triumph. Despite a general air of cooperation, tales of rivalry and competition found their way into retellings. After the shots had been fired at Kennedy, Merriman Smith of UPI and Jack Bell of the Associated Press rushed for a telephone to report the story. Seated in the front of the pool car, Smith accomplished the task first by radiophone. William Manchester later provided the following account of that incident:

> [Smith decided that] the longer he could keep Bell out of touch with an AP operator, the longer that lead would be. So he continued to talk. He dictated one take, two takes, three, four. Indignant, Bell rose from the center of the rear seat and demanded the phone. Smith stalled. He insisted that the Dallas operator read back the dictation. The wires overhead, he argued, might have interfered with his transmission. No one was deceived by that. Everyone in the car could hear the cackling of the UPI operator's voice. The relay was perfect. Bell, red-faced and screaming, tried to wrest the radiophone from him. Smith thrust it between his knees and crouched under the dash . . . [then] surrendered the phone to Bell, and at that moment, it went dead.[35]

There was also a flip side to the triumphs of technology for the reporters who experienced them. As NBC reporter Tom Pettit said of the minutes after his live televised broadcast of Oswald's murder, "when other reporters were free to go inside police headquarters to get more information, I still was tied to the live microphone."[36] Pettit saw himself limited by the very instruments of technology that had earned him, in the words of *Broadcasting* magazine, a "place in television history."[37]

Stories of journalistic mishap surrounding the assassination were thus largely thematized through technology. On the one hand, normative upsets—missing scoops, becoming secondhand witnesses, or interfering with events—were construed as having been redressed by technology, which often facilitated additional standards of action that allowed journalists to hold onto their authority as professionals. On the other hand, journalists admitted their incomplete mastery of technology. All of this gave the media a way to air concerns through narrative about the insufficiency of formalized cues of professionalism and to rethink standards of journalistic practice and authority.

Stories of Triumph

Journalists did not see only the problematic aspects of the assassination story. While tales of mishap allowed them to air concerns about the limits to their authority raised by the assassination coverage, in tales of triumph they celebrated their overcoming of such limits by valorizing on-the-spot judgment calls and hunches as signs of a "true" professional. This claim was contradictory, for while reporters couched improvisational and instinctual behavior as practice that came "naturally," it was in effect acculturated behavior, imposed by the journalistic community around them. Claims about acting "by instinct" therefore served less to absolve individuals of errors and more to uphold the importance of the surrounding journalistic culture. Authority was derived in effect from the journalistic community.

Tales of triumph generally assumed one of three forms. Journalists variably claimed to be "the first," "the best," and "the only."

Being the First

The Kennedy assassination required journalists to act in ways that were unpredictable and unroutinized, and were also the focus of extended and exclusive media attention. These circumstances gave journalists the opportunity to implement a series of "firsts" in covering the story. Authority was assumed to have derived from such coverage.

Journalists used tales of "being the first" to reference the presentational style that prevailed after the Kennedy story had been told. "Being the first" in the event of Kennedy's death differed from media presentations of other events. For example, while radio's role in the death of President Harding had challenged existing notions of journalistic practice, it did not provide the kind of sustained stage that Kennedy's assassination did. Television journalists had not yet had the opportunity to play a central part in presenting such an event, and certainly not in the protracted manner of the coverage of the assassination weekend.[38]

This situation set up various guidelines against which journalists could consider their authority for covering the assassination story. First, most journalists lacked the professional experience with comparable events that might have helped them "rehearse."[39] Second, the sustained nature of media coverage during the assassination required many journalists to act in unfamiliar ways for extended periods of time. The quality of "firstness" the Kennedy assassination offered was therefore unique not only because it set up circumstances that were different from those of normal coverage but also because it sustained them.

The differences in journalistic practice that these circumstances entailed extended notions of appropriate professional practice. For example, interrupting scheduled programming and sustaining the interruption was seen as a different kind of "first" that enhanced the stature of broadcasting networks.[40] Similar feats took place in other media, such as replating magazine copy or issuing second newspaper editions.[41]

The event's newness was best articulated by NBC reporter Robert MacNeil on the evening of the assassination: "This is one of those days that a reporter finds himself musing about when he's half asleep. . . . What is likely to happen at this moment is that sometimes your mind drifts to the most extreme thing that could happen but you hastily dismiss it, because the most extreme thing never does happen. You pull your mind back to the ordinary things that always do happen."[42] When the most extreme thing did happen, journalists had to find new ways of generating authoritative interpretations. This was because "old ways" had been rendered unhelpful, with sources nowhere to be found, circumstances uncertain, and tried methods of fact verification unworkable. At the same time, institutional pressures on journalists to provide information persisted. Providing information thus became as much an institutional necessity as a professional goal. This was entwined with the new demands created by new technologies.

Valorizing Improvisation

Journalists told of reinstating their authority for assigned tasks by improvising, redoing completed tasks, and reorganizing around last-minute changes. *Journalism Quarterly* hailed the way local WBAP-TV reporter Robert Welsh, refused entry to Parkland Hospital by the police, drove over the curb, through the barricade, and up to the hospital entrance.[43] In looking back, Meg Greenfield recalled how stories were "hysterically remade on deadline."[44]

The press did not go unpraised. On Friday alone, newspapers issued as many as eight "extras."[45] The press set new sales records, with the *New York Times* selling 1,089,000 papers on 26 November, nearly 400,000 more than its normal sales.[46] Replating, resetting, redoing written accounts were all seen as substantial sacrifices of the usual order of printing a newspaper.

Weekly magazines were hailed for having worked around Friday afternoon deadlines. Staff members at the three major newsmagazines were lauded for "getting everything into their issues in spite of incredible deadline problems" in the middle of the assassination weekend.[47] Editorial staffs tore out huge holes at the front of their magazines, with *Newsweek, Time,* and *U.S. News and World Report* adding tens of pages of fresh type at the last minute. Both *Time* and *Newsweek* were praised for having replated twice—once after Oswald's murder and once after the *Dallas Morning News* published a photograph of that event.[48] *Look* magazine, sent early to the newsstands with a cover article entitled "Kennedy Could Lose," issued paste-over labels to distributors.[49]

NBC correspondent Bill Ryan was preparing the 2 P.M. radio newscast when

> an unnerved staffer burst into his office, shouting, "Get back to TV right away! The President has been shot!" It was 1.45 P.M., and NBC was off the air for its daily noon break. . . . Technicians had to hastily rig a patchwork of telephone lines before NBC could tell America that President JFK had been shot in Dallas. Even then, NBC couldn't tell an anxious nation whether Kennedy was alive or dead. It didn't know. In 1963, there were no satellite links, no microwave relays, no you-heard-it-here-first reports from on-the-scene correspondents. Seated in a closet-size studio, Ryan and Chet Huntley scrambled not only to report the news but also to learn it.[50]

These stories reflected awkward but successful attempts at improvisation. Journalists conveyed how well they had adapted to last-minute changes, even redoing completed tasks. Ultimately their ability to do so reflected well on the organizations that employed them.

One comprehensive attempt at improvisation was a decision by the broadcasting industry to offer continuous coverage of the procession of mourners viewing Kennedy's casket. This decision, culminating in NBC's marathon forty-two-hour broadcast of lines of mourners (shown as hushed music played in the background), was seen as a "first" in broadcasting that was called "television's finest hour."[51] Journalists were lauded for their good taste and sensitivity, for the "unobtrusive coverage of the final rites [which] underscored broadcasting's dignity and maturity in covering the news."[52] These comments suggested a high regard for the improvisational skills of television journalists, despite their adaptation to the events of mourn-

ing in a way that contradicted the investigatory and intrusive practices favored by members of the profession.

Valorizing Instinct

Other stories of "being the first" focused on the journalistic "hunch,"
or the instinct that guided journalists in their work. A lack of obvious
rules for covering the assassination and its unpredictable circumstances meant that journalists did not always know what to do. Tom
Wicker felt he had relied on instinct when he heard from another
reporter that Kennedy had been shot:

> Marianne Means of Hearst Headline Service hung up a
> telephone, ran to a group of us, and said, "The President's
> been shot. He's at Parkland Hospital." One thing I learned
> that day. I suppose I already knew it, but that day made it
> plain. A reporter must trust his instinct. When Miss Means
> said those eight words—I never learned who told her—I
> knew absolutely that they were true. Everyone did. . . .
> That day a reporter had none of the ordinary means or time
> to check or double-check matters given as fact. He had to
> go on what he knew of people he talked to, what he knew
> of human reaction, what two isolated "facts" added to in
> sum—above all what he felt in his bones.[53]

Harry Reasoner's "instincts told him it would be better not to broadcast" an item that Oswald had been shot by a black man.[54] Reporters
confessed to having had journalistic hunches that Dallas would turn
into a "big story"; at their regular news briefing before the assassination, CBS news executives had discussed the possibility of a hostile
demonstration in Dallas.[55] While still at the airport, *Time* reporter
Hugh Sidey, who "as a rule disregarded airport crowds, left his press
bus seat; he felt a general air of tension."[56] Henry Brandon of the
London Sunday Times made the trip to Dallas because he thought there
might be trouble.[57] An Austin editor predicted that Kennedy would
not get through his trip to Dallas without something happening to
him, and the two Dallas newspapers ran editorials calling for restraint
of public sentiments against the president.[58] Relying on instinct also
had its tangible rewards, as when CBS reporter Dan Rather urged his
network to assign extra reporters to cover Kennedy's Dallas trip. By
at least one account, that premonition earned him rapid promotion
through the ranks at CBS.[59]

While it is difficult to ascertain in retrospect how the journalistic
hunch crept into journalists' tales, the "I told you so" position it implied helped them regain authority for an event whose unpredictabil-

ity had made it unwieldy. The ability to anticipate events through instinct was seen as bona fide professional activity. In using tales of instinct to anchor the uncertainty surrounding situations of "being the first," journalists offset their partial knowledge about the event. Equally important, these stories allowed reporters to couch their assassination coverage as natural and derived from instinct. Doing so reinforced their claims to authority and appeared to absolve them of some of their errors, despite the fact that their reliance on instinct was in effect an acculturated dimension of journalistic practice.

Thus, stories of "being the first" to a large extent displayed how, through narrative, journalists valorized improvisational and instinctual behavior as the true mark of the professional. The abilities to respond quickly to unpredicted circumstances, bend established rules and procedures on a hunch, and do so correctly were touted as signs of professionalism. In telling how they had effectively covered the assassination story by relying on improvisation, redefinition, and instinct, journalists made claims of professionalism for behavior not necessarily valorized by formalized cues of professional practice. In so doing, they constructed an alternative authoritative role for themselves in retelling the assassination story.

Being the Best

While tales of "being the first" highlighted the improvisational and instinctual dimensions of journalistic practice, tales of "being the best" let journalists expound on the range of their activities. "Being the best" in covering Kennedy's shooting meant quick relay, for example; in covering his funeral it meant reverent, slow-paced, and hushed reportage. "The best" was differently reflected in James Reston's condolence column the day after the assassination and in Frank McGee's choked-up relay of the news that Kennedy was dead.

For television journalists, in particular, Kennedy's funeral presented a way to tell tales of "being the best." How television journalists adapted to the decision to broadcast processions of mourners gave rise to numerous stories of behavior that was different yet acceptable. For instance, the broadcasting industry was praised for having canceled advertisements, at a cost, according to one estimate, of some $3 million in direct spending and ten times that in advertising revenue loss.[60] Television was complimented for having efficiently "played to the largest audience in its history."[61] Such praise was often set against a background of professional expertise. As one trade journal, *Broadcasting* magazine, stated, "were it not for the experience that broadcasters have acquired in the day-to-day practice of their form of journalism, their coverage of the wholly unexpected events of Nov. 22–25 would have been impossible."[62]

Ironically, tales of "being the best" legitimated what elsewhere might have been considered lapses in professional behavior. In the 1964 United Artists documentary "Four Days in November," a local reporter was shown rushing into a Dallas television station, with the statement "you'll excuse me if I'm out of breath but. . . . " The comment, which the reporter breathlessly delivered both to the anchorperson and to the television audience, constituted his introduction to news of Kennedy's assassination.[63] In addition to successfully conveying the import of the news, the delivery suggested how inappropriate was the collected demeanor of the professional television commentator. Similarly, tales of "being the best" implied that other, possibly unusual, qualities were required to cover the assassination in a professional manner. In a special column entitled "If You Can Keep Your Head When All about You . . . ," the *Saturday Review* evaluated the performance of journalists by highlighting their "special talent" and "training." Editor Richard Tobin maintained that it had taken "coolness under the fire of highly-charged events" to carry out reportorial tasks.[64]

But "being the best" did not mean the same thing to all journalists, and no one set of rules characterized all assassination coverage. This was displayed in the range of journalists' stories of "being the best," which provided reporters with a variety of backgrounds against which to display their tales of what they saw as superlative practice.

Being the Most Dedicated

For many journalists, "being the best" meant "being the most dedicated," measured by the degree of personal deprivation experienced in accomplishing assigned tasks. This ranged from loss of sleep and skipped meals to an affectation of coolness. Meg Greenfield, walking around with other journalists in a "disembodied, high-octane state," told how she did not go home until Saturday.[65] The president of the ABC News Division said late-night planning conferences prevented staff people from getting more than three or four hours of sleep,[66] and reporter Bill Seamans "was forced [after thirty-six hours] to take a break when his eyes became so irritated from lack of sleep that he couldn't force them open all the way."[67] NBC correspondent Bill Ryan held back his emotions until he was off the air, when he "cried like hell."[68] Walter Cronkite did not realize until he was relieved from his anchoring duties that "I was still in my shirtsleeves, although my secretary hours before had draped my jacket over the back of my chair."[69] A sense of dedication, in each case, was derived from the reporter's ability to place the public's right to know above basic personal needs.

Being the Most Human

For other journalists, "being the best" meant "being the most human," displaying the ability to momentarily abandon professional demeanor. Voices shook as news of the assassination was relayed. One rewrite man "dissolved. He couldn't go on. They had to put another rewrite man on."[70] NBC's Frank McGee and CBS's Walter Cronkite both became choked up while on the air. As Cronkite told the news to the audience, "his voice broke with emotion and he wiped a tear from his eye."[71] He removed his eyeglasses, then distractedly put them back on.

Cronkite delighted later in telling how, on his first break from anchoring the Kennedy shooting, he answered a studio phone whose caller admonished CBS for allowing Cronkite to anchor the broadcast. "This is Walter Cronkite," he said angrily, "and you're a goddamned idiot." Then he slammed the receiver down.[72] The proliferation of these tales suggests that journalists used them to work out the personal and professional incongruities imposed by the assassination coverage.

Being the Most Technologically Adept

Journalists dwelled on technology in many of their stories, and in these "being the best" meant "being the most technologically adept." These stories conveyed journalists' triumphs over the technologies with which they worked. Often this meant using technologies other than one's own in reporting stories. Tom Wicker incorporated into his written account of Kennedy's shooting an eyewitness interview that he saw while watching television in the Dallas–Fort Worth airport.[73] Frank McGee of NBC cradled a telephone in his hand while on the air and repeated verbatim the words of a correspondent on the other end.[74] Press reporters huddled around radios as they waited for information outside Parkland Hospital.[75]

Journalists described how they had been able to carry out their tasks despite technological limitations. Wicker made reference to the fact that he—a newspaper reporter—was without a notebook that day in Dallas.[76] NBC correspondent Bill Ryan made the same point when he later remembered the precise conditions of the flash studio and its "lack of technical sophistication." "We didn't even have a regular news studio," he said. "We had to go to what they called the flash studio in New York, a little room where they had one black-and-white camera set up."[77] Dan Rather also later turned a tale about using the telephone from a tragedy into a triumph. Attempting to verify the fact of Kennedy's death by telephone, at one point he was simultaneously talking to both local reporter Eddie Barker in Dallas and his New York office on different lines. Rather recounted the situation as follows:

> In one of my ears, Barker was repeating what the Parkland Hospital official had told him at the Trade Mart. I was trying to watch and listen to many things at once. My mind was racing, trying to clear, trying to hold steady, trying to think ahead. When Barker said again that he had been told the President was dead, I said "Yes, yes. That's what I hear too. That he's dead." A voice came back, "What was that?" I thought it was Barker again. It wasn't. The "what was that" had come from a radio editor in New York. . . . At that point I heard what my mind then recognized clearly as someone in New York announce, "Dan Rather says the President is dead." . . . I began shouting into the phone to New York, shouting that I had not authorized any bulletin or any other kind of report. Confusion burst anew. I was told that I had said not once but twice that Kennedy was dead. Now it came through to me: Those weren't Barker's questions I had been answering.[78]

Rather recalled contemplating the possible repercussions of what he had done, saying that "it dawned on me that it was possible I had committed a blunder beyond comprehension, beyond forgiving." It took a full half-hour before official confirmation of Kennedy's death came through, and the waiting was tense. He knew "that if the story was wrong, I would be seeking another line of work."[79] The fact that Rather was right, though shaken, helped make his tale a story about the proper use of technology.

References to instruments of technology—notepads, pencils, cameras, or studios—were invoked by journalists to suggest that they had tried to be professional about their assassination coverage. The ways reporters worked to compensate for the primitive state of affairs thus formed one cornerstone of discussions of professionalism. Journalists saw themselves legitimated as professionals because they had mastered the limitations of technology, making technology work for them. Such claims were not incidental to establishing their authority in retelling.

Tales of "being the best" thus legitimated a range of practices by which journalists made claims to journalistic professionalism. In tales of "being the best," journalists expanded the range of improvisational and instinctual activities by which they reinstated their authority in retelling the story of the assassination.

Being the Only

Tales of "being the only" offered a way for journalists to parade their performances as individual reporters. While the media were full of stories about how journalists mastered coverage by valorizing instinctual behavior over formalized professional cues, tales of "being the only" concentrated on the individual dimension of such behavior. To a large extent, these tales marked the personalities who would emerge as the celebrities of the assassination story.

Stories of "being the only" celebrated the tales and practices of certain reporters and news organizations over others. In daily news "being the only" tends to be a temporary category, since a journalist's interest in a story is validated by other journalists doing similar stories. Thus by the Friday afternoon of the assassination, there would be many confirmations of Kennedy's death to follow the first report. Nevertheless, the reporters who initially confirmed the report were accorded special stature.

For a time, Merriman Smith of UPI was the only reporter to have relayed news of the president's shooting, a distinction due largely to his aforementioned telephone dispute in the pool car. Said William Manchester:

> [The] bulletin was on the UPI printer at 12:34, two minutes before the President's car reached Parkland. Before eyewitnesses could collect themselves, it was being beamed around the world. To those who tend to believe everything they hear and read, the figure of three [shots] seemed to have the sanction of authority and many who had been in the plaza and had thought they heard only two reports later corrected their memories.[80]

While Smith ceased to be "the only reporter" to convey the news of Kennedy's shooting once the pool car reached public telephones, this did not affect the status he derived from his accomplishment. It later earned him the Pulitzer Prize, and UPI reproduced his account in its in-house organ *UPI Reporter*. UPI called the coverage "an historical memento . . . for what it shows about how a top craftsman dealt with the fastest-breaking news story of his generation."[81]

Another tale of "being the only" concerned the activities of Eddie Barker, director of KRLD-News (a CBS affiliate). It was Barker who initially reported that Kennedy was dead:

> A doctor I know who is on the staff at Parkland Hospital came to me, and he was crying. . . . He had learned that President Kennedy was dead. When I announced this over the air, the network panicked. No official announcement had yet been made, and the validity of my source was questioned. However I knew that this man was trustworthy, so I kept repeating that the President was dead.[82]

Barker's decision to announce the president's death without official confirmation was, in one observer's eyes, possibly "the most important journalistic event of the period . . . one of the greatest snap evaluations of a source in the history of broadcast journalism."[83]

Other stories of "being the only" remained exclusives long after the events that occasioned them. Walter Cronkite's removal of his eyeglasses to shed a tear set the limit for anchoring the news, yet few journalists looked upon it as behavior to be emulated. In contrast, Thomas Thompson's exclusive interview with Oswald's wife and mother, held before the police had found them, put his scoop "high on the list of *Life* interviews."[84] Theodore White's postfuneral discussion with Jacqueline Kennedy that named the Kennedy years "Camelot" was hailed for years afterward by the journalistic community.[85] In that interview, Jacqueline Kennedy revealed that her husband had enjoyed playing the record of the musical "Camelot" before going to bed.

Sometimes stories of "being the only" offered journalists a way to turn mishaps into triumphs. Harry Reasoner was working at the CBS anchor desk on the morning Oswald was murdered:

> At the moment Oswald was shot, CBS was broadcasting a live report from Washington . . . Reasoner, who was watching the Oswald story on a closed-circuit monitor, saw it happen—or saw, at least, that something had happened. Although seldom given to emotional outbursts, Reasoner began jumping up and down in his chair, screaming for the control room to switch to Dallas. A few seconds later, the switch was made. . . . Thanks to videotape, CBS soon was able to broadcast an "instant replay" of the shooting.[86]

Interestingly, the fact that CBS "missed" original coverage of the event became intriguing from an institutional point of view, because the scene was recorded by the CBS cameraperson but was not replayed on national television until after the fact. The "presence" of journalists thus existed but was not institutionally legitimated or supported.

Journalists also told more literal tales of "being the only": Richard Stolley was "the only reporter" among Secret Service agents to view the Zapruder film;[87] Henry Brandon the only foreign correspondent in Dallas on 22 November;[88] James Altgens the only professional cameraperson to catch spot pictures of Kennedy's shooting.[89] Entwined within these tales was the notion of having left one's personal signature on history: Tom Pettit "made TV history at the scene of the shooting of Oswald" precisely because he had been "the only television reporter" on live television.[90]

Thus, journalists' use of mediated narratives about covering the assassination revealed much about existing parameters of journalistic practice. When cues for covering the assassination were found to be unavailable in formalized professional codes, journalists used tales of mishap to air their concerns about the adequacy of their coverage and tales of triumph to valorize their on-the-spot judgment calls and hunches. Embedded within both sets of tales was a discourse about professionalism, technology, and alternative ways of upholding journalistic authority.

Journalists used their narratives to replay positive self-assessments in three ways. One, stories of "being the first," opened up formalized codes of professional behavior by emphasizing journalists' instinctual and improvisational actions. A second, stories of "being the best," expounded upon the range of activities that allowed journalists to act instinctually and on the basis of improvisation. A third, stories of "being the only," connected individual journalists with improvisational and instinctual cues of professionalism. The reliance of these tales on notions of being the first, the best, and the only revealed how short a distance journalistic professionalism had moved from baser notions of competition.

The proliferation of mediated discourse about the assassination coverage suggested its consolidation as an incident critical to professional journalists. It was no coincidence that the use of discourse to rearrange existing standards of practice was made possible by the informal networks among reporters. Such networks helped strengthen journalists' status as an independent interpretive community. The boundaries of that community were in turn strengthened by the circulation of narratives that authenticated its members.

SIX

"Covering the Body"
by Professional Forum

The media were not the only site where journalists assessed their coverage of Kennedy's death. At the same time, narratives in trade publications and professional forums were suggesting the centrality of the incident for journalists themselves. Members of professional and trade circles showed particular interest in marking assassination coverage as a professional triumph, and their narratives, like those that appeared in mediated discourse, discussed instinctual and improvisational behavior as a way of turning the assassination coverage into a story of journalistic professionalism. As with mediated discourse, in which journalists often invoked the same attributes of coverage for both positive and negative appraisals, the stories that circulated in trade publications and professional forums displayed an ambivalence about journalists' coverage that was linked to the complex nature of the story.

The emphasis in trade publications was on how the demand for information did not ease up throughout the weekend of the assassination. The unceasing demand was complicated by the fact that television journalism was just coming into its own as a legitimate medium for news. With the journalistic community trying to legitimate itself as an authoritative interpretive group, these circumstances made professional assessments—particularly about television—a critical part of retellings in professional forums.

In Praise of Coverage

In the first year after Kennedy's death, the assassination story caught the attention of nearly every professional journalistic forum. During their 1963–64 meetings, the American Society of Newspaper Editors (ASNE), National Association of Broadcasters (NAB), and Radio and Television News Directors Association each independently considered what would have constituted appropriate coverage of the Kennedy assassination. Trade and semitrade publications, including the *Columbia Journalism Review, Editor and Publisher, The Quill, Broadcasting,* and *Television Quarterly*, devoted special sections to the assassination. Several of them, such as the *Columbia Journalism Review*, reprinted large sections of original assassination coverage for their readers.[1] The 1964 meetings of the Association for Education in Journalism convened a general panel on the "Aftermath of the Ruby Trial: The Courts, the Press and Fair Trial."[2]

Professional forums differed from mediated forums in that they allowed journalists to focus upon the professional attributes of their activities with little direct linkage to their newsworthiness. In some cases, this facilitated reconstructions of what had happened in actual coverage. Through such reconstructions, journalists were able to anchor their discussion and negotiation of consensual standards of action.

One particularly illustrative example of this reconstructive work in professional forums took shape a few years after the assassination, at which point news photographers' missed scoop in covering Kennedy's shooting had already been recast by trade journals as a professional triumph. A 1968 *Quill* article, entitled "Professionalism in News Photography," featured a picture of bystanders crouched atop the grassy knoll near the assassination scene. The following caption accompanied the picture: "Seconds after the John F. Kennedy assassination bullets hit their mark, news photographers kept on working as bystanders 'hit the dust' for protection. Photographers, including the one who took this picture, reacted instantly as professionals should."[3] On-the-spot accounts of the shooting showed, however, that this was not the case. With one exception, professional photographers totally missed the Kennedy shooting, and photographic work had initially been credited to amateurs.[4] It is significant that the recasting of this mishap as a professional triumph was engineered by a trade journal, where the need for professional legitimation may have been greater than in mediated forums. Such reconstructive work was typical of professional assessments of the assassination coverage, in which the facts of coverage were often adjusted to meet professional aims of legitimation or credentialing.

At the time of the assassination, professional forums were generally quick to laud journalists for their coverage. The *Columbia Journalism Review* said, "Like no other events before, the occurrences of November 22 to 25, 1963, belonged to journalism, and specifically to the national organs of journalism."[5] In its annual report, the Associated Press called the assassination the "major national news event of 1963" and boasted that it had "thrown more resources into covering the assassination than any single news-event in its history."[6] An editorial in *Editor and Publisher* called the story "the most amazing performance by newspapers, radio and television that the world has ever witnessed."[7] Self-congratulatory advertisements filled the pages of *Editor and Publisher* and *Broadcasting* magazine.

Laudatory remarks were directed at all media. Trade journals hailed the press for canceling columns of scheduled advertising in the press.[8] Journals were congratulated for holding up the publication of articles that were seen as insensitive in the aftermath of the assassination.[9] Newsmagazines were singled out for their resourceful coverage of the weekend. As the *Columbia Journalism Review* said, "These magazines made over whole sections—in some cases interrupting press runs to add late developments—and still reached most of their readers on time."[10] In its view, this demonstrated that magazines "were in many ways more flexible than most Sunday newspapers."

News photographers were praised for capturing the weekend's main events. Significantly, while originally only photographer James Altgens had been congratulated for his shot of a Secret Service officer sprinting over the back of the presidential car,[11] the more generalized performance of photography quickly came to be seen in a favorable light. Discussions generally centered on the "historic" shot of Johnson's swearing-in or the pictures of Oswald being shot. Robert Jackson of the *Dallas Times-Herald* won a Pulitzer Prize for his picture of Oswald crumpling under the bullet's impact.[12] This fueled an intense discussion about professionalism among photographers, in which coverage by amateurs was dismissed in comparison to the role played by professional photographers. As one article saw it, "the actual shooting down of the President was caught mainly through out-of-focus pictures taken by non-professional photographers. But the actual shooting of his accused assailant was recorded in full view of press photographers with their cameras trained right on him and this produced pictures which may rank with the greatest news shots of all time."[13] The fact that most trade publications juxtaposed the amateur photographic coverage of Kennedy's shooting with professional pictures of Oswald's murder suggests the problem posed by these amateur photos. As *Editor and Publisher* noted in a moment of professional vindication, "If President Kennedy's death was left for the amateur photographers to record, the situation reversed itself on Sunday, November 24."[14]

Of all media, the broadcast element received special attention. *Broadcasting* magazine claimed that "in those four terrible days, television came of age and radio reasserted its capacity to move to history where it happens."[15] Broadcast coverage "was one of superlatives—the most people, the most hours, the biggest losses and the most raw emotion that broadcasting had ever known."[16] Radio was hailed for broadcasting more than eighty hours of continuous coverage.[17] Trade journals praised the dignity and deportment of the broadcast media.[18] The radio-television industry received a special Peabody Award, given for public service in radio and television by the University of Georgia School of Journalism.[19] Televised coverage of Kennedy's funeral was voted the best foreign program of the year by the British Guild of Television Producers and Directors.[20] The NAB sent its subscribers a full-page newspaper advertisement that echoed praise accorded the broadcasting industry.[21]

Not surprisingly, most professional forums felt that the assassination coverage displayed bona fide professional behavior. The editor of the *Saturday Review* hailed "as professional a job . . . as one could care to see."[22] An editorial in *Broadcasting* magazine noted that the last-minute reorganization of reporters and the energetic and creative ways in which they revamped existing set-ups to meet the pace of the event "was not a job that amateurs could have done. . . . It was a job for professionals."[23] As with mediated discourse, the ability to improvise, and to reorganize, redo, and anticipate events through instinct, was cast by professional forums as the activity that legitimated journalists as professionals.

At the same time, embedded within these appraisals was recognition of a new form of news coverage. *Television Quarterly* spoke of the "full emergence of a televised documentary form [in which] the conditions which define the role and function of the artist and reporter in television journalism have begun to take shape."[24] This was borne out years later, as the ways in which journalists had covered the assassination story determined the parameters of action for similar stories. Covering Kennedy's assassination, for instance, taught journalists how to approach assassination attempts on Gerald Ford and Ronald Reagan.[25] Coverage of Kennedy's funeral showed journalists how to cover the funeral of Egyptian President Anwar Sadat.[26]

All of this suggests that, like mediated discourse, professional forums regarded assassination coverage as professional activity, despite the fact that it was not necessarily valorized by formalized cues of professional practice. Assessments centered on television technology and on the ability of reporters to develop new practices in conjunction with it. Unlike mediated discourse, however, professional assessments were quick to move from discussions of coverage into discussions about fundamental questions of professionalism. In other words, the coverage itself was quickly turned into a debating ground over what constituted professional behavior. This upheld the status of the assassination story as a critical incident for journalism professionals. Not surprisingly, it also led to certain critical observations of what journalists had accomplished in Dallas.

In Critique of Coverage

Within a few weeks of the assassination, professional groups began to critique problems caused by journalists' coverage of Kennedy's death. One major organization, ASNE, discussed the events of 22 November 1963 in a special program at its annual convention the following year. In the proceedings of that convention, members of the association criticized reporting that was "sloppy, bad, inaccurate, sensational."[27] Similarly, they found evidence of a "raw, planned distortion of facts."[28] The questions facing the professional community concerned whether or not journalistic practice had met the challenges posed by the Kennedy assassination. As one observer summed it up, "The central question is whether the best tradition of the press is good enough. . . . The lesson of Dallas is actually an old one in responsible journalism: Reporting is not democratic to the point that everything posing as fact has equal status."[29]

Editor and Publisher printed a detailed consideration of legal questions raised by the assassination story. Under the headline "Assassination Story Raises Legal Snares," it discussed the "gross departures from constitutional standards" displayed by reporters' coverage.[30] Other forums debated the "herd behavior" of journalists. As one local Dallas editor testified before the 1964 ASNE conference:

> Newspaper, radio and television offices [in Dallas] were invaded. Reference files were scattered over newspaper offices; some permanently lost. Photo departments bulged with outsiders wanting to process film, buy photographs and so forth. Magazine and foreign newspaper representatives "hustled" individual photographers with very tempting offers for exclusive pictures.[31]

Professional forums lamented what they saw as a loss of basic manners and integrity among journalists involved in the assassination story. In particular, critiques of the assassination coverage centered on the media's activities in covering the death of Lee Harvey Oswald.

A Closer Look: The Imbroglio over Oswald

There were two main charges about the Oswald case. One held that the media actually contributed to his murder; the other that had he lived, the media would have prevented a fair trial.[32] Chapter 5 explored the ways in which journalists faulted themselves on both counts. They saw themselves as not having been easily identifiable to local police, possessing intrusive equipment, and arriving in numbers too large for the police to handle. Oswald's homicide and its coverage shed new light on the problematic boundaries of journalistic obligations, rights, and privileges in covering criminal cases.

Discourse about the role of journalists was not limited to the journalistic community. The *Warren Report*, issued by the first official investigation of Kennedy's death, played an active part in crystalizing some of the salient problems raised by the assassination coverage. In a special section called "The Activity of Newsmen," the report traced what the commission saw as the events that had led up to Oswald's murder:

> In the lobby of the third floor, television cameramen set up two large cameras and floodlights in strategic positions that gave them a sweep of the corridor in either direction. Technicians stretched their television cables into and out of offices, running some of them out of the windows of a deputy chief's office and down the side of the building. Men with newsreel cameras, still cameras and microphones, more mobile than the television cameramen, moved back and forth seeking information and opportunities for interviews. Newsmen wandered into the offices of other bureaus located on the third floor, sat on desks and used police telephones; indeed, one reporter admits hiding a telephone behind a desk so that he would have exclusive access to it if something developed. . . . The corridor became so jammed that policemen and newsmen had to push and shove if they wanted to get through, stepping over cables, wires and tripods.[33]

A detective was quoted as saying that the journalists were "asked to stand back and stay back but it wouldn't do much good, and they would push forward and you had to hold them off physically. . . . The press and television people just took over."[34] When Oswald was brought into view of the journalists, "his escorts . . . had to push their way through the newsmen who sought to surround them . . . when [he] appeared, the newsmen turned their cameras on him, thrust microphones at his face and shouted questions at him."[35]

On Sunday morning, when Oswald was to be transferred from the city to the county jail, the situation was repeated. Again the press corps arrived in large groups, and an estimated fifty persons crowded into the basement of the city jail by 10 that morning.[36] The transfer began, and Jack Ruby stepped out from the group of journalists. His shot hit Oswald straight in the abdomen. The *Warren Report* concluded that partial responsibility for Oswald's death "must be borne by the news media,"[37] and it called on journalists to implement a new code of professional ethics.

Such an idea was already circulating among professional forums. *Editor and Publisher* had published an editorial in late 1963 entitled "'Accused' or 'Assassin,'" in which it considered whether the journalistic community had judged Oswald too rapidly.[38] In January 1964, the leader of ASNE, Herbert Brucker, had plaintively called for media curbs. Laying out his views in a *Saturday Review* article entitled "When the Press Shapes the News," he stated that "pressure from the press . . . had set the stage for [Oswald's killing, with] . . . little doubt that television and the press must bear a share of the blame."[39] In his view, the murder was "related to police capitulation in the glare of publicity . . . to suit the convenience of the news media . . . [the problem grew] principally out of something new in journalism . . . the intrusion of the reporter himself in the news."[40] Brucker held broadcasting equipment responsible for creating the sense of intrusion around Oswald's murder. He compared the incident with an earlier one involving the introduction of radio—the 1937 trial of Bruno Richard Hauptmann for the kidnapping and murder of the Lindbergh baby—stating that "the new medium of radio, together with news photographers' flashbulbs, made a circus of the trial."[41] Brucker's comments suggested a link between the legitimation of new media and the boundaries separating public from private space, boundaries that the journalistic community saw as being altered by television's active presence.

Brucker was not alone in his critique of television. ASNE's annual conference in 1964 began with testimony from the head of the National Press Photographers Association, who claimed that "putting live cameras on the scene on those rare occasions of major news stories makes it certain that the worst possible side of the communications industry is brought into the living room. Then, by replaying the event, television makes it doubly certain that anyone who may have missed the scene on the first broadcast has any number of additional opportunities to view it."[42] The speaker went on to lament what he saw as "one of the most serious and threatening problems journalism

has had to face in many generations."[43] For as long as he could remember, he said, people had been

> badgered by reporters, hounded into a corner and plied
> with questions, some relevant and many inconsequential
> and downright foolish. However, there was no radio or
> live television in those days. . . . As a result, by the time
> the story or the interview appeared in print, all of the ir-
> relevant questions had been distilled from the story. The
> public never knew the badgering circumstances under
> which the answers to the questions had been obtained.[44]

His remarks centered not upon the fact that journalistic practice was
problematic but rather upon the fact that television displayed how
problematic it was. Television offered an excessively revealing view of
the conduct of journalists, a view which he felt necessitated careful
consideration of journalistic standards of action.

Independently considering where—and if—they had gone wrong,
trade publications discussed what the *Columbia Journalism Review* labeled "judgment by television."[45] A forum conducted in 1964 by *Current* magazine, entitled "The Life and Death of John F. Kennedy,"
concluded with a final section called "Trial by Mass Media." In that
forum it asked, "In their competitive eagerness to report every aspect
of the story, did the media ignore and trample the rights of Kennedy's
accused assassin?"[46] The section included statements by members of
the American Civil Liberties Union, *Editor and Publisher,* and several
media critics, all of whom pondered the role of publicity in changing
legal process.[47]

By early 1964, pressure was mounting for professional forums to
address some of the questions raised by the Oswald murder. CBS
President Frank Stanton offered funds to the Brookings Institution to
establish a voluntary intermedia code of fair practices.[48] In October
of that same year, ASNE convened a meeting of seventeen top
news organizations—including the American Newspaper Publishers
of America, the Associated Press Managing Editors Association,
Sigma Delta Chi, the NAB, UPI, the National Press Photographers
Association, and the Radio and Television News Directors Association—to discuss complaints about journalistic practice.[49] Ten days
later, the group issued a statement that warily conceded the news
media's influence over events. It echoed earlier reservations about
journalistic practice voiced by ASNE: "If developing smaller TV cameras is beyond our control, we can certainly try by our own example
to teach the electronic newsmen larger manners and a deeper under-

standing of the basic truth that freedom of information is not an un-limited license to trample on individual rights."[50] While allowing for pooled coverage under certain circumstances, the statement stopped short of calling for codes of behavior or other external bars on media performance.[51]

The idea that external forces would regulate journalism seemed anathema to the notion of a free press. A *Washington Post* editor urged journalistic self-restraint in preference to "magic codes" to curb excesses typical of Dallas.[52] *New York Times* editors Turner Catledge and Clifton Daniel separately called on members of the press corps to use their own judgment in covering similar events.[53] The president of the Associated Press Managing Editors Association complained that the Warren Commission should have lauded the press instead of scoring it.[54] And television reporter Gabe Pressman, in a *Television Quarterly* forum on ethics, journalism, and the Kennedy assassination, complained that his medium was being used as a scapegoat. "Because we have the capability of telling a story efficiently, dramatically, and with a maximum amount of impact—because we have the ability to satisfy the need of the American public for instantaneous journalism in this modern age—does it follow that we have to be paralyzed because people react badly?"[55] Published under the title "The Responsible Reporter," the article examined the effect of television on journalistic practice. It considered whether television journalists could carry out their job without intruding on others, despite their "cumbersome equipment," and suggested focusing journalists on "the matter of reportorial taste and judgment, as well as the respect for the individual in an open society."[56] In one interchange, the article mentioned that television's newness magnified the irritation caused by TV cameras: Pressman responded that "the camera is used as a newspaperman uses his pad and pencil. And yet, the camera is the most faithful reporter we have. The video-tapes don't lie and the film doesn't lie."[57]

At the heart of these discussions were two assumptions about this new medium for news—that the camera equipment to which Pressman and others referred made for a better journalism, and that television was capable of providing a more truthful and hence more authoritative form of reportage than other media. Whether Ruby had shot Oswald, for instance, was not debatable, for the camera had recorded it. These assumptions were increasingly being taken for granted in most journalists' accounts of their assassination coverage. Equally important, while the discourse about the intrusiveness of television technology monopolized public assessments of the assassination coverage for months following the event, it was absent from later journalistic accounts of the assassination. This suggests that journalists ceased to view television as a technological interference in events, that this picture no longer fit journalists' collective perceptions about themselves.

It is worth noting that legal organizations picked up the professional controversy about journalistic performance and condemned the press's insistence on the right to know. They claimed that journalists had seriously interfered with Oswald's right to a free and private trial and hampered police efforts to transfer the accused. The director of the American Civil Liberties Union held that Oswald was "tried and convicted many times over in the newspapers, on the radio and over television."[58] When Jack Ruby's trial necessitated quick decisions about acceptable parameters of press coverage, District Judge Joe Brown consulted only with press representatives before ruling to prohibit television, radio, and still photographers from the courtroom. Said Brown:

> The microphone and the television camera in open court are intrusions that no judge or defendant should have to put up with. There is enough ham acting by prosecutors, defense lawyers and even judges without this further invitation. Reporters bearing pads and pencils, photographers carrying candid cameras are enough. They give the public the news the public is entitled to.[59]

Television journalists grumbled about the judge's decision, but generally did little else to contest it. Their reluctance to act possibly stemmed from the salience of more general criticism about their coverage of Oswald's murder.

The media's behavior at Jack Ruby's trial again drew the attention of professional forums. At the annual conference of the ASNE, one participant noted that

> quite naively the judge of the court agreed, after a conference with the networks, to permit the televising of the verdict only. He said later he had their promise that immediately after their verdict was announced, they would go off the air. He adjourned the court, dismissed the jury, left the courtroom. If you were a privileged American television viewer that day, you then saw the pandemonium.[60]

Journalists were criticized for exhibiting behavior similar to that which they had displayed when covering Oswald. On a day when Ruby had been questioned about his mental fitness, journalists behaved in a particularly unruly fashion:

> [on] his return late in the afternoon to the Dallas County
> Jail, while mentally and physically exhausted, he was sur-
> rounded by a mob of news reporters, including radio,
> press and television with a multitude of flashing lights. . . .
> The news media representatives were simultaneously
> shouting questions to him involving his mental illness and
> many other questions that were entirely inappropriate, ir-
> responsible and in complete disregard of the rights of this
> individual.[61]

This suggested that despite criticism of the behavior of journalists in
covering Oswald, they repeated the same behavior only a few months
later.

What do the two opposite appraisals of journalistic practice, as occasioned by Oswald's murder, suggest? Significantly, certain observers
used attributes of coverage to condemn journalism, while others used
the same attributes to praise it. The instruments of technology—
cameras, cables, microphones—both facilitated live coverage and
were held responsible for facilitating Oswald's death. This indicates
that journalists were seen as having used technology to conduct their
work in a professional manner, but that the thoughtless use of technology was seen as a hazard. Within this discourse about technology
two distinct assessments of assassination coverage originally prevailed, assessments that revealed the extent to which the acceptable
parameters of journalistic professionalism were still being debated at
the time of the assassination.

One assessment, exemplified by the Warren Commission and court
decisions barring television cameras from courtrooms, emphasized
the flaws of television. It advanced the view that journalistic coverage
had overextended itself and that the technology on which television
journalists based their struggles for legitimation was more of a hin-
drance than a help. By emphasizing the negative aspects of television
technology, the imbroglio about Oswald threatened to upset the
shaky legitimacy of practitioners within the new medium: if the journalistic community agreed with the points raised by the Oswald
controversy, they would have invalidated the very qualities that distinguished television journalism from print.

That is why this specific discourse—about journalists facilitating
Oswald's death—has simply disappeared over time. The cables, microphones, cameras, and the discourse they generated about the
appropriateness of television journalism and journalistic professionalism are no longer referenced in contemporary discussions of the
Oswald case, whether mediated or professional. The fact that the

technology of television was hailed for producing live coverage of Oswald's murder (by one view) meant that its instruments—the cables, microphones, and cameras—could not be held responsible for facilitating his death (by another view). In other words, it was not possible for both positive and negative views of coverage to have persisted, because the same attributes of television were being simultaneously used both to condemn journalism and to praise it.

At stake in professional discourse about Oswald's murder was a larger discussion about the relationship between professionalism and technology. The question of whether journalists had made themselves more professional through technology—and whether they had done so by succumbing to technology or by mastering it—influenced debates not only about coverage of the Oswald homicide but also and more generally about covering Kennedy's death. Being a professional meant using instruments of technology effectively. The Oswald homicide gave rise to questions about journalistic claims of authority, television technology, and the practices of television journalists. This made it necessary to recast journalistic retellings as narratives legitimating journalistic professionalism. Because the specific events of Kennedy's death embedded problems of journalists' authority in much of the assassination coverage, retelling their part in covering the story called for reconstructions of their performances as effective professional triumphs or as understandable—but salvageable—professional mishaps. It was thus necessary for contemporary renditions of the Oswald story to recast it as the professional triumph that was implicit in the scoop of having caught the murder on live camera.

Thus over time most journalists, in both professional and mediated forums, have preferred the view that emphasized the attributes of television and, not coincidentally, saw journalists as having acted professionally in their coverage. It also, significantly, allowed reporters to generate a narrative that told of their successful adaptation to the new technology of television. As one critic lamented, "broadcasting resembles the little girl in the nursery rhyme. When it is bad, it is horrid. But when it is good it is very very good." [62] Differing assessments of journalists' behavior encouraged professional discourse about covering Oswald's murder; the thrust for rhetorical legitimation marked one assessment for an early death.

Mastering Coverage by Mastering Technology

At the heart of many of the professional assessments of journalistic coverage lay discussions about technology. Through technology, journalists were able to set forth arguments that reinstated their authority for telling the story of the assassination. Television technology in particular offered journalists alternative ways of repairing their professionalism, by helping them to classify as professional a number of activities that were largely improvisational. The technology was thus seen as facilitating—and as hindering—the emergence of collective and individual professional identities.

How the Oswald imbroglio figured in professional assessments of the assassination reveals much about the embedded discourses of technology, professionalism, and journalistic authority through which journalists sought to position themselves as authoritative spokespersons for the events in Dallas. In mediated forums journalists set the stage for self-authorization through discourse about professionalism; they bolstered that discourse in professional forums.

Mediated discourse depended on the circulation of similar assumptions about journalistic performance in professional circles. It was necessary for individual mediated accounts to be supported by larger institutional agendas, as they were shaped by trade publications, proceedings of professional meetings, and agendas of journalism associations and organizations. It was thus no surprise that already in the weeks following the assassination, journalists made use of professional forums to transform their assassination coverage into a marker of professional accomplishment. In so doing, reporters strengthened the status of the assassination story as a critical incident for professional journalists.

Journalists' discourse thus helped to consolidate the journalistic community around certain issues central to its professionalism. Such assessments upheld journalists as an authoritative interpretive community, underscoring collective notions about the improvisational and instinctive nature of journalistic practice, the value of informal networks, and the innovative uses to which technology could be put. Implicit within these assessments were considerations about how the individual journalist, the organization and institution, and the structure of the profession all fit together within one interpretive community. Professional assessment—in both mediated and trade discourse—thereby signaled what it meant for journalists to speak authoritatively not only about the assassination but about themselves. By embedding notions of authority in professionalism and technology, it set up an effective base for the creation of assassination tales and signaled the boundaries of the interpretive community from which such tales would emerge.

Part Three: Promoting Assassination Tales

SEVEN

De-authorizing Official Memory:
From 1964 to the Seventies

At the time of Kennedy's death, the media competed with other groups to be seen as the preferred retellers of the assassination tale. Over the years, as historians and independent critics put forward their own versions of what had happened, this competition persisted and, if anything, increased.[1] This chapter shows how the tales that evolved were a function of this interaction. It discusses the more general concerns and tensions that facilitated and hindered the journalists in becoming a central part of the assassination story. It thus digresses from the role played by journalists to address the activities of historians and independent critics in retelling the story.

Death Creating Life: The Assassination and Readings of Kennedy

Once called the "most fascinating might-have-been in American history,"[2] the deceased John F. Kennedy was seen by many Americans as having "infinitely more force than Kennedy living."[3] Details of the president's death were brought directly into the growing national repertoire of Kennedy stories, and the Kennedy tale was recast as one of tragedy.

Early Readings of Kennedy's Death

For many observers interested in tracking the details of Kennedy's reign as president, the Kennedy myth came into being only after he died, "and then only as a means of coping with his death."[4] One sociologist recalled that "all those splendid great expectations that we are now convinced we had back in the early 60s were discovered for the first time after the assassination."[5] Historian Daniel Boorstin made a similar point in 1988, when he contended that Kennedy's "untimely death reminds us of how history assesses public figures who die too soon. In the making of historical reputations, there are advantages and opportunities to brevity."[6]

Two popular readings of Kennedy's death persisted in the public eye, both, according to Christopher Lasch, rooted in the intellectual climate of the 1950s.[7] On the one hand, observers lamented the promise of Camelot that was cut short in Dallas; on the other, notions of conspiracy emphasized the underside of Kennedy's public existence. Because the assassination brought together these "two elemental themes of American history," journalist Jefferson Morley contended, its "anniversary [endured] as a national rite."[8] The assassination story reflected basic disjunctions within Kennedy's life itself.[9]

Those endorsing the first perspective admitted that Kennedy's time in office had been too brief for him to carry out all of his envisioned program. They were quick to laud Kennedy's support of the Peace Corps, the Alliance for Progress, and legislation on civil rights. They also used Kennedy's death to soften criticism about some of his activities as president. Memories of his death were brought to the forefront of evaluations of his administration, to explain and rationalize what some held as having gone wrong.

These observers held Kennedy in lofty, almost mythic regard, a sentiment fueled by Kennedy's inner circle—Theodore Sorensen, Arthur Schlesinger, Jr., and Pierre Salinger—and by Kennedy's widow. Years later, when writer Theodore White recalled how Jacqueline Kennedy had "wanted Camelot to top the story" of Kennedy's administration, he admitted that "Camelot, heroes, fairy tales, legends were what history was all about. . . . So the epitaph on the Kennedy administration became Camelot—a magic moment in American history. Which of course is a misreading of history. The magic Camelot of JFK never existed."[10] While the "selling of Camelot" was seen by some as "too insistent, too fevered, accompanied by too much sentimentality and too little rigorous thought,"[11] it made the president's death the "sacrificial offering . . . to the forces of bigotry, irrationality and fanaticism."[12] In Henry Steele Commager's view, Kennedy's death dramatized "lawlessness and violence, fear, suspicion and hatred."[13] Ben H. Bagdikian claimed three weeks after the event that it was the result of "a destructive internal force . . . an obsession."[14]

The second popular view of Kennedy's administration was put forward by the Cold War advocates. Early appraisals faulted Kennedy from both Right and Left. He was seen as a Communist agent, "killed because he failed to fulfill Moscow's decisions quickly enough."[15] On the Left, he was criticized for an array of mistakes, including a failure to lead Congress effectively, faulty administration, and the Bay of Pigs invasion.[16]

The persistence of both views in the early years after the assassination was reflected in the *New York Times* best-seller list during one week in 1964. Its selection of titles included Kennedy's celebratory *Profiles in Courage* and Victor Lasky's critique of Kennedy, entitled *JFK: The Man and the Myth*.[17] Both titles emphasized the centrality of issues related to the slain president. Yet another Kennedy-related title was also on the best-seller list that week—*Four Days*, a UPI–*American Heritage* book about the assassination.[18] Its position underscored journalists' continuing efforts to retell the assassination.

Alternative Readings: Journalists, Critics, Historians, and the Family

In the years following Kennedy's death, many groups began to put forward competitively their versions of the assassination story. The Kennedy family in large part blocked popular attempts to retell it. This was most evident during the mid 1960s, when it set in motion what one newsmagazine called "the biggest brouhaha over a book that the nation has ever known."[19] The family agreed to let writer William Manchester publish an authorized history of Kennedy's death, and then reneged on the agreement.[20] The book, said *Time* magazine, "was to be a *rara avis*: a history that would be independent but would still carry the authorization of the Kennedys and require their approval before publication."[21] The family denied approval, however, and it delayed publication until Manchester agreed to make some changes to the manuscript.[22] One 1967 overview of the incident commented that the charge against the Kennedy family was no longer one of managing news, but rather of managing history.[23]

The incident characterized a more general pattern of image management by the Kennedys. Family members sought to sever images of the president's death from appraisals of his life, to the extent that they engaged in their own commemorative practices or boycotted certain public memorial services.[24] By the seventies, the family had begun to avoid dedication services in Dallas and to call for national commemorations not on November 22, the date of Kennedy's death, but on his birthday instead.[25] Few journalists agreed.[26]

Kennedy's in-house historians at first upheld the family's perspective. Arthur Schlesinger, Jr.'s *Thousand Days* and Theodore Sorensen's *Kennedy* provided generally sympathetic views on the presidency from persons who had served on the White House staff.[27] Excerpts in popular magazines ensured the availability of their accounts to wider audiences.[28] Their accounts placed the assassination within a general context rather than directly address it. This exemplified a general tendency not to address Kennedy's death too soon. One exception was an appraisal of Kennedy offered by scholar William Carleton in 1964. Called "Kennedy in History," the article was accompanied by a footnote in which Carleton justified his attempt to "historicize" Kennedy before sufficient time had passed.[29] Other historians incorporated mention of the assassination, usually in epilogues. For example, William Manchester reissued his book *Portrait of a President* with a revised epilogue that tracked the effect of the president's death on those around him.[30]

Journalists, too, had begun to implant and perpetuate images about Kennedy in collective memory. News organizations and journalists were quick to produce books, films, and articles on Kennedy's administration. The *New York Times* published *The Kennedy Years;* journalists Tom Wicker and High Sidey issued *Kennedy Without Tears* and *John F. Kennedy, President,* and Pierre Salinger and Sander Vanocur published a book of tributes to the president.[31] *Life* magazine issued a special memorial issue on Kennedy's "life, words, deeds."[32] A few years later NBC News issued *There Was a President.*[33]

Some of these productions focused directly on Kennedy's death. The United Artists/UPI documentary film *Four Days in November* premiered in 1964.[34] The *New York Times*'s book *The Kennedy Years* came with a forty-eight-page booklet on the assassination.[35] UPI and *American Heritage* magazine published *Four Days,* which described the assassination and its immediate aftermath.[36] The Associated Press published its own version of the assassination, *The Torch Is Passed. . . .*[37] Books began to appear on the event's anniversaries.[38] Twenty years later, Americans were still being treated to what one journalist called "a media bath of reassessment."[39]

While making efforts to construct their own record, journalists also voiced some dissatisfaction with the record construction of others. They particularly debated whether Arthur Schlesinger, Jr.'s work constituted more "gossip" than "history": in 1965 one writer discussed his memoirs under the title "Peephole Journalism," making the somewhat caustic comment that "he has made the most of a few occasions when he was permitted to see more than the average reporter."[40] Elsewhere, reporter Meg Greenfield argued that "Any reporter can tell you how hard it is to recall even a brief quotation word for word after an interview, and the fact that certain memoirists repaired to their diaries in the evening is not even mildly reassuring in view of the extensive verbatim exchanges they have produced."[41] Such a response by journalists reflected what appeared to be their concerns over the privileged place already being given to historians in retelling the tale.

At the same time another group interested in the details of Kennedy's death had begun to emerge. Commonly known as "the assassination buffs," these independent critics were bothered by the public record concerning Kennedy's death, and they set out to document its inconsistencies. Three weeks after Kennedy was assassinated, one of the first articles doubting the received version of the assassination was published. Appearing in the *New Republic* under the title "Seeds of Doubt," the article raised questions about five different categories of evidence.[42] At about the same time, critic Mark Lane, who would later be singled out by Gerald Ford for his critiques of the Warren Commission,[43] wrote a defense brief lamenting the fact that Oswald had not enjoyed a presumption of innocence.[44] Other articles appeared in obscure journals with generally limited readership, such as a journal called *Minority of One* that published a detailed discussion of the shots that killed Kennedy.[45] The critics' ranks included salespersons, graduate students, and homemakers, many of whom turned a lay interest in Kennedy's death into an avocation as sleuth. Their interest in the assassination challenged the ability of other, professional groups—such as journalists and historians—to position themselves as the story's authoritative spokespersons.

At the heart of alternative readings of Kennedy's death were questions about who was authorized to retell the story, and in what way. Historians had only begun to document their part of the record. Journalists faced a professional dilemma that was not to their liking: in their attempts to simultaneously appraise Kennedy's presidency and understand his death, the more attention they paid to the events of the assassination, the more holes in collective memory they revealed. This created a situation ripe for the emergence of independent critics, who hoped to tell the authoritative, and final, story of what had really happened. All these efforts highlighted the assassination, making it an essential part of memories about Kennedy.

An Absence of Closure

Official agencies had also begun to investigate the unresolved angles of Kennedy's death shortly after it occurred. But in making certain documents public and concealing others, as well as failing to provide answers to questions that arose, they generated a climate of suspicion among many other retellers. This made the assassination story of greater interest to journalists, independent critics, and historians.

The Warren Commission

Within two weeks of the assassination the Warren Commission, a seven-member body put together at the behest of President Lyndon B. Johnson, had begun to investigate Kennedy's death.[46] The largest official group charged with investigation, it addressed six areas: basic facts, identity of the assassin, Lee Harvey Oswald's background, possible conspiratorial relationships, Oswald's death, and presidential protection.[47] The commission examined hundreds of reports and documents and interviewed more than 550 witnesses. By the time it concluded its deliberations in late 1964, it had produced more than 17,000 pages bound in a report and twenty-six accompanying volumes of hearings and exhibits.[48] Its final report held that Kennedy was killed by a lone gunman, Oswald.

The commission's speedy resolution of the assassination, however, left unanswered some vital questions concerning how and why the murder took place. This was due in part to the time pressures surrounding deliberation, which left large holes in the official record. Questions persisted concerning the reasons for Oswald's involvement, the mechanics of that involvement, and the contradictory eyewitness testimony that suggested the involvement of others. Other problems with the Warren Commission also emerged. These included its uncertain ties with both the CIA and FBI, and internal inconsistencies in the selection and questioning of witnesses and the handling of evidence.[49]

It is significant that, regardless of the problems surrounding the Warren Commission that arose over time, it initially enjoyed considerable public support. The national media, both print and broadcast, praised its work.[50] Much of its documentation was made available to the public, either through media reports or for direct purchase at seventy-six dollars.[51] Abridged editions, less cumbersome than the report and its accompanying twenty-six volumes, were also available.[52]

In the beginning, the efforts of news organizations were intertwined with those of the commission. The *New York Times* issued its own version of the report, with a preface by journalist Harrison Salisbury.[53] The Associated Press did the same and appended to its edition what it called "An AP Photo Story of the Tragedy," a series of fourteen pictures of Kennedy's final moments.[54] In a footnote, the editors sought to offset possible criticism arising from their decision to merge the documents, one seemingly nonpartisan, the other official: "As indicated, the supplement of pictures inserted in the front section of the book is not a part of the Commission's report. It was added in order to recall more vividly the tragic four days which made the report necessary."[55] The ideological assumptions implicit in the merger, however, were not addressed.

The independent critics were critical of the *Warren Report* almost from the beginning. While "most Americans did not even want to listen to any theories that contradicted [the Commission],"[56] critical articles were published in national journals like *Esquire* and the *New Republic* and local journals like the *Texas Observer* within months of the commission's report of its findings.[57] By the end of the decade, the critics had aired conspiracy theories involving pro-Castro and anti-Castro proponents; the Dallas police; the CIA, FBI, and Secret Service; organized crime; Texas right-wingers; and oil magnates.[58]

The critics' efforts displayed both ingenuity and unity of purpose. They ranged from that of Sylvia Meagher, who on "finding the commission's index next to useless prepared and published her own,"[59] to that of Edward J. Epstein, who turned his master's thesis into a best-selling discussion of the Warren Commission.[60] Four books in particular—Epstein's *Inquest,* Josiah Thompson's *Six Seconds in Dallas,* Meagher's *Accessories after the Fact,* and Mark Lane's *Rush to Judgment*—presented alternative perspectives on Kennedy's death that raised fundamental questions about what had actually happened.[61] They particularly questioned the premises on which the commission had based its pronouncement of Oswald's guilt. While some of the issues they raised helped discredit the report over time, they went largely unnoticed by the mainstream media. Even the popular name given to the independent critics, the "buffs," implied "a harmless fixation like collecting old cars."[62] One reporter exemplified a tendency toward dismissiveness when he maintained that "clearly the pattern with Warren Commission critics is: If the experts agree with you, use them. If they don't, ignore them."[63] Interestingly, the fact that the same had been often said about the media did not lead journalists to the same kind of self-evaluations.

The critics were as critical of journalists as journalists were of them. In particular, they faulted journalists for their support of the commission and for their reluctance to incorporate critics' accounts within their assassination retellings. The most strident critiques addressed the mainstream media's failure to lend closure to the story by resolving its unanswered questions. "Reporters were everywhere in Dallas that day," said one critic, but the record they provided "still remains inexplicable." [64] Another said that after the assassination, "we all thought, 'it's almost going to break. This is just too blatant and obvious. There are bright newsmen working on this thing.' Well, of course it didn't break." [65]

Particularly fervent complaints about the media were made by critic Mark Lane, whose book *A Citizen's Dissent* was framed as a call to journalistic conscience. European reporters, he said, "were puzzled by the obvious endorsement of the [Warren Commission] document by the American press . . . they asked how the independent American newspaperman had been silenced or cajoled into supporting the Report." [66] Calling American journalists a "biddable press," Lane lambasted the media "for their many efforts to endorse the Report." [67] Lane called to reopen the official investigation, saying that "the heroes of journalism are not those who crusade for the popular, who attack the weak and who are awarded the much-sought prizes. They are those who calmly assess the evidence, those who do not permit a sense of self to interfere with their professional obligations. They are too few; they are a disappearing breed." [68]

Lane's claims were important for two reasons: they not only undermined the authority of journalists with regard to the assassination, as appeared to be his intention, but also they cast the critics as investigative reporters. References to "heroes of journalism," attempts to frame the critics' work as the best kind of journalism, and more general discussions of the critics within a larger discourse about journalists and journalism suggested how closely related were the two spheres of practice and how central were journalists to retelling the assassination story. Lane's comments also underscored the ways in which issues of professionalism undercut the assassination retellings. By framing his discussion as journalism, he successfully elevated the amateurism of the critics and detracted from the journalists' professionalism.

Individual journalists also drew commentary from the critics. UPI reporter Merriman Smith was castigated for what they saw as his selective memory of what had happened. In Lane's words, Smith "had been awarded the Pulitzer Prize for his eyewitness reporting of the assassination. If ever one wishes to develop an argument against such awards, one need merely reread the Smith dispatches from Dallas in the light of the facts now known, making allowance for the fact that standards which an historian might be expected to adhere to cannot be applied to a reporter." [69] Dan Rather of CBS News was criticized for his interpretation of the Zapruder film, the amateur film that recorded the president's shooting. Allowed to view the full film shortly after Kennedy died, Rather gave network viewers a verbal description of what he had seen. He said that the president's head "fell *forward* with considerable violence," a statement that caused consternation among those contesting the lone-gunman theory, since it did not indicate that a shot had been fired from in front of the president.[70] The conspiracy theories the critics favored instead rested on claims that an additional shot had come from in front of the president and therefore that his head had jerked backward.

It was not long before the *Warren Report* began to come under fire from selected official and semi-official quarters. In 1966 former Kennedy aide Richard Goodwin called for an independent assessment of charges of inadequacy against the Warren Commission.[71] Two years later a team of medical practitioners appointed by the attorney general, known as the Clark Panel, began its investigation of the autopsy photographs and x-rays. The panel revealed "serious discrepancies between its review of the autopsy materials and the autopsy itself."[72] New Orleans district attorney Jim Garrison brought the assassination into the public eye when he accused a prominent local business leader, Clay Shaw, of involvement.[73]

Certain journalists began to reconsider their backing of the commission. Epstein in particular

> inspired a surge of assassination-related activity, not only by "buffs," but by investigative journalists and other members of the press, which had, to then, applauded The Warren Report as the final word. Epstein had academic credentials, he was not considered biased, his book was accompanied by an introduction by Richard H. Rovere, the respected New York writer, and it was favorably reviewed and widely read.[74]

In September 1966 reporter Tom Wicker publicly criticized the commission for failing to address public concerns raised by its report.[75] In November, *Life* magazine published its copy of the Zapruder film sequence under the title "A Matter of Reasonable Doubt." By showing in detail the moments when both Kennedy and Texas governor John Connally were hit by bullets, the printing of the sequence raised questions about the validity of the lone-bullet theory.[76] The magazine called on the government to set up a new investigative body. At about the same time, *Esquire* published a "Primer of Assassination Theories" that set out thirty versions of Kennedy's murder at odds with official documentary record.[77] A television panel pitted critics of the commission against its defenders for an on-air debate.[78]

The following year the *New York Times* decided to reinvestigate the assassination. Journalist Harrison Salisbury justified the decision on the basis of "the torrent of conspiracy yarns, challenges to the Warren Commission Report and general hysteria about the assassination."[79] In the *Washington Post*, reporter Jack Anderson exposed CIA plots to assassinate Castro.[80] More mainstream discussions of questions raised by the assassination began to appear in journals like the *New Yorker*, the *Saturday Evening Post*, and the *American Scholar*.[81] And CBS aired a four-part special arising from its own seven-month probe of the *Warren Report*.[82]

The publicity surrounding the CBS program was telling. Billed as "very well the most valuable four hours you ever spent with television,"[83] the program was touted by CBS News President Richard Salant in a press release as "professional" and a work of "genius."[84] *TV Guide* ranked it "a major journalistic achievement . . . a masterful compilation of facts, interviews, experiments and opinions—a job of journalism that will be difficult to surpass."[85] This suggests that already at that point, a technical discourse addressing the failings of the official process of documentation was being hailed as the best of investigative journalism.[86]

This did not mean that all media were ready to take up the call. Considerable efforts were still being directed at discrediting the independent critics. They were viewed as a group that had built its assassination libraries from newspaper clippings,[87] a "media offspring."[88] In effect, their usage of journalistic documents underscored the success of journalists' efforts to position themselves as authoritative retellers. The reliance on journalists' accounts made them a necessary part of alternative views about what had happened. But such reliance was problematic for critics trying to establish their own authority as an independent interpretive community.

In 1967 the independent critics' efforts prompted journalist Charles Roberts to direct a particularly scathing attack at what he considered a threat to the Warren Commission's integrity:

> Who are the men who have created doubt about a document that in September 1964 seemed to have reasonable answers. . . . Are they bona fide scholars, as the reviewers took them to be, or are they, as Connally has suggested, "journalistic scavengers?" . . . unlike Émile Zola and Lincoln Steffens, who rocked national and local governments by naming the guilty, the Warren Report critics never tell us who's in charge of the scheme that has victim-

ized us all. Nor are they able to define its purposes, although they offer half a dozen conflicting theories.[89]

Roberts's decision to frame his criticism of the independent critics on professional grounds, comparing them with the most renowned writers and journalists of the muckraking tradition, on the one hand, and with academics, on the other, was telling, because most critics were neither scholars nor journalists. Rather, most were laypersons who, despite the demands of other professional callings and other activities, had voluntarily decided to investigate the assassination. Roberts's attempt to classify them as a group recognized for its documentary exploration only reinforced how extraordinary was their intervention. Their attempts to retell the assassination thus strongly challenged the attempts of other groups to do so.

From the beginning, then, the assassination record lacked closure. Characterized by incompleteness and incongruities, it drew groups trying to put forward competitively their authoritative views of what had happened. The thrust toward questioning its premises, led by the independent critics, was accompanied by fundamental questions about professionalism, amateurism, and the access of private citizens to public official record. While journalists initially joined forces with recognized institutions in generating favorable documentation about the commission, by the end of the decade they too had begun to call for reconsideration of its findings. The increasing volume of claims of inadequacy helped establish a preliminary groundwork for laypersons, amateurs, and private citizens to begin to comment authoritatively upon the official version of Kennedy's death.

Interim Years

The tenth anniversary of Kennedy's death fell in the midst of the Watergate scandal, a fact that allowed his admirers to contrast their hero's actions with Nixon's stealth.[90] A *New York Times* writer contended that Kennedy was on his way to becoming great when killed.[91] At the same time, Kennedy was dubbed "unimaginative and perhaps even conservative," and was held responsible for the arms race, military entanglements, racial turmoil, and abuses of power.[92] By some accounts the Kennedy shrine was beginning to show its "cracks and termites."[93] This meant that the two perspectives by which Kennedy was remembered in the sixties persisted into the following decade. The sentiments of Camelot still lingered, although they were tempered, and they were accompanied by revisionist readings that regarded the former president more critically, usually as a conventional Cold War warrior.

This "coarsening of the collective memory"[94] was shaped by developments in society at large. The late sixties was "a period when entrenched authority was to be challenged and confronted,"[95] a "tearing-loose—the active beginning of the end of life within the old institutions."[96] Vietnam, Watergate, and other scandals of the seventies shook trust in public institutions to such an extent that, by the middle of the decade, skepticism of things official had extended to a "popular mistrust of official history."[97] As *Ramparts* magazine commented in 1973,

> We have learned (or should have) much about ourselves in the past decade. We slaughtered women and children in Vietnam and then covered it up; there was bombing in Cambodia and then a coverup; there was massive espionage at Watergate and then a coverup. Given the atmosphere in Dallas in 1963, and the admitted inadequacies of the Warren Commission Report, is it not equally possible that the assassination of President Kennedy was followed by a coverup? . . . It is clear that a reopening of the assassination investigation is now in order.[98]

Many Americans began to abandon either-or interpretations of Kennedy's death and entertain a more complex and critical view of the assassination than that suggested by the Warren Commission's lone-gunman theory. In 1975, *U.S. News and World Report* argued that while the tendency of many Americans in the sixties

> was to regard attacks on the Warren findings as the ideas of "kooks" or "cranks" or of "profiteers" seeking to exploit the great public interest in the Kennedy case. . . . [now] cynicism generated by the Watergate affair, the Vietnam War, and revelations about CIA operations have made both officials and the American public more inclined to accept a "conspiracy" theory as possible.[99]

Questioning the assassination record thus had its roots in larger cultural and political enterprises that cast doubt on governmental institutions and recognized forms of documentation.

But developments directly related to the assassination also prompted its reconsideration. Knowledge of the activities of the independent critics began to reach increasing numbers of people. By 1969, a *Ramparts* discussion claimed that the critics "were doing the job the Dallas police, the FBI and the Warren Commission should have done in the first place."[100] Articles in marginalized journals began to give way to mainstream treatments in *Newsweek* and *Time*.[101] Books continued to accumulate, from the cautious (Albert Newman's *Assassination of John F. Kennedy: The Reasons Why*) to the surprising (Hugh McDonald's *Appointment in Dallas*, which pointed to the existence of a second Kennedy assassin as told by a former CIA contract agent) to the sensational (the Harold Weisberg *Whitewash* series).[102]

By the mid seventies, the critics occupied a central role in the reopening of the assassination record. The Assassination Information Bureau drew thousands of people to Massachusetts for the first major public showing of Abraham Zapruder's film of the shooting.[103] In 1975, optics technician Robert Groden showed certain frames of the Zapruder film on national television and argued that Kennedy was the victim of crossfire.[104] Critic Mark Lane organized a Citizens Commission of Inquiry, whose intent was to pressure Congress to reopen the assassination investigation.[105]

As time wore on, and other quarters failed to address the issues they raised, the involvement of the critics generated questions about whether officials were needed to interpret the record. The *Saturday Evening Post* commented that the new headlines about Kennedy's assassination brought "a new national resolve to have a final satisfactory accounting of this American tragedy."[106] Groups of citizens began gathering signatures for petitions that urged the investigation's reopening.[107] Novels and films fed the growing interest in the events of Kennedy's death.[108]

At focus of such activities were considerations about the role of amateurs and private citizens in a world generally run by experts and officials. Observers were uncertain about the meaning of poorly evaluated evidence in a context where tidy official piles of documentation presumably worked best. As one critic said, "It's possible that [what I've found] is completely unscientific. But my answer to people saying 'you're no expert' is 'where are the experts?'"[109]

At about the same time, official quarters began to focus on possible irregularities in CIA and FBI activities. The Rockefeller Commission, formed in 1975 to investigate domestic activities by the CIA, basically upheld the Warren Commission report yet left unanswered many questions about the workings of American intelligence.[110] The following year, a U.S. Senate Select Committee chaired by Senator Frank Church was formed to study the relationship between the government and federal intelligence agencies.[111] The Church Committee was charged with exploring the performance of intelligence agencies in regard to Kennedy's death. A subcommittee led by Senators Richard

Schweiker and Gary Hart confirmed the federal intelligence agencies' failure to examine conspiracy leads. It also pointed to illicit sexual connections between Kennedy and one Judith Campbell Exner, a link to possible involvement of organized crime in the assassination.[112]

Other irregularities were also suggested. It was revealed that FBI documents had been concealed from the Warren Commission[113] and that reports of CIA plans to assassinate Castro were kept from commission members. These revelations made a reconsideration of the assassination case more palatable, if not essential. The presence of ambiguities, falsities, reports of mishandled information and witnesses also made it crucial to reappraise the Warren Commission. Retellers who had actively doubted the official record now found themselves attractively positioned.

The actions of the media in such a context gave rise to different views. While the media were instrumental in giving voice to a variety of reports, it was unclear whether they had been fair to spokespersons of all sides. On the one hand, journalists were faulted for not lending sufficient credence to critiques of the lone-gunman theory. Independent critics called the media "one-sided":[114]

> Although there have been indications that our national media may make a large contribution to the mounting public pressure to reopen the investigation of the Kennedy assassination, certain pitfalls remain. One problem is that sensational charges are often more newsworthy—and more easily understood and communicated—than the subtle discoveries of long-term research. The only way the press will appreciate the significance of the less sensational research is through its own sustained investigation.[115]

Others held that for the sake of expediency, journalists bought "Castro did it" yarns and ignored leads suggesting more complex explanations.[116] The *New York Times* was faulted for having previewed the findings of the commission three months before it completed taking testimony.[117] Reporter Jack Anderson was charged with having CIA connections.[118] Questions lingered about the media's readiness to investigate the unsolved aspects of Kennedy's death.

Yet as reports increasingly critiqued the findings of the Warren Commission, journalists became increasingly coopted in the move to reopen the assassination investigation. In some cases, they themselves put forward alternative claims about Kennedy's death. Veteran CBS reporter Daniel Schorr published *Clearing the Air*, which tracked the links between Kennedy's death and the CIA's plots to murder Castro.[119] TV anchorperson Walter Cronkite in 1975 showed parts of an interview with Lyndon Johnson that had been deleted years earlier at the president's request; the omitted portions indicated that he suspected international involvement in Kennedy's assassination.[120] Investigative sequels on the assassination were shown on network news programs, and assassination articles began to appear more frequently in the mainstream press.[121] When in March 1975, the entire Zapruder film was first shown on network television, it displayed for millions of American viewers the graphic footage that had originally documented Kennedy's fatal head wound.[122] In one historian's view, "this episode convinced many that the Warren Commission had erred."[123]

At the same time, the inactivities of another group of retellers—the historians—were drawing attention. While the start of the decade after Kennedy's death might have been expected to generate the beginnings of a historical record, few historians at the time were willing to address the issue. David Halberstam, himself the practitioner of a hybrid form of chronicling that was both journalistic and historical, produced *The Best and the Brightest*, a work that dealt with Kennedy but not with his death.[124] History textbooks were criticized for not discussing the assassination in detail.[125] As one historian said years later, professional scholars "neglected the assassination, as if it never occurred. This lack of attention has created a vacuum filled by journalists, freelance writers and others, most of whom have examined the assassination more for its sensational value than for its objective value."[126] The assassination story had too many loose ends to take final form as part of the historical record.

One direct challenge to historians' role in telling the assassination story came from writer Theodore White. White had enjoyed a long relationship with Kennedy while writing *The Making of the President, 1960*, and his relatively easy access to Kennedy's thousand days in office made him a familiar face at the White House. On this basis Jacqueline Kennedy had asked him to write about the slain president. "She wanted me to make certain that JFK was not forgotten in history. She thought it was up to me to make American history remember. . . . She wanted me to rescue Jack from all the 'bitter people' who were going to write about him in history. She did not want Jack left to the historians."[127] White's memorable account of Kennedy's administration, which first dubbed it "Camelot," made a journalist, not a historian, responsible for popularizing Kennedy's memory. That fact was energetically stressed in journalists' chronicles.[128]

Underlying all of these discussions was the representation of different groups of assassination retellers, each seen to have its own agenda. Embedded in their retellings were assumptions about the perspective taken in telling the story, the narrative practices chosen to structure its telling, and the demarcations separating one group of retellers from others. These issues made professionalism central to the story's retellings.

As these discussions continued, much of the American public increasingly came to perceive an absence of closure in the assassination record. At the same time as official forums for documentation had visibly faltered in their attempts to make a final accounting of what had happened, other groups, led by the independent critics, made alternative theories a more popular reading of Kennedy's death. Their interpretations of the existing documentary record showed that professional expertise and training did not necessarily produce the most authoritative perspectives on Kennedy's death. These groups not only underscored the value of private access to official documents but intensified a thrust toward questioning the validity of those documents. Although journalists generally followed the lead of the independent critics, as members of the media with routinized access they remained a necessary part of attempts to reopen the assassination record.

The House Select Committee

Increasingly critical readings of the assassination, growing recognition of the value of questioning the official documentation, and questions raised by the Schweiker-Hart subcommittee and Rockefeller Commission all produced a climate by the end of the decade that favored reopening the Kennedy investigation and directly affected the images of Kennedy that persisted. Camelot was deromanticized, "portrayed as a hoax, [and] conspiracy [came to be seen] as realism." [129]

This did not imply that all retellers were comfortable with a more critical perspective. Interestingly, in some quarters it was seen as an abandonment of "appropriate" journalistic practice. "[It was] as if the epistemology of the *New York Times* and the *Washington Post* had been replaced by that of the *National Enquirer* and *People* magazine. Camelot, it seemed, could never again appear to be the pristine place its celebrants had claimed—there were simply too many Mafia dons and party girls dwelling within its precincts." [130] For some journalists, undermining the Warren Commission was implicitly encoded as an undermining of traditional standards of journalism.

That changed, in large part, with Watergate, which lent renewed relevance to the events of Kennedy's death. Independent critics in particular found links and parallels between the two. One cogent discussion of the Dallas-Watergate connection was put forward in a 1976 book by academic critic Carl Oglesby, entitled *The Yankee and Cowboy War*.[131] Oglesby, who had been a key intellectual figure of the New Left during the sixties, contended that at the heart of both Dallas and Watergate were persistent splits between northern Yankees and southern Cowboys. These tensions, he claimed, produced a merger between anti-Castro Cuban exiles, organized crime, and "a Cowboy oligarchy" that had conspired to murder the president. At about the same time, another academic, Peter Dale Scott, argued that the connection between organized crime and American intelligence was not only responsible for both events but had helped mire the United States in Vietnam.[132] His claim was particularly interesting given his former status as a Canadian diplomat. Edward Epstein's *Legend* documented the intelligence connections of Lee Harvey Oswald.[133] Journalist Seth Kantor produced his own version of the Dallas-Watergate link, which saw both investigations as weak attempts to sidestep larger issues about the influence of organized crime.[134]

Publications like these altered public notions about the meaning of "conspiracy." Earlier appropriations of conspiracy as an oppositional reading of Kennedy's death had made it seem unidimensional. Yet links to Watergate suggested a deeper complexity than had been suggested initially. Rather than adhere to earlier views that largely equated conspiracy with the political Left, Oglesby's book suggested that it not only came from the Right but continued to permeate then-current political affairs. This made "conspiracy" into a more complicated, multidimensional notion, at the same time as it reinforced generalized doubts about the reliability of official documentary process and the authority of official documents.

Within such a climate, official efforts to reinvestigate the assassination began to move faster. They were prompted by new acoustic testimony, which suggested that there had indeed been crossfire. In 1976 a second federal investigation was officially opened. Known as the House Select Committee on Assassinations, the 170-member House committee linked the killings of Kennedy and Martin Luther King and sought to address the unresolved aspects of both deaths. The committee's convening was framed as a mission by which its members were "out to restore credibility, just as the Watergate hearings . . . restored belief in our government."[135] In the case of Kennedy's assassination, most subpoenas were directed at CIA- and FBI-held files.[136]

The House committee took two years to reach its deliberations. According to historian Michael Kurtz, its mandate was fourfold. It was to uncover:

> 1) Who assassinated President Kennedy? 2) Did the assassin(s) receive any assistance? 3) Did United States government agencies adequately collect and share information prior to the assassination, protect President Kennedy properly, and conduct a thorough investigation into the assassination? 4) Should new legislation on these matters be enacted by Congress? [137]

News of the committee's deliberations reached the media on 30 December 1978.

The committee strongly disputed the findings of the Warren Commission. The *Warren Report* was not, it said in its final report, "an accurate representation of all the evidence available to the Commission or a true reflection of the scope of the Commission's work, particularly on the issue of possible conspiracy in the assassination. It is a reality to be regretted that the Commission failed to live up to its promise." [138]

The committee ruled that there had probably been a second gunman in the killing of Kennedy and noted that Kennedy was "probably assassinated as a result of a conspiracy." [139] It presented extensive documentation about who might have been interested in pulling a second trigger—the Cuban government, the Kremlin, right-wing Cuban exiles, organized crime, the CIA, the FBI, or the Secret Service. Conceding that it could not specify the identity or extent of a possible conspiracy, it strongly suggested the involvement of a combination of anti-Castro elements and organized crime. [140]

The committee's efforts attempted to sidestep pat definitions and easy answers. Its final report, for instance, discussed at length the problematics surrounding the term *conspiracy:* "while the word 'conspiracy' technically denotes only a 'partnership in criminal purposes,' it also, in fact, connotes widely varying meanings to many people, and its use has vastly differing societal implications depending on the sophistication, extent and ultimate purpose of the partnership." [141] The committee called on the Justice Department to act on the leads its deliberations provided. In his introductory remarks to the final report, Chief Counsel G. Robert Blakey noted that "the government, to live up to the meaning of justice, can do no less than to pursue the course the committee has charted." [142]

Observers were divided in their appraisals of the committee's efforts, offering both praise and condemnation. The negative criticism came from two fronts: certain scholars, independent critics, and journalists either remained unconvinced of the committee's suggestions or felt that the committee had not gone far enough in supporting alternative explanations of the assassination. The latter characterized the committee's efforts as "an exercise in bathos."[143] It was argued that

> The investigation uncovered some new evidence, particularly the acoustical analysis, but on the whole it proved as limited as that of the Warren Commission. . . . The committee's refusal to operate publicly, its lack of expert cross-examination of witnesses, its failure to attach the proper significance to numerous pieces of evidence resulted in an investigation of the assassination that raised more questions than it originally sought to answer.[144]

This view held that, while it had displaced the commission's lone-gunman theory with notions of conspiracy, the committee had not lent closure to the story. It had not definitively implicated the agents of Kennedy's assassination;[145] nor had it opened many of the documents that were sealed from public scrutiny. The committee was therefore held responsible for doing little to set straight the record that had been obfuscated by the Warren Commission.

Those who remained unconvinced of the committee's efforts carefully laid out their skepticism. One such example was a preface by journalist Tom Wicker that was appended to the Bantam edition of the committee's final report. In nearly ten pages, Wicker gave his reasons for doubting the committee's findings. "What the Committee gives us with one hand—a second gunman and a conspiracy—it tends to take away with the other," he said.[146] Wicker faulted the report for excessive sensationalism, assumptions, and interpretations. Significantly, the curious inclusion of such a negative preface to the report's published version implied the continued importance of larger questions about legitimating different versions of what had happened.

A second appraisal of the committee was more supportive. This view, adopted by many independent critics, argued that the committee had significantly clarified a complex issue. The failure of the committee to document the gunman's identity mattered less than the fact that conspiracy had been put forward as a reasonable explanation of what had happened. Within this view, the media were viewed as instrumental in having spread notions of the committee's ineffectiveness. Alternately seen as either generally uninterested or too eager to grasp quick and tidy solutions, they were criticized for overlooking the real significance of the committee's findings.[147] As British journalist Anthony Summers noted,

> The American press, to its discredit, has generally played down the achievements of the Assassination Committee or brushed its conclusions aside. This lethargy may stem in part from the fact that—sixteen years ago—there was no serious attempt at investigative reporting of the Kennedy assassination. In those days, before Vietnam and Watergate, investigation was left to the government.[148]

Summers added that after the committee "drew sarcastic comment from the press," the Kennedy case was "abandoned by the mainstream media, except when the anniversary comes round each year."[149] The complexities of the case further increased two years after the committee's report, when Chief Counsel G. Robert Blakey wrote his own version of the case, which pointed in the direction of organized crime.[150] Interestingly, that book too was generally ignored by prominent journalists and news organizations.

Regardless of the view one adopted, the case of Kennedy's assassination still remained unsolved. Rather than achieving closure, new information diminished it, generating questions where there had previously been answers. As critic Josiah Thompson said, while normal investigatory procedure of homicides tended to produce a convergence of the evidence, in Kennedy's homicide, "things haven't gotten any simpler; they haven't come together."[151] Despite their status as legitimate and recognized holders of assassination memories, official documentary agencies were unable to provide a complete account of what had happened.

Its official memories de-authorized, the assassination story was thus opened up for reconsideration. Implicitly or explicitly, the inability of official documentary process to lend closure to the story invited other retellers to do so. While some of these groups, particularly independent critics, had been active along the way, the path for their continued involvement was increasingly legitimated.

EIGHT

Negotiating Memory: From 1980
to the Nineties

As it was increasingly accepted that no one version of President Kennedy's death could document all of its angles, the competition among different groups of retellers persisted. Now, however, television began to position journalists over both historians and independent critics as preferred retellers of the assassination story. This chapter discusses how journalists used television to put forward their own retellings in favorable ways.

The Recognition of Alternative Retellers

During the eighties the body of assassination literature continued to grow, although not everybody remembered, or cared about, the events of Kennedy's death. By 1988 writer Pete Hamill was able to observe that "an entire generation had come to maturity with no memory at all of the Kennedy years; for them, Kennedy is the name of an airport or a boulevard or a high school."[1] One photograph in 1987 showed two visitors at Kennedy's grave on the anniversary of his death,[2] a far cry from the hordes of people that had gathered there in earlier years.

But for the many who did still care, readings of the presidency oscillated between the two proven themes, favorable and unfavorable. On the one hand, Camelot still reigned. Thirty-four percent of Americans in a 1988 poll said that Kennedy had been the country's most effective president.[3] National amnesia seemed to have erased many tawdry revelations of the seventies.[4] Relatively few Americans associated John F. Kennedy with either sexual misconduct or plots to murder foreign leaders.[5] The period saw nostalgic TV series like "Kennedy" and books like William Manchester's *One Brief Shining Moment*, a tribute to the president that mentioned few problems in Camelot.[6] The twentieth assassination anniversary "received even more media exposure than had the anniversaries of 1973 or 1978—much of it devoted to nostalgia about the Kennedy family and the Kennedy charm. The underside of Camelot was also acknowledged, dismissed as unimportant."[7] Articles were written under titles like "Camelot Revisited" and "Camelot on Tape," which detailed how Kennedy had taped White House conversations.[8] The notion of Camelot remained intact, despite its acknowledged failings.

At the same time revisionists demoted Kennedy from a "great" president to a merely "successful" one. In this view, "A dry-eyed view of his thousand days [suggested] that his words were bolder than his deeds."[9] Herbert Parmet's book on the presidency succeeded in thoroughly documenting the underside of Kennedy's presidency but stopped short of castigating him for his failings.[10] Gary Wills's *Kennedy Imprisonment* and Peter Collier and David Horowitz's *Kennedys* paid close attention to the dark side of Kennedy's life.[11] Newsmagazines were filled with more realistic rereadings of the Kennedy presidency.[12] In 1985, Hofstra University held a conference on Kennedy called "John Fitzgerald Kennedy: The Promise Revised." The conference director maintained that the theme was chosen to provide a fair evaluation of the former president.[13]

Accounts in this vein that directly addressed the assassination tended to favor some form of conspiracy theory. New books on the assassination suggested different angles on old information: one posited Texas Governor John Connally as the assassin's target rather than Kennedy;[14] others gave new reasons for organized crime wanting to kill Kennedy, for CIA involvement, and for the incompleteness of the Warren Commission.[15] Don DeLillo's 1988 novel *Libra* and the NBC mini-series "Favorite Son" were further examples of a critical appraisal.[16]

An Emphasis on Process

Retellings in the eighties were appraised in two ways. Some observers felt they offered few revelations concerning the assassination record. "There are no new facts about the Kennedys," said one journalist, "only new attitudes."[17] Reporter Jefferson Morley found an impatience with the ambiguities of the story and argued that "Camelot and conspiracy in Dallas were domesticated for prime time: 'Who shot JFK?' became 'Who shot J.R.?' "[18] Media forums ranging from the *Washington Post* to *Newsweek* were content to admit that they would never find the truth in the assassination story.[19] At the same time, other observers, such as the independent critics, felt that retellings continued to unravel the numerous tangled threads of a complicated tale. There were new explanations, new interpretations, and new frameworks for considering decades-old evidence. Attention turned from uncovering new facts about the assassination to the processes by which the assassination record had been documented.

In an article called "The Life of Kennedy's Death," Christopher Lasch detailed the story's lingering effect on views not about Kennedy or the assassination but about those who promoted such views.[20] The assassination, according to Lasch, remained a national obsession because it validated conflicting historical myths about insiders and outsiders, professionals and laypersons. Understanding the manipulation of the record was thus as important as understanding the circumstances that caused Kennedy's death. In such a view it made sense that retellings would focus on the process of recording the assassination as well as on the crime itself. Cover-up actions in recording the events of Kennedy's death offered fresh angles to various theories of conspiracy, just as the experience of the Ervin Committee had suggested the value of focusing "on the cover-up rather than on the crime itself" in the Watergate story during the preceding decade.[21]

Growing interest in the processes by which the assassination was documented—the meta-discourse about the record of the record—helped to focus attention on alternative forms of documentation. Retellers began to document the documents of others. No longer able to access the original assassination story, retellers instead sought documents that had previously been sealed and examined old testimony within different parameters and circumstances. Access to secondary sources of information came to be seen as equal in importance to access to the original crime. When told he had no new evidence, one critic of the eighties replied that his argument came from rereading the documents themselves.[22] His comment underscored the worth of secondary access, or the rereading of old texts, as a documentary technique. It also suggested the central role laypersons could play in interpreting what had happened in Kennedy's death.

The reliance of new theories and interpretations on rereadings of many of the same documents and statements focused attention on one alternative form of documentation—professional memories. Memories of persons present in some professional capacity at the events of Kennedy's death offered a potentially authoritative perspective on tales that had been told many times over. These recollections, by journalists, independent critics, and historians, frequently began to be set up in competition with official accounts that had failed. The recollections had popular appeal, independent of the degree of substance they offered.

Journalists, in particular, began to comment with increasing frequency on their own documentation and that of others. A 1988 episode of "Nova" traced the kinds of evidentiary practice that had figured over the years in readings of Kennedy's death.[23] Using Walter Cronkite as narrator, it explored twenty-five years of investigatory efforts through changing categories of evidence and expertise. Which assassination reading people adopted was shown to depend largely on the categories of evidence, testimony, and expertise in which they believed. Assassination retellings thus became framed as a *Rashomon*-like narrative. As David Lifton suggested in his book about the assassination, "What you believe happened in Dallas on November 22, 1963, depends on what evidence you believe."[24] This placed the alternative retellers squarely at the forefront of the assassination story.

Forms of Memory

As the assassination story crossed into the eighties, its retellings assumed familiar forms. The independent critics continued to push for further investigation. Books by David Lifton, James Reston, Jr., Anthony Summers, and Robert Groden and Harrison Livingstone provided a many-angled lens through which to view the events of Kennedy's death.[25] More "respectable" views, by academics or former officials, were also tendered.[26] They helped enhance public regard for the independent critics.

Official investigations culminated in a document issued by the Department of Justice in 1988, which stated that it had found no evidence in support of conspiracy. The document, requested by the House Select Committee on Assassinations nearly a decade earlier as a way to address outstanding questions that had been raised in committee, was a five-page refutation of the significance of some of the acoustics testimony. Former committee counsel G. Robert Blakey blasted the document, contending that "instead of science, it was an effort to lay to rest inconvenient information."[27]

Historians, particularly popular historians, began to address the assassination in their chronicles. In the early eighties, books by Herbert Parmet, Gary Wills, and Peter Collier and David Horowitz tracked the Kennedy myth and how it was affected by the events in Dallas.[28] Assassination narratives were incorporated as part of larger narratives about the Kennedys. Other than two noteworthy exceptions—Michael Kurtz's *Crime of the Century* and Thomas Brown's *JFK: History of an Image*[29]—the assassination story did not generate its own historical literature. The absence of historical record did not go unnoticed by other retellers. Historians were criticized for "missing the boat." "Historians Lost in the Mists of Camelot" was how one article in the *Los Angeles Times* described readings of Kennedy's administration and assassination.[30]

But during the eighties retellings by the media increased in number. Journalists began to experiment with the narrative formats by which they told the story. Some reporters adopted the kind of assassination retelling that until then had been largely confined to the independent critics—the book.[31] Others continued to publish articles. In both cases, journalists began to reference their own assassination memories with increasing frequency. Newspapers filled with eyewitness articles under titles like "Many Remember the Scene as It Was."[32] Reporter Robert MacNeil, employed at the time of the assassination by NBC News, published a book that detailed his memories of the year Kennedy died, and elsewhere books were published that compiled recollections of Kennedy's death.[33] Presence, both actual and symbolic, was crucial. As journalist Mary McGrory said in an article entitled "You Had to Be There to Know the Pain," "Those who did not know him or did not live through his death may find it difficult to understand the continuing bereavement of those who did."[34]

To a certain extent, the salience of journalistic memories was simply one version of the "where were you when Kennedy was shot?" game. Memories did not provide a more accurate, truthful, or fact-ridden investigation of events, but in some ways they were not expected to make sense of everything. As Christopher Lasch observed, truth had given way to credibility, "facts to statements that sound authoritative without conveying any authoritative information."[35] Journalists' access to the media, and their technologies of dissemination, promised a way of replaying Kennedy's death in convincing and plausible memory-based narratives, regardless of whether they brought in new information.

In 1983 ABC News produced its first two-hour-long retrospective on the president, which included the memories of Ben Bradlee, David Halberstam, and others.[36] The same year, an episode of "Good Morning, America" featured the personal and professional memories of reporters and photographers who had been with the president in Dallas.[37] The speakers each established where in the presidential motorcade they had been and what they remembered. Significantly, the entire program consisted of their recollections, suggesting that by 1983 memories alone had begun to be considered sufficient documentation of the events in Dallas. Five years later, journalists' recollections again made up central segments of a PBS documentary called "JFK: A Time Remembered," which was billed as a "collection of reminiscences about the fall of Camelot."[38] Journalists like Nancy

Dickerson, Charles Bartlett, Tom Wicker, Sarah McClendon, and Dan Rather relayed what they had seen, heard, and remembered. By 1988, journalistic presence—symbolic or physical—at the events of Kennedy's death was being extensively referenced across media. Journalists' memories began to be legitimated over those of other groups of retellers.

Indeed, by the twenty-fifth anniversary of the assassination, televised institutional recollections of Dallas included nearly every facet of recollection possible and was more the norm than the exception. Journalists' regular media appearances helped thrust them into the forefront of the assassination story. While the early years featured blow-by-blow accounts of what had happened in Dallas,[39] later years saw several programs that more generally addressed the assassination.[40] News organizations produced retrospectives that ranged from one-hour recaps—like NBC's "JFK: That Day in November"—to long, six-and-a-half-hour reconstructions of events.[41] Televised recollection also pervaded existing programs. Regular news shows were filled with small commemorative segments, from a ten-minute production called "Kennedy Remembered" on Philadelphia's "Action News," to a special hour-long edition of ABC's "Nightline," to an eight-part CBS series on the assassination.[42] Tabloid television recounted the assassination on programs hosted by Oprah Winfrey, Mort Downey, Jack Anderson, and Geraldo Rivera.[43] Programs like "Entertainment Tonight" and Philadelphia's "Evening Magazine" even carried their own assassination-related segments.[44] As one reporter observed in 1988, "the amount of coverage [given the assassination story] suggests how strongly television executives believe the event still grips the American population."[45]

In most cases, each anniversary of the assassination received greater and more varied media attention than the ones preceding it.[46] This prompted one reporter to note somewhat caustically that "if you don't come to Dealey Plaza this year, the assassination is very much as it was 25 years ago: reality framed by a television set."[47] Television had become central in documenting the lore of assassination memories, particularly those of journalists. The assassination was by now "not only the stuff of history but . . . the fabric of memory."[48] Journalists headed the list of those eager to share their tales.

Competing for Memory

Journalists were not the only group with memories, of course. The role of other retellers—independent critics and historians—remained central. This meant that credentialing often took place not only among one's own interpretive community but at the expense of others'. This process revealed not only how shaky was the ground on which all retellers stood, but how valued a terrain it was.

The Contest for Authorization

Retellers were motivated by a regard for history that was embedded in the very act of retelling the assassination. History was seen as the ultimate locus of the assassination record, and retellers were "aware of the place in history reserved to whoever solves the puzzle" of Kennedy's death.[49] Their emphasis on history was facilitated by what had been Kennedy's own interests. In an article called "History on His Shoulder," *Time* correspondent Hugh Sidey recalled that Kennedy "knew he was on history's stage."[50] Jacqueline Kennedy was quoted as saying that "history made Jack what he was."[51] Some retellers, particularly historians, regarded the historical record with such caution that they hesitated to add to it before sufficient time had passed. Journalists often tried to frame their retellings as historical record. Independent critics were generally indifferent to the cracks their accounts introduced into the record. "Only in textbooks was history tidy," said one editorial.[52]

Until the story "became history," however, the positioning of retellers in it was uncertain. The story's many loose ends did not yet call for "a historian's detachment."[53] This raised questions of a professional nature: Was it the journalist's, critic's, or historian's mission to report history? At what point would the story "belong" to historians? And what would happen to the other retellers—the journalists and independent critics—when the historians took over? While historical accounting implied an authority to be applied "after the fact," precisely what constituted "after the fact" in the case of Kennedy's death remained unclear. Chronological and linear demarcations were somewhat blurred by the story's persistence, a circumstance that encouraged others to contest the right to tell the story's authoritative version. This made the mission of "reporting history" a goal for all retellers. The historical record not only worked against renewed considerations of the assassination story, but also failed to underscore the importance of memory as a viable way of documenting it.

Doubts thus arose concerning the viability of the notion of one definitive history of the assassination. Was one history possible, attainable, or desirable? The ensuing skepticism rested in part with the kaleidoscopic quality that assassination retellings had taken on, which implied the viability of many versions of Kennedy's death. It also rested with the growing, if uneasy, recognition of the fact that the critics addressed points about the assassination that historians and journalists had failed to see. This became particularly problematic as the volume of critics' retellings increased over time, taking the place generally assumed by the historical record. A third factor was the blurring of traditional differences separating journalists from historians. Traditional distinctions, such as issues of perspective or temporal distance, did not bear out in the assassination's retelling.

All of this intensified the contest for authorization among the different groups seeking to authenticate themselves professionally through the tale's telling. This contest took on a particularly popular dimension in 1991, when Hollywood director Oliver Stone brought out his version of events in the film *JFK*. The film was by and large initially censured by the mainstream media, which castigated the filmmaker for blurring fact and fiction, for promoting himself as a historian, and for offering a flawed version of what had happened in Dallas.[54] At the heart of their discussions were concerns not only about Stone's authority to retell the assassination story, but about the challenge he posed to their own authority as preferred retellers. As one writer had earlier admonished, "Establish your right to the mystery, document it, protect it."[55] That challenge was taken up by all retellers of the assassination, but it was one to which the media appeared particularly well suited.

Television: Referencing Presence through Technology

The ultimate difference between most historians and independent critics, on the one hand, and many journalists, on the other, was what the lore of professional memories rested upon—presence. In the final reading, much of the authority of retelling derived from a reteller's ability to establish the fact of "actually [having been] present."[56] In such a light, critic David Lifton said that "watching the images come up to full contrast [in a photograph taken of the grassy knoll], I felt I was joining the ranks of the eyewitnesses—a year and a half after the event."[57] Many years earlier, journalist Meg Greenfield had phrased it more bluntly:

> If the author stood somewhat outside the event, has he let us take this fact into account—or done so himself? Is there evidence that [as a historian] he has made some effort to

> fill in fairly those parts of the story he knew he had missed? Or has he taken advantage of the ingenuousness of a public that can hardly be expected to realize that he speaks with different degrees of authority on different subjects—a public that is already inclined to invest any insider with broad oracular powers on the vaguely understood ground that he was there?[58]

Greenfield's comments suggested the importance of being there as a way of legitimating authority. Documenting one's presence at the events of Kennedy's death thus imparted much of the authority for retelling its story. It thereby became an unvoiced goal of retellers to lend a sense of their presence to the story.

Attempts to construct presence where there was none, and to imply presence through authoritative retellings, ultimately gave journalists an advantage over other groups of speakers. Two circumstances—their presence, and a systematic means by which to invoke and perpetuate a sense of that presence—served journalists well. It gave them the kind of framework that ensured their words would be heard and remembered.

This did not mean that journalists simply created their role in the story because of their access to technological and institutional support. Their professional memories, narratives, particular mode of storytelling, and media technologies were all predicated on presence. Unlike most historians or independent critics, many journalists who retold the assassination story actually had been present at some of its events. In cases when they had not been there, their technologies and narrative strategies allowed them to construct their tales as if they had been. The record by which journalists constructed their assassination retellings was thus devoted to constructing a sense of proximity to the events of Kennedy's death.

To a large extent, television made this possible. Television helped journalists reference their presence as if it were a given in the assassination story. Professional memories and the journalistic presence they implied were solidified by television technology. Mere attentiveness to television's role developed into an extensive self-referential discourse, by which reporters, particularly TV journalists, sought to document extended aspects of the role the medium played.

Journalists' tendency over time to amass their recollections of their coverage into that kind of record—which had begun immediately after the assassination—encouraged them to portray themselves as particularly active players in the assassination story. This was particu-

larly the case with television, where journalists made considerable
efforts at aggrandizement. As television's status as a legitimate medium for telling news grew, so did the weight given journalistic
appraisals of television's role in covering Kennedy's death.

It was therefore no surprise that by 1988, recollections of Kennedy
were intimately linked with the media, in general, and with television, in particular. To some extent this was inevitable; as one historian
commented, "Kennedy was cut off at the promise, not after the performance, and so it was left to television and his widow to frame the
man as legend."[59] But the linkage was strengthened by the "anniversary spate of books and TV specials"[60] that produced extensive accounts linked to the medium. As *Newsweek* maintained, television
helped create a flashbulb memory, the indelible freeze-framing of the
event in its most trivial incidental detail. "The Kennedy in that freeze-
frame is the Kennedy of Camelot, not the man who miscarried the
Bay of Pigs invasion or shared a Vegas playgirl with a Mafia don; it is
as if the shadows had been washed away by the flashbulbs or the
tears."[61]

Television's role in perpetuating journalistic presence was emphasized across media. A special commemorative edition of "Good Morning, America" proclaimed that the assassination had made television
into "irreversibly the most important medium for communication":
"The death of our first television President marked the beginning of
the age of television as the dominant medium in our lives."[62] Newspaper recountings of the assassination in 1988 proclaimed television's
triumph under headlines like "TV Retells the Story of Slaying," "CBS
Replays November 22," "JFK and a Tribute to TV," and "TV: The
Ghost of a President Past."[63] According to one such article, "television has marked the 25th anniversary of the assassination of President Kennedy in a wave of programming that is as much a reminder
of how large a role television played in reporting the tragedy and its
aftermath as it is a retelling of the event."[64] Such efforts confirmed
the linkages among JFK, his administration, his assassination, and
television. At the heart of these links were journalists, who lent the
story its narrative form.

The persistent emphasis on television as the medium that most effectively memorialized Kennedy enhanced the authority of journalists, particularly television journalists. Despite being initially squeezed
in alongside the critics and historians who were working out their
own memories, journalists found their position further enhanced by
their access to many stages on which they could present their versions of Kennedy's death. Such a position in part displaced lingering

criticism over the degree to which the mainstream media had actively investigated the event's unsolved questions.

Situating the Journalist as Preferred Reteller

Journalists gained the upper hand among retellers not only because they possessed easy and continued access to the media. Rather, their central role in making public the tales of all retellers, including historians and independent critics, turned them into mediators of a record-in-the-making. In this capacity, journalists secured their central position in the story and reinforced their authority by adopting four journalistic stances, each suggesting a different role in the assassination's retelling: eyewitness, representative, investigator, and interpreter. These roles allowed journalists a repertoire of ways to situate themselves in association with Dallas, providing different foundations for the claim to be legitimate tellers of its story. By highlighting different dimensions of practice that were central to the professional codes of journalism, each role linked journalists with ongoing discourse about journalistic practice, professionalism, and the legitimation of television news.

The Journalist as "Eyewitness"

Journalists continued their use of the eyewitness role that they had adopted at the time of Kennedy's death. It allowed them to generate personalized narratives by which they established themselves as preferred retellers of the assassination story. Being an eyewitness carried with it the authority of having "seen" what happened. That position became important in light of increasingly prevalent debates about conspiracy in the Kennedy assassination.

Reporters like Hugh Sidey, Tom Wicker, and Robert MacNeil recollected Dallas through their experiences as eyewitnesses. Sidey recalled that "perhaps we knew when the first sound reached the press bus behind President Kennedy's limousine. A distant crack, another. A pause, and another crack. Something was dangerously off-key." [65] Wicker recounted how he was "sitting on the press bus, I think the second press bus, with a local reporter from Texas. He observed this, people running and so forth, and he dashed up the front of the bus and then came back to me and said, 'Something's happened. The President's car just sped away, they just gunned away.' " [66] Robert MacNeil recalled how "We heard what sounded like a shot . . . I jumped up and said, 'They were shots! Stop the bus! Stop the bus!'

The driver opened the door, and I jumped out . . . I couldn't see the president's car but I really started to believe there was shooting because on the grass on both sides of the roadway people were throwing themselves down."[67] The eyewitness role was also invoked from Washington, where journalists awaited arrival of the plane carrying Kennedy's body. As NBC correspondent Nancy Dickerson recalled, "We were on the air, talking, and Air Force One arrived and I saw them. They were all confused as far as I was concerned. They weren't doing it the right way. Instead of opening the front door of Air Force One, they were opening the back door. And they had a hydraulic lift there, and of course they were taking the body out the back door in a casket."[68] NBC News correspondent Sander Vanocur was standing outside the White House's west wing when he saw Kennedy's rocking chair being brought out and LBJ's mounted saddle brought in. "Power changes very quickly and very brutally in Washington," said Vanocur. "I'll never forget the exchange of those two pieces of furniture within a 20 minute period."[69]

By situating themselves as eyewitnesses, journalists were legitimated for having been in the *same time* and *same place* as the events of Kennedy's death. The time and place that characterized these personalized narratives took journalists from Dallas to Washington, where the assassination culminated in Kennedy's funeral.

The Journalist as "Representative"

Journalists also gained authority for the assassination story by adopting a second role in their narratives, that of representative. By mentioning their professional affiliation as reporters, journalists invoked the role of representative when they could not claim eyewitness status, that is, when they had not worked on the assassination story in either its Dallas or Washington frames. One NBC retrospective used John Chancellor's experiences during the assassination weekend as a focal point for its footage of events in Dallas, even though Chancellor had not been present. "I was NBC's correspondent in Berlin then," he later recalled. "Kennedy had been there a few months before his death, and he was idolized by Berliners. . . . The people there were devastated by [Kennedy's] death. In West Berlin, you would get in a taxi, give your destination, and the driver would say 'America?' If you said yes, the meter would be turned off and you rode free."[70] The irrelevance to the assassination of Chancellor's experiences as a Berlin correspondent was not openly addressed. Instead, his professional standing at the time of the assassination credentialed him to speak about Dallas. Even if his personal memories of the events in Dallas were tendered from the less-than-ideal perspective of Berlin, NBC incorporated them because they offered another authoritative way of retelling the assassination weekend.

Professional standing was thus invoked to justify how seemingly "unconnected" reporters could nonetheless authoritatively interpret events of the assassination weekend. As one reporter said, "When the shots were fired, I was working for *Life* as a reporter in the education department."[71] She was then flown to Hyannis Port to spend the day with Rose Kennedy.

Other reporters were never even assigned to the story. Peter Jennings introduced an item on the assassination as "a reporter who [had] covered [the South] in the mid-60s," around the time of Kennedy's death.[72] Journalist Chuck Stone, featured on a Philadelphia news station in 1988, "recalled being a Washington newsman covering Kennedy."[73] In the news item, Stone held up a framed photograph of Kennedy at one of his news conferences, and the implication was that Stone had been present, although that was not made clear. One former reporter for the *Philadelphia Bulletin* recalled in a 1988 television interview how "we sat there. We couldn't believe what had happened. We asked members of the police department, 'could it happen here?'"[74] None of these reporters was anywhere near Dallas during the assassination; nor were they in any way connected with the story elsewhere. Yet the fact that they had been reporters at the time of the assassination thrust them into a position years later of authoritatively retelling its story. Using their words to index the assassination reinforced journalists' ability to act as preferred spokespersons.

Journalists were thus credentialed as representatives for having been in the *same time* but a *different place* as the events in Dallas. The relevance of professional affiliation at the time of the assassination implicitly supported the growing status of journalists as the story's authoritative retellers and expanded the access of reporters whose stories had no direct spatial link to the events in Dallas.

The Journalist as "Investigator"

A third role allowed journalists to invoke authority in retelling the assassination—that of investigator. Their activities as investigative reporters were increasingly supported by growing discourse about conspiracy in Kennedy's death. In particular, the heightened role of the independent critic in the years following the assassination gave momentum and increased credence to tales of the investigator. As Hugh Aynesworth, the reporter who held claim to having worked longest on the assassination story, said, "The story would die down for a while and then crop up again. Something was always coming up."[75]

The notion of reporters as investigators was implicit in journalistic coverage of the assassination from the start. It was implied in the way that journalists crowded Dallas police headquarters the night of the assassination, hoping to catch a glimpse of Kennedy's accused killer, Lee Harvey Oswald. One specific dialogue was then widely recounted across the media:

> REPORTER: Did you kill the president?
> OSWALD: No. I have not been charged with that, in fact nobody has said that to me yet. The first thing I heard about it was when the newspaper reporters in the hall asked me that question.
> REPORTER: You have been charged.
> OSWALD: Sir?
> REPORTER: You have been charged.[76]

The role of journalist as investigator was thereby foregrounded from the first days of the assassination story.

Tales of the investigator flourished because Kennedy's death was "an incomplete story."[77] One reporter remarked that "having covered the story as a working journalist on the scene, I cannot accept as proven facts the incoherent conglomeration of circumstantial evidence against [Oswald]."[78] The assassination story was full of "loose strands, improbable coincidences, puzzling gaps," which made deciphering difficult.[79] Columnist Nora Ephron commented that "only a handful of reporters [were] working the assassination story. . . . This is a story that begs for hundreds of investigators, subpoena power, forensics experts, grants of immunity: it's also a story that requires slogging through twenty-seven volumes of the Warren Commission Report and dozens of books on the assassination. . . . The whole thing is a mess."[80] Attempting to resolve the story's unknowns gave journalists a way to authenticate themselves as professionals.

Journalists and news organizations portrayed themselves as having made "exhaustive" and "painstaking" efforts to unravel the assassination story.[81] *Life* magazine was hailed for having led the call among news organizations to reopen the Warren investigation.[82] Geraldo Rivera referred on the air to the years he had spent investigating the story.[83] *New York Times* editor Harrison Salisbury maintained that journalists at the *Times* continued to actively investigate the assassination story "to the limits of the correspondents' ability." Ultimately, boasted Salisbury, "there was little likelihood" that other evidence would materially change the fundamentals the *Times* had established in its initial reporting.[84] Jack Anderson hosted his own special on the assassination, which credentialed him as a "Pulitzer Prize-winning journalist" and detailed his "twenty-year investigation of the crime of the century."[85] Walter Cronkite summed up a special edition of "Nova" by saying that its investigation had "explained many but not all of the questions about the assassination."[86] Tales of the investigator thus made reference to career trajectories in which reporters conducted independent investigations into various unsettled aspects of Kennedy's assassination. Implicit in these discussions were references to practices of exploration, discovery, and scrutiny.

It is important to realize, however, that the media faced considerable criticism for the degree of investigative activity in which they engaged. The independent critics, in particular, assailed mainstream journalists and news organizations for not having played out their investigative role sufficiently. This discourse was particularly prevalent around the 1991 screening of the movie *JFK*.

Situating themselves as investigators nonetheless gave journalists authority for having returned to the place of the assassination to conduct their investigations. Their tales—tales of the *same place* but a *different time*—created a way for journalists who had not taken an active part in covering the assassination weekend to authoritatively retell aspects of its story. Such tales legitimated journalists who associated themselves with the assassination story by reopening its record years after the events in Dallas. They ensured journalists' access to the assassination's retelling by emphasizing place over time.

The Journalist as "Interpreter"

The final role adopted by journalists was that of interpreter. Borrowing from the experiences of eyewitnesses, representatives, and investigators in making interpretive claims about the assassination, the role of interpreter implied that it was unnecessary to have been in either the same place or the same time as the events in Dallas in order to make authoritative claims about the assassination story.

Adopting the role of interpreter not only allowed journalists to speak authoritatively about events from such distant positions as, for example, New York anchorpersons or news editors; it also legitimated persons who had little association with the assassination when it took place. The role of the journalist as interpreter was foregrounded a few weeks after the assassination. Wrote reporter Marya Mannes concerning the press corps, "For four interminable days, I listened to the familiar voices of . . . so many who never failed us or history during their greatest possible ordeal. Shaken as they visibly were, infinitely weary as they became, they maintained calm and reason and insight throughout the marathon of madness and mourning."[87] References to journalists' interpretive role blurred both the temporal and physical distance from which they pronounced judgment on the events of Kennedy's death.

This meant that many reporters who assumed the interpretive role had no other visible linkage to the story. The best example was ABC's Forrest Sawyer, who conducted a one-hour retrospective on the assassination on "Nightline" in 1988. Other than mentioning that "for those of us who are old enough, this has been a day of remembering, recalling the glamour of the Kennedy presidency and how it felt then,"[88] Sawyer made no obvious attempt to credential his interpretation of the assassination story.

Similarly, writer Lawrence Wright concluded his book on the sixties, which dealt in part with Kennedy's assassination, with the observation that "it began as an essay for *Texas Monthly* about growing up in Dallas in the years preceding the assassination of President Kennedy. I did not intend to make myself a character so much as a guiding sensibility to the thoughts and passions of the moment."[89] Journalist Nicholas Lemann wrote an article about the effect of the assassination, saying that it "lingers, at least in my mind, far more stubbornly than [Kennedy's] achievements."[90] Lemann credentialed his experiences as a young boy in 1963 through his contemporary affiliation as "a national correspondent of The Atlantic." In all cases, the apparent "connection" to the assassination story was a contemporary professional affiliation with journalism. Whereas the role of representative was authenticated by a journalist's professional association at the time of the assassination, the role of interpreter was credentialed by having journalistic status at the time of the assassination's recollecting. The shift was significant, for it helped to grant authority to retellers of the assassination who lacked any direct link to the story.

Journalists thereby situated themselves as interpreters of the Dallas story despite the fact that they told their tales in a *different time* and *different place*. Invoking the role of interpreter allowed journalists to become authoritative spokespersons despite—or perhaps because of—their spatial and temporal distance from the events. In one independent critic's view, this resulted in a breed of journalists years after the assassination who could approach the story without bias.[91] Legitimating a stance of spatial and temporal distance thus permitted more journalists to act as authoritative interpreters of the assassination story, likening their role as spokespersons to that of historians.

The four roles in which journalists narratively positioned themselves with regard to the assassination thus created several bases on which they could rhetorically connect themselves to the story. The eyewitness role legitimated journalists for having been in the same place and time as the events in Dallas; the representative role credentialed them to speak about the time of the assassination but from places other than Dallas; the investigator role allowed them to perpetuate stories from the same place but a different time; and finally the interpreter role made it possible for journalists to recollect the assassination despite the fact that they had been in neither the same place nor time period as the events in Dallas. As professional stances, these roles reinforced journalists' authority in retelling the story. They allowed journalists to legitimate themselves as spokespersons not only through the role they originally played in covering the assassination but also through a wide range of activities that took place in times and places beyond it. These roles thereby expanded the range of practices that constituted professional journalism, which helped the media turn assassination stories into stories about themselves.

Marginalizing the "Unauthorized" Reteller

A slew of factors was involved in journalists' emergence as preferred spokespersons of the assassination story. The official failure to lend the story closure; continuous professional backbiting between journalists and other "interested" spokespersons (notably, the independent critics and historians); journalists' ready access to the media, which allowed them to present their versions of the story to mass audiences; the recognition of memory as a viable alternative to documenting the events of Kennedy's death; and the ascent of television and televisual memory as an effective way to perpetuate that documentation—all were contributing factors. Once journalists' position was consolidated, they then adopted journalistic stances that further enhanced their authoritative role.

Yet in doing so, the media marginalized other voices. Their reluctance to critique the Warren Commission and indifference to the House Select Committee suggest that they failed to fulfill their fundamental responsibilities to act as a check on governmental process. Equally important, as systematically as they worked to legitimate themselves, they marginalized many of those—especially the independent critics—who contradicted the perspectives they were invested in perpetuating.

This was particularly evident during the early nineties in the controversy surrounding Oliver Stone's film *JFK*. While the surge of public discourse around the movie suggested the continued vitality of a number of independent critics, the attempts by many mainstream journalists to censure independent efforts to tell the story displayed the degree to which such efforts challenged their own authority as retellers. A similar scenario developed around the screening of an independently produced five-part TV series, "The Men Who Killed Kennedy." The series was screened on the Arts and Entertainment network in September and October of 1991, but only after reported unsuccessful attempts to screen it on the major networks.[92] Similarly, although to a lesser extent, journalists attempted to marginalize historians, whom they cast as professionally problematic because of their delay in addressing the events of Kennedy's death. While this certainly upheld the positioning of mainstream journalists and news organizations, it also de-authorized many other writers—whether independent critics or historians—who lacked the institutional support of mainstream media establishments.

In a sense, then, retelling Kennedy's death suggested additional questions about the boundaries of journalistic authority: at issue were not only the limits of preferred professional practice, but definitions about who was allowed to practice journalism and who was disallowed, and the question of what became of those who were barred from practice. In this way journalists pushed forward in the contest over authorization, marginalizing more or less successfully those lacking institutional support and media access. This was particularly critical given the outstanding questions over whether the mainstream media had indeed sufficiently investigated Kennedy's death. As the following chapters will show, journalists found ways of perpetuating their assassination tales that implicitly linked them to American journalism. As the tales were lodged in collective memory, journalists reworked them in ways that celebrated the role of the individual reporter, the news organization and institution, and the structure of the profession of journalism. Such tales often displaced more general questions about the degree to which they had effectively covered Kennedy's death and had actively investigated it in the years that followed.

Part Four: Recollecting Assassination Tales

NINE

The Authority of the Individual:
        Recollecting through Celebrity

Stories about individuals, particularly famous ones, offered a useful way of perpetuating the assassination story in collective memory. They ensured that individual reporters would be incorporated as an integral part of recollections of Kennedy's death. As one scholar commented, "to be talked about is to be part of a story, and to be part of a story is to be at the mercy of storytellers. The famous person is thus not so much a person as a story about a person."[1] Since Kennedy's death, these recollections have produced what are here called tales of celebrity, which let journalists promote the stature of individual reporters alongside the stories they told. This meant that celebrity became a cornerstone of journalistic authority, which helped reporters not only perpetuate their presence in the story but also gain leverage from it. Celebrity also had particular bearing on journalists' constitution as an interpretive community, since the community itself placed a strong emphasis on the individual.

The Workings of Celebrity

At the time of Kennedy's death, television had begun to generate its own form of journalistic storytelling that wove reporters' celebrity directly into popular forms of TV news presentation.[2] An emphasis on the visual, dramatic, and personal, which produced an authority based on style, personality, and flair,[3] made it possible for reporters to gain celebrity status through journalistic practice. Later efforts to enhance the popular recognition of journalists—through forums like televised interviews that linked news to faces—would build on these practices.

   In addition to the flurry of public attention to television reporters caused by their use of the relatively new medium, concerns about journalistic professionalism also gave rise to celebrity. The legitimation of television called for the rearrangement of familiar professional roles. Television made possible—and necessary, if institutional intermedia competition were to survive—new forms of authoritative storytelling and new professional identities, which generated new ways of achieving celebrity. Celebrity, a quality that made "persons well-known for their well-knownedness,"[4] gave journalists idealized notions about how they should be or act, at the same time as it reflected "shifting definitions of [their] achievement."[5] Celebrity was thus as much an institutional as an individual concern, dependent on the interpretive community of journalists for its perpetuation.

In recollecting their assassination coverage, journalists constructed stories of celebrity by systematically "plugging" different reporters into the assassination story via tales about technology and professionalism. Individual reporters were made the pivotal point of criss-crossing discourses about the assassination, on the one hand, and technology and professionalism, on the other. These tales privileged the individual over the organization, institution, or profession. Over time, they offered assassination retellers an effective way of both perpetuating their own presence within assassination tales and gaining stature independent of them. This further delineated the appropriate boundaries of journalistic community and made celebrity a fruitful way for journalists to gain more general stature as cultural authorities.

The Context for Journalistic Celebrity

The assassination was fertile ground for tales of journalistic celebrity, in that the Kennedy administration itself had catered to journalists' celebrity status. In recalling his coverage of Kennedy's reign, *Washington Post* reporter David Broder maintained that the president's live television conferences attracted reporters who generally avoided such institutionalized set-ups. "Some of those [reporters] Kennedy recognized regularly became TV stars themselves, and that status—reinforced by invitations to White House parties and dinners—did nothing to hurt the administration," he said.[6] Kennedy's administration was "an American court where the rich, the glamorous and the powerful congratulated each other. It was a pantheon of celebrity."[7] The president created an atmosphere that made celebrity a viable context for remembering his life and death.

Journalists' retellings of Kennedy's assassination followed these parameters.[8] Certain reporters became celebrities through their post-assassination reconstructions of Kennedy's reign, while others found that retelling the assassination was a vantage point from which to perpetuate their renown. For example, writers Theodore White and Hugh Sidey were labeled "Kennedy's elegists."[9] Assassination narratives often displayed the names of individual reporters as emblems of authority for the events in Dallas.

This was done in a fashion that highlighted discourses then relevant to American journalists. Four particular reporters—Tom Wicker, Dan Rather, Walter Cronkite, and Theodore White—were consistently mentioned by the journalistic community in conjunction with assassination retellings. While they were not the only journalists to emerge from the assassination as celebrities, each one's rise to fame involved issues of concern to professional journalists. At the same time, other journalists—such as Hugh Aynesworth, Geraldo Rivera, and Jack Anderson—experienced celebrity's downside, largely because the issues about journalism they raised did not fit in with the concerns of the journalistic community. This suggests that retelling the Kennedy assassination gave journalists a stage on which to gain and maintain status. Their records of the assassination allowed them to narratively reconstruct its events in ways that reinforced their own celebrity.

The Indicative Dimension: Wicker and Rather

Narratives about Tom Wicker and Dan Rather provided an indicative dimension to the celebrity tale that documented the "as is" of coverage. These tales illustrated how individual journalists had acted in covering the assassination.[10] These narratives served not only to elevate the individual's role, but also to demonstrate how other journalists viewed his or her actions.

Tales about Wicker showed how members of the print media felt about having successfully covered Kennedy's death. Journalists told of Wicker being on the scene continuously for the first day's events, filing his report at day's end from an airport terminal. His actions were constructed as an ideal instance of journalistic practice, for they showed how the goals of speedy coverage, eyewitness reporting, and terse prose could lead to professional success.

Years later, colleague Harrison Salisbury praised Wicker's on-the-scene reporting by saying that

> The coverage had begun with classic reportage—Tom Wicker's on-the-scene eyewitness. It could not be beat. [I told him to] . . . just write every single thing you have seen and heard. Period. He did. No more magnificent piece of journalistic writing has been published in the *Times*. Through Tom's eye we lived through each minute of that

fatal Friday, the terror, the pain, the horror, the mindless
tragedy, elegant, blood-chilling prose.[11]

One telling aspect of Salisbury's comments is located in the phrase,
"the horror, the mindless tragedy, elegant, blood-chilling prose." Salisbury quietly moved from telling the horror of the event to telling the
elegance of the writing in which it was inscribed. In so doing, he
reinforced an intrinsic association between Wicker's role in telling
Kennedy's death and the actual events of the death. Salisbury made
it appear as if Wicker himself were an integral part of the assassination story, a pattern frequently repeated in tales of journalistic
celebrity.

Narratives about Wicker were predicated upon just such an association—Wicker in Dallas was part of the Dallas story. Wicker's reporting that afternoon, in one view, "will live longer than any novel, or
play, or essay, or piece of reportage that he has ever written or will
ever write."[12] Wicker's actions in Dallas were repeatedly referenced
in subsequent stories of his own career trajectory. For example, media
observer Gay Talese contended that "Wicker was a product of events,
an individual whose career had been advanced by the reporting of
the John Kennedy assassination . . . after the assassination story that
day, and the related stories that followed, Wicker's stock rose sharply
in the *New York Times*."[13] One year later he was selected to succeed
James Reston as the Washington bureau chief.[14] Nearly thirty years
later, Wicker's actions in Dallas were still being used for personal credentialing, as in his discussion of Oliver Stone's movie *JFK*, which
was published with the information that Wicker "covered the assassination of John F. Kennedy for the newspaper."[15] The *New York Times*
sought to uphold and perpetuate its reporter's celebrity status because that status also justified fundamental organizational decisions,
such as employing him and sending him to Dallas.

Tales of Wicker the celebrity were thus linked by the journalistic
community with highly topical discourses about what it meant to be
a print-media professional in the age of television. This tale of individual celebrity allowed larger discourses about television journalism
and journalistic professionalism to intersect with assassination narratives. It underscored the viability of print journalism and showed
the relevance of different media in the making of journalistic
community.

Narratives about the actions of Dan Rather in Dallas were also
linked with similar discourses, but from the perspective of television.
Tales about Rather addressed attempts to legitimate television corre-

spondents as bona fide reporters. Rather too was on the spot when Kennedy was killed:

> Keep in mind that I had heard no shots. I didn't know what was wrong. I only knew that something appeared to be very wrong . . . and so I began running, flat out running, sprinting as hard as I could the four blocks to our station . . . I got through to Parkland Hospital. And the switchboard operator was not panicked but not calm. And very quickly she told me it was her understanding that the President had been shot, and was perhaps dead. And I'll never forget her saying that. And I followed up with that, and tried to talk to one of the doctors and a priest at the hospital, both of whom said that the President was dead. But nobody had said this officially.[16]

Instead of remaining on the scene, as Wicker had done, Rather rushed to the nearest CBS affiliate, where he succeeded in providing rapid, up-to-date relays of what was happening in the city. As Rather later recalled, "Among the first lessons I learned in journalism . . . No story is worth a damn unless you can get it out. . . . I had to hotfoot it back to the station."[17]

The comparison between Rather and Wicker is telling. While Wicker anticipated the deadlines of printing by following the story to the airport, where he labored to write elegant prose in less than ideal conditions, Rather anticipated the demands of television technology by rushing *away* from the story and *toward* the technology of its telling—to the nearest affiliate station. His success in filing the story depended directly on his subordinates, who remained on the scene to supply him with information.

Narratives about Rather credited his cool-headed performance in Dallas with earning him a White House posting, "over the heads of several more experienced Washington reporters."[18] Media lore held that "he came to national prominence through his coverage of the Kennedy assassination."[19] In one view, the day that Kennedy died was "in career terms, the most important day in Dan Rather's life. His swift and accurate reporting of the Kennedy assassination and its aftermath that weekend transformed him from a regional journalist into a national correspondent."[20] Institutional discourse thus attributed Rather's professional success to his assassination coverage.

But celebrity had repercussions for more than the individual reporter. Tales of Rather the celebrity were also put forward in organizational overviews of CBS News and more general discussions of the legitimacy of television journalism. Because they reflected larger attempts to legitimate television correspondents as bona fide reporters, tales of Rather's activities were important to the journalistic community. His story demonstrated that it was possible to gain celebrity status through the broadcast media.

By foregrounding the indicative dimension of journalistic practice, tales about both Tom Wicker and Dan Rather played an important role in marking the boundaries of the American journalistic community. They served as a frame of reference for journalistic practice, at the same time underscoring the linkage between the broadcast and print media.

The Subjunctive Dimension: Cronkite and White

While tales of Wicker and Rather underscored the propriety of standard journalistic practice across media, other narratives focused on higher levels of practice that outlined journalism "as it might be." Examples are the narratives about Walter Cronkite's performance on the Dallas story and Theodore White's coverage of the days immediately following the assassination.

Narratives about Cronkite created a reference point for discussions not only of assassination coverage but also of the evolution of American TV journalism. Cronkite stayed on the air for much of the first day of events, and he was responsible for conveying to the public the news that Kennedy was dead. His emotional relay of that fact was coupled with behavior that emphasized how distraught he was— notably, removing his eyeglasses in a distracted fashion and forgetting to put on his suit jacket.[21] His actions showed how it was possible to define professionalism through improvisational and instinctual behavior. Cronkite cried, seemed shaken, appeared emotionally moved, and then composed himself to carry the nation through its evolving crisis. He transcended his own personal distress to guide the public throughout the four-day ordeal.

Cronkite's activities were important for the authentication of anchorpersons as journalists. Discourse centered on both his deeds and his words. One 1983 *Newsweek* article on the assassination stated that "Walter Cronkite broke into a popular CBS soap opera, 'As the World Turns,' with the first TV bulletin of the attack on JFK."[22] The next sentence noted that Cronkite was "for 19 years anchorman of the CBS Evening News." Like other institutional recountings of the assassination, *Newsweek* in this way reinforced the link between the anchorperson's role in covering the assassination story and his personal career trajectory. Another 1983 discussion of coverage of the Kennedy assassination was entitled "The Age of Cronkite."[23] A print retro-spective of television's fiftieth anniversary hailed Cronkite for having taken the American people through assassinations, conventions, and space shots:

> [his] reputation for being the TV news authority had evolved in the early 60s and was underscored by his cov-erage of the assassination of President John F. Kennedy on November 22, 1963. For four straight days, beginning on Friday afternoon, Cronkite sat in the anchor chair, some-times in his shirt sleeves and sometimes in tears, through the Monday when JFK was buried at Arlington National Cemetery.[24]

Seen as creating a "new persona" for American journalists, Cronkite and the image of solid integrity that he projected would thereafter be emulated by journalists across the country. It was "Cronkite's perfor-mance that was invariably cited" when admiration was expressed "for the restraint, the taste and the all-around professionalism of TV's coverage that weekend."[25] As one history of CBS News began, "Some of the things he did that day would pass into folklore and become part of the legend. More than a decade later, journalism professors would still be telling their students, who were mere children at the time, how Walter Cronkite cried on the air when he had to report the official announcement that President John F. Kennedy was dead."[26] The centrality of the Cronkite tale in journalistic lore depended as much on institutional efforts at commemorating his deeds and words as on his original performance in covering the assassination.

The legitimation of television anchorpersons, as exemplified by dis-cussions of Cronkite's celebrity, thus became a central dimension of many assassination tales. Tales of Cronkite as celebrity created, and reinforced, not only his individual status but also the legitimate pres-ence of television journalists and the consoling role of anchorpersons in times of crisis. Cronkite's activities on the Dallas story made him a celebrity by upholding the improvisational and instinctual behavior that journalists looked upon as the mark of the true professional, and tales about him underscored the recasting of professional paradigms that was suggested by the coverage of Kennedy's death. This was important for evolving discussions about the relevance of anchorper-sons as a separate yet functional breed of journalists. Tales of Cronk-ite's celebrity upheld the subjunctive mood of journalistic practice by exemplifying "what might be" to members of the community.

Narratives about Theodore White worked in much the same way

for print journalists. As tales of Cronkite reflected the highest forms of broadcast journalistic practice, narratives about White signified more refined dimensions of practice in the print media. White's performance on the assassination story was coopted within discussions of the glory of the journalistic written word, the effectiveness of which had been brought into question following what was perceived to be the successful televised coverage of Kennedy's death.

Although White was not present during the immediate events of Kennedy's death, his summons by Jacqueline Kennedy one week later drew him into the public eye. His appearance at Jacqueline Kennedy's Hyannis Port home a week after Kennedy's death was portrayed in fictionalized form in an ABC Circle film called *Jacqueline Bouvier Kennedy*, where their meeting was used to signify Kennedy's death.[27] White's narrative recounting of her experiences in Dallas, coupled with the labeling—at her behest—of the Kennedy administration as "Camelot," made White one of the more visible storytellers of the time. White's success with the written word rapidly gained him status as a journalistic celebrity, and his archetypal narrative structure was emulated by journalists across media. One journalist said that "he invented the form. He absorbed politics and hymned it in an act of reportage and imagination that was a variation on Walt Whitman. White's descriptions of the 1960 race are bardic, Homeric."[28]

All of this drew White away from periodized journalism and toward book publishing. He remained interested in the larger, more general issues that lay behind the making of current events, and his series of books on presidential campaigns was well regarded by other journalists. Nonetheless, he continued to define himself—and to be defined by others—as a journalist. His eulogy, published in *Time* in 1986, called him "a reporter in search of history."[29]

Within larger discussions of journalistic community and authority, narratives about White as celebrity suggested again how it was possible to cast the boundaries of professional journalism in different ways. His self-defined interest in history, his search for general impulses in society, and his exemplary writing style all reconfigured the supposed limits of good print journalism. In much the same way that Cronkite epitomized the anchorperson as an emblem of unity and source of consolation, White exemplified the print reporter as a person who not only wrote well but was concerned with issues beyond immediate news reporting. In both their indicative and subjunctive moods, these tales emphasized the importance of emulation in journalistic professionalism. Circulating celebrity narratives was important for journalists trying to authenticate themselves as an interpretive community. Significantly, both subjunctive and indicative dimensions of journalistic celebrity were embodied in the individual reporter. This suggested the centrality of the individual within the collective lore by which the journalistic community authenticated itself.

The Downside of Celebrity

While discourses connecting many journalists with the events of the assassination weekend were ultimately legitimated, other discourses —and journalists—were discarded. Certain journalists who were actively associated with Kennedy's assassination failed to receive general acclaim for their association. Some journalists even lost their jobs due to their assassination coverage. Robert Pierpoint of CBS was rumored to have lost his Washington posting to Dan Rather, because Pierpoint's cumulative experience did not match Rather's skill in covering Dallas.[30] Tom Pettit of NBC, whose on-site, on-air coverage of Oswald's murder was hailed in 1963 by *Broadcasting* magazine as "a first in television history,"[31] was rarely featured in later journalistic chronicles.

Other journalists were shunted into collective oblivion. Reporter Hugh Aynesworth, for example, whose assistance to more renowned reporters working the assassination story earned him the title of being its "longest running reporter," was rarely discussed with the same degree of interest as those journalists with greater celebrity status.[32] Penn Jones, who uncovered a series of mysterious deaths related to the assassination, was called "a sign of hope for the survival of independent journalism,"[33] but such cries of acclaim were confined to the nonmainstream press. Geraldo Rivera first ran a frame-by-frame analysis of Zapruder's footage of Kennedy's shooting on nationwide television, in a series he hosted in the mid 1970s called "Good Night, America," but his tabloid-style performance rendered him marginal to the mainstream reporters working the story.[34] French journalist Jean Daniel published interviews conducted shortly before the assassination with Fidel Castro and Kennedy, which pointed to a shared belief in U.S. capitalism and Cuban communism, but mainstream media discussions of Daniel's journalistic performance invariably labeled him as being "too involved in politics."[35] Leads by reporter Jack Anderson about Mafia involvement occupied columns of the *Washington Post* during the 1970s but were eventually marginalized in more tabloidlike formats. Anderson's 1988 assassination documentary displayed a "900" telephone number that viewers could call if they wanted to reopen the investigation, a touch that was a far cry from the hard-news formats with which Anderson had earlier been associated.[36]

These journalists' actions made them marginal to consensus about appropriate journalistic performance, substituting notoriety for celebrity status. The fall of certain journalists from acclaim despite admirable assassination coverage revealed patterns by which celebrity worked as a memory system. Reporters fell from fame because their performances did not attend to larger discourses about journalism—specifically, those favored by the mainstream journalistic community. Dan Rather's performance, for example, highlighted a journalistic agenda—the legitimacy of television journalism—that was more salient than the role of investigative journalism within the assassination story, a topic addressed by both Penn Jones and Hugh Aynesworth. The latter pair were marginalized by other journalists for being too political, too left-wing, too "tabloid," or too local. Marginalization denied them the kind of institutional backdrop necessary to perpetuate their tales and promote their celebrity status.

The failure of certain noteworthy performances to achieve celebrity status and the success of less praiseworthy performances speaks about the workings of celebrity as a memory system. It suggests that journalistic celebrity depended less on actual journalistic actions than on institutional agendas and surrounding discourses about journalism. Celebrity status for journalists was derived not only from the quality of their actions but from larger agendas motivating their involvement in the story.

Assassination recollections thus led to uniform narratives that featured journalists with tenable celebrity status. Recollections that reinforced the celebrity status of certain reporters were perpetuated, while tales documenting the presence of lesser known journalists were left out. By weaving the lives and careers of certain reporters into recollections of the assassination story, the journalistic community perpetuated narratives that highlighted the professional activities of well-known journalists, particularly certain national television journalists, in covering the story. This allowed journalists to facilitate the growth of their celebrity status. It also reinforced hidden institutional agendas about nascent features of journalistic professionalism and television journalism, setting out both indicative and subjunctive dimensions about what constituted appropriate journalistic practice.

Institutionally Perpetuating Celebrity

In the final analysis, the transformation of retellers into celebrities depended on the institutional backdrop against which journalists told their tales. Gaining status for retelling the assassination thus depended on media backing.

News organizations played an active part in legitimating reporters' celebrity status. In some cases, journalists crossed media boundaries to perpetuate their authority for retelling the story. In 1988, for example, reporter Robert MacNeil compiled a pictorial history of the assassination entitled *The Way We Were*. Discussions of the book were used as part of "Good Morning, America"'s commemoration of the twenty-fifth anniversary of Kennedy's assassination, where MacNeil was introduced as having been "in Dallas on this day 25 years ago when President Kennedy was assassinated."[37] One PBS documentary about Kennedy featured print reporter Tom Wicker recounting his own narratives almost verbatim.[38] In both cases, the crossover was made possible by reporters' celebrity status.

News organizations effectively perpetuated journalistic celebrity through two arenas of activity—commemoration and recycling. Both were used alone and in tandem to cement journalists' celebrity status.

Commemorative Activity

Commemoration allowed for the inclusion of assassination discourse on predetermined and routinized dates. Generally organized around anniversaries, commemoration marked assassination memories as well as the individuals who bore them. Thus both Gary Wills and William Manchester published their books on Kennedy on the twentieth anniversary of the events in Dallas.[39] As one journalist remarked, commemoration produced its own genre of news story—"anniversary journalism."[40]

Anniversaries offered journalists a wide range of media formats by which to associate themselves with the assassination story. In print, journalists used recognized and routinized dates as a reason for publishing special commemorative issues about the assassination, special sections in journals, and commemorative volumes.[41] Commemoration ranged from reconstructions of the assassination story to extensive "where were you" articles that featured prominent individuals' recollections.[42] In the broadcast media, journalists coordinated the production of media retrospectives around assassination anniversaries.[43] The tone and content of televised recollections not only reflected existing trends in news programming but also tied into larger moods and concerns at the time of each anniversary. Issues of technology, for instance, were first discussed in a 1967 CBS series about charges of conspiracy and the assassination. They were doubly revived in 1988, when CBS's "Four Days in November" stressed the technological triumphs and limitations of television, and PBS used scientific technology to reexamine the evidence in Kennedy's death.[44]

Commemorative efforts like these helped journalists perpetuate their chronicles as an independent, longstanding record. That record increasingly incorporated journalists as its narrators. On television, early assassination retrospectives were narrated by actors like Cliff Robertson, Larry McCann, Hal Holbrook, and Richard Basehart, while later efforts employed the skills and talents of journalists such as Edwin Newman, Walter Cronkite, Dan Rather, Nancy Dickerson, Tom Brokaw, and John Chancellor. The choice of journalists over actors as narrators was an indication of the emerging authority of journalists as legitimate assassination retellers.

Commemoration also highlighted "the club" of reporters who had originally covered the story. Such collective status perpetuated the stories of a few reporters as representative of tales of the many. It also underscored the importance of the norm in consolidating professionals into one cohesive group, which had direct relevance for the consolidation of journalists as an interpretive community.

This community convened in November 1988 to commemorate the events of twenty-five years earlier.[45] The reporters who had covered the assassination attended the gathering, an indication of the story's persisting centrality. Similarly, nearly all the later television retrospectives concluded with long lists of names of those journalists who had participated in the original coverage. One 1988 PBS documentary proposed to identify people "by their positions or affiliations in the fall of 1963," creating an "as if" mood for the recollections they embodied.[46] One trade magazine published lengthy lists of correspondents, management personnel, and technical crew who had participated in the coverage of the assassination story on radio and television.[47] NBC's "JFK Assassination: As It Happened" ended with "a note to more than 500 people who pooled their efforts to provide continuous and extensive coverage." Slides showed names of the "key members of the team."[48]

Within "the club," lead status was assigned certain journalists. For example, columnist Walter Lippmann's words of interpretation were moved to front-page columns alongside actual assassination coverage.[49] The *New York Times*'s James Reston was also frequently cited.

Reston, whose consolatory columns in the days following the assassination were lauded across media, was hailed in a 1987 ABC celebrity profile that called him the "most influential journalist in the country": "There is no way in television, sadly, to preserve Reston's prose or capture the real essence of his influence, for burdened by the pain of loss for millions of people, Reston has made the world less confusing." [50] In the profile, anchorperson Peter Jennings quoted verbatim from Reston's assassination coverage, seen against still pictures of John-John saluting his dead father. The juxtaposition of Reston's written words against the visual images supplied by television fit well into larger discourses about celebrity, technology, and professionalism. It was ironic that the medium of television honored a print journalist for covering the assassination, yet such media crossbreeding was facilitated by Reston's celebrity status.

Commemorative activity thus gave journalists routinized ways to promote their association with the assassination story. News organizations gave budding celebrities the opportunity to consolidate their status at the same time as they strengthened and reinforced journalists' stature.

Recycling Activity

Recycling activity was a second arena that let both print and broadcast journalists perpetuate their stories, presence, authority, and, ultimately, celebrity in conjunction with Kennedy's assassination. Each medium tended to recycle tales that originally appeared in it. The decision to recycle discourse was thus often dependent on appraisals of its worth by media organizations.

In the press, discourse was often recycled through reprinting. Special issues of magazines, journals, newspapers, and books systematically borrowed the words of reporters that had originally graced their pages. The dispatches of certain journalists were circulated in in-house journals; for example, Merriman Smith's dispatch of November 23 was reproduced in the *UPI Reporter* and later reissued as part of a special UPI book entitled *Four Days*. [51] It was also reproduced in the trade publication *Editor and Publisher,* together with a letter in which UPI editors praised Smith's coverage as "an historic memento, an example of narrative style at its best." [52] The words of Associated Press correspondent Jack Bell were featured in the organization's 100-page book *The Torch Is Passed*. [53] The *Columbia Journalism Review* published an extensive compilation of reporters' original assassination accounts under the title "The Reporters' Story." [54] Reprintings reinforced the importance of original accounts as well as their links with the original tellers.

One journalist whose words were frequently reprinted was Tom Wicker. One of Wicker's first pieces about the assassination, entitled "That Day in Dallas," was reprinted in December in the *New York Times* house organ, *Times Talk,* and again reprinted one year later in the *Saturday Review.* [55] Wicker used the space provided him to question the validity of eyewitness testimony, journalistic clarity, even the cability to remember what went on during those four days. "Even now, I know of no reporter who was there who has a clear and orderly picture of that surrealistic afternoon," he commented.[56] Wicker's piece raised questions about the standards of appropriate journalistic practice during the assassination; its reprinting reflected lingering questions about those standards.

But other words of Wicker's were also reprinted. Seven months after the assassination he penned an article for *Esquire* entitled "Kennedy Without Tears,"[57] which was acclaimed as outstanding journalism and called a "non-textbook history" of the 1960s.[58] While that label attested to the already burgeoning tensions between journalists and historians, it also reinforced Wicker's celebrity for having covered the original assassination story. The piece was subsequently reprinted as a book within the year and in *Esquire* ten years later,[59] where it was described as follows: "Tom Wicker's brilliant (and heartbreaking) coverage of the assassination for the *New York Times* moved *Esquire* to ask him to write this essay seven months later in June 1964. Mr. Wicker went on to become chief of the Washington bureau and an associate editor of the *Times.*"[60] Notes about the author commented that he "covered most of the events of the Kennedy administration and was riding in the Presidential motorcade when John Kennedy was murdered in Dallas."[61] Wicker's presence at the assassination thus became embedded in tales of the events of that November. The career trajectory by which he covered the assassination and went on to journalistic glory was facilitated by the institutions that reprinted his words.

In some cases reprinting original assassination accounts allowed journalists to make mention of other narratives. For example, a special commemorative volume on Kennedy, issued twenty-five years after his death, was linked to the events in Dallas by its reprinting of two articles by Theodore White—an essay he had written twenty-five years earlier for *Life* and his famous postassassination interview with Jacqueline Kennedy.[62] It was no accident that the label "Camelot" became part of the title of the commemorative volume, which was itself sponsored by Time-Life Books, the parent company of *Life* magazine. Other Time-Life publications, including *Time* magazine, also reprinted parts of the original White essay.[63]

The decision by news organizations to reconstruct the events in Dallas by reprinting original assassination accounts has implications for the authority derived from journalistic presence. Recollections of the assassination assumed an authority through recapturing—and reproducing—the events "as they were." Yet the decision to reprint the story's original tellings also embedded the names of original tellers within institutional recollections. Reprinting thus reinforced associations between the assassination story and certain reporters in a way that allowed journalists to uphold their celebrity status. The proliferation of reprintings around the assassination's anniversaries only reinforced how central to the original story journalists had become.

Media retrospectives were another example of recycling activity that accomplished for the broadcast media what reprinting did for print. The media retrospective helped journalists narrate, and thus reconstruct, their original stories of coverage. The incorporation of contemporary voice-overs into original film clips underscored journalists' celebrity status.

Dan Rather was regularly featured in broadcast media retrospectives. Many CBS retrospectives employed him as narrator: he narrated a three-part news series in 1983 investigating the myths and realities behind Kennedy's assassination, an eight-part news series in 1988, and a two-hour documentary called "Four Days in November," which aired on the twenty-fifth anniversary of Kennedy's death.[64] Rather concluded his narration of the documentary with "a personal note, based on the many years CBS News and I have spent investigating, thinking about those four days. It was a day we haven't shown that also has a lot of meaning for me—the fifth day. Tuesday. On Tuesday, America went back to work. . . . So it is Tuesday I often think of."[65] That line, labeled "Rather Blather" by one observer,[66] nonetheless reinforced Rather's role as an authoritative interpreter of the assassination story. Connections between the assassination narrative, his interpretation of it, and his status as a journalist were thus underscored by media retrospectives. The incorporation of stories of his assassination coverage in chronicles of his career equally showed how that authority helped make him into a journalistic celebrity.

Similar aims were achieved by self-quoted discourse. Self-quoting let journalists incorporate original tales within larger contemporary recollections. They were able to look back and comment upon their own words and views. Like other kinds of recycling activity, self-

quoting needed media backing. Anticipated already when reporters interviewed other reporters on the night of the assassination,[67]
self-quoted discourse was most effective when realized over time.

Reporters' appearances on talk shows and documentary specials
and frequent interviews in the press all made certain individuals
seem more authoritative because they commented on their own performances from afar. Radio reporter Ike Pappas took part in the following televised exchange with Geraldo Rivera about his coverage of
Oswald's murder twenty-five years earlier:

> PAPPAS: My job that day was to get an interview with this
> guy, when nobody else was going to get an interview.
> And I was determined to do that. . . . So I said the only
> thing which I could say, which was the story. Tell the
> story: "Oswald has been shot. A shot rang out. Oswald
> has been shot."
>
> RIVERA: Is that the single most profound or dramatic mo-
> ment of your life?
>
> PAPPAS: It's an extraordinary story. Probably the most ex-
> traordinary story I'll ever cover.[68]

The exchange referenced Pappas's professionalism, contextualized
the assassination as a critical incident, and pointed to his ensuing
celebrity status. Later reviews of Pappas's professional career focused
on his coverage of the Kennedy assassination.[69]

Self-quoting lent an air of simultaneous presence and distance to
narrative. It positioned the reporter as an interface between the past
events and their later retelling. Phrases like "the crime of the century," "the end of innocence," or "Camelot" were paraded about—
and commented upon—by journalists years after their original
coinage. For example, accounts of *Time* correspondent Hugh Sidey
were partly quoted, partly paraphrased by the same magazine twenty-
five years after Dallas.[70] In narrating CBS's "Four Days in November,"
Dan Rather pointedly commented that "back then, this is what we
knew, and this is how I reported it."[71] The documentary was filled
with clips of Rather's coverage from Dallas, conveying the impression
that he had almost singlehandedly mastered the entire assassination
story. Reporter Steve Bell introduced an on-air repeat of an original
film clip of himself standing in front of the Texas School Book Depository twenty-five years earlier.[72] In a 1977 *Esquire* piece, Tom
Wicker wrote that "within weeks of the assassination in Dallas—
which, as the *New York Times* White House correspondent, I'd covered on November 22, 1963, I had written for *Esquire* a long article

that the magazine ran as a cover piece."[73] Wicker then quoted two lengthy paragraphs from his original assassination coverage. He repeated the practice in another essay, where he commented that "I wrote that morning [of November 23] what I thought about the way things were, and would be."[74]

Self-quoting helped reporters set up their version of "who Kennedy was" or "what happened during the assassination" in order to revise it. In Wicker's case, later articles detailed where he had earlier erred, allowing him to conduct a dialogue with his own earlier discourse. This self-referencing not only emphasized the authority of reporters for the events of Kennedy's death, but it also connected their original words, revised with hindsight, to later discourses.

This institutionally backed activity thus helped perpetuate the image of certain journalists as celebrities. Commemoration gave news organizations convenient, recognizable, and routinized ways to highlight and perpetuate the status of certain reporters. Recycling maintained a focus on their words, while deflecting attention from those of others. Tales were generally recycled in the medium where they had originally appeared, then made the subject of extensive institutional efforts to reproduce them. With time, the investments surrounding such efforts justified recognition of the tale's original tellers as celebrities in their own right.

The Viability of Recollecting through Celebrity

The activities of commemoration and recycling attest to the viability of celebrity as a memory system. Positioning individual reporters as pivotal points for crisscrossing discourses about the assassination and about technology and journalistic professionalism was an effective way to perpetuate collective memories. Walter Cronkite's actions became important in discussions about televised journalistic practice, because they authenticated the consoling role of anchorpersons. Dan Rather's coverage reflected growing attempts to legitimate television correspondents as bona fide reporters. Theodore White's coverage highlighted the glory of the written word, which faced competition following the effective televised coverage of much of the assassination story. Tom Wicker's performance promoted the old guard of American journalism, showing that traditional objectives of speedy coverage, eyewitness reporting, and terse prose remained worthy goals. Tales of celebrity attested to both the subjunctive and indicative dimensions of individual journalistic practice, using narrative to mark appropriate standards of action.

Other activities, related to ongoing investigatory agendas or uncovering conspiracies, had less to do with the workings of celebrity because they did not touch on recognized tensions for mainstream
American journalism. Celebrity, then, constituted an effective memory system for the journalistic community precisely because it used
the individual reporter to focus attention on issues crucial to the
community. Celebrity gave journalists idealized, but institutionally
correct, notions of how to act or be. In other words, as a memory
system, celebrity helped mold journalists within the contours of institutionally supported agendas.

In his work on celebrity, Leo Braudy has commented that "the
urge to fame is not so much a cause as a causal nexus through which
more generalized forces—political, theological, artistic, economic,
sociological—flow to mediate the shape of individual lives."[75] The
establishment of journalistic celebrity through assassination tales
revealed a matrix of activity around a variety of issues. Tales that
became markers of journalists' celebrity status clustered around professional issues central to the journalistic community.

The emphasis on individual personalities within assassination tales
underscored an important dimension of journalistic community—
the significance of the individual. Journalists' ability to constitute
themselves as an independent interpretive community through their
assassination retellings depended on how individuals delineated
boundaries of practice and authority. The featured presence of the
individual reporter within assassination narratives thus keyed members of the community into boundary changes. Celebrity thereby not
only provided a set of shared perceptions and recollections about Dallas through which certain reporters were systematically thrust over
others into the public eye, but it also helped mark memories of the
assassination in a way that signaled the status of individual bearers of
memory.

Recollecting the assassination through celebrity tales thus effectively blurred distinctions between "the event" and "the event as
told" in journalistic accounts of the assassination, allowing journalists
as tellers-of-the-event to become a valued part of the assassination's
retelling. Invoking celebrity as a memory system encouraged journalists to remember the events of Kennedy's death by recalling the
Walter Cronkites, Dan Rathers, and Tom Wickers who gave them
voice. Equally important, recalling the Cronkites, Rathers, and Wickers became a goal in its own right.

TEN

The Authority of the Organization
and Institution: Recollecting through
Professional Lore

Another memory system that helped unite journalists as an interpretive community was professional lore, the body of knowledge that journalists and news organizations systematically circulated among and about themselves. Professional lore gave the media a way to perpetuate institutionally supported perspectives on their actions, providing a set of texts, discourses, and practices that helped them tailor their assassination memories into a celebration of their own professionalism. Unlike tales of celebrity, these tales privileged the organization and institution over the individual or the structure of the profession.

Themes of Professional Lore

The relevance of professional lore for establishing journalistic authority was suggested directly after the assassination, when covering Kennedy's death was systematically turned into a story of professional triumph. Problems raised by the assassination coverage enhanced the need for professional lore that would emphasize the professional stature accrued from having covered the story. Professional lore thus helped journalists and news organizations mark the appropriate standards of practice and, by implication, authority. Through its function as a memory system, it offered journalists a way to perpetuate the authority of the news organization and institution by linking it to assassination tales. Tales of the organization and institution thereby acted as a socializing agent that circulated collective notions about practice and authority.[1]

Like other memory systems, professional lore worked by a substitutional rule. It allowed members of the journalistic community to "plug" different news organizations and institutions into collective memory—implying, for example, that what CBS did today, NBC could do tomorrow. Just as the individual reporter was made the pivotal point of tales of celebrity, in professional lore the news organization and institution were positioned at the intersection of larger discourses about journalism and discourses about covering Kennedy's death.

In retellings of the assassination story over time, only certain dimensions of professionalism were sustained within professional lore. Narratives that attested to the viability of certain news organizations or institutions persisted. Selecting the assassination story as a locus for illustrating professional codes and practices gave professional lore the air of a backward-looking discourse, a self-retrospective that systematically glorified certain points within its own history from the vantage points of those who could afford to look back. Lost in the shuffle was the perpetuation of any critical perspective on the original coverage of Kennedy's death. What remained were clear-cut messages about those dimensions of professionalism that had effectively helped journalists perpetuate themselves as an authoritative interpretive community.

Tales of the Novice

In one way or another, all interpretive communities are maintained through origin narratives, which give members of groups collective ways of referencing themselves and their shared heritage, tradition, and values.[2] They constitute an important part of professional lore, setting the parameters of successful entry into the community. At the same time, professional lore constitutes fertile ground for origin narratives, often in the form of tales of professional acclimatization. These tell the story of untried individuals making their way into the community. Such tales attest both to the worth of the community and, by implication, to that of the professional lore that records its impulses.

Assassination narratives were used by journalists to generate such tales of acclimatization. The route by which naive and unknowing novices made their way into the journalistic profession was located years later by many journalists in the coverage of Kennedy's death. Their tales legitimated the professional journalist at the same time as they helped displace amateurs. Journalists' need to view the assassination as a locus for the onset of their professional behavior made tales of the novice a necessary part of professional lore.

One example was provided by reporter Meg Greenfield, who wrote a commemorative piece about the assassination for *Time* magazine twenty-five years later. Entitled "The Way Things Really Were," the article traced Greenfield's professional identity to the day Kennedy was killed. It was, she said, the day when she began to think and act like a journalist. "I date everything back to November 22, 1963, so far as my adult working life is concerned. . . . What I experienced that day, for the first time, was our peculiar immunity as a trade. We became immune by a crush of duty . . . allowed, even expected to function outside the restraints of ordinary decent behavior. We had a job to do. Our license was all but total."[3] Recalling the detached and disembodied "high-octane state" in which she and her colleagues operated in the aftermath of Kennedy's death, Greenfield detailed the frenzy that pushed them into action and kept them going. Her tale recounted the displacement of emotion, the intrusive nature of journalistic work, and the semblance of indifference that characterized journalists' activities during those four days.

Similarly, Barbara Walters recalled her own past as a writer on the "Today Show," where she heard the news that Kennedy had been shot. "That next Monday, I had one of my first on-the-air assignments, reporting on the funeral of President John F. Kennedy, and being still a novice, I wondered how I could possibly manage to keep the tears out of my voice."[4] Her ability to transcend the anxieties of a first-time broadcast qualified her as a competent journalist.

Even former anchorperson Jessica Savitch, then a high school student anxious to break into journalism, was construed as having reacted "with a curious mixture of personal horror and professional excitement . . . As soon as she heard the news, she raced to a pay phone and called in a report to WOND on the reactions of Atlantic City high school students. Jessica and Jeff Greenhawt thought of trying to do a special edition of *Teen Corner*, but in the end they were overtaken by the dimensions of the event. The show was canceled."[5] Although not yet employed as a reporter, Savitch already displayed the proper attributes of a journalist—intensity, drive, motivation, and ingenuity.

Implicit in each of these narratives was a view of the assassination as a professional testing ground of the reporter's untried journalistic acumen. Interestingly, tales of the novice upheld the "known" dimensions of journalistic practice. Unlike Walter Cronkite, who wept while on the air, or the various reporters who reshaped notions of professional practice in order to provide coverage, tales of the novice played directly into accepted and recognized standards of action. Journalists could emerge as new members of the community by proving themselves within already defined parameters of professional journalistic practice.

Tales of the novice thus relayed a story of professional validation and personal transformation that was portrayed as being intrinsically

tied to the assassination story. Novice reporters, upholding professional codes, were transformed by their coverage into journalists with
first-rate professional experience. This made the assassination story a
fruitful locus for discussions about journalism, journalistic professionalism, and the legitimation of television news. As Dan Rather
later said, "If that weekend, beyond the trauma, became a shared
experience in journalism, it was because without exception those
called on responded so well to the pressure."[6] In other words, the
novice's ability to respond effectively to the circumstances of Kennedy's death was instrumental in maintaining the appearance of journalistic professionalism that came to be associated with the event.

Greenfield made a similar point in her narrative, which by its end
had set her, too, solidly within the ranks of veteran reporters. In concluding, she called the ongoing efforts to commemorate Kennedy's
death "anniversary journalism." The title was apt, for it suggested
how journalists had positioned themselves within assassination tales.
Because tales of the novice generally recounted the transformation of
untried cub reporters into hard-nosed journalists, recalling the events
of Kennedy's death became a way of marking this transformation in
professional lore. Tales of the novice thus were important less for
what they said about the career trajectories of individual reporters
and more for what they implied about the organizations and institutions of journalism. This suggests that professional lore constituted
an important dimension by which journalists consolidated themselves as an interpretive community.

Memory and the Tools of Technology

A second theme central to professional lore was the relationship between memory and technology. In retellings of the assassination, an
emphasis on the technologies used in reporting helped journalists
link their tales retrospectively to discussions about the legitimacy of
technology, often that of television.[7]

This meant that assassination tales were refracted through the
technologies that helped perpetuate them. For example, journalists
readily admitted to the vagaries and inconsistencies of human memory, citing faulty recall of that weekend's particulars and mentioning
their reliance on aids to memory.[8] They admitted that they used certain tools of technology to keep their assassination tales fresh. The
mention of such tools within professional lore suggested that journalists partly shaped their own identities through the technologies

they used. They saw themselves as more professional for having used them.

Early tales in which journalists recounted their assassination coverage played up the importance of technology. Tales of triumph—in which reporters praised themselves for having been "the first," "the best," and "the only" in covering Kennedy's death—set up a context that allowed them over time to celebrate their professionalism in conjunction with technology.[9] Immediately after the assassination, in an early defense of television, one journalist claimed to use the camera just as a newspaper reporter used his pad and pencil.[10] This suggests that even then reporters attended to the reconfiguration of practices necessitated by different technologies.

Recollections of assassination coverage frequently mentioned the practice of note taking. In both print and electronic media, journalists recounted at length how they took copious notes of events. Note taking was seen as stabilizing memory, and setting down on paper what one had seen or heard appeared to validate one's recollections.

One television item bore this out particularly well. Reporter Steve Bell, called upon in 1988 to anchor a Philadelphia TV station's commemoration of the assassination anniversary, did so by incorporating a repeat broadcast of his original coverage of Kennedy's death. As Bell recalled that "we were on a round-the-clock vigil for information, and Police Chief Jesse Curry was the primary source of information," the picture of Curry faded to one of Bell taking notes years before in Dallas.[11] The semiotic message conveyed by the image was its ability to authorize him twenty-five years later to speak about the assassination.

Another example was provided by Harrison Salisbury of the *New York Times,* who edited his newspaper's coverage of the assassination. In an impassioned chronology of his reportorial career, Salisbury recollected the role of notes in setting down his assassination memories. "On November 27, 1963, five days after Kennedy was killed, the first moment I had time and strength to put down what I felt, I wrote a memorandum to myself. I said that in the year 2000 the Kennedy assassination would still be a matter of debate, new theories being evolved how and why it happened."[12] References to his notes rendered Salisbury's memories a valuable recording of events, and he proceeded to quote from the memorandum he had penned two and a half decades earlier. But rather than link his thoughts with personalized discourse about himself as a journalist, he connected them to lore about journalistic professionalism. "I had concluded before going to work for the *Times* in 1949 that the essence of journalism was reporting and writing," he said. "I wanted to find things out—particularly things which no one else had managed to dig out—and let people have the best possible evidence on which to make up their minds about policy." [13] The decision to take notes thus allowed Salisbury to see himself as "more professional." This implied an interest in posterity, perhaps in history, and at the very least a recognition that note taking facilitated accuracy and stabilized memory.

New York Times reporter Tom Wicker similarly recollected how he "had chosen that day to be without a notebook. I took notes on the back of my mimeographed schedule of the two-day tour of Texas we had been so near to concluding. Today, I cannot read many of the notes; on November 22, they were as clear as sixty-point type." [14] Two years later, he recounted how

> I sat in a stuffy, cramped room in the Baker Hotel in Dallas on the morning of November 23, when the great plane had borne its burden of mortality back to Washington, and the fact of death was palpable and tearful in every heart, and Lee Harvey Oswald was snarling his tiny pathetic defiance a few blocks away in the Dallas jail. I wrote that morning what I thought about the way things were, and would be. [15]

Wicker's references to his attempts to write down what he saw signified his efforts at stabilizing memory. The activity of note taking referenced his presence as a professional at the site of Kennedy's death. Note taking was thus a particularly visible attribute of journalistic professionalism.

Failure to take notes worked to the disadvantage of other reporters. *Washington Post* editor Benjamin Bradlee, for instance, prefaced his *Conversations with Kennedy,* published twelve years after the president's death, with the claim that although he had not kept regular notes of his meetings with the late president, he could, unbelievably, "still quote verbatim whole chunks of conversations with him." [16] Reporter Jean Daniel, the foreign editor of the French weekly *L'Express,* neglected to take notes during a series of interviews with Fidel Castro and John Kennedy shortly before Kennedy's death. When Daniel contended that both men had said they shared a belief in American capitalism and Cuban communism, he was discredited because "no one else was present, and Daniel, by his own account, took no notes." [17] His zeal was held to have "outperformed his memory," which implies that his failure to take notes made him appear unprofessional.

Other tools of technology mentioned in professional lore were those surrounding photography. The filmed and photographic sequencing of the events of Kennedy's death was widely used to anchor different reporters' accounts. For example, the CBS documentary "Four Days in November" incorporated still photographs, particularly of Oswald being shot, within its filmed footage.[18] Elsewhere, Edwin Newman recalled how

> Americans went to sleep with images of assassination spinning in their heads. It all seemed some horrible dream from which we would awaken. But it wasn't. We would awaken to more and more images, images that would become forever burned in our memories. We remember Jacqueline Kennedy, her dress stained with her husband's blood, standing beside LBJ as he took the oath of office. We remember her, kneeling with her daughter to kiss the flag-draped casket. We remember a little boy's salute to his father. We remember the riderless horse Blackjack.[19]

Repeated references to assassination images made the image-making technology a relevant tool in circumscribing memory. Photographic and film technology became central to professional lore because photographs and films gave journalists a strategy for retelling their assassination role.

By the end of the assassination weekend, journalists had readily adopted the sequencing supplied by television technology: the assassination narrative was transformed into one long story that stretched over four days of seemingly continuous happenings rather than maintained as piecemeal accounts of discrete moments of coverage.[20] Such sequencing appeared in accounts of memory as well, making the celebration of television technology an integral part of journalists' definitions of professional behavior. By borrowing the characteristics of television technology referenced by certain journalists, reporters in other media in effect became second-class tellers of the assassination narrative.

This suggests that the tales by which journalists sought to promote themselves as professionals implicitly recognized the dependence of professionalism on technology and reporters' effective use of it.[21] Use of the tools of technology bolstered journalists' collective memories of the event, in much the same way as it supported their professionalism at the time of the assassination.

Recycling Organizational and Institutional Tales

Just as tales of journalistic celebrity were perpetuated through extensive recycling, so too were organizational and institutional tales. How a narrative made its way from one context to others reveals significant patterns of legitimation by which the journalistic community solidified its boundaries. Here again, tales became a central part of collective lore through reprintings and retrospectives, all of which emphasized the organizations and institutions where individuals worked. The growth of professional lore was thus partly the result of an organization's own decision to recycle its tales.

This was exemplified by Time-Life, which devoted extensive efforts to recycling its own lore on the assassination. *Life* magazine published a twenty-fifth anniversary issue that reprinted its original memorial edition. An outer leaf was affixed to the magazine, bearing a picture of the earlier cover and the word *reprint* slashed diagonally across it. The outer leaf proclaimed that "we recall him 25 years later with this historic issue," and a brief insert ran as follows:

> The first copies of this magazine, published two weeks after John F. Kennedy's killing, sold out immediately as a grieving America, seeking a memoir of its sadness, turned to *Life*. . . . We believe this account to be richer than any anniversary review could be. So we have reprinted our original for the 100 million Americans who are too young to remember—and for those too old to forget—the assassination of a President.[22]

Except for these alterations, and a price raised from $.50 to $3.95, the issue was reprinted exactly as it had been published twenty-five years earlier. Similar practices were found in books and in-house journals.

Time-Life also recycled the most popular part of assassination lore, photographs: shots of Johnson being sworn in as president, of Jacqueline Kennedy leaning over her husband's casket, of Oswald crumpling under a murderer's bullet, of Caroline touching her father's coffin were reproduced in magazines, journals, and commemorative volumes. One such volume, a Time-Life book entitled *Life in Camelot*, concluded with two pictures taken from the assassination and pre-assassination coverage—one of John-John saluting his father's casket, the other of Kennedy walking on the sand dunes near Hyannis Port. The accompanying text read, "This is how *Life* ended its special JFK memorial following the assassination. In this retelling of Camelot so many years later, it still seems fitting to let these two pictures close the story."[23] Many of these pictures had appeared twenty-five years earlier in *Life* magazine,[24] etched into collective memory by earlier organizational efforts, and the commemorative volume was careful now to include pictures of the photographers who had photographed Kennedy.[25] Other subsidiary companies supported Time-Life's effort at organizational legitimation, as when *Forbes* magazine told its readers:

> In the November *Life* are some of the most vividly famous photographs of the instant and stunning aftermath [of Kennedy's death] . . . the First Lady in her blood-soaked pink suit standing by as Lyndon Johnson is sworn in as President on Air Force One . . . the coffin being lowered from the plane for the dead President's last White House sojourn . . . John-John saluting the coffin. De Gaulle, towering, as they walk behind the caisson to Arlington.[26]

The validation of Time-Life was repeated in other news organizations, as when CBS introduced a special eight-part series on the assassination in 1988 with a color montage of the event's best-known photographs, most of them from *Life* magazine.[27] This upheld not only the stature accorded photography in recollecting the assassination story but the role played by Time-Life as well.

Similar patterns of recycling were found in other news organizations. Film clips from assassination footage, for example, were replayed in televised news programs, special documentaries, and media retrospectives. These televised sequences, which showed the funeral caisson, the riderless horse, the procession of mourners, and the murder of Oswald, were put forward as part of organizational lore, despite the fact that they were often compiled under different names, thereby allowing news organizations to profit several times from the same footage. NBC, for instance, reused one basic compilation of NBC assassination coverage under two different titles: "JFK Assassination: As It Happened," screened on the Arts and Entertainment cable network in 1988; and "The Week We Lost John F. Kennedy," sold as a three-part set on the private market one year later.[28] Although different narrators introduced the clips, the coverage presented was nearly identical.

The context in which an assassination narrative was recycled by news organizations thus indicated the specific nature of its importance. For example, the incorporation of the narrative about Dan Rather in Dallas within CBS's organizational lore revealed how important the story was to CBS. The same narrative's incorporation within histories about television as a news medium reflected its function in determining the legitimacy of television journalism. The fact that assassination tales were recycled in a variety of contexts underscored the effectiveness of professional lore in revealing patterns of authority. It showed how the establishment of journalists as an authoritative interpretive community depended on the continuous recirculation of narratives through professional lore.

Texts of Organizational Memory

News organizations recycled assassination narratives in two main groups of organizationally bound texts—overviews of specific news organizations, such as histories of CBS or the *New York Times*, and biographical and autobiographical perspectives about life within such organizations. Both types were used to lend a valorized past to the organizations.

One example was the professional lore surrounding CBS. Gary Paul Gates's history of CBS News, *Air Time*, began with a chapter entitled "Kennedy's Been Shot," which detailed how CBS had covered the assassination.[29] The chapter's placement reflected the centrality of the assassination for members of the organization. In a semiotic sense, framing the book around the assassination highlighted the role the tragedy played in legitimating CBS News.

Like other accounts found in professional lore, Gates's recounting of the assassination story was laced with praise for television technology. He traced how CBS was able to produce its coverage of Kennedy's death. The 1962 opening of three new CBS bureaus (one in Dallas), the expansion of network news coverage from fifteen minutes to thirty, and the employment of communications satellites and videotape were all seen to have been necessary elements. This contextualized CBS's successful coverage of the story as a natural evolution, grounded in organizational decision making that had embraced advances in technology. Gates's focus on CBS's adoption of technological advances and organizational expansion made it seem that the assassination coverage had been the result of organizational foresight. This coopted the assassination story within a larger discourse legitimating the news organization.

Similar stories were featured in the professional lore about NBC. One biography of former NBC anchorperson Jessica Savitch described how NBC had set the scene for broadcast coverage of the assassination when executive Robert Kintner decided that NBC would yank all scheduled programming, including commercials, after Kennedy was shot. "His competitors at CBS and ABC followed suit, but NBC garnered the credit for public-spiritedness," went the account.[30] The same story was featured in other overviews of NBC News,[31] suggesting that organizational decisions at NBC helped make the assassination story into the special-event coverage that it became. This focus supported links between the assassination story and NBC's prestige as a news organization.[32]

In each case the assassination story was used to bolster the prestige of the organization from which the tale emerged. As one television retrospective maintained, "It was at times like these that a news organization finds out how good it is, whether it can do the hard jobs, the grim ones."[33] Professional lore helped perpetuate the critical nature of the event for most news organizations. The recycling of organizational tales functioned much like the recycling of individual celebrity tales discussed earlier: while recycling the celebrity tale served individual journalists by heightening and solidifying their personal stature, recycling of organizational tales served news organizations by stressing the gains they had made in covering Kennedy's death.

Texts of Institutional Memory

At the same time, assassination narratives were recycled extensively in institutional overviews, including discussions about national journalism and the evolution of television news. In such cases, assassination narratives were coopted within more general discourses that helped create a valorized past for certain institutions. As one leading trade journal said at the time of Kennedy's death, the events "belonged to journalism and specifically to the national organs of journalism."[34] The assassination was seen as a national story, and institutional texts played it as such.

Most institutional texts linked the Kennedy assassination with discussions of journalistic professionalism. Compilations of news stories, such as those found in a volume called *American Datelines*, included assassination accounts as some of the major news stories in American history; *Esquire* magazine used an entire section of assassination stories, originally published in the magazine, to compile its own "history of the sixties"; and *Ramparts* magazine used a piece on assassination investigations to show good muckraking reporting.[35] Trade journals, such as *The Quill*, reprinted early assassination coverage.[36] Most institutional texts also stressed the role of television, and one frequently repeated claim held that the Kennedy assassination occurred just when television news was capable of covering such an event. The central place of this claim in professional lore was borne out in works such as that of Erik Barnouw, who devoted nearly ten pages of a volume on the evolution of television to discussion of assassination coverage.[37] The Associated Press's *History of Television* used tales of the assassination to signify the medium's coming of age.[38] Nearly every institutional overview of the medium of television made mention of the Kennedy assassination.

Authorizing Television

The nuances of associations between television and the Kennedy assassination were significant, because in account after account, assassination retellers and television were construed as having legitimated each other. In large part this was because 1963 was a pivotal year for television. Not only did more people than ever before say that they got their news from television rather than from newspapers, but, in one view, the advent of the half-hour newscast intensified the "bond of familiarity and dependence between anchor and viewer."[39] Coverage of the Kennedy assassination was seen as capping what had become an advantageous situation:

> Television had already proved its ability to cover large-scale events that were pre-planned, but never before had it attempted to keep up with a fast-breaking, unanticipated story of this magnitude. . . . Remarked one executive at the time, "I think we were frightened when we saw our capability." In a medium not noted for its dignity or restraint, the commentators and reporters also performed admirably, conscious perhaps of their role in keeping the nation calm and unified. What the networks lost in commercial revenues during the four days was more than compensated for by the good will generated.[40]

In a special issue celebrating television's fiftieth birthday, *TV Guide* held that the assassination story was a turning point in the medium's legitimation.[41] A CBS documentary recalled how America needed a calming influence, which television was able to provide through its coverage. "Hour after hour, day after day, from murder to burial, the flow of images and pictures calmed the panic. Someone has said that those four days marked the coming of the age of television."[42] Similar claims were made in narrative histories about American media, such as David Halberstam's *Powers That Be.*[43]

In much the same way that organizational tales contextualized the assassination as the result of organizational foresight, institutional tales viewed it as the consequence of institutional developments in technology, and of the social, economic, political, and cultural legitimation of television. Television was seen as an active player in the assassination drama. The assassination coverage helped audiences understand television in a way that prepared them "for the many

murders to come, for the 'living room war' of Vietnam, for the constitutional lessons of Watergate, and finally, monotonously, for the local
murders of the ten o'clock news."[44] As one observer said, "On that
day, American television changed forever."[45]

Implicit in these comments was a recognition that television had
changed the forms by which the American public would remember
major events. Television solidified its status as "a collective reference
point" and shaper of American memories.[46] It was not only that, as
one analyst observed, by bringing the assassination and its aftermath
"vividly into the national consciousness . . . far more graphically than
the printed page, the video screen [had] depicted some of the most
unforgettable scenes in recent history."[47] Equally important, television made certain dimensions of those scenes available for collective
perpetuation—a status well suited to journalists' attempts to uphold
themselves as an authoritative interpretive community.

The assassination was thus contextualized as one of the first situations in which journalists showed they were capable of acting in a
way demanded of them by television technology. This made the authorization of television a central part of professional lore about the
assassination. Within institutional texts, television thus reigned
supreme.

Peopling Technology

Broader considerations of television technology as an issue of concern
to the journalism profession did not erase more specific consideration
of the individual reporter's usage of technology. Technologies of all
kinds provided a human element in professional lore, in that stories
remained peopled with the individuals who used them. In narrating
the 1988 CBS documentary "Four Days in November," Dan Rather
cautioned viewers that they were about to watch a "hastily prepared
biography CBS News broadcast that weekend. Tapes and films were
rushed from our vaults, and my colleague Harry Reasoner improvised from notes."[48] A 1988 Associated Press dispatch discussed the
earlier performance of NBC correspondent Bill Ryan: "It was Ryan
who read the AP flash that Kennedy was dead. 'It's jarring when
somebody comes up to you and says, "You're the one who told me
President Kennedy was dead,"' Ryan said."[49] The article recounted
the circumstances of technical naivete Ryan was expected to overcome in covering the story. "We didn't even have a regular news studio," he said, observing that "it wasn't like today, where you could
punch up the whole world by satellite in a minute and a half."[50]

Both accounts tracked the improvement of television technology since the days of the assassination. Such tracking made the claim that, even without the sophisticated equipment of contemporary television, television journalists had acted as professionals in covering Kennedy's death. Stories about the legitimation of journalists as professionals were thus put forward in—although they were not dependent on—stories about television technology.

This may explain why Rather chose to introduce that same CBS retrospective with a detailed overview of the state of television technology at the time of the assassination:

> In 1963, television news was broadcast in black and white. Lightweight portable tape equipment did not exist. Our signals moved mostly by hardwire or microwave relay. In some film clips which follow, you will see watermarks, looking like rain on the screen. The film had no chance to dry out. It was broadcast from wet stock. But the message went out across the country.[51]

The embedded message suggests the triumph of reporters over what was then an undeveloped technology. When separated from the visual images that documented the story of Kennedy's death, Rather's words told in addition the story of the evolution of television and of the reporter's triumph in it.

Other technologies were similarly woven into the story of Kennedy's death. Overviews of photojournalism, for example, praised the assassination story's photographic footage. A special *Time* survey of 150 years of photojournalism included the Oswald shooting as one of the ten greatest images in the history of the field.[52] Another essay in that same issue noted that in 1963, "as historical events darkened, photojournalism regained some of its tragic power. . . . A Dallas *Times-Herald* photographer caught the instant of Lee Harvey Oswald's death."[53]

Yet the professional claims of photojournalists to the story of Kennedy's death took second place to those of television journalists. As the same essay noted, television's capture of the moment of Oswald's death prompted photojournalists to ask whether "picture taking, no longer history's first witness, [would] ever again be more than stenography?"[54] The systematic and repeated incorporation of assassination narratives within institutional overviews about journalism suggested that the answer to that question was negative. The fervor with which organizational and institutional memory made television technology the central element in recountings of the assassination story left little space for competing claims about the status of other professional groups.

Radio suffered a similar fate. While people told of receiving their first accounts of Kennedy's death from radio,[55] many had turned to television by the time the assassination weekend was over. This suggested that radio fulfilled an important but transient function. The disappearance of references to radio's role in assassination retellings was connected with the rise of interest in television technology. Alongside the extensive texts that referred to television's glorious success, little room remained for narratives about radio. This perhaps explains why even in professional lore, the role of radio received short shrift in institutionally bounded narratives about the assassination. Radio became seen as a local medium next to the more nationalized medium of television. Similar circumstances explain the disappearance of narratives about local media of all sorts.

Thus the assassination story was systematically perpetuated within discourse about television technology, particularly national television. This reinforced the need to view Kennedy's death as a locus for professional behavior and technological legitimation. Just as the celebrity tale promoted individual reporters, organizational and institutional tales helped valorize specific news organizations and institutions. The repeated and systematic cooptation of these tales within professional lore helped journalists create a past that elevated the stature not only of journalistic professionalism but of television news as well.

On Memory and Professionalism

In 1989, Walter Cronkite was asked to comment on television's fifty years of broadcasting. He reflected on the use of television to look back at television, and said, "You'll be amazed at how much you've forgotten that you remembered."[56] Claims such as this, which underscored the ability of television to bring back forgotten events, were instrumental to members of the American journalistic community. They formed their self-definitions as professionals in conjunction with that view and others like it.

Journalists thereby used professional lore to turn themselves into an interpretive community. Pivoting assassination retellings on professional lore in addition to individual tales of celebrity enhanced the importance of the profession's organizational and institutional loci. Individual reporters were cast as players who upheld proven parameters of professionalism, while organizations and institutions provided frames both for their activities at the time of the assassination and for their retellings years later. Journalists' professional memories were thus derived not only from individuals but from their organizational and institutional contexts. Through all dimensions, the media were able to constitute themselves as an independent, authoritative community.

In an essay about photojournalism, writer Lance Morrow considered certain technologically generated intersections of memory and professionalism. "The pictures made by photojournalists have the legitimacy of being news, fresh information . . . [But] it is only later that the artifacts of photojournalism sink into the textures of the civilization and tincture its memory: Jack Ruby shooting Lee Harvey Oswald, John-John saluting at the funeral."[57] Morrow's comments reflect how professional journalists refashioned the assassination narrative through organizational and institutional tales. They used it to create the kinds of memories that most directly benefited their organizational and institutional concerns. These concerns focused on news organizations, particularly mainstream ones like CBS, the *New York Times,* and *Life* magazine, and on institutions, particularly national television news. It was within this context that assassination narratives took shape over time, and they became an integral part of how the journalistic community continued to look at itself.

ELEVEN

The Authority of the Profession:
Recollecting through History

What is accessible to all of us is the memory of ourselves during that bleak November weekend.[1]

The tale of President Kennedy's death was, of course, more than a
story about journalism. This meant that journalists needed to do more
than perpetuate narratives that emphasized their own authority for
the story: they needed to account for other authorities too.

Nearly three decades after the assassination, journalists' competition with the independent critics had taken on familiar forms. Some
critics had either voluntarily abandoned the story or been marginalized by mainstream journalism. Those who continued to investigate
it coexisted with reporters tensely, in recognized, circumscribed channels. Historians, on the other hand, who had not yet played an active
part in recording the assassination, had no such familiar patterns of
interaction with journalists. Yet history remained the main discipline
with a clear claim to the tale. Journalists were attentive to the fact that
historians had not yet fully addressed the story, and they began to
consider the role of history in its retelling. History gave journalists a
way to tailor their assassination memories into a consideration of the
structure of their own profession. These tales privileged considerations of the profession of journalism over those of the individual, organization, or institution.

History: Privileged Record or Anachronism?

The relevance of the historical record for all retellers derived from its
ability to lend depth and context to the events it retold. In one view,
history was a "discipline which [seeks] to establish true statements
about events which have occurred and objects which have existed in
the past."[2] In terms of perspective, narrative standard, and analytical
method, historians were recordkeepers of a system predicated on distance.[3] They focused on the long rather than short term, favored

structure over event, and viewed themselves as effective providers of context.

Such a perspective was at odds with larger developments of the time that had shaped assassination records. Traditional understandings of the workings of history contradicted the self-reflexivity of chronicles of the sixties. The assumed distance of the historical perspective failed to account for the relevance of history among those seeking new boundaries of cultural authority. More important, the prospect of history taking over the assassination story remained problematic because traditional historians did not make room for memory. As one observer remarked, "Memory has always been difficult for historians to confront . . . [It] is considered an information source to be confirmed by scholarship."[4]

Among traditional historians, memory and history offered "mutually opposed ways of appreciating the past."[5] Memory was expected to give way to history, and its subjective images to yield "to the historian's description of objective facts."[6] Over time, then, memory would become a tool in the historian's hands; but as long as memory remained vital, history could not assume an authoritative role in discourse.

For assassination retellers, history thus offered significant advantages but a mode of recordkeeping that was not valorized. While these advantages—perspective, stability of interpretation, sensitivity to the context—successfully separated historical writing from other assassination chronicles, retellings of the assassination story needed to address the issues of reflexivity and questioning of documentary process that had been readily adopted by other chroniclers of the time. It was thus no surprise that for assassination retellers, most of whom had lived through the events, tensions about historical record persisted. As the story moved into the historian's domain, it was expected that memories would decrease in importance.

Yet from the beginning journalists resisted giving up the role of historian. As one historian admitted, in the case of Kennedy, the "efforts of the historians are not likely to have a considerable effect . . . for he has already become part not of history but of myth."[7] Since journalists' professional codes, modes of storytelling, and technologies for telling tales were all predicated on their presence within the assassination story, the historical record implied an eradication of the journalist's role as recollector. Reporters therefore set about proving they could play the role of historian better than historians themselves. It was an "event in history," proclaimed one trade publication just one week after Kennedy's death.[8] Four years later, *Newsweek* already contemplated the story's status under the title "Assassination: History or Headlines?"[9] History and news were thus set up in direct competition with each other.

Justifying Journalistic Record as History

Journalists recollected the assassination through the memory system of history by referring to the historic nature of the events they were narratively reconstructing. "Historic photographs" were referenced across media; "historic films" became media triumphs.[10] "Historic coverage" was one frequently used label for journalistic coverage of the assassination story.[11]

The tension between journalism and history was grounded firmly in collective lore. Writer Theodore White defined reporters as "servants of history, offering up our daily or passing tales for them to sort out."[12] Journalists were seen as responsible for covering the events of today, historians for chronicling those of yesterday. One observer remarked that the tension between the two groups was an old one, the only difference being "a difference of time; today's journalism is tomorrow's history."[13] It was within such a context that journalism became known as the "first rough draft of history." That comment, offered by *Washington Post* publisher Philip Graham,[14] was widely quoted throughout the assassination literature.

The Distinction between Journalism and History

Recollecting the assassination through the eye of the historian was linked with journalists' uncertainty over the distinction between the two professions. Initially journalists saw themselves as helping historians to retell the assassination. Immediately after Kennedy's death, one trade publication held that "never before has there been such documentation of history-in-the-making."[15] Another admitted that if "future historians will have a full record of events," it was because "they will know exactly what Lee Harvey Oswald looked like."[16] This implied that television, by disseminating images of the assassination, was supporting the recording of history. Journalists, particularly TV reporters, viewed themselves as offering the American public a "new dimension in understanding history."[17]

Defining themselves as aides to historians encouraged journalists to emphasize differences between journalistic and historical retellings of the assassination story. These centered on temporal demarcation. Journalists saw themselves as providers of a "first draft"; their accounts were preliminary yet essential to the final draft to be written by historians. One article in the *Progressive* noted that "the commentators, responding in the tragic passion of the moment, have had their say about Mr. Kennedy, and the historians, writing in the coolness of time, will have theirs one day."[18] History was expected to take up where journalism left off, by offering a finite end point that would discard or immobilize contradictory claims to the story. But it was unclear where or when that point would be.

Television documentaries became occupied with the point at which "history reexamined the facts."[19] Journalism lingered as a form of uncooked history, where "the participants' memories haven't yet entirely faded and the historians haven't yet taken over."[20] Because journalists were closer to the story and their authority was derived from their presence, they began to recognize the advantage they had over historians, whose authority would come only after the facts became clear.

This advantage was derived from several circumstances, all of which blurred traditional distinctions between journalists and historians. Journalists' continued presence in the assassination story was to a large degree supported by the timing of the event, occurring as it did before the president had completed a first term. Kennedy's time in office was too short for historians to gauge his reign, yet journalists had been granted easy access to the 1,000 days of Kennedy's administration. This placed them in the position of becoming its preferred evaluators. This was certainly the case with Theodore White, whose stature with the Kennedy family later gave him access to the assassination story.[21] As Norman Mailer said, "Much of what we had to say, intended to have the life of contemporary criticism, [became] abruptly a document which speaks from . . . a time which is past, from history."[22] Journalists were thus cast as instant historians by the circumstances of Kennedy's death.

But there were other circumstances that derived from the insufficiency of traditional modes of recordkeeping. While historians became less competent to tell the story as its retellings persisted, due to their discomfort with the reflexive quality of sixties-era narratives, their detached mode of storytelling, and their assumption that the assassination's contradictory events could be woven into a coherent narrative, the distinctions between contemporaneous and after-the-fact accounts also became less relevant. It was unclear where journalism ended and history began. "Past events," said one reporter, "become history when the public forgets its details. America has not yet let go of the details of that afternoon."[23]

This was in part because the media kept replaying them. Indeed, news reports themselves seemed to lack a temporal finiteness: "*The [New York] Times* would not be thrown away by readers a day later, it was a collectors' item. . . . It would pass on, as a family heirloom or a relic or a vague testimony to existence on the day a President was shot."[24] Media accounts took on a historical cast. One compilation of assassination coverage collected years later by the *Dallas Morning News* was flagged on the back cover by the following statement: "Much has been written and recorded about the assassination of John F. Kennedy, but no source in the world has more to offer on the events of November 22, 1963 than the *Dallas Morning News*. Here . . . is a permanent record of coverage from the city's largest newspaper."[25] The state of limbo in which historians were expected to wait before they began their analysis of Kennedy's death never ended. Instead, the story's persistence prevented them from "being able to complete a coherent account of this extraordinarily complex event."[26] This put them in the peculiar position of having a "nonrole" in the assassination's retelling. It also meant that expectations that the historical record would finalize the interim nature of news were not upheld. This raised serious questions about how long journalists were expected to retain their positions as spokespersons for events, and when historians were expected to take over.

All of these points that worked to the disadvantage of historians worked simultaneously to the advantage of journalists: proximity and presence upheld their professional perspective, their mode of storytelling was valorized within larger attempts to reconsider the assassination record, and the memories they provided were seen as a legitimate mode of recordkeeping. Rather than define themselves as aides to historians, journalists began to see themselves as independent makers of the historical record.

Other Challenges to Traditional Historical Authority

Traditional historians also faced other challenges than those posed by journalists. Pragmatic challenges to traditional historical authority came from the independent critics, who contested limitations on the right to reconsider the official documentary record. The critics' activities fit in with the reflexivity of the time and supported a larger appeal to history in making everyday life meaningful. As time passed and the volume of material produced by the critics increased, their presence within the assassination story contrasted with the role generally played by historians.

Other challenges came from within the discipline of history itself, where scholars like Philippe Ariès, Fernand Braudel, and Pierre Nora reconceptualized the relationship between memory and history in a way that suggested a more complicated link between the two.[27] A surge of work by scholars like Hayden White and Hans Kellner addressed the literary qualities of historical writing and its function in reality construction.[28] Other pragmatic challenges came from the professionals situated between historians and journalists—a hybrid alternatively called participant historians, historians of popular memory, or popular historians. Individuals such as David Halberstam and Gary Wills sought to achieve an alternative mode of documenting history, one that attended to their own participation in it. Unlike traditional historians, who were wont to sift through documents from a temporal distance, popular historians made use of their experience *within* events.

Popular historians lent a fresh perspective to retellings of the assassination, particularly by the early eighties. Their views and actions became a legitimate part of the stories they wrote, a point that linked them with ongoing discourses about participation, self-reflexivity, and the relevance of memory. For example, although it did not address Kennedy's death, Halberstam's *Best and the Brightest* documented the trappings of American politics in a way that left little doubt about his own perspective on them, and he wrote it while events relevant to his chronicle were continuing to take place.[29]

This trend worked to enhance the authority of the assassination's chroniclers. Books like Gary Wills's *Kennedy Imprisonment*, John H. Davis's *Kennedys*, and Peter Collier and David Horowitz's *Kennedys: An American Drama* implanted the assassination within larger contexts that were generally concerned with issues of corruption, power, and domination. While Collier and Horowitz tracked the effect of the assassination on family members, Davis incorporated an epilogue in 1984 that addressed the Justice Department's investigation of the assassination.[30] Herbert Parmet concluded one of his books about Kennedy with a detailed description of the events in Dallas and consideration of its flawed investigation.[31] Even challenges from oral historians, memoirists, and biographers—all of whom emphasized the value of memory as preferred documentation of the past—suggested a mode of historical recordkeeping that was more in tune with the assassination story. Their versions were less detached and often "based on remembered experiences."[32] This meant that challenges to traditional views of historical recordkeeping were taking place within the discipline itself.

All of this had direct relevance for the journalistic community, whose method of recordkeeping and perspective on events were closely aligned to those suggested by other challenges to traditional modes of historical recordkeeping. Even in discourse about history, then, journalistic practice was seen as a possible resolution to problems surrounding historical recordkeeping.

Journalism's Critique of History

The existence, however tentative, of challenges to traditional modes of recordkeeping suggested that there was room for flexibility in defining the role to be played by historians. This caused journalists to rethink the criteria that distinguished them from historians. It also generated revealing tensions between journalists and those popular historians, memoirists, and biographers who did address the assassination.

As that work began to punctuate the record, journalists tended to criticize it for the very qualities that made it different from that of their traditional colleagues. Popular historians' accommodation of their own reflexivity was met with skepticism among many reporters. Journalists lambasted them for being subjective, too close to events, too hasty, and not sufficiently detached.[33] Their attempts to adopt either a more participatory stance on events or a less analytically remote perspective were harshly appraised. This was perhaps because reporters felt that nontraditional historians were encroaching on their domain. Popular, or participant, historiography especially was seen as being too similar to journalism.

In that light, William Manchester's publication of *The Death of a President*, touted as the official history of the assassination, was brushed off in media reviews during the late sixties as "compelling narrative but hardly impartial history."[34] When columnist Mary McGrory examined biographers who produced, in her view, "early, perhaps hasty, memoirs," she asked whether it was possible to "once see Kennedy plain."[35] Reporter Meg Greenfield questioned "the proprieties and improprieties of all this secret-baring" in the chronicles of Kennedy's biographers.[36] She argued that they had overstepped the boundaries of appropriate participation:

> History—even somewhat precipitately written—has its claims. . . . The circumstances under which these books were written would dictate that they meet the same set of criteria: that the history at a minimum be accurate, the as-

sessments be reasonably fair, and that the disclosures be
made for some recognizably serious purpose.[37]

Greenfield accused the biographers of undermining their commitment to accuracy, and concluded that drama had been served "at the
expense of history."[38]

Arthur Schlesinger, Jr., bore the brunt of the journalistic community's scorn. "Brief, Not a History" was the headline of *Newsweek*'s
critique of Schlesinger's *Thousand Days*, published in 1965.[39] His
attempts to tamper with the historian's detachment and so-called
objectivity ruffled many journalistic observers. Said Andy Logan:

> It's all right to be taken aback when Schlesinger in the *Life*
> serialization of *A Thousand Days* has the President crying in
> his wife's arms after the Cuban setback and then removes
> the scene from his published book. . . . Apparently where
> John Kennedy is concerned, the previous winner of the
> Bancroft, Parkman and Pulitzer prizes in history thinks of
> historic material as something that may be tried this way,
> turned around and tried that way, and balled up and dis-
> carded if it doesn't seem entirely becoming to the subject.[40]

An accompanying drawing portrayed Kennedy and his "instant historians"—including Schlesinger, Theodore Sorensen, William Manchester, and Pierre Salinger—as Jesus and his disciples.[41]

Thus attempts by historians to infuse their own chronicles with a
reflexive, participatory mode of analysis were denigrated by the journalistic community. Journalists paid little attention to the corrective
this offered to traditional historiography. Their criticism had to do in
no small part with the fact that popular historiography brought historians substantially closer to journalists' own mode of chronicling.
By adopting alternative modes of historical recordkeeping, historians
interested in accommodating their own reflexivity seemed to be step-
ping into the journalists' domain.

Historians' growing involvement in the assassination story in ways
that resembled the reportorial mode of storytelling thus encouraged
journalists to define clearly their own involvement in the story. Rather
than contextualize their activities as assisting in the making of the
historical record, journalists began to see themselves as its makers.
They moved from acting as facilitators of historians to becoming historical facilitators. This suggests that retellings gave journalists authority not only among themselves but among other interpretive
communities as well, underscoring basic assumptions about the structure of the journalistic profession.

Journalists' narratives about the Kennedy administration and assassination thus addressed notions about history and the historical
record overlooked by historians. They began to promote themselves
within the larger corpus of historiography. One reporter in 1988
asked whether history was "beyond the reach of ordinary Americans." [42] Memoirs, biographies, and popular histories were penned by
reporters and writers such as Theodore White, Hugh Sidey, Henry
Fairlie, Benjamin Bradlee, and Pierre Salinger.[43] They continued to
define themselves as reporters despite their forays into historical
interpretation.

Journalists felt that they were capable of addressing points in the
record that historians missed, and they stressed that they were doing
the work of historians. Media critic Gay Talese said that for reporters,
"the test in Dallas was like no other test . . . [*New York Times* correspondent Tom] Wicker was writing for history that day." [44] A *New
York Times* book called *The Kennedy Years* was labeled a "history prepared by *New York Times* staff under H. Faber's direction." [45] Referring
to his hunger "to contribute to the recording of contemporary history," reporter Benjamin Bradlee recounted how he was motivated by
his "unique, historical access" to the Kennedy administration: "I
knew enough of history to know that the fruits of this kind of access
seldom make the history books, and the great men of our time are
less understood as a result." [46] Bradlee seemed to maintain that he had
been compelled to act as a historian by the larger force of history. His
comments also implied that his history would be preferred to that
offered by professional historians. A similar view was implicit in comments about Tom Wicker's articles and books about Kennedy, which
were called "non-textbook histories." [47] In that view, Wicker was
praised for having worked against the distortions effected by the historical record on memories of Kennedy.

Journalists made attempts across media to recast their retellings as
history. In 1988 reporter Jack Anderson justified his televised report
on Kennedy's death by lamenting the suspended involvement of historians. "The government has sealed the most sensitive files on the
Kennedy assassination—the key CIA file, the critical FBI file—all in
the name of national security. By the time these files are jarred loose
from the agencies that could be embarrassed by them, the information will be ancient history, and only the historians will care, but we
care now." [48] Anderson felt that journalists could provide a degree of
participation that historians had missed.

One particularly illustrative example was NBC's set of videocas-
settes about Kennedy's administration and assassination, produced

in 1989. The blurb on the back of the tapes, entitled "The Week We Lost John F. Kennedy," went as follows:

> To commemorate the 25th anniversary of JFK's death, NBC News has opened its archives to make available "The Week We Lost John F. Kennedy" . . . perhaps the most important video document of our time. From more than 70 hours of live, on-the-air coverage, the most dramatic, crucial segments have been skillfully woven in a special production by NBC News to give you a moment-by-moment account of the Kennedy assassination and its aftermath. This is history exactly as it happened . . . and happened to you. As you saw it then.[49]

Implicit here was the notion of providing the "real" eyewitness version of events. In the next paragraph, the possibility of "owning history" was raised, when the tape was called "an extraordinary piece of history that you could not own until now." By recasting its retellings as history, NBC News made explicit an underlying aim in journalists' attempts to credential themselves as spokespersons for Kennedy's death: the aim of legitimating themselves as historians. Putting themselves forward as the event's rightful historians thus became part of perpetuating their authority for the events in Dallas.

This suggests that rather than regard history as an untouchable terrain, journalists reworked the notion of history as a semisacred space inside which journalistic chronicles had their own legitimate resting place. Larger discourses about both the increased accessibility of history and the legitimacy of gaining access to records of the record worked in their favor. They cast a positive light on journalistic attempts to access history. In such a way, journalists' involvement in the assassination story undid the notion of history as a haven where the events of Kennedy's death could eventually be properly articulated. It implied that there was something between contemporary retellings and historical record, narratives in which the meaning of the event could be negotiated not only as an interim arrangement but also as a long-term one.

In such a light, journalists also negatively regarded attempts by other retellers to call themselves historians. Oliver Stone, director of the 1991 film *JFK*, claimed to be a "cinematic historian" who wanted history to be turned back to the American people.[50] Such claims were in effect ignored by media critics of the film, perhaps because these claims infringed on their own objectives.

Journalists thus tried systematically to perpetuate themselves as alternative keepers of the historical record. They fancied themselves as a different kind of chronicler—one who was validated by presence, participation, and proximity, rather than the remote and detached objectivity advocated by traditional historians. Alongside independent critics, popular historians, memoirists, and biographers, journalists established themselves as scribes of the historical record and tried to set themselves up as its preferred chroniclers. Within larger discourses about access to history, the salience of professional memories, and the viability of accessing records, this development made sense. It set up a framework by which journalists could perpetuate their assassination tales within narratives about the structure of their own profession. Within this final frame, through which journalists legitimated themselves as authoritative spokespersons for the assassination story, the act of perpetuating their retellings showed the need for securing professional legitimation not only within journalism but beyond it as well.

The Custody of Memory

Because the assassination story remained vital and contested among so many groups of retellers, historians were seen as unable to uphold the privileged status of history in its retelling. It was no coincidence that assassination historian William Manchester complained of not being consulted in the making of Oliver Stone's 1991 movie *JFK*.[51] His work, *The Death of a President*, was seen as potentially outdated and too wedded to the nuances of the time in which it had been written. Journalists' activities—which appeared to be more open and self-reflexive—made them particularly well suited to adopt the historian's role, if not entirely, then at least in tandem with those historians and independent critics whose accounts were similarly motivated.

The attempt to uphold the media as retellers of the story thereby suggested an authority that exceeded the recognized bounds of journalism. By the very activity of perpetuation, journalists extended their authority beyond the immediate temporal frame in which the assassination had occurred, and beyond the temporal frame in which they could be expected to interpret its events. This blurring of the distinction between the journalistic and the historical modes of recordkeeping—making journalists not only responsible for contemporaneous events but also for those of the past—highlighted journalists' role in retelling the story. As time passed, and journalists continued to show reluctance about turning the events of Kennedy's death over to historians, the distinction finally became irrelevant. The media's declared interest in perpetuating certain versions of the assassination story, as well as their role in it, broke down the boundary between the two professional communities.

This in turn blurred distinctions about where the journalistic record ended and the historical record began. In his novel *Libra,* Don DeLillo relayed how the investigator of Kennedy's murder took refuge in his recordkeeping strategies. "The notes are becoming an end in themselves . . . it is premature to make a serious effort to turn these notes into coherent history. Maybe it will always be premature. Because the data keeps coming. Because new lives enter the record all the time. The past is changing as he writes." [52] Journalists' unwillingness to surrender the story to historians was rooted in concerns that they would impose closure on the tale, perhaps prematurely. The possibility of historians' involvement thus became a threat to journalists' own involvement in the story.

Journalists thus refused to turn the assassination story over to historians in part because they wanted to remain its authoritative spokespersons. As long as the story remained part of their domain, the perpetuation of their authority remained a realistic objective. By invoking history, and passing off journalistic practice as being historically motivated, journalists transformed themselves into historians.

And what kind of history did they write? Unlike historians, who tended to make sense of what other people remembered, journalists made use of their own memories, recording historical events through lived recollections. It was significant that the distinction between journalists and historians pivoted on the issue of memory, because through memory journalists assumed the role of historians. Their assumption of that role was facilitated by television technology.

The repeated images and recastings of events provided by technology allowed journalists to gain access to the record of the record in a way that made its surrender to historians less appealing. Television coverage made it easier to enter the archives of memory provided by television networks or newsmagazines than to go back to the original documents. As John Connally said in 1988:

> I don't think the time has come when history will really look at the Kennedy administration with a realistic eye. And how could we? When you see a beautiful little girl kneeling with her hand on her father's coffin, and when you see a handsome little boy standing with a military salute by his slain father, how can you feel anything but the utmost sympathy? It's a scene of pathos, of remorse, of tragedy, and that's the way we now view President Kennedy. [53]

Television interfered with historical progression by not allowing
memories to move beyond the images it repeatedly showed. In Halberstam's view, "Television had no memory, it was not interested in
the past, it erased the past, there was never time to show film clips of
past events, and so, inevitably, it speeded up the advent of the future."[54] The idea of a history frozen by images worked to the advantage of journalists.

In this way television helped journalists offer and perpetuate their
own version of historical narrative. One observer recalled how ABC
used a re-creation of the shooting of Lee Harvey Oswald as a promo-
tional trailer for a Kennedy-related mini-series. He noted that "as the
fictional clip was rebroadcast over and over again, the memories of
the real event faded away. A clone had taken its place."[55] Television
relied, in Pierre Nora's words, on "the materiality of the trace, the
immediacy of the recording, the visibility of the image."[56] It led to a
mode of historical recording that was based on archives of memory.
Becoming a "veritable history machine, spewing out a constant
stream of historical, semihistorical and pseudo-historical recrea-
tions,"[57] television helped journalists create an archive of their memories that was now referenced as history itself. It was for this reason
that discussions around Oliver Stone's movie *JFK* were so heated:
Stone, in effect, was using technology to authorize his own version of
events in a way that resembled journalists' use of television.

As long as journalists' memories remained, reporters were reluctant to yield the authority they lent. The emergence of journalists as
custodians of memory about the assassination made them into archivists of its story. Journalists did their best to build a history of the
story through memory. In short, memory became the basis of the
preferred retelling of the assassination story.

By perpetuating their assassination tales through the memory system offered by history, journalists emerged as retellers through issues
vital to the structure of the profession. They perpetuated their retellings by contextualizing archetypal journalistic tales as a vital part
of history. Drawn by the privileged status of history, they created a
record of the assassination that suggested not only the depth, perspective, and stability of interpretation of historical record, but also
the proximity, personal memories, and experience of journalistic accounts. Journalists thus personalized the history of the assassination
through their own professional codes of practice, collective memory,
and journalistic authority. They gave texture to the historical record
of Kennedy's death.

It was once said that "most historians would give a great deal to have had the chance of being actually present at some of the events they have described."[58] The proximity journalists cherished as their right to the assassination story could be assumed by no other retellers of the tale. Journalists' possession of what other retellers wanted—power, media access, visibility, authority—made their experience of covering Kennedy's death a preferred mode of retelling the assassination. As one reporter said, "Those of us who shared it will never forget."[59] In recollecting the assassination through tales that highlighted the authority of the profession, journalists made certain that journalism would not be forgotten.

TWELVE ◾ Conclusion: On the Establishment of Journalistic Authority

[handwritten annotation:] Assuming the Right to speak authoritatively = declaring one has a STANDING w/ audience

You are, among other things, what you remember, or believe you remember.[1]

This book began with somewhat amorphous and tentative thoughts on the workings of journalistic authority, by which the media assume the right to present authoritative versions of events. Journalistic authority was approached as a construct implicitly but identifiably located within the practices of American journalists.

These pages have shown that journalistic authority is neither amorphous nor tentative. It exists in narrative, where journalists maintain it through the stories they tell. By varying who tells these stories, how they tell them, and what they do or do not tell, journalists enact their authority as a narrative craft, embodied in narrative forms. These narratives are then transported into collective memory, where they are used as models for understanding the authoritative role of the journalist and journalistic community. Specific narratives signal different boundaries of appropriate journalistic practice and help clarify the boundaries of cultural authority across time and space. This is what Jürgen Habermas, Max Weber, and others called rhetorical legitimation, the ability of retellers to legitimate themselves through the stories they tell in public discourse.

Rhetorical legitimation was shown here to work in a circular fashion: Narratives beget authority, which begets memories, which beget more narratives, which beget more authority, and so on. At the heart of this circular process are journalists, who, like Hayden White's makers of historical discourse, produce a second-order fiction that attends through its craft to the needs of its chroniclers.[2]

The workings of journalistic authority were explored here through one critical incident, the assassination of John F. Kennedy. By examining how the media narratively reconstructed their role in covering Kennedy's assassination, these pages considered a range of narrative practices by which journalists upheld their own stature, credentials, and positioning as the authoritative spokespersons of the story. By contextualizing, telling, promoting, and recollecting assassination tales, journalists—especially the emerging cadre of television journalists—fashioned themselves into an authoritative interpretive community.

This does not suggest that journalistic authority exists in complete form in any given narrative or memory system. Authority exists in bits and pieces, fits and starts. It is a construct in continual tension with its creators, never becoming embodied by one practice. Parts of journalistic authority exist everywhere. But without the other parts, it exists nowhere.

The Argument, Refined

Three threads were shown to be relevant to the establishment and perpetuation of journalistic authority:

Journalistic authority emanates from context. This includes contextual factors both at the time of Kennedy's death and in the years that followed. At the time of the assassination, context included discourses about the boundaries of cultural authority and historical relevance, journalistic professionalism and the nascent medium of television news, and the ties between journalists and the Kennedy administration. In addition, covering Kennedy's death created specific circumstances that journalists used as a springboard for narratively upholding their authority. In the years that followed, larger questions about documentary process and consequent changes in the recognized forms of cultural authority also left an imprint on assassination retellings: official memory was de-authorized and professional memories, particularly those of journalists, were made relevant. In each case, collective assessments about journalism proved crucial to the eventual promotion of journalists as a preferred and authoritative presence in the assassination story.

Journalistic authority depends on collective memory. Journalistic authority derives from memory systems, or shared ways of recollecting events across time and space. Memory systems give journalists a way to connect with ready-made interpretations of their tales: individual tales stressed celebrity, organizational and institutional tales emphasized professional lore, and tales about the structure of the profession underscored the role of history. These ways of remembering consolidated the role of journalistic recollectors as cultural authorities.

Journalistic authority depends on narrative. The craft of narrative brings together the other two threads, memory and context. Through narrative, journalists linked contexts—about the sixties, television, the changing authority of official documents—with memory systems—about celebrity, professional lore, history. Narrative allowed journalists to connect discourses situated outside journalism with developments taking place within it. More important, narrative implicitly and explicitly focused on the people who generated it, the journalists.

Journalists worked these three threads together to create what I call journalistic authority. Through these threads they turned the assassination story on angles crucial to their own legitimation. Often the results bore little connection to the lingering public criticisms of many journalists' performance.

Context, Memory, Narrative, and Critical Incidents

Not all events covered by the media are central to their establishment as cultural authorities. But certain events function as critical incidents, which journalists use to display and negotiate the appropriate boundaries of their profession. During the sixties and early seventies, for example, a number of critical events embodied distinctive "sixties perceptions" about everyday life: its fusion with history and historical relevance, shifting boundaries of cultural authority, growing demands on professionalism, and a spirit of self-reflexivity. Journalists' efforts to define the appropriate boundaries of their profession prompted them to use narratives about these events to air relevant concerns. Watergate, for example, the scandal that journalists uncovered, displayed the appropriate boundaries of investigative journalism. Vietnam, the war that television brought into American homes, gave rise to questions about the responsibilities and roles of journalists in conducting wartime coverage. Space exploration televisually connected American audiences with new frontiers. Like such events as the Civil War in the nineteenth century or the Teapot Dome scandal in the earlier twentieth, each of these critical incidents highlighted issues that were central to journalism at the time of its unfolding, issues that were refracted as the event was retold.

By illuminating relevant rules and conventions about journalistic practice and authority, critical incidents give the media alternative ways in which to discuss, challenge, and negotiate boundaries of appropriate journalistic practice. This in turn allows journalists to set up collective notions about journalistic practice and thereby uphold themselves as an authoritative interpretive community.

In such a light, narratives about the Kennedy assassination constitute one stage among many on which journalists evaluate, challenge, and negotiate consensual notions about what it means to be a reporter. Journalists used the assassination story to address changing rules of their profession, their approaches to new technologies of news gathering, their role in determining historical record, and finally the importance of their own memories in establishing and perpetuating their role as cultural authorities. In retelling assassination tales journalists thus attended to several agendas, many of which had little to do with the events of Kennedy's death.

The Craft of Journalistic Authority

The establishment and perpetuation of journalists as authoritative spokespersons for the assassination story was no small feat. As this book has shown, "The process of adjusting the fit [between what actually happened and received narratives about the past] is an ongoing one, subject to continual debate and exchanges in which memory and history may play shifting, alternately more or less contentious roles in setting the record straight."[3] The tale's original recasting as a story of professional triumph rather than mishap was only the first order of reconstructive work. Journalists' reconstruction of their presence, participation, and memories required careful attention over the decades following Kennedy's death. The transformations of journalists' narratives and memories in accordance with larger discourses about cultural authority were systematic, constant, and inventive. Problematic dimensions of the original coverage of Kennedy's death were erased as larger collective questions about professionalism, technology, and authority came into play. Narrative retellings of the assassination thus took place in the face of other developments that assisted journalists in their establishment as cultural authorities.

Journalistic authority was achieved through both the form and content of journalists' narratives. Form refers to the narrative practices that journalists used; content, to the types of stories those practices embodied. Form and content in turn displayed features that were internal (within the narrative itself) and external (existing beyond the narrative). Portrayed graphically, the craft of journalistic authority might resemble the figure opposite.

In their tales, journalists systematically and strategically incorporated references to their authoritative presence across all four domains. In attending to form, they used narrative strategies of synecdoche, omission, and personalization to adjust their tales internally in a way that accommodated their presence. Externally, they used strategies of commemoration and recycling to gain stature. Similarly, journalists manipulated issues of internal content in stories about being the first, the best, and the only, at the same time as they manipulated issues of external content to address themes about journalistic professionalism, the impact of television technology, the validity of official documents, and the importance of memory. Journalists' ability to uphold their authoritative presence in both internal and external dimensions of the form and content of their narratives left little doubt about their positioning as preferred spokespersons.

Journalists further maintained their authoritative presence as their tales were disseminated across time and space. Taking on the roles of eyewitness, representative, investigator, and interpreter ensured that, regardless of their own proximity to the events of the assassination tale, journalists were able to speak authoritatively about it. The appeal to memory systems also helped fasten journalists in authoritative roles. They used tales of celebrity to uphold the stature of individual journalists, tales of professional lore to promote the stature of news organizations and institutions, and tales about the role of journalism in serving as a historical chronicle of the nation's impulses to promote the structure of the profession. In each case, memory was codified, then fed back to its codifiers, who codified it yet again. Journalists thereby perpetuated a tightly knit cycle of self-legitimation through narrative. This suggests the central role of discourse in determining the community's boundaries.

	FORM (Practices of)	CONTENT (Stories about)
Internal to each narrative	synecdoche omission personalization	being the first being the best being the only
External to each narrative	commemoration recycling	journalistic professionalism television technology validity of official documents professional memory

Technology, Professionalism, and Memory

Discourse about the Kennedy assassination was refracted through lenses of journalistic professionalism and technology. Technology helped the media classify improvisational activities as professional, at the same time as it gave reporters a way to establish custody over memories. Mastering the technology became almost as important as mastering the events of the coverage, linking cultural authority with the successful use of technology.

In retelling the assassination, journalists referenced three functions of technology: transmission (conveying information), documentation (providing new means for testing evidence), and storage (preserving assassination tales so that they could be retold). To establish their mastery over the tales they told, journalists at times reordered these technological functions. For example, Walter Cronkite's use of new technologies—imaging processes with which he reexamined assassination documents—exemplified his creative use of technology on a "Nova" segment. This tactic prevented assassination tales from being classified as tales about faceless, unmanned "great machines." Journalists turned tales of unpeopled technologies into stories about how individuals strategically used technology to accomplish professional and social aims in new and improvised ways.[4] Similarly, journalists' reworking of the assassination story into a tale about the rise of television was a testament to their persistent efforts to remain active players within it.

This was true of the retellings of other events too. Journalists drew upon their mastery of satellite-fed technology to tell the story of the 1991 war in the Persian Gulf.[5] The story of the Vietnam War focused on the technological devices that helped the media record graphic dimensions of the war and its effects. It is no coincidence that media critic Michael Arlen coined the term "the living-room war" for the Vietnam experience, thereby defining it through its technology of transmission.[6] Journalists' tales of covering these stories were thus largely determined by their relationship to technology.

Tales of technological mastery are therefore crucial for revealing journalists as willing and able to manipulate the technology at hand in the name of professionalism. While certain technologies gave rise to more plausible stories than others, embedded within each story of technology is a journalist who makes it work. Technology also enhanced the media's capacity for storytelling not only at the time of the event but later too. Over time, many tales of technological mastery helped journalists create archives of memory, making the use of such archives necessary for audiences and other retellers to gain access to the memory. As Natalie Zemon Davis and Randolph Starn have suggested, "Whenever memory is invoked, we should be asking ourselves: by whom, where, in what context and about what."[7]

Thus we have a discourse not only about Kennedy's death but also about the technologies that have transmitted and stored collective memories about his death. Journalism becomes a primary archive or repository of collective memories, many of which are also about journalists themselves.[8] The ease with which retellers can gain access to the memory archives created by journalists and news organizations has turned these archives into a mode of documentation preferred over the original documents. As Halbwachs maintained, "The reality of the past is no longer in the past."[9] Rather, it is in a present narrated and largely controlled by the American media.

Within these developments, the media emerge as the archivists of memories about the events whose stories they tell. Public memory is turned into what Mary Douglas called "the storage system for the social order."[10] As custodians of such a storage system, journalists foster a tightly constructed view of their activities that turns away competitive presences. In other words, by linking issues of professionalism and technology through collective memory, journalists have established themselves as cultural authorities for retelling not only the story of John F. Kennedy's death, but also the stories of a host of other public events, such as the Civil War, Watergate, and the massacre in Tiananmen Square.

The Shape of Journalistic Community

What kind of journalistic community is implied by assassination retellings? Part of the answer lies in those sectors of the community that have been filtered *out* of retellings. Gone are most radio journalists, who played a part in the original coverage of Kennedy's death. Gone too are many local reporters who assisted their national counterparts in covering the story. Gone are those less renowned reporters who are no longer around to tell their tales. The journalists who remain are national reporters, usually employed by television. More important, the journalists who remain continue to have access to the media and to possess the kind of organizational and institutional support necessary for perpetuating their tales. The journalistic community is thus to a large degree shaped by access, technology and medium, individual stature, and position within a news organization. It accedes to the powerful and vocal members among its constituents, and it tells stories in such a vein. Well-known, nationally employed (television) journalists are put forward as the vanguard and prototype of the journalistic community.

This is borne out too by the memory systems through which the media have perpetuated their retellings. In tales that have emphasized the individual journalist, the organization and institution, and the structure of the profession, reporters have developed parallel

categories of who is "allowed" in and who is shunted aside. The retellings that received the most play over time were those that attended
to all three dimensions. Tales about Dan Rather, for example, concerned not only his career (the level of the individual journalist) but
also his news organization and the status of television news (the or-
ganizational/institutional level) and the ability of journalism to retell
public events (the level of the structure of the profession). On the
other hand, tales that addressed only the level of the individual journalist, such as stories about the investigative reporting of local Texan
reporter Penn Jones, may have died out because they were not supported on the level of the organization or institution. The popular
emphasis on differences between press and television reporters or on
different reportorial roles therefore may not be as relevant here as the
relationship between the individual, the organization/institution, and
the structure of the profession. Journalists appear to structure their
discourse along such dimensions to address what they see as relevant
to them as an authoritative interpretive community.

Patterns of crossbreeding support this point. In retellings, journalists stressed how they regularly crossed lines between news organization, and journalistic function. Journalists wrote books and
appeared on talk shows, served as anchorpersons instead of reporters, and acted as columnists rather than on-the-spot chroniclers. In
this effort, journalists ignored commonly held boundaries about
reportorial tasks and involved themselves independent of predetermined tasks, definitional roles, or formal demarcations. Distinctions
between generalists and specialists, or anchorpersons and print columnists, emerged as secondary to the consolidation of journalists as
one interpretive community that favored the powerful and vocal. This
does not imply that a columnist functioned with the same authority
as an anchorperson or beat reporter. But that distinction emerged in
journalists' tales as secondary to what they felt they shared as a
group.

All of this harks back to the role of discourse in serving a cultural,
or ritual, function for journalists. Discourse provides a locus where
journalists have been able to come together as a community, but not
necessarily in accordance with formalized professional cues. While
not the only event to do so, the assassination tale has given journalists a way to articulate and negotiate the shifting boundaries of their
community. Discourse has made it possible to address problems and
issues of concern to members of the profession. There is reason to
assume that a similar pattern exists for other kinds of spokespeople
in other kinds of discourse. It is thus in the interfaces between social

groups that the significance of cultural authority may ultimately rest.

Implicit in the crafting of journalistic authority are questions about the acquiescence of the American public to the power of the media. Journalistic authority can thrive only with a relatively uncritical and inattentive public. The ability of the media to adjust stories to agendas having little to do with the effective relay of information depends on audiences that pay little heed, protesting only when such adjustments violate or contradict their own experience. Yet most public events preclude the primary audience experience of them. The lack of a mechanism for encouraging and facilitating audience decoding of media narratives thus helps to consolidate journalistic authority. In the case of assassination retellings, in many ways this factor helped establish journalistic authority despite lingering questions about the efficacy of journalistic performance, both at the time of Kennedy's death and in the years that followed.

Acts of Transmission, Narratives of Solidarity: The Role of Discourse in Shaping Community

The discussion in these pages has established that journalists use narrative to maintain their position and stature as an authoritative interpretive community. This notion comprises two points: Journalists function as an interpretive community that authenticates itself through its narratives, and authority has cultural dimensions designed to consolidate journalists into a cohesive group. Both points suggest how narrators might use narrative to establish collective understandings of themselves as cultural authorities. Authority not only helps narrators consolidate themselves into an independent interpretive community, but also it helps them remember events in a way that enhances their collective dignity as professionals.[11]

Was the tale of "covering the body" of John F. Kennedy a unique event for American journalists? On one level, it appears to have been. Its extreme and unpredictable nature forced reporters to employ improvisational and instinctual behavior to reassert their control. Yet beyond actual coverage, patterns of retelling the event suggest that it had ordinary, recognizable, patterned elements. Journalists' ability to create narrative patterns shaped the assassination into a recognizable news tale, allowing them to reassert through narrative the control they had lost in coverage.

The employment of narrative to make sense of the one type of incident that has been least explained by media researchers—what Gaye Tuchman called "what a story"[12]—suggests that journalists have developed their own ways to cope with insufficiently developed codes of practice and knowledge. The journalistic community is engaged in constant interpretive activity about its standards of action. When formalized standards of practice fail to function as a blueprint for such action, certain events become critical incidents for journalism professionals.

This highlights the communal and cultural dimensions of journalistic retellings. Journalists use their narratives to address dimensions of their own activity that have been overlooked by formal socializing agents. Discourse about critical incidents allows journalists to air professional concerns raised by certain events. Their constitution as an interpretive group is thus bolstered through discursive practice. Narrative gives journalists stages upon which to rethink the hows and whys of the profession at various points in time and space, according to their own agendas and priorities.

Journalists are better equipped than others to offer a "preferred" version of events because they themselves perpetuate the notion that their version of reality is a preferred one. By codifying their versions in repetitive and systematized mediated narratives, journalists place themselves ahead of other potential retellers, narratively attending to critical events in ways that uphold their authority. This was particularly crucial in retelling the Kennedy assassination, where questions lingered about the media's performance.

This is not to suggest that the transmission of information is irrelevant to the larger picture of establishing cultural authority. The decoding of public events by audiences in particular ways is what lets journalists' authority flourish. But the transmission of information often becomes secondary to the use of that same information for the group that collected it. The extent to which the realization and articulation of community have been critically embedded within the routinized relay of news narrative highlights how it is possible to address aims irrelevant to the efficacy of transmission.

This embedding of "narratives of solidarity" within "acts of transmission" reveals the real workings of cultural authority in discourse. Through narrative, retellers set up an extensive self-referential discourse through which they address, air, challenge, negotiate, and alter the parameters of their standards of action. Authority becomes a marker of collective practice, delineating for other members of the group what is appropriate and preferred.

This suggests a view of authority as a construct anchored within community. Authority generates "a self portrait that unfolds through time . . . and allows the group to recognize itself through the total succession of images" it generates.[13] Authority thus plays a central part in authorizing acts of transmission and also in legitimating narratives of solidarity. It allows collectives of retellers to uphold themselves as viable, authoritative, interpretive groups.

On Cultural Authority, Memory, and Community

This study has suggested that cultural authority emerges through a circular system of practices that codify knowledge across time and space. Such a view, welding the perspectives of Durkheim, Giddens, and Halbwachs, has been examined through one practice—that of narrative. This analysis suggests that "the function of narrativity in the production of the historical text"[14] constitutes a viable and effective way for narrators to position and uphold themselves as authorities in culture.

Journalists are one group among possibly many others who use narrative to effect rhetorical legitimation. These pages have shown how they use rhetorical legitimation to address larger issues about their own authority. Such a process is made possible not only by the internal adjustments within every tale of critical incidents, but by the positing of adjustment as a legitimate mode of constructing reality. In other words, rhetorical legitimation underscores basic assumptions about the latitude allowed retellers in all kinds of public discourse.

Particularly in the workings of public discourse, the establishment and perpetuation of authority are tied in with media practices. This book has shown how authority results from an unequal concentration of power among those with media access. Media provide certain retellers with effective ways to display their authority, both to themselves and to others. While journalists are best able to use the media in order to recycle collective codes of knowledge about what makes them an authoritative interpretive community, often their codes do not mirror their experience of events. This makes a consideration of rhetorical legitimation particularly significant. That significance is enchanced because rhetorical legitimation is also used by other groups—such as politicians, academics, and the clergy—who seek to uphold their own authority.

Clifford Geertz tied knowledge to situations of practice, saying that "if you want to understand what a science is, you should look at what the practitioners of it do."[15] Geertz's comment emphasizes the importance of practice in determining the boundaries of cultural authority. This study's emphasis on the people behind what has been termed the "assassination mythology" suggests that an extensive network of strategic practices fastens that mythology in place.[16] In making use of the assassination tale, people not only give life to the story; they also give life to their own authority to act as spokespersons. More important, they affirm their authority for new generations of onlookers, who will adopt the versions of the tales they tell and accept the appropriations of journalistic practice and authority that their tales imply.

While the construct of professionalism remains important for examining the American journalistic community, this study has suggested that journalists also function as an interpretive community. They share features with other communities of potential retellers, with historians, politicians, and ordinary private citizens—a fact that raises questions about the workings of cultural authority in all kinds of public discourse. What are the mechanisms by which different retellers legitimate themselves through their stories? Why do certain individuals and groups become legitimated over others as spokespersons for events? What are the strategic practices by which they codify knowledge and use it to realize collective gains? And, finally, why does the public cede to retellers the authority they need to construct reality? This study suggests that retellers of all sorts act to legitimate themselves as authoritative interpretive communities, and that they use other groups to do so. In a sense, then, authority is realized by mechanisms for recycling knowledge not only across members of one community but across many communities, not least of all the public.

Journalists' attempts at rhetorical legitimation have generated their own constitutive narratives about American journalism, minimizing what is problematic and emphasizing what is admirable. Retelling the incidents that are critical to the American journalistic community offers an exemplary case of the circular codification of knowledge, by which retellers strategically authenticate themselves as cultural authorities. Discourse, therefore, not only affects group consolidation by achieving community and commonality, it also guides and directs people into their own future. This, then, is how authority acts as a source of codified knowledge, and how the tale of the assassination of America's thirty-fifth president gave rise to one of the major constitutive narratives of American journalism.

Epilogue: Beyond Journalistic Authority to the Shaping of Collective Memory

As this book was being shaped into galleys, the retellings of John F. Kennedy's assassination took a new twist. In December of 1991, Hollywood director Oliver Stone's film *JFK* was released to cinemas across the nation. Over the next few months, his version of the assassination story gave rise to extensive public discussions that made the workings of cultural authority an explicit topic of popular discourse and popular culture. This chapter explores how the events of late 1991 and early 1992 provide additional evidence about the establishment of cultural authority in the assassination tale, thereby both supporting and extending the central arguments of this book.

The early nineties displayed many of the patterns of assassination retelling exhibited in earlier years. The public distrust of government grew and, in part due to scandals like Irangate, the October Surprise, and the BCCI affair, so did belief in the possibility of conspiracy activities among high government officials. The continuing contest for authority now was complicated by energetic and seemingly credible efforts from retellers in popular culture. This gave rise both to renewed questions about who was authorized to tell the story of Kennedy's death, and to new questions about the role of popular culture as an appropriate and legitimate domain of telling. Both sets of questions affected the ability of the media to continue asserting their role as preferred spokespeople for the assassination tale.

The Renewed Contest for Authorization

This book has argued that the lack of closure surrounding the assassination tale gave rise to an ongoing contest for authorization, by which different groups attempted to promote their version of what happened in Dallas in order to promote themselves. The book addressed particularly the legitimation of American journalists as authoritative spokespersons for the assassination story, a status made possible by their routinized media access and institutional support. Journalists' efforts were accompanied by those of the independent critics, who, despite being marginalized by officials and the mainstream media, continued to address the story within circumscribed and limited channels, and by those of the historians, who incorporated bits of the assassination tale as part of the historical record. Each of these groups was engaged in a contest with the others for the authority to tell the story of what had happened.

By late 1991, however, this contest needed to accommodate the increasingly central activities of another party—the fictionalizers. Following the lead set years earlier by novelists like Loren Singer and Don DeLillo, and by films like *Executive Action* and *The Parallax View*, Oliver Stone used the cinematic apparatus to challenge existing assassination accounts. His penchant for tackling outstanding issues in popular history had been displayed in his earlier films, including *Platoon, Born on the Fourth of July,* and *The Doors.*

Yet Stone was a curious addition to the contest. Unlike other fictionalizers, he had stature, prestige, media interest and access, finances, proven celebrity talent—in short, many of the institutional trappings upon which journalists had long built their preferred presence in the tale. Furthermore, in using accounts by the independent critics to suggest conspiracy involvement, Stone's filmmaking effort gave institutional support to a generally marginalized group of retellers, bringing their claim straight into cinemas across America.[1] Stone went even further to claim that he was acting as historian in retelling the story of Kennedy's death.[2] By obscuring the boundaries across which the different groups of retellers—the journalists, independent critics, and historians—had long competed, Stone equally challenged the authoritative presence of each.

Retellers whose longstanding claims to the story did not fit Stone's version were bothered by the unexpected presence of a filmmaker in their midst. Predictably, their concern quickly became a featured topic of journals, newspapers, and television talk shows. Discussions focused on the content of Stone's film, which journalists criticized while it was still being edited. *Washington Post* correspondent George Lardner, Jr., played an instrumental part in fueling the debate when he charged in May of 1991 that Stone was merely "chasing fiction."[3] Other writers called the film an "attempt to rewrite history," a "strange, widely disputed take on the assassination," and "Dallas in Wonderland," all before it left the editing table.[4] In response, some independent critics and a few journalists protested what they saw as precensorship, although still others, anxious to shed light on their own views, decried Stone's perspective.[5]

These patterns persisted once the movie opened. Historian Arthur Schlesinger, Jr. argued that, despite Stone's journey into fantasy, "history will survive,"[6] as did assassination historian William Manchester, author of *Death of a President*. Manchester both complained that no one working on the film had consulted him and asserted that "there was no evidence whatever" of a conspiracy.[7] Anthony Lewis of the *New York Times* reviewed each of Stone's claims and declared that "facts will dispel Oliver Stone's fantasy."[8] *Newsweek* labeled the film "twisted history,"[9] and its cover promised readers that they would understand "Why Oliver Stone's New Movie Can't Be Trusted."

Competing for Memory: Stone, Wicker, and Rather

Journalists who had covered Kennedy's death were quick to assail Stone. In a lengthy piece in the *New York Times,* Tom Wicker derailed the theory that Stone propounded.[10] "It is a measure of Mr. Stone's heavily weighted storytelling," Wicker said, "that he gives [us] only a fleeting glimpse" of an NBC documentary which had sharply criticized New Orleans District Attorney Jim Garrison, the hero of Stone's film, during the 1960s. He added that the film treats "matters that are highly speculative as fact and truth, in effect rewriting history."[11] "Mr. Stone insists on one true faith about November 22, 1963," he said, "as though only he and Mr. Garrison could discern the truth, among the many theories of what happened that terrible day. Moreover, he implies that anyone who doesn't share his one true faith is either an active part of a cover-up or passively acquiescent in it."[12] Wicker carefully pointed out both *JFK*'s factual inaccuracies and his own statements and activities that had either supported or disconfirmed the evidence as Stone presented it. Given the linkage of his professional identity with the assassination story—the byline specifically said that he "had covered the assassination of John F. Kennedy for the newspaper"—these statements relayed the impression that Wicker had not abandoned the topic but had simply found no new evidence worth considering.

CBS's Dan Rather also invested considerable efforts in addressing *JFK* and Oliver Stone. In February of 1992 Rather devoted a special program of "48 Hours" to an investigation of Kennedy's death, where he paid special attention to the controversy surrounding Stone's movie.[13] Breaking from its usual format of covering activities within a 48-hour time frame, the program took up the topic in part "because of the intense personal interest of Mr. Rather. He has been covering the Kennedy assassination since November 22, 1963, when he reported the news that the President was dead."[14] In prescreening publicity, Rather asserted his own expertise over that of Stone. "Long after Oliver Stone has gone onto his next movie and his next movie," he said, "and long after a lot of people who have been writing about this now have stopped, I'm going to keep coming on this one."[15] Another preview of the show told readers that Rather had "witnessed the awful day in Dallas. And tonight in a special '48 Hours,' the CBS newsanchor re-examines the assassination. But please—don't equate him with Oliver Stone."[16] The "48 Hours" producer said that for Rather, the Kennedy assassination was a "journalistic passion. Dan's been involved with this story from the beginning. He's a bona fide expert."[17]

Rather concentrated on displaying his expertise from the first few moments of the show. In his introductory remarks, he said that "an act that took only a few seconds has been dissected by thousands of investigators, scholars, journalists, amateur sleuths and even Hollywood. . . . Tonight, in this special '48 Hours,' we build on more than 28 years of reporting on the Kennedy assassination, including three separate investigations by CBS News."[18] Rather departed from usual practice to interview Stone himself for the program. Similar self-credentialing framed his concluding remarks, where the reporter said that "We do know a lot and there is much to support the Warren Commission's conclusions, but unanswered questions also abound. Not all of the conspiracy theories are ridiculous. . . . They explain the inexplicable, neatly tie up the loose ends, but a reporter should not, cannot find refuge there. Facts, hard evidence are the journalist's guide."[19] Rather thus carefully distinguished between journalists, who respected hard facts, and other retellers, who seemingly were taken in by conspiracy theories that lacked such facts.

In one sequence, Rather asked Stone why he faulted the media. The interchange went as follows:

> RATHER: I don't understand why you include the press as either conspirators or accomplices to the conspiracy.
> STONE: Dan, when the House Report came out implying that there was a probable conspiracy in the murder of both Kennedy and King, why weren't you running around trying to dig into the case again? I didn't see you, you know, rush out there and look at some of

these three dozen discrepancies that we present in our movie.

RATHER: It's on the record, 1964, late 1960s, 1975, again in the late 1970s and again the '80s. The fact that we could not come to answers, that we didn't find solutions— you seem to be—take as proof positive that somehow— that we have knowingly or unknowingly been part of the conspiracy.[20]

By suggesting that Rather had not sufficiently investigated the story, Stone threatened Rather's integrity as a professional journalist. Rather's outline of his earlier investigations mirrored previous efforts to set his career trajectory and professional image firmly within the context of the assassination.

Other reporters who had been present at Kennedy's death made similar attempts to credential their versions over Stone's. One television reporter, who "flew to Dallas just hours after President Kennedy was assassinated" to work on the assassination story, "[discounted] assassination theories." Although he had not seen *JFK*, the reporter nonetheless told the public that Stone's theory was "off the wall."[21]

Certain news organizations examined the movie from within larger agendas. Thoughtful cover articles in *Life, Esquire,* and *Details* considered the movie's attempt to renew outstanding assassination-related questions.[22] ABC's "Nightline" featured two programs on the issues surrounding the movie.[23] The gay media faulted *JFK* for being homophobic, while one former official decried it for being "obscene in the sense of paranoia."[24] As with earlier attempts to retell the assassination story, discussions of Stone's film began to appear on tabloid television and various talk shows.[25]

All of this discourse, seemingly about the content of the film, sidestepped what appeared to be the real issue at hand: cultural authority. Debate over *JFK*, said one observer, failed to differentiate between "Stone's theory . . . [and] his right to have his theory."[26] At the root of discussions about the film was the question of whether Stone possessed sufficient credentials to set forth a view of the assassination. Stone's film was seen as problematic not only because of its content, but also because it was framed as an attempt to generate discussion about issues on which many sectors of the public had long been silent. "Whether you accept my conclusion is not the point," he said. "We want people to examine this."[27] Because the film was suggested as a way to open rather than close dialogue, offered a nonmainstream account of what had happened, and derived from a filmmaker, its very positioning as a potentially authoritative account challenged the authority of other retellers, regardless of the film's message.

JFK undermined the authority of nearly everyone who had been associated with the assassination story—the independent critics, the historians, and, most notably, the mainstream journalists. As talk show host Larry King said, "Film critics are raving. Historians are raving mad. Way before this movie was done, the establishment press was going after Stone for wrapping his theory in the trappings of truth. The fear: Perhaps Stone's version may be more convincing to some than the Warren Commission's."[28] Critic Robert Groden predicted that "the movie will raise public consciousness. People who can't take the time to read [books] will be able to see the movie, and in three hours they'll be able to see what the issues are."[29] Robert Sam Anson wondered whether reporters could take up the investigative challenge posed by the story.[30] For one of the few times in the history of the assassination, retellers were publicly debating the parameters of their own cultural authority in its retelling.

On the Importance of Credentialing

Credentialing activity thus became positioned at the core of discussions about *JFK*. Independent critics reduced George Lardner, Jr., the reporter who had set the debate in motion, to having an "axe to grind," due either to his assumed anti-Garrison bias or his reported intelligence contacts in Washington;[31] Reporters dismissed Garrison as obsessed with his own publicity;[32] Stone was considered too intent on credentialing himself as a historian.[33] No one was assumed capable of having an untainted interest in the film or the story behind it.

This pattern was furthered somewhat in January of 1992, when Stone, whose movie had been seen by nearly 50 million viewers and would garner him a Golden Globe award for best director and two Academy Awards,[34] appeared before the National Press Club. His address, broadcast live by C-Span, gave him a stage on which to call for the release of declassified documents and to accuse the media, the government, and the historians of zealously holding onto essentially faulty versions of events.[35] In so doing, he brought the issue of credentialing to the forefront of attempts to tell the tale, turning discourse about the movie from criticism about his specific theory to discussions of his right to put that theory forward. In attempting to legitimate his own authoritative presence in the tale's retelling, it was inevitable that he encroach on the activities of other retellers.

Existing perspectives on the assassination, he said, were a "myth that has sustained a generation of journalists and historians who have refused to examine it, who have refused to question it, and above all who close ranks to criticize and vilify those who do."[36] When, he asked, "in the last twenty years, have we seen serious research from Tom Wicker, Dan Rather, Anthony Lewis?" For them, one must not disturb "this settled version of history . . . lest one call down the venom of leading journalists from around the country." Anger over his film thus came from "older journalists [on the Right and Left], political journalists. . . . Newsmen's objectivity is in question here."[37] Stone saw the media criticism as being both institutionally derived and supported, as was made evident in the following exchange on "Larry King Live":

> KING: Why do you think the Wickers, the Rathers, the
> Gerald Fords in an op-ed piece in a newspaper—in the
> *Washington Post*—why do you think they're so mad?
> STONE: Well, they're the official priesthood. They have a
> stake in their version of reality. Here I am—a film-
> maker, an artist—coming onto their territory and I
> think that they resent that.
> KING: Are you surprised at it?
> STONE: I think they blew it from day one.[38]

Interestingly, the reporters so labeled by Stone answered the film-maker by suggesting that he followed a different standard of action. In Rather's view, artists "have a different value system than journalists: Journalists try to stick to the facts and bear witness."[39] Such a comment again positioned filmmakers as fictionalizers, making them less credible spokespeople for the tale than journalists. It also reinforced, not coincidentally, the preferred position of journalists.

Yet the greater challenge for journalists came from Stone's attempt to set forth a vision of himself as historian: "We can move forward . . . and [show] that people can be trusted with their own history," he said.[40] "If you read American history books, it's disgusting . . . two paragraphs . . . I think that kids have a right to know a little more about their history."[41] Stone had long presented himself as "one who does not believe in official history."[42] In an earlier interview in *American Film* he had even allowed that he preferred to examine history that the larger culture ignored or glossed over.[43]

It was here that his claims became most problematic, for they suggested that he was setting forth not just fiction but some version of historical truth. As Tom Wicker complained, "This movie . . . claims truth for itself. And among the many Americans likely to see it, par-

ticularly those who never accepted the Warren Commission's theory
of a single assassin, even more particularly those too young to remember November 22, 1963, 'JFK' is all too likely to be taken as the
final, unquestioned explanation."[44] In a column titled "The Problem
With 'JFK' Is Facts," Ellen Goodman lamented "the sense that Stone
has a claim on 'exclusive rights' to JFK's death."[45] Stone's comments
about assuming a historical role in the tale's retelling in effect challenged journalists on two fronts—not only for having insufficiently
investigated Kennedy's death, but also for having made their own
claims to the historical role. In upholding himself as historian, Stone
made the same general claim to cultural authority that journalists had
been making for nearly thirty years.

The threat posed by Stone to journalistic authority increased as discourse around *JFK* appeared to have a considerable effect in official
and semiofficial quarters. Although former Commission lawyer Arlen
Specter maintained that the film mangled the facts,[46] there were hints,
however muted, of interest and support. The real legacy of "nearly
three decades of revisionist Kennedy-assassination investigation,"
said one observer, was "a darker, more complex, less innocent vision
of America."[47] In line with this view, members of the Kennedy family
called to open the remaining assassination files, as did former FBI and
CIA director William Webster and a panel of the Warren Commission
lawyers.[48] Louis Stokes, who had chaired the House Select Committee, led lawmakers in both houses of Congress to support the files'
release.[49] A *New York Times* editorial also called for their declassifi-
cation.[50] Such interest was viewed favorably by many retellers. As
journalist Robert Sam Anson commented, "it shouldn't be up to the
buffs to spend their entire lives, and God bless them for doing this
kind of stuff. The federal government should be investigating this
crime, and the press, of which I am a member, should be going at
this hammer and tong."[51]

The discussions about *JFK* also cast a positive light on the independent critics, with whom Stone was grouped and to whom he referred
as "the research community."[52] The *New York Times Book Review* published a three-page "readers' guide" to conspiracy literature.[53] One article in *Time* magazine discussed the subculture of "the band of mostly
self-appointed experts who zealously pursue theories of a wider
plot."[54] At a major national conference of independent critics, conference organizers circulated a questionnaire that queried participants
about their views on *JFK*.[55] Issues that were formerly marginalized
as the interests of kooks or crackpots became generalized and more
mainstream. As one observer commented, "whatever else the Ken-

nedy assassination buffs have accomplished, they have made their favorite subject into the nation's No. 1 question about its history."[56]

The public appeared to take an active part in the discussions. The National Archives, where much of the evidence concerning Kennedy's death was located, reported a surge in public requests to inspect evidence.[57] The readers' letters in much of the national media appeared to favor Stone's film more strongly than did most professional journalists.[58] In one week late in January of 1992, the *New York Times*'s best-seller lists included four assassination-related titles.[59] By February an NBC poll reported that a full fifty-one percent of the American public believed, as the movie had set forth, that the CIA was responsible for Kennedy's death. Only six percent believed the Warren Commission.[60]

All of this suggested that the authorization of additional retellers of the story was embedded within discussions of Stone's movie. At the heart of discourse about the film were fundamental questions about the right to challenge orthodoxy, official record, and marginalization. Discussions had as much to do with Stone's presumption that he was sufficiently authoritative to make a movie on the subject as with the actual version of events he set forth.

For journalists to support Stone's presence in the tale therefore would have undercut their own authority. Yet because he enjoyed access to channels of media access and institutional support, Stone was able to challenge them on many of their own terms. By giving the formerly marginalized independent critics an institutionally supported voice, he invited evaluation of journalistic authority's validity in the assassination story, in some of the same channels that the media had used to celebrate themselves.

Thus, the battle for authorization that *JFK* faced extended a contest that had been ongoing since Kennedy's death. As this book has shown, all parties to that contest held fast to their own accounts and attempted to delegitimate and marginalize others. Oliver Stone, and the making of *JFK*, were no exception. Yet in directly addressing the workings of cultural authority, Stone revealed many of the ways by which the media had authenticated themselves in the assassination story's retelling.

The Authority of Popular Culture

In making the assassination a topic of popular discourse, Stone's movie also made explicit a second issue—the degree of authority that the American public was willing to cede to popular culture in retelling the American public was willing to cede to popular culture in retelling the story of Kennedy's death. The movie differed from the earlier cultural productions associated with the assassination story, like *Executive Action*, *The Parallax View*, or even *Taxi Driver*, which had used some aspect of Kennedy's death to embellish dissimilar plot lines. *JFK* was the first major cinematic treatment of the assassination story in docudrama form, operating with a $40 million budget and employing Hollywood stars in both major and minor roles.[61]

Other domains of popular culture rallied around Stone's efforts. Book publishers brought out old titles of assassination-related literature, which began to occupy their own corners in some mainstream-bookstores.[62] Trading cards displayed the facts and figures of the conspiracy theories. Interviews with other independent critics ran in newspapers and on television shows.[63] A five-part series on the "Today Show" about the alternative conspiracy theories culminated in a viewer survey of favorite theories.[64] A movie about Oswald, *Libra*, began filming in early 1992, while another film, *Ruby*, opened in March of 1992 with publicity that declared its protagonist to be "The Man Who Shot the Man Who Shot JFK." Through this variety of popular cultural forms, the public gained increased access to the assassination story in all its complexities, nuances, and unresolved dimensions.

Other retellers, bothered by the intrusion of popular culture, focused their criticisms on Stone's "movie version of history" and its fictionalization of real-life events.[65] As Dan Rather asked rhetorically on the "CBS Evening News," "What happens when Hollywood mixes facts, half-baked theories, and sheer fiction into a big budget film and then tries to sell it as, quote, 'truth' and 'history'?"[66] In an article that recounted the "historical realities that Stone stretches and caricatures in *JFK* to support his own theories," one journalist said that Stone's movie, "historically considered, is in fact sensationalist claptrap."[67] That article was tellingly titled, "With 'JFK,' Filmmaker Oliver Stone Shows He Isn't Up to the Job of Historian." *Newsweek* complained that *JFK* was propaganda, while former President Gerald Ford called it "commercial fantasy."[68]

Much criticism centered on what was seen as Stone's inappropriate use of the visual image. Admitting that he "wanted to blur the distinction between what's real and what's recreated,"[69] Stone positioned real film sequences alongside fictionalized ones, thereby violating viewer expectations as to what constituted the "real." There were "real-life film clips, grainy reenactments, black-and-white imitations, dramatizations. Every trick in the bag of 'reality-based' programming [was] employed."[70] Stone used "trick photography and spurious evidence" to set forth controversial assumptions about real-life events.[71]

Numerous criticisms of the movie complained that it failed to represent itself as fiction. "Is Hollywood remaking history?" asked one observer.[72] Sam Donaldson said that "critics are outraged that 'JFK' portrays itself as a work of history rather than fiction."[73] Ted Koppel opened one edition of "Nightline" with the following scenario:

> If I were to say on the broadcast tonight that the assassination of President Kennedy was the product of the conspiracy involving officers of the CIA, the FBI, high-ranking members of the Pentagon and former vice president Lyndon Baines Johnson, you would have every right to say, "Prove it. Substantiate it. Document it. Or at the very least, quote your sources." There are, in other words, certain ground rules that even journalists are expected to observe. Indeed, if Oliver Stone, the filmmaker, had produced a documentary rather than a feature film, he would have been expected to observe a similar discipline. Instead he produced a film in which he simply made up what he couldn't prove or substantiate. In film-making, that is called "artistic license." In statecraft it's called "propaganda." Either way, it carries a lot of impact.[74]

Filmmakers and artists, answered Stone, had "a right, and, possibly, even an obligation, to step in and reinterpret . . . events."[75] But many observers raised questions about the appropriateness of using visual technology to retell the past. Tom Wicker said that Stone "uses the powerful instrument of a motion picture, and relies on stars of the entertainment world, to propagate the one true faith."[76] Ellen Goodman commented that

> those of us who are print people—writers and readers—are losing ground to the visual people—producers and viewers. . . . A newspaper column is one of five or six voices on a page. A $40m. movie is not seen on a split screen with another $40m. movie. For those in my Cineplex, Oliver Stone's theory may become the only version and Lee Harvey Oswald may forever look like actor Gary Oldman. So the fuss over "JFK" is about facts, yes, but also about media and messages, the past and future.[77]

Before the film opened, Stone had attempted to mute some of the criticisms. In a series of prescient moves, he had employed as film consultants private citizens who had been eyewitnesses to the assassination, including detective Jim Leavelle (the white-hatted man who was standing alongside Oswald when he was shot);[78] had used Garrison himself to play the part of Chief Justice Earl Warren;[79] and had directed extensive efforts at recreating the Dealey Plaza of 1963.

Yet Stone's particular use of visual documents to authenticate his version of events was problematic for other retellers, notably the journalists, because it paralleled their own practices. Particularly during the spate of televised retrospectives of the late eighties, the media had used fictionalized portrayals of the events of Kennedy's death, calling them "simulations."[80] Stone's so-called faulty use of images to authenticate his story raised questions about the boundaries of responsibility in shaping any popular cultural production about the past.[81]

The discourse surrounding Stone's movie thus tackled the appropriateness of using popular culture to address a controversial event of the past, raising issues about representation, subjectivity, and the responsible use of the visual image. Since popular culture was able to remake the past in ways that rendered it more entertaining, compelling, and often controversial, it suggested its own making, and remaking, of history. For many observers, this constituted the crux of the problem: the reality-based claims of the story were threatened by the intrusion of fictionalizers, who upset the already precarious balance of authority that derived from the story's controversial, nonconsensual nature. Just as he had made explicit the renewed contest for authorization, Stone also made explicit the authority of popular culture, and he brought discussions of its workings directly into popular discourse.

Beyond Journalistic Authority
to the Shaping of Collective Memory

All of this suggests that the controversy over Stone and *JFK* is as much about the shape of public discourse about the past—who is let in, and why; who is kept out, and why—as it is about the story of Kennedy's death. In maintaining that the film "is a lot closer to the truth than the Warren Commission was,"[82] Stone not only underscored the "mythic" quality of the official record but played up—and legitimated—the fictionalizing activity characteristic of most popular culture.

Stone's presence in the tale challenged the recognized parameters for telling the story. He used the media access, institutional support, and visual technology that were common to journalists; he used the arguments typically put forward by the independent critics; and he called himself a historian. This suggests the inevitability of establishing cultural authority not only within one interpretive group, but across many such different communities. As this book has argued, it is in the interfaces across interpretive communities that cultural authority takes shape. Entrusting one's memories to others—whether the media, the historians, the official agencies, or other private citizens—remains controversial because it is punctuated with fundamental insecurities about the past, and our placement in it. The retellings of Kennedy's assassination thus offer only one example of the strategizing by which people attempt to come to terms with their history. As historian Michael Kammen recently observed,

> the media convey a fair amount of what passes for history and memory. In so doing, they frequently mediate between people and historical events, sites, or situations. The press, radio, television, and film have assumed (or achieved) an ever larger responsibility for explaining America, as well as the meaning of America, to Americans and others. In so doing they have reduced the role of [others] and have diminished the felt need for full knowledge of American history as a basis for understanding national identity.[83]

If Stone's film succeeds in changing the status quo in the assassination story, he will have succeeded also in posing the ultimate challenge to American journalists, who typically regard themselves as the true fourth estate. In contesting the versions of events that reporters have set forth, *JFK* has also contested the journalistic authority their versions imply. This makes reporters' public criticism of *JFK* not only predictable but essential to their integrity as an authoritative interpretive community.

Thus, the controversy surrounding *JFK* extends the arguments of this book in two ways: it suggests a renewal of the ongoing contest for authorization that surrounds the assassination retellings, and it emphasizes the rising role of popular culture to resolve this particular event of the past. On both counts, Stone has made explicit the workings of cultural authority by addressing them in popular discourse and popular culture.

Regardless of its inaccuracies or faults, Stone's film thus provides a countermemory or counterauthority to more mainstream views of the assassination story. It does so in both content and form, challenging the account of what happened and the recognized agents of its retelling. On both counts, it acquaints the American public with the workings of cultural authority in this particular tale, and illustrates the mesh of voices that shape public discourse in a variety of tales. Due to the collective memories that arise from such discourse, there is need to account for how these voices blend and clash, the points on which they contradict, the arguments which they introduce that have little relevance to the topic at hand.

For, as one writer observed, "the crime of the century is too important to be allowed to remain unsolved and too complex to be left in the hands of Hollywood movie makers."[84] Just as the move to reopen the assassination files need not end in the lap of Hollywood filmmakers, neither should the American public lose sight of the discursive workings of cultural authority and collective memory. For as long as the public fails to question journalists' cultural authority, it will be unable to question, challenge, or limit it. The story of America's past will remain in part a story of what the media have chosen to remember, a story of how the media's memories have in turn become America's own. And if not the authority of journalists, then certainly the authority of other communities, individuals, and institutions will make their own claims to the tale. As this book has shown, it is from just such competition that history is made.

Notes

1. Introduction: Narrative, Collective Memory, and Journalistic Authority

1. Peter L. Berger, *Invitation to Sociology: A Humanistic Perspective* (New York: Anchor Press, 1963), p. 57.

2. Emile Durkheim, *The Elementary Forms of the Religious Life* (New York: Free Press, 1965 [1915]). Also see Serge Moscovici, "The Phenomenon of Social Representations," in *Social Representations*, ed. Robert M. Farr and Serge Moscovici (Cambridge: Cambridge University Press, 1984), pp. 3–69.

3. Victor Turner, *The Ritual Process* (Ithaca, N.Y.: Cornell University Press, 1969).

4. Roger Abrahams, "Ordinary and Extraordinary Experience," in *The Anthropology of Experience*, ed. Victor Turner and Edward Bruner (Urbana: University of Illinois Press, 1986), p. 45.

5. Anthony Giddens, *Central Problems in Social Theory* (Berkeley: University of California Press, 1979), p. 69.

6. James W. Carey, "A Cultural Approach to Communication," *Communication* 2 (1975), p. 6. See also James W. Carey, *Communication as Culture* (Boston: Unwin Hyman, 1989).

7. G. H. Mead, *The Philosophy of the Present* (Chicago: University of Chicago Press, 1932).

8. Maurice Halbwachs, *The Collective Memory* (trans. of *La mémoire collective* [Paris: Presses Universitaires de France, 1950]) (New York: Harper and Row, 1980), p. 33. The quotation is from Natalie Zemon Davis and Randolph Starn, "Introduction," *Representations* (Spring 1989), p. 4.

9. Ralph Lowenthal, *The Past Is a Foreign Country* (Cambridge, Mass.: Cambridge University Press, 1985).

10. Barbara Kruger and Phil Mariani (eds.), *Remaking History* (Seattle: Bay Press, 1989).

11. Richard Johnson et al. (eds.), *Making Histories: Studies in History-Writing and Politics* (Minneapolis: University of Minnesota Press, 1982).

12. George Lipsitz, *Time Passages* (Minneapolis: University of Minnesota Press, 1990).

13. David Middleton and Derek Edwards (eds.), *Collective Remembering* (Beverly Hills: Sage, 1990).

14. Pierre Nora, *Les lieux de mémoire* (Paris: Editions Gallimard, 1984–); Michael Kammen, *Mystic Chords of Memory: The Transformation of Tradition in*

American Culture (New York: Alfred A. Knopf, 1991). See also Fred Davis, *Yearning for Yesterday* (New York: Free Press, 1979).

15. Special issue on "Social Memory," *Communication* 11(2) (1989); special issue on "Memory and Counter-Memory," *Representations* (Spring 1989); special issue on "Memory and American History," *Journal of American History* 75 (1989).

16. John Nerone and Ellen Wartella, "Introduction: Studying Social Memory," special issue on "Social Memory," *Communication* 11(2) (1989), pp. 85–88.

17. Claude Lévi-Strauss, *The Savage Mind* (Chicago: University of Chicago Press, 1966), p. 259.

18. George Gerbner, "Cultural Indicators: The Third Voice," in *Communications Technology and Social Policy: Understanding the New "Social Revolution,"* ed. George Gerbner, Larry Gross, and William Melody (New York: John Wiley, 1973), p. 562.

19. Bradley Greenberg and Edwin Parker (eds.), *The Kennedy Assassination and the American Public* (Palo Alto: Stanford University Press, 1965); Darwin Payne, "The Press Corps and the Kennedy Assassination," *Journalism Monographs* 15 (February 1970).

20. For example, see Tom Pettit, "The Television Story in Dallas," in *Kennedy Assassination,* ed. Greenberg and Parker, pp. 61–66; Ruth Leeds Love, "The Business of Television and the Black Weekend," in *Kennedy Assassination,* ed. Greenberg and Parker, pp. 73–86; Tom Wicker, "That Day in Dallas," *Times Talk* (*New York Times* internal publication) (December 1963); Meg Greenfield, "The Way Things Really Were," *Newsweek,* 28 November 1988, p. 98.

21. This point is made by Stephen Knapp, who says that "socially shared dispositions are likely to be connected with narratives preserved by collective memory" (Stephen Knapp, "Collective Memory and the Actual Past," *Representations* [Spring 1989], p. 123).

22. Ulric Neisser, "Snapshots or Benchmarks?" in *Memory Observed,* ed. Ulric Neisser (San Francisco: W. H. Freeman, 1982), p. 45.

23. Greenberg and Parker, *Kennedy Assassination.*

24. These include Payne, "Press Corps"; Richard K. Van der Karr, "How Dallas TV Stations Covered Kennedy Shooting," *Journalism Quarterly* 42 (1965), pp. 646–47; and Thomas J. Banta, "The Kennedy Assassination: Early Thoughts and Emotions," *Public Opinion Quarterly* 28(2) (1964), pp. 216–24. One exception to the effects studies is Leland M. Griffin, "When Dreams Collide: Rhetorical Trajectories in the Assassination of President Kennedy," *Quarterly Journal of Speech* 70(2) (May 1984), pp. 111–31.

25. See, for example, Magali Sarfatti Larson, *The Rise of Professionalism* (Berkeley: University of California Press, 1977); Eliot Friedson, *Professional Powers* (Chicago: University of Chicago Press, 1986); Philip Elliott, *Sociology of the Professions* (London: Macmillan, 1972); Morris Janowitz, "Professional

Models in Journalism: The Gatekeeper and the Advocate," *Journalism Quarterly* 52 (Winter 1975), pp. 618–26.

26. See Larson, *Rise of Professionalism*. Also see Wilbert Moore, *The Professions: Roles and Rules* (New York: Russell Sage Foundation, 1970); and Terence Johnson, *Professions and Power* (London: Macmillan, 1972). Johnson (p. 31) cites Everett Hughes's much-cited and relevant reformulation of "Is this occupation a profession?" as "What are the circumstances in which people in an occupation attempt to turn it into a profession and themselves into professional people?"

27. J. Johnstone, E. Slawski, and W. Bowman, *The News People* (Urbana: University of Illinois Press, 1976); David Weaver and G. Cleveland Wilhoit, *The American Journalist* (Bloomington: Indiana University Press, 1986). Also see Lee Becker et al., *The Training and Hiring of Journalists* (Norwood, N.J.: Ablex, 1987). Says one news editor: "Now, of course, we have schools of journalism. Most publications these days—not all, thank God—recruit from schools of journalism. This means they are recruiting from the bottom 40% of the population, since, on the whole, bright students do not go to schools of journalism" (quoted in Irving Kristol, *Our Country and Our Culture* [New York: Orwell Press, 1983], p. 82).

28. Both Clement Jones, *Mass Media Codes of Ethics and Councils* (New York: UNESCO, 1980), and Robert Schmuhl, *The Responsibilities of Journalism* (Notre Dame, Ind.: University of Notre Dame Press, 1984), address this issue. Also see Tom Goldstein, *The News at Any Cost* (New York: Simon and Schuster, 1985), p. 165. Licensing, or credentialing, comes into play for journalists on a more pragmatic level: The limited credentials issued by police departments for reasons of "security," for instance, are often used by journalists to gain access to events with which said credentials have no obvious link. As David Halberstam once said, "Your press card is really a social credit card" (quoted in Bernard Rubin, *Questioning Media Ethics* [New York: Praeger, 1978], p. 16).

29. Weaver and Wilhoit, *American Journalist*, p. 106.

30. Ibid., p. 145.

31. One recent formulation of this perspective was provided by Tony Rimmer and David Weaver, "Different Questions, Different Answers: Media Use and Media Credibility," *Journalism Quarterly* 64 (Spring 1987), pp. 28–36, who examine "how credible (trustworthy, unbiased, complete, accurate) newspapers and television news were perceived (by audiences) to be" (p. 36). Other examples include Eugene Shaw, "Media Credibility: Taking the Measure of a Measure," *Journalism Quarterly* 50 (1973), pp. 306–11; and R. F. Carter and Bradley Greenberg, "Newspapers or Television: Which Do You Believe?" *Journalism Quarterly* 42 (1965), pp. 22–34.

32. This includes a rich body of material from sociology. See Gaye Tuchman, *Making News* (New York: Free Press, 1978); Mark Fishman, *Manufacturing the News* (Austin: University of Texas Press, 1980); Herbert Gans, *Deciding What's News* (New York: Pantheon, 1979).

33. Warren Breed, "Social Control in the Newsroom," *Social Forces* 33 (1955), pp. 326–35.

34. See Gaye Tuchman, "Making News by Doing Work: Routinizing the Unexpected," *American Journal of Sociology* 79 (July 1973), pp. 110–31; Edward J. Epstein, *News from Nowhere* (New York: Vintage, 1974); Edward J. Epstein, *Between Fact and Fiction: The Problem of Journalism* (New York: Vintage, 1975); Jeremy Tunstall, *Journalists at Work* (Beverly Hills: Sage, 1971); Harvey Molotch and Marilyn Lester, "News as Purposive Behavior," *American Sociological Review* 39 (February 1974), pp. 101–12.

35. Included here would be scholarship in critical studies, work by the Center for Contemporary Cultural Studies in Birmingham, and research on news discourse. Examples include Stuart Hall, "Culture, the Media and the Ideological Effect," in *Mass Communication and Society*, ed. James Curran, Michael Gurevitch, and Janet Woollacott (Beverly Hills: Sage, 1977), pp. 315–48; John Fiske, *Television Culture* (London: Methuen, 1987); and John Hartley, *Understanding News* (London: Methuen, 1982). Also see Todd Gitlin, *The Whole World Is Watching* (Berkeley: University of California Press, 1980), who contends that "journalism exists alongside—and interlocked with—a range of other professions and institutions with ideological functions within an entire social system" (p. 251).

36. See, for instance, Margaret Gallagher, "Negotiation of Control in Media Organizations and Occupations," in *Culture, Society and the Media*, ed. Michael Gurevitch et al. (London: Methuen, 1982), pp. 151–73. Also see Gunther Kress and Robert Hodge, *Language as Ideology* (London: Routledge and Kegan Paul, 1979); and the Glasgow University Media Group, *Bad News* (London: Routledge, 1976) and *More Bad News* (London: Routledge, 1980).

37. Tuchman discusses the promotion of "trained incapacity" among journalists (Gaye Tuchman, "Professionalism as an Agent of Legitimation," *Journal of Communication* 28[2] [Spring 1978], pp. 106–13). Schudson says news professionalism emerges from specific methods of work (particularly, identifying and verifying facts) rather than answering to a combination of (supposedly laudatory) predetermined traits or conditions. See Michael Schudson, *Discovering the News* (New York: Basic Books, 1978). This perhaps explains why contemporary journalists still cling to the notion of a fully describable "objective" world, despite the increasing popularity of philosophical and sociological views to the contrary. See James Carey, "The Dark Continent of American Journalism," in R. K. Manoff and Michael Schudson (eds.), *Reading the News* (New York: Pantheon, 1986), pp. 146–96; Schudson, *Discovering the News;* and Dan Schiller, *Objectivity and the News* (Philadelphia: University of Pennsylvania Press, 1981).

38. Robert E. Park, "News as a Form of Knowledge," *American Journal of Sociology* 45 (March 1940), pp. 669–86.

39. Dean O'Brien, "The News as Environment," *Journalism Monographs* 85 (September 1983), p. 1.

40. Michael Schudson, "What Is a Reporter? The Private Face of Public

Journalism," in *Media, Myths and Narratives*, ed. James W. Carey (Beverly Hills: Sage, 1988), pp. 228–45. Also see Michael Schudson, *Watergate in American Memory: How We Remember, Forget and Reconstruct the Past* (New York: Basic Books, in press).

41. See Peter Blau and M. Meyer, *Bureaucracy in Modern Society* (New York: Random House, 1956). For applications in news organizations, see Tuchman, *Making News;* Fishman, *Manufacturing the News;* and Gans, *Deciding What's News.* Also see Bernard Roshco, *Newsmaking* (Chicago: University of Chicago Press, 1975).

42. Tunstall calls this a "non-routine bureaucracy." See Tunstall, *Journalists at Work.* Also see Itzhak Roeh, Elihu Katz, Akiba A. Cohen, and Barbie Zelizer, *Almost Midnight: Reforming the Late-Night News* (Beverly Hills: Sage, 1980). Joseph Turow examines the workings of such a collective frame elsewhere. See Joseph Turow, "Cultural Argumentation Through the Mass Media: A Framework for Organizational Research," *Communication* 8 (1985), pp. 139–64.

43. These points are suggested in a range of sources, including Goldstein, *News at Any Cost;* and Carey, "Dark Continent."

44. Hymes delineates seven factors at play in a speech community— sender, receiver, message, channel, code, topic, and context (Dell Hymes, "Functions of Speech," in *Language in Education: Ethnolinguistic Essays* [Washington, D.C.: Center for Applied Linguistics, 1980], p. 2).

45. Stanley Fish, *Is There a Text in This Class?* (Cambridge, Mass.: Harvard University Press, 1980), p. 171.

46. In folklore, scholarship on the folk group and narrative is exemplified by Alan Dundes, "What Is Folklore?" in *The Study of Folklore* (Englewood Cliffs, N.J.: Prentice-Hall, 1965), pp. 1–3; and Linda Degh, "Folk Narrative," in *Folklore and Folklife*, ed. Richard M. Dorson (Chicago: University of Chicago Press, 1972), pp. 53–83.

47. Robert Bellah et al., *Habits of the Heart: Individualism and Commitment in American Life* (Berkeley: University of California Press, 1985), p. 153.

48. A few exceptions are Robert Darnton, "Writing News and Telling Stories," *Daedalus* 120(2) (Spring 1975), pp. 175–94; Michael Schudson, "The Politics of Narrative Form: The Emergence of News Conventions in Print and Television," *Daedalus* 3(4) (Fall 1982), pp. 97–112; special issue on "News as Social Narrative," *Communication* 10(1) (1987); Barbie Zelizer, " 'Saying' as Collective Practice: Quoting and Differential Address in the News," *Text* 9(4) (1989), pp. 369–88; and Zelizer, "Where Is the Author in American TV News? On the Construction and Presentation of Proximity, Authorship and Journalistic Authority," *Semiotica* 80(1/2) (1990), pp. 37–48. Several recent scandals addressing the fact-fiction continuum have made reporters more cautious about using storytelling practices—the Janet Cooke scandal, the reportorial invention of a British army gunner in Belfast, or the case of Christopher Jones, the *New York Times Magazine* reporter who plagiarized portions of his (fictitious) report on the Khmer Rouge from a novel by André Malraux. See

David Eason, "On Journalistic Authority: The Janet Cooke Scandal," *Critical Studies in Mass Communication* 3 (1986), pp. 429–47; and Shelley Fishkin, *From Fact to Fiction: Journalism and Imaginative Writing in America* (Baltimore: Johns Hopkins University Press, 1985).

49. See Eviatar Zerubavel, *Hidden Rhythms* (Berkeley: University of California Press, 1981); Erving Goffman, *Forms of Talk* (Philadelphia: University of Pennsylvania Press, 1981).

50. Barney Glaser and Anselm Strauss, *The Discovery of Grounded Theory* (New York: Aldine, 1967). The logic of this method as a viable sociological tool is implicit in both Weber and Simmel. See Max Weber, *Max Weber: Selections in Translation* (Cambridge: Cambridge University Press, 1978); George Simmel, *The Sociology of George Simmel* (New York: Free Press, 1950). Also see Charles L. Bosk, *Forgive and Remember* (Chicago: University of Chicago Press, 1979).

51. These included the *New York Times Index, Washington Post Index, Current Guide to Periodical Literature*, the Vanderbilt Television News Archive, CBS News Archives, and NBC News Archives.

52. Journals and news organizations surveyed included ABC News, CBS News, NBC News, *Newsweek, Time*, the *New York Times*, and the *Washington Post*.

53. Other institutions that provided documentary material for this project included the John F. Kennedy Memorial Library, Sherman Grinburg Library, Journal Graphics, Inc., ABC News Transcripts, and the Investigative News Group.

2. Before the Assassination

1. See Sohnya Sayres et al. (eds.), *The 60s Without Apology* (Minneapolis: University of Minnesota Press in cooperation with *Social Text*, 1984), for an extended discussion of this theme. In line with many writers of the time, I suggest examining the sixties as a heuristic construct rather than a chronological category.

2. Morris Dickstein, *Gates of Eden: American Culture in the Sixties* (New York: Penguin, 1989), pp. v, 137.

3. Todd Gitlin, *The Sixties: Years of Hope, Days of Rage* (New York: Bantam, 1987), p. 7.

4. Jacob Brackman, "The Sixties: Shock Waves from the Baby Boom," *Esquire*, June 1983, p. 198; rpt. from *Esquire*, October 1968.

5. Norman Mailer, "Enter Prince Jack," *Esquire*, June 1983, p. 208; excerpted from "Superman Comes to the Supermarket," *Esquire*, November 1960.

6. Lance Morrow, "Of Myth and Memory," *Time*, 24 October 1988, p. 22.

7. Peter Stine, "Editor's Comment," *Witness* 2(2/3), special double issue on "The Sixties," (Summer/Fall 1988), p. 9.

8. Lawrence Wright, *In the New World: Growing Up with America from the Sixties to the Eighties* (New York: Vintage, 1983), p. 48.

9. Thomas Brown, *JFK: History of an Image* (Bloomington: Indiana University Press, 1988), p. 2.

10. Casey Hayden, "The Movement," *Witness* 2(2/3) (Summer/Fall 1988), p. 245.

11. Tom Schachtman, *Decade of Shocks: Dallas to Watergate 1963–1974* (New York: Poseidon, 1983), p. 62.

12. Dickstein, *Gates of Eden*, p. 136.

13. Fredric Jameson, "Periodizing the 60s," in Sayres et al. (eds.), *The 60s Without Apology*, p. 184.

14. Gitlin, *The Sixties*, p. 20.

15. Introductory remarks to Brackman, "The Sixties: Shock Waves," *Esquire*, June 1983, p. 197.

16. See Tom Wolfe, *The New Journalism* (New York: Harper and Row, 1973); or Dickstein, *Gates of Eden*, pp. 132–35.

17. See David Halberstam, *The Powers That Be* (New York: Laurel Books, 1979), pp. 640–56.

18. Ibid., p. 561.

19. Pierre Salinger, "Introduction," in *Kennedy and the Press*, H. W. Chase and A. H. Lerman (New York: Thomas Y. Crowell, 1965), p. ix.

20. Gary Wills, *The Kennedy Imprisonment* (New York: Pocket Books, 1983), p. 155.

21. Pierre Salinger, *With Kennedy* (New York: Doubleday, 1966), p. 31.

22. Ibid., pp. 32–33.

23. Quoted in Lewis Paper, *The Promise and the Performance* (New York: Crown, 1975), p. 253.

24. Hugh Sidey, quoted in Philip B. Kunhardt, Jr. (ed.), *Life in Camelot: The Kennedy Years* (New York: Time-Life Books, 1988), p. 6.

25. Tom Wicker, *On Press* (New York: Berkley, 1975), p. 125.

26. Ibid., pp. 125–26.

27. Stories of extramarital affairs, Addison's disease, crude language, and early marriages were systematically wiped from public record as Kennedy began to rise in the political world. The singlemindedness with which problematic aspects of his life were erased from memory continued after his death, evidenced by bitter legal battles between the custodians of his memory, Robert and Jacqueline Kennedy, and assassination historian William Manchester. Such battles expanded the extent to which Kennedy's memory would be systematically managed, yet they were already linked with efforts at image management during Kennedy's early political career.

28. Henry Fairlie provides a detailed discussion of the problems raised by Kennedy's ties with journalists. See Fairlie, "Camelot Revisited," *Harper's*, January 1973, pp. 67–78.

29. Benjamin Bradlee, *Conversations with Kennedy* (New York: W. W. Nor-

ton, 1975). *Newsweek,* for instance, called it a "fond memoir of JFK" (*Newsweek,* 17 March 1975, p. 24).

30. Taylor Branch, "The Ben Bradlee Tapes: The Journalist as Flatterer," *Harper's,* October 1975, pp. 36, 43.

31. These details were prominently featured in Goddard Lieberson (ed.), *JFK: As We Remember Him* (New York: Atheneum, 1965).

32. John F. Kennedy, *Profiles in Courage* (New York: Harper and Row, 1956). Kennedy's reputation as a reporter and writer has come under fire from several critics. Both Herbert S. Parmet, *Jack: The Struggles of John F. Kennedy* (New York: Dial, 1980), and Wills, *Kennedy Imprisonment,* relate the anecdotes by which the reputation was created. "When the Ambassador arranged for his son to travel to useful places with press credentials, [*New York Times* columnist Arthur] Krock celebrated him as a brilliant young journalist. Krock even claimed that Kennedy as a journalistic stringer in England predicted the surprise 1946 defeat of Winston Churchill . . . John Kennedy the writer was almost entirely the creation of Joseph Kennedy the promoter" (Wills, *Kennedy Imprisonment,* p. 135). Wills and Parmet also convincingly argue that Kennedy wrote *Profiles in Courage* with excessive assistance from Arthur Krock and Theodore Sorensen, while Wills contends that an earlier book, *Why England Slept* (New York: Funk and Wagnalls, 1961 [1940]) was heavily edited by Krock and overused the ideas of economist Harold Laski (see Wills, *Kennedy Imprisonment,* pp. 133–40).

33. *Editor and Publisher,* 12 November 1960, p. 7.

34. Joseph Kraft, "Portrait of a President," *Harper's,* January 1964, p. 96.

35. Quoted in Peter Goldman, "Kennedy Remembered," *Newsweek,* 28 November 1983, p. 66. Kennedy's voracious reading habits were cited at length by journalists. Joseph Kraft at one point generously classified the president's regular reading material as comprising most of the journalistic community's news "accounts, editorials and columns" ("Portrait of a President," p. 96). Even the fact that this sometimes worked to their disadvantage—as evidenced by former CBS correspondent George Herman's story about the president "chewing out a reporter for a footnote that was buried in a long story"—was subordinated to the interest he appeared to take in their work (see Paper, *Promise and the Performance,* p. 324).

36. David Halberstam, "Introduction," in *The Kennedy Presidential Press Conferences* (New York: Earl M. Coleman Enterprises, 1978), p. ii.

37. David S. Broder, *Behind the Front Page* (New York: Touchstone, 1987), p. 157.

38. Christopher Lasch, "The Life of Kennedy's Death," *Harper's,* October 1983, p. 33. Lasch also contended that Kennedy was already made a hero during the 1950s, because the "academic establishment, journalists and opinion makers had decreed that the country needed a hero" (p. 33).

39. This is detailed in Paper, *Promise and the Performance,* p. 326.

40. See Kenneth P. O'Donnell and David F. Powers, *"Johnny, We Hardly Knew Ye"* (Boston: Little, Brown, 1970), p. 408.

41. Bradlee, *Conversations with Kennedy*, pp. 20–25.

42. Broder, *Behind the Front Page*, p. 158.

43. Charles Roberts, "JFK and the Press," in K. W. Thompson (ed.), *Ten Presidents and the Press* (Lanham, Md.: University Press of America, 1983), and cited in Broder, *Behind the Front Page*, p. 158.

44. "News Managing Laid to Kennedy," *New York Times*, 25 February 1963, p. 5. The article discussed Krock's assertions as they were about to be laid out in *Fortune* magazine. See Arthur Krock, "Mr. Kennedy's Management of the News," *Fortune*, March 1963, pp. 82, 199–202.

45. I. F. Stone, "The Rapid Deterioration in Our National Leadership," in *In a Time of Torment, 1961–67* (Boston: Little, Brown, 1967), p. 6.

46. Fairlie, "Camelot Revisited," p. 76.

47. Halberstam, *Powers That Be*, p. 444.

48. Ibid., p. 447.

49. Notice of the fact that the results of the debate between Kennedy and Nixon were perceived differently by radio and television users has been traced to a Philadelphia polling firm.

50. At the time the debates were held, the polls gave Nixon 48 percent of the vote and Kennedy 42 percent.

51. John Weisman, "An Oral History: Remembering JFK, Our First TV President," *TV Guide*, 19 November 1988, p. 2.

52. Theodore H. White, *The Making of the President, 1960* (New York: Atheneum, 1961), pp. 340–44.

53. Quoted in Weisman, "Oral History," p. 2.

54. Halberstam, *Powers That Be*, pp. 461, 477.

55. Quoted ibid., pp. 558–59.

56. Salinger, *With Kennedy*, p. 53. Kennedy's estimations of what he could lose by implementing the conferences, as chronicled by Salinger, were revealing: "[he] would not even have the temporary protections of a transcript check. . . . He could not go off the record. He could accuse no one of misquoting him" (p. 56).

57. Quoted in Lieberson, *JFK: As We Remember Him*, p. 118.

58. Ibid., p. 173.

59. Arthur M. Schlesinger, Jr., *A Thousand Days* (Boston: Houghton Mifflin, 1965), p. 716.

60. Wicker, *On Press*, p. 126.

61. Quoted in Henry Fairlie, *The Kennedy Promise* (New York: Doubleday, 1972), p. 174.

62. Barbara Matusow, *The Evening Stars* (Boston: Houghton Mifflin, 1983), p. 84.

63. Halberstam, "Introduction," p. iv. The possibility of wide public access was at best only a partial hope. Kennedy's statement on the Cuban missile crisis was one of his few scheduled appearances on prime-time television. Most of the president's news conferences were held at noontime, when television viewing audiences were small.

64. Paper, *Promise and the Performance*, p. 234.

65. Bradlee, *Conversations with Kennedy*, p. 123.

66. Ibid., p. 123.

67. The film was "Crisis: Behind a Presidential Commitment," produced by Drew Associates in 1963. It was shown in 1988 by PBS as part of the series "The American Experience," under the title "Kennedy v. Wallace: A Crisis Up Close."

68. See Mary Ann Watson, *The Expanding Vista* (New York: Oxford University Press, 1990), pp. 139–44. Watson provides a detailed look at the links between Kennedy and television.

69. "John Fitzgerald Kennedy," special section, *Newsweek*, 2 December 1963, p. 45.

70. Halberstam, *Powers That Be*, p. 502.

71. Ibid., p. 485.

72. Gary Paul Gates, *Air Time* (New York: Harper and Row, 1978), p. 5.

73. Matusow, *Evening Stars*, p. 85.

74. Ibid. This was similar to the situation of radio in the 1930s.

75. Ibid., p. 86.

76. "International Press Institute Rejects Move to Admit Radio-TV Newsmen," *New York Times*, 8 June 1963, p. 52.

77. Theodore White, *Making of the President, 1960*, pp. 335–36. While television news made inroads in the sixties, it did have an earlier history. Already in 1941, CBS was broadcasting two fifteen-minute daily newscasts to a local New York audience. The newscasts generally offered unsophisticated footage with talking heads, and film was taken from newsreel companies. Although John Cameron Swayze went on the air daily with NBC's "Camel News Caravan," the onset of "See It Now" in 1951 quickly made Edward R. Murrow and Fred Friendly journalistic celebrities. Their probing coverage of McCarthyism helped underscore the potential importance of television news. Television's coverage of the 1952 presidential elections not only set up the venerable team of David Brinkley and Chet Huntley on NBC but also coined the term *anchorman* for the role played by Walter Cronkite on CBS. See Eric Barnouw, *Tube of Plenty* (London: Oxford University Press, 1975). Also see Gates, *Air Time*; and Mitchell Stephens, *A History of News* (New York: Viking Press, 1988).

78. This is discussed in Matusow, *Evening Stars*, p. 82.

79. *New York Times*, 27 August 1963, p. 1.

80. Halberstam, *Powers That Be*, p. 569.

81. Pierre Salinger, quoted in Weisman, "Oral History," p. 6.

82. Matusow, *Evening Stars*, p. 107. A growing realization among journalists and others that television might be capable of offering a different background for news exacerbated an already existing rivalry between CBS and NBC. To the disadvantage of ABC, at that time still a fledgling operation, CBS and NBC competed over which would take first place in the news world. NBC's enterprising team of Chet Huntley and David Brinkley reportedly held

the largest share of the news audience, and their wit, earnestness, and intelligence made the program a popular mainstay. Furthermore, CBS's woeful, and wrong, prediction of the 1960 elections—giving Nixon a victory over Kennedy by odds of 100 to one—had made CBS executives realize that they needed to catch up with the other network. Steps were taken to help them capture first place: being first to adopt the expanded half-hour format for news; opening new bureaus, such as one in Dallas that was headed by an up-and-coming correspondent named Dan Rather; and adopting technologically sophisticated equipment that they hoped would help them combat NBC's Huntley and Brinkley.

83. Halberstam, *Powers That Be*, p. 539.

84. Matusow, *Evening Stars*, p. 85. This also worked in the reverse direction, as in the Bay of Pigs, which was called a total disaster but "not a televised disaster, there were no cameras on the scene; and although the response to the Bay of Pigs was televised, Kennedy had the power, and the authority, and the cool to handle it, putting off all serious questions about why it had happened in the first place on the basis of national security" (Halberstam, *Powers That Be*, p. 539).

85. Halberstam, *Powers That Be*, pp. 506–7.

86. Matusow, *Evening Stars*, p. 85.

87. Wicker, *On Press*, p. 2.

88. Ibid.

89. Quoted in Theodore H. White, *America in Search of Itself* (New York: Warner, 1982), p. 175.

90. Ibid.

91. Schachtman, *Decade of Shocks*, p. 47.

92. Theodore White, *America in Search of Itself*, p. 174.

93. Wilbur Schramm, "Communication in Crisis," in *Kennedy Assassination*, ed. Greenberg and Parker, p. 11.

94. *Broadcasting*, 2 December 1963, pp. 44–45.

95. "Kennedy Retained Newsman's Outlook," *Editor and Publisher*, 30 November 1963, p. 65.

3. Rhetorical Legitimation and Journalistic Authority

1. John L. Lucaites and Celeste Condit, "Reconstructing Narrative Theory: A Functional Perspective," *Journal of Communication* 35(4) (Autumn 1985), pp. 93–94.

2. Weber, *Max Weber: Selections*.

3. Jürgen Habermas, *The Theory of Communicative Action*, vol. 1 (Boston: Beacon Press, 1981), pp. xxiv–xxv.

4. Robert Wuthnow, James Davison Hunter, Albert Bergesen, and Edith Kurzweil, *Cultural Analysis* (London: Routledge and Kegan Paul, 1984), p. 190.

5. See particularly Hayden White, "The Value of Narrativity in the Repre-

sentation of Reality," in W.J.T. Mitchell (ed.), *On Narrative* (Chicago: University of Chicago Press, 1980), pp. 1–23; Lucaites and Condit, "Reconstructing Narrative Theory"; Walter R. Fisher, "Narration as a Human Communication Paradigm," *Communication Monographs* (March 1984), pp. 1–22; Peter L. Berger and Thomas Luckmann, *The Social Construction of Reality* (New York: Anchor Press, 1967); and Fish, *Is There a Text in This Class?*

6. Roland Barthes, "Introduction to the Structural Analysis of Narratives," in *Image, Music, Text* (New York: Hill and Wang, 1977), pp. 79–124.

7. Hayden White, "Value of Narrativity," p. 18.

8. See Barbara Herrnstein Smith, *On the Margins of Discourse* (Chicago: University of Chicago Press, 1978); Robert H. Canary and Henry Kozicki (eds.), *The Writing of History* (Madison: University of Wisconsin Press, 1978); Hans Kellner, *Language and Historical Representation: Getting the Story Crooked* (Madison: University of Wisconsin Press, 1989); or Hayden White, "Value of Narrativity." Work in folklore has also been concerned with the dissemination of narratives across time and space. See particularly Richard Bauman and Roger Abrahams (eds.), *'And Other Neighborly Names'* (Austin: University of Texas Press, 1981).

9. Hayden White, "Historical Pluralism," *Critical Inquiry* 12 (Spring 1986), p. 487.

10. Studies of journalism's narrative dimensions include Carey, *Media, Myths and Narratives;* Schudson, "Politics of Narrative Form"; Darnton, "Writing News"; and Graham Knight and Tony Dean, "Myth and the Structure of News," *Journal of Communication* 32(2) (Spring 1982), pp. 144–61.

11. Friedson, *Professional Powers.* Also see Larson, *Rise of Professionalism.*

12. This argument has been most forcefully advanced by technological determinists, who contend that forms of authority in public discourse are directly determined by the attributes of the medium in which the discourse is conveyed. See Harold A. Innis, *Empire and Communications* (Toronto: University of Toronto Press, 1972); Marshall McLuhan, *Understanding Media* (London: Routledge and Kegan Paul, 1964). For a related argument, see Stephens, *History of News.*

13. This point is suggested by Smith, *On the Margins of Discourse.* Communication studies in this area include work by the Center for Contemporary Cultural Studies in Birmingham (Stuart Hall et al. [eds.], *Culture, Media, Language* [London: Hutchinson, 1980]; James Curran, Michael Gurevitch, and Janet Woollacott [eds.], *Mass Communication and Society* [Beverly Hills: Sage, 1977]), the Glasgow University Media Group (*Bad News* and *More Bad News*), and work in critical linguistics (Kress and Hodge, *Language as Ideology;* Roger Fowler, *Language in the News* [London: Routledge, 1991]). Each perspective focuses upon the workings of language and authority in institutional and mediated settings.

14. Andy Logan, "JFK: The Stained Glass Image," *American Heritage Magazine,* August 1967, p. 6; Frank Donner, "The Assassination Circus: Conspira-

cies Unlimited," *The Nation*, 22 December 1979, p. 658; Herbert S. Parmet, *JFK: The Presidency of John F. Kennedy* (New York: Penguin, 1983), p. 348.

15. Dan Rather, quoted in "Four Days in November: The Assassination of President Kennedy," CBS News, 17 November 1988.

16. Charles Roberts, *The Truth about the Assassination* (New York: Grosset and Dunlap, 1967), p. 15.

17. As *John F. Kennedy, President* went into its second printing, author and reporter Hugh Sidey added a note that included the sentence: "I was with him in Dallas, Texas, on November 22, 1963" (Hugh Sidey, *John F. Kennedy, President* [New York: Atheneum, 1964], p. vi). Tom Wicker made similar mention in his book *Kennedy Without Tears* (New York: William Morrow, 1964), "About the Author," n.p.

18. Retrospectives of this sort included Kunhardt, *Life in Camelot;* and Jacques Lowe, *Kennedy: A Time Remembered* (New York: Quartet/Visual Arts, 1983).

19. Steve Bell, "John F. Kennedy Remembered," "KYW Eyewitness News, Channel Three Eyewitness News Nightcast," Philadelphia, 22 November 1988.

20. "Four Days in November: The Assassination of President Kennedy," CBS News.

21. "JFK Assassination: As It Happened," NBC News, shown on Arts and Entertainment Network, 22 November 1988.

22. For a more general discussion of spatial strategies that underscore the authority of reporters in network news, see Zelizer, "Where Is the Author."

23. Kathleen Hall Jamieson's *Eloquence in an Electronic Age* (New York: Oxford University Press, 1988) discusses how news conventions incorporate synecdochic representations of events.

24. Tom Wicker, "A Reporter Must Trust His Instinct," *Saturday Review*, 11 January 1964, p. 81.

25. Tom Pettit, NBC News, 24 November 1963.

26. Bert Schipp, quoted in John B. Mayo, *Bulletin from Dallas* (New York: Exposition Press, 1967), p. 142.

27. See Greenberg and Parker, *Kennedy Assassination*, for a thorough collection of essays on this subject. Also see Payne, "Press Corps."

28. See Greenberg and Parker, *Kennedy Assassination*. Also see Daniel Dayan and Elihu Katz, *Media Events: The Live Broadcasting of History* (Cambridge, Mass.: Harvard University Press, 1992).

29. Wicker, "Reporter Must Trust His Instinct," p. 81.

30. More detailed support for this statement can be found in chapters 4, 5, and 6. An extensive description of the problems faced by journalists in Dallas is found in Payne, "Press Corps."

31. See *Warren Report: Report of the President's Commission on the Assassination of President John F. Kennedy* (Washington, D.C.: U.S. Government Printing Office, 1964; hereafter cited as *Warren Report*) for a detailed description of testimony given by lay eyewitnesses.

32. The only professional photographer to capture Kennedy's death in stills was an Associated Press photographer hailed by the trade press as "the lone pro" on the scene ("Lone 'Pro' on Scene Where JFK Was Shot," *Editor and Publisher*, 7 December 1963, p. 11).

33. William Manchester, *The Death of a President* (New York: Harper and Row, 1967), p. 116.

34. "Oswald Shooting a First in Television History," *Broadcasting*, 2 December 1963, p. 46.

35. This role is discussed at length in Dayan and Katz, *Media Events*.

36. "JFK," ABC News, 11 November 1983.

37. Van der Karr, "Dallas TV Stations"; Karl J. Nestvold, "Oregon Radio-TV Response to the Kennedy Assassination," *Journal of Broadcasting* 8(2) (Spring 1964), pp. 141–46.

38. Rick Friedman, "The Weekly Editor: The Kennedy Story," *Editor and Publisher*, 7 December 1963, pp. 44–46.

39. Nestvold, "Oregon Radio-TV Response," p. 146.

40. "A World Listened and Watched," special report, *Broadcasting*, 2 December 1963, p. 40.

41. In his autobiography, Dan Rather relates how he and Barker maintained intermittent contact in trying to verify what had happened. See Dan Rather with Mickey Herskowitz, *The Camera Never Blinks* (New York: Ballantine, 1977), pp. 123–28.

42. "Television's Fiftieth Anniversary," special issue, *People*, Summer 1989, p. 100.

43. Matusow, *Evening Stars*, p. 105.

44. Gates, *Air Time*, p. 3.

45. See, for example, *Warren Report*; also see "At Issue: Judgment by Television," *Columbia Journalism Review* (Winter 1964), pp. 45–48. This topic is covered extensively in chapter 6.

46. "At Issue: Judgment by Television"; also see "News Media Act to Study Charges," *New York Times*, 9 October 1964, p. 21.

47. "The Activity of Newsmen," *Warren Report*, pp. 201–8.

48. Charles Roberts, "Eyewitness in Dallas," *Newsweek*, 5 December 1966, pp. 26–28.

49. Sidey, *John F. Kennedy, President*, pp. vi–vii.

50. Tom Wicker, *JFK and LBJ* (New York: William Morrow, 1968), p. 299.

51. Roberts, "Eyewitness in Dallas," p. 26.

52. Roberts, *Truth about the Assassination*.

53. Steve Bell, "John F. Kennedy Remembered," "KYW Eyewitness News."

54. Pierre Salinger, "John Kennedy—Then and Now," *MacLean's*, 28 November 1983, p. 20.

55. Edwin Newman, "JFK Assassination: As It Happened," NBC News, shown on Arts and Entertainment Network, 22 November 1988.

56. John Chancellor, *The Week We Lost John F. Kennedy*, three-tape series, NBC News, March 1989.

57. Harrison E. Salisbury, "The Editor's View in New York," in *Kennedy Assassination*, ed. Greenberg and Parker, pp. 37–45.

58. Marya Mannes, "The Long Vigil," *The Reporter*, 19 December 1963, p. 16.

59. Similar recollections were voiced elsewhere. One observer mentioned how "in the days immediately following the assassination, voices of men like Huntley, Brinkley and Cronkite became more prominent than those of my own parents" (John P. Sgarlat, "A Tragedy on TV—and the Tears of a Crestfallen Nation," *Philadelphia Daily News*, 22 November 1988, p. 35). Again, mention was made not of on-site reporters but of the anchorpersons who monitored their words.

4. "Covering the Body" by Telling the Assassination

1. *The Reporter*, 5 December 1963, p. 19.

2. Routinizing the unexpected is discussed at length in Tuchman, *Making News*, pp. 39–63.

3. Ibid., pp. 59–63.

4. Gans, *Deciding What's News*, p. 157.

5. Manchester, *Death of a President*, p. 329. Because Manchester's book provides the most detailed chronological account of what initially happened, I have elected to use it to set the background against which journalists' tales were initially told.

6. *Warren Report*, p. 201.

7. This work strategy has been underscored in most sociological examinations of the journalistic workplace. See particularly Tuchman, *Making News*; Gans, *Deciding What's News*; Fishman, *Manufacturing the News*; and Roshco, *Newsmaking*.

8. Wicker, "Reporter Must Trust His Instinct," p. 81.

9. Payne, "Press Corps."

10. Unidentified radio newscaster, 22 November 1963; quoted in "25th Anniversary of JFK Assassination," "Good Morning, America," ABC News, 22 November 1988.

11. Robert MacNeil, NBC News, 22 November 1963; shown on "JFK Assassination: As It Happened," NBC News.

12. Wicker, "Reporter Must Trust His Instinct," p. 81.

13. Tom Wicker, "Kennedy Is Killed by Sniper as He Rides in Car in Dallas," *New York Times*, 23 November 1963, p. 2.

14. Jack Bell, "Eyewitnesses Describe Scene of Assassination," *New York Times*, 23 November 1963, p. 5. The headline of this article is telling, for it put Bell in the position of an "eyewitness"—someone who could be either professional or amateur—rather than labeling him explicitly as a professional journalist. See chapter 5 for more on this point.

15. Ibid.

16. Ibid.

17. Ibid.

18. Quoted in Saul Pett, AP Log (Associated Press internal publication); rpt. in "The Reporters' Story," Columbia Journalism Review (Winter 1964), p. 8.

19. "Reporters' Story," p. 11.

20. "Lone Pro," p. 11.

21. Merriman Smith, "The Murder of the Young President," distributed by United Press International, 23 November 1963; rpt. in "Reporters' Story," p. 7.

22. Manchester, Death of a President, pp. 167–68.

23. "Unresolved Issues," Columbia Journalism Review (Winter 1964), p. 27.

24. Schramm, "Communication in Crisis," p. 11.

25. "I Just Heard Some Shots . . . Three Shots," Editor and Publisher, 30 November 1963, p. 14.

26. Walter Cronkite, CBS News, 22 November 1963; shown in "Four Days in November: The Assassination of President Kennedy," CBS News.

27. Unidentified radio newscaster, ABC Radio, 22 November 1963; quoted in "JFK," ABC News.

28. Schramm, "Communication in Crisis," p. 4.

29. Manchester, Death of a President, p. 190.

30. Van der Karr, "Dallas TV Stations."

31. Wicker, "Reporter Must Trust His Instinct," p. 82.

32. Elmer Lower, "A Television Network Gathers the News," in Kennedy Assassination, ed. Greenberg and Parker, p. 71.

33. Wicker, "Kennedy Is Killed by Sniper," p. 2.

34. Manchester, Death of a President, pp. 222, 242.

35. Ibid., p. 222.

36. For a discussion of how discourse about Kennedy's bodily wounds has generated discourse about the body politic, see Barbie Zelizer, "From the Body as Evidence to the Body of Evidence," in Bodylore, ed. Katharine Young (American Folklore Society and University of Tennessee Press, in press).

37. Wicker, "Kennedy Is Killed by Sniper," p. 2.

38. Wicker, "Reporter Must Trust His Instinct," p. 82.

39. Ibid.

40. This chapter attends only to those aspects of the assassination story which figured prominently in chronicles of journalistic practice. Other units of coverage—such as the murder of Officer Tippit and the apprehension of Oswald—played an important part in defining the tone of coverage but are less central to discussions of appropriate journalistic practice.

41. Manchester, Death of a President, p. 222.

42. Jim Bishop, The Day Kennedy Was Shot (New York: Bantam, 1968), p. 266.

43. Smith, "Murder of the Young President"; rpt. in "Reporters' Story," p. 15.

44. Ibid., p. 16.

45. Ronnie Dugger, "The Last Voyage of Mr. Kennedy," *Texas Observer*, 29 November 1963; rpt. in "Reporters' Story," p. 16.

46. Rick Friedman, "Pictures of Assassination Fall to Amateurs on Street," *Editor and Publisher*, 30 November 1963, pp. 16–17, 67.

47. Wicker, "Kennedy Is Killed by Sniper," p. 2.

48. "Huntley-Brinkley Report," NBC News, 22 November 1963.

49. Roberts, *Truth about the Assassination*.

50. *Warren Report*, p. 202.

51. Ibid., p. 208.

52. *Warren Report*, p. 213. Because the *Warren Report* provides the most comprehensive step-by-step account of how journalists covered Oswald's murder, I have elected to use it here in providing a chronology of events around his death.

53. Ibid., p. 216.

54. Ibid., p. 227.

55. Pettit, "Television Story in Dallas," p. 63.

56. "Oswald Shooting," p. 46.

57. "World Listened," p. 37.

58. Ike Pappas, quoted in "On Trial: Lee Harvey Oswald," London Weekend Television, shown on Fox Network, 22–23 November 1988.

59. "The Day Kennedy Died," *Newsweek*, 2 December 1963, p. 21.

60. Friedman, "Pictures of Assassination," pp. 17, 67.

61. Ibid., p. 16.

62. "Oswald Shooting," p. 46. Oswald's murder was not the first murder recorded on television. In one similar case, in October 1960 a Japanese political leader was knifed on a public stage in Tokyo. Videotaped recordings were played back on Japanese television ten minutes later (*New York Times*, 25 November 1963, p. 1). However, the audiences that viewed Oswald's death live were considerably larger and more attentive than were those of the earlier incident.

63. "Oswald Shooting," p. 46.

64. Gates, *Air Time*, p. 254.

65. "Oswald Shooting," p. 46.

66. Ibid.

67. "Press, Radio and TV," *Editor and Publisher*, 30 November 1963, p. 6.

68. "*Parade* Reprints Because of Death," *Editor and Publisher*, 30 November 1963, p. 73.

69. "World Listened," p. 36. The flip side of this reorganization was the pressure brought to bear on news organizations unable to do so. How they justified it was exemplified in an "Office Memo" published on the front page of *The Progressive* (1 January 64, p. 1):

> The December issue was irrevocably in the mails early on November 22. If you felt it was strange that the December issue, reaching you in late November or early December, carried not a word of the world's irrevocable loss of JFK, please understand how it happened. Daily newspa-

pers, despite crushing problems of their own, faced no such problems. Weekly magazines could reach their readers in a matter of days after the tragedy. Other monthlies fared worse than *The Progressive*, or somewhat better, depending on their publication and mailing dates. It is a minor irony that we had advanced our mailing date to Friday November 22, to get the magazine to the post-office before the weekend, as a way of overcoming the expected slowness of the mails during the following week of the Thanksgiving holiday.

70. "World Listened," p. 42.
71. Schramm, "Communication in Crisis," p. 12.
72. Nielsen Co., *TV Responses to the Death of a President* (New York: Nielsen, 1963); cited in "World Listened," p. 37.
73. Schramm, "Communication in Crisis," p. 25.
74. Greenberg and Parker, *Kennedy Assassination*, p. 382.
75. "Radio-TV's Deportment," *Broadcasting*, 2 December 1963, p. 54.
76. Edwin Newman, NBC News, 22 November 1963; shown on "JFK Assassination: As It Happened," NBC News.
77. James Reston, Jr., "Why America Weeps," *New York Times*, 23 November 1963, pp. 1, 7.
78. See particularly Richard L. Tobin, "If You Can Keep Your Head When All about You . . . ," *Saturday Review*, 14 December 1963, p. 54. On 31 July 1987, ABC broadcast a "Person of the Week" segment on Reston, in which it hailed his column on Kennedy's death.
79. Friedman, "Weekly Editor," p. 44.
80. "TV: A Chapter of Honor," *New York Times*, 6 November 1963, p. 11.
81. "World Listened," p. 37.
82. "TV: A Chapter of Honor," p. 11.
83. Ibid.
84. "Comments on Coverage: 'Well Done,'" *Broadcasting*, 2 December 1963, p. 50.
85. Tobin, "If You Can Keep Your Head," p. 53.
86. As the *New York Times* said, "Whatever a viewer wanted to see next, a camera was ready to show it." See "TV: A Chapter of Honor," p. 11.
87. Charles Collingwood, quoted in "The Four Dark Days: From Dallas to Arlington," CBS News, 25 November 1963.
88. Ibid.
89. This point is discussed in Dayan and Katz, *Media Events*.

5. "Covering the Body" by Mediated Assessment

1. Payne, "Press Corps," p. 1.
2. Tom Wicker, quoted in Lieberson (ed.), *JFK: As We Remember Him*, p. 223.
3. Wicker, "That Day."
4. Friedman, "Pictures of Assassination," p. 16.

5. Ibid.

6. Ibid.

7. "World Listened," p. 37.

8. "The Assassination of President Kennedy," *Life*, 29 November 1963, p. 24.

9. Richard B. Stolley, "The Greatest Home Movie Ever Made," *Esquire*, November 1973, p. 134.

10. Payne, "Press Corps," pp. 8, 26.

11. Love, "Business of Television," in *Kennedy Assassination*, ed. Greenberg and Parker, p. 84.

12. See particularly Elizabeth F. Loftus, *Eyewitness Testimony* (Cambridge, Mass.: Harvard University Press, 1979). How journalists visually (and often fictitiously) construct their proximate status to events is discussed in Zelizer, "Where Is the Author."

13. Roberts, "Eyewitness in Dallas," p. 26.

14. Manchester, *Death of a President*, p. 191.

15. Roberts, *Truth About the Assassination*, pp. 12–13.

16. Ibid.

17. Ibid., pp. 13, 15.

18. Ibid., front cover.

19. Ibid., back flap.

20. Ibid., p. 129.

21. Roberts, "Eyewitness in Dallas," p. 26.

22. Wicker, "Kennedy Is Killed by Sniper," p. 2.

23. Interestingly, the *New York Times* appended an account by Associated Press reporter Jack Bell on a later page of the same issue, under the headline "Eyewitnesses Describe Scene of Assassination." Bell's dispatch was displayed together with the words of a "man from suburban Willowdale" (originally published by the Canadian Press) and an eyewitness report by a fourteen-year-old boy (originally published by the *Chicago Tribune*). This seemed to deprive Bell of his privileged status as a professional eyewitness (i.e., a journalist) and instead contextualized him as an ordinary bystander (Bell, "Eyewitnesses Describe Scene," p. 5).

24. Mannes, "Long Vigil," pp. 15–17.

25. "The Marxist Marine," *Newsweek*, 2 December 1963, p. 27.

26. "President's Assassin Shot to Death," *New York Times*, 25 November 1963, p. 1.

27. Tobin, "If You Can Keep Your Head," p. 54.

28. Turner Catledge, "Until Proven Guilty," letter to the editor, *New York Times*, 27 November 1963, p. 36

29. William Rivers, "The Press and the Assassination," in *Kennedy Assassination*, ed. Greenberg and Parker, p. 57.

30. Roberts, *Truth about the Assassination*, p. 19.

31. Van der Karr, "Dallas TV Stations," p. 647.

32. Quoted in Alan Robinson, "Reporting the Death of JFK," Associated

Press dispatch printed in the *Philadelphia Inquirer*, 22 November 1988, p. 8E.

33. Ibid.

34. Gates, *Air Time*, p. 3.

35. Manchester, *Death of a President*, p. 168.

36. Pettit, "Television Story in Dallas," p. 66.

37. "World Listened," p. 42.

38. Schramm, "Communication in Crisis," p. 3.

39. One journalist with such experience was David Brinkley, who recalled having mispronounced the word *cortège* during the broadcast of President Franklin D. Roosevelt's funeral eighteen years earlier. Left alone in NBC's Washington office when word arrived that Roosevelt had died, the twenty-five-year-old correspondent had been reprimanded for his gaffe (Manchester, *Death of a President*, p. 144). The experience haunted him while he was covering Kennedy's funeral.

40. *Broadcasting* discussed at length the ways in which television networks produced record-breaking broadcasts. See "World Listened," pp. 36–46.

41. This included canceling columns of advertisements ("Press, Radio and TV," p. 6).

42. Robert MacNeil, NBC News, 22 November 1963; shown in "JFK Assassination: As It Happened," NBC News.

43. Van der Karr, "Dallas TV Stations," p. 647.

44. Greenfield, "Way Things Really Were," p. 98.

45. "Newspapers: Hunger for Print," *Columbia Journalism Review* (Winter 1964), p. 20.

46. Ibid.

47. Tobin, "If You Can Keep Your Head," p. 53.

48. Ibid.

49. "Magazines: Good Luck and Bad," *Columbia Journalism Review* (Winter 1964), p. 24.

50. Robinson, "Reporting the Death."

51. Herbert Brucker, "When the Press Shapes the News," *Saturday Review*, 11 January 1964, p. 77.

52. Tobin, "If You Can Keep Your Head," p. 53; "Radio-TV's Deportment," p. 54.

53. Wicker, "Reporter Must Trust His Instinct," p. 81. The problematic nature of relying on instinct was conveyed in Jim Bishop's reconstruction of a similar scene: "Wicker hurried a little and caught up to Hugh Sidey of *Time* magazine. 'Hugh,' he said, puffing. 'The President is dead. Just announced on the radio. I don't know who announced it but it sounded official to me.' Sidey paused. He looked at Wicker and studied the ground under his feet. They went on. Something which 'sounds official' meets none of the requirements of journalism" (Bishop, *Day Kennedy Was Shot*, p. 264).

54. Gates, *Air Time*, p. 9.

55. "World Listened," p. 40.

56. Manchester, *Death of a President*, p. 130.

57. Ibid., p. 38.

58. *Warren Report*, p. 41.

59. Gates, *Air Time*, p. 10.

60. John Horn, "Television: A Transformation," *Columbia Journalism Review* (Winter 1964), p. 18.

61. Tobin, "If You Can Keep Your Head," p. 53.

62. *Broadcasting*, 2 December 1963, p. 108.

63. "Four Days in November," David L. Wolper for United Artists and United Press International, originally shown 7 October 1964; reshown by Combined Broadcasting Corp., November 1988.

64. Tobin, "If You Can Keep Your Head," p. 53.

65. Greenfield, "Way Things Really Were," p. 98.

66. Elmer Lower, quoted in "World Listened," p. 38.

67. Lower, "Television Network Gathers the News," p. 68.

68. Bill Ryan, quoted in Robinson, "Reporting the Death," p. 8E.

69. Walter Cronkite, quoted in "Ten Years Later: Where Were You?" *Esquire*, November 1973, p. 136.

70. "Reporters' Story," p. 13.

71. Matusow, *Evening Stars*, p. 105.

72. Gates, *Air Time*, p. 6.

73. Wicker, "Reporter Must Trust His Instinct," p. 81.

74. Frank McGee, NBC News, 22 November 1963; shown in "JFK Assassination: As It Happened," NBC News.

75. "Four Days in November," United Artists and United Press International, 1964.

76. Wicker, "Reporter Must Trust His Instinct," p. 81.

77. Bill Ryan, quoted in Robinson, "Reporting the Death," p. 8E.

78. Rather with Herskowitz, *Camera Never Blinks*, pp. 126–27.

79. Ibid., pp. 127, 128.

80. Manchester, *Death of a President*, p. 168.

81. Quoted in *Editor and Publisher*, 30 November 1963, p. 7; the coverage by Merriman Smith was reprinted in *UPI Reporter* on 28 November 1963.

82. Quoted in Van der Karr, "Dallas TV Stations," p. 647.

83. Ibid.

84. Kunhardt, *Life in Camelot*, pp. 13–14.

85. Ibid., p. 14.

86. Gates, *Air Time*, p. 8.

87. Stolley, "Greatest Home Movie," p. 134. In fact, Dan Rather was also present for part of the screening. See Rather with Herskowitz, *Camera Never Blinks*, pp. 132–33.

88. Manchester, *Death of a President*, p. 38.

89. "Lone Pro," p. 11.

90. "World Listened," p. 42.

6. "Covering the Body" by Professional Forum

1. "Reporters' Story," pp. 6–17.
2. Association for Education in Journalism, "Official Minutes of the 1964 Convention," *Journalism Quarterly* 42 (Winter 1965), p. 152.
3. "Professionalism in News Photography," *The Quill*, November 1968, p. 55.
4. Friedman, "Pictures of Assassination," p. 16.
5. "The Assassination," *Columbia Journalism Review* (Winter 1964), p. 5.
6. "Kennedy, Vietnam Topped '63 News," *New York Times*, 29 March 1964, p. 16.
7. "Press, Radio and TV," p. 6.
8. Ibid.
9. "*Parade* Reprints," p. 73.
10. "Unresolved Issues," p. 24.
11. "Lone Pro," p. 11.
12. Payne, "Press Corps," p. 12.
13. Friedman, "Pictures of Assassination," p. 16.
14. Ibid., p. 17.
15. *Broadcasting*, 2 December 1963, p. 108.
16. "World Listened," p. 36.
17. Ibid.
18. "Radio-TV's Deportment," p. 54.
19. *New York Times*, 30 April 1964, p. 71.
20. *New York Times*, 16 December 1964, p. 21.
21. "Comments on Coverage," p. 51.
22. Tobin, "If You Can Keep Your Head," p. 53.
23. *Broadcasting*, 2 December 1963, p. 108.
24. A. William Bluem, "Looking Ahead: The Black Horse," editorial, *Television Quarterly* 3(1) (Winter 1964), p. 86.
25. This is suggested in "The Washington Shoot-out," *The Quill*, May 1981, pp. 8–13.
26. Dayan and Katz, *Media Events.*
27. "Dallas Revisited," in *Problems of Journalism*, Proceedings of the 1964 Convention of the American Society of Newspaper Editors, 16–18 April 1964 (Washington, D.C.: ASNE, 1964), p. 23.
28. Ibid., p. 26.
29. Rivers, "Press and the Assassination," p. 59.
30. "Assassination Story Raises Legal Snares," *Editor and Publisher*, 14 December 1963, p. 12.
31. Felix R. McKnight, quoted in "Dallas Revisited," p. 27.
32. Ibid., p. 23.
33. *Warren Report*, p. 202.
34. Ibid., p. 204.
35. Ibid., p. 206.
36. Ibid., p. 208.

37. Ibid., p. 240.

38. "'Accused' or 'Assassin,'" editorial, *Editor and Publisher*, 14 December 1963, p. 6.

39. Brucker, "When the Press Shapes the News," p. 76.

40. Ibid., pp. 75–76.

41. Ibid., p. 77.

42. Joseph Costa, quoted in "Dallas Revisited," p. 24.

43. Ibid.

44. Ibid.

45. "At Issue: Judgment by Television," p. 45.

46. "The Life and Death of John F. Kennedy," *Current*, January 1964, p. 43.

47. Ibid., p. 44.

48. "At Issue: Judgment by Television," p. 47.

49. "News Media Act," p. 21.

50. Quoted in *Television Quarterly* (Spring 1964), p. 27.

51. *New York Times*, 18 October 1964, p. 53.

52. *New York Times*, 7 April 1964, p. 71.

53. *New York Times*, 16 April 1964, p. 41; 20 November 1964, p. 76.

54. *New York Times*, 20 November 1964, p. 76.

55. Gabe Pressman, Robert Lewis Shayon, and Robert Schulman, "The Responsible Reporter," *Television Quarterly* 3(2) (Spring 1964), p. 17.

56. Ibid., p. 6.

57. Ibid., p. 15.

58. Quoted in *Editor and Publisher*, 14 December 1963, p. 12.

59. Quoted in Brucker, "When the Press Shapes the News," p. 77.

60. "Dallas Revisited," p. 30.

61. Ibid., pp. 39–40.

62. Brucker, "When the Press Shapes the News," p. 77.

7. De-authorizing Official Memory: From 1964 to the Seventies

1. A variety of terms have been applied to persons who, without professional claim or institutional backing, sought to investigate the events of Kennedy's death. Some prefer to label them "assassination buffs," and others press for names implying more rigorous research activities, such as "independent analysts" or "independent researchers." In selecting "independent critics," I have tried to choose a term that minimizes the group's marginalization yet remains somewhat in the middle of possible alternatives.

2. Tom Wicker, "Kennedy Without End, Amen," *Esquire*, June 1977, p. 69. The phrase appeared to be a neatly turned version of a remark made by James Reston the day after the assassination: "What was killed in Dallas was not only the President but the promise. The heart of the Kennedy legend is what might have been" (Reston, "Why America Weeps," p. 1). It also became the title of a much-acclaimed article by Reston one year later ("What Was Killed

Was Not Only the President But the Promise," *New York Times*, 15 November 1964, section 6, p. 1).

3. Gore Vidal, "Camelot Recalled: Dynastic Ambitions," *Esquire*, June 1983, p. 210; excerpted from "The Holy Family," *Esquire*, April 1967. For an overview of readings of Kennedy's death in folklore, see S. Elizabeth Bird, "Media and Folklore as Intertextual Communication Processes: John F. Kennedy and the Supermarket Tabloids," in *Communication Yearbook 10*, ed. Margaret McLaughlin (Newbury Park, Cal.: Sage, 1987), pp. 758–72.

4. Andrew M. Greeley, "Leave John Kennedy in Peace," *Christian Century*, 21 November 1973, p. 1150.

5. Ibid.

6. Daniel Boorstin, "JFK: His Vision, Then and Now," *U.S. News and World Report*, 24 October 1988, p. 30. Such a view was expressed by many observers.

7. Lasch, "Life of Kennedy's Death," p. 33.

8. Jefferson Morley, "Camelot and Dallas: The Entangling Kennedy Myths," *The Nation*, 12 December 1988, p. 646. Lasch similarly distinguished between "Kennedy's style" and the "unsuspected flaws in the national character" (Lasch, "Life of Kennedy's Death," p. 34).

9. Lasch, "Life of Kennedy's Death," p. 40.

10. Theodore H. White, "Camelot, Sad Camelot," *Time*, 3 July 1978, p. 47.

11. Pete Hamill, "JFK: The Real Thing," *New York Magazine*, 28 November 1988, p. 46.

12. Brown, *JFK: History of an Image*, p. 104.

13. Henry Steele Commager, "How Explain Our Illness?" *Washington Post*, 1 December 1963; rpt. as "The Pervasiveness of Violence," *Current*, January 1964, pp. 15–18.

14. Ben H. Bagdikian, "The Assassin," *Saturday Evening Post*, 14 December 1963, p. 22.

15. Brown, *JFK: History of an Image*, p. 45; also "Birch View of JFK," *Newsweek*, 24 February 1964, pp. 29–30.

16. This is traced in William G. Carleton, "Kennedy in History: An Early Appraisal," *Antioch Review* 24 (Fall 1964), pp. 277–99.

17. Victor Lasky, *JFK: The Man and the Myth* (New York: Dell, 1977 [1963]); Kennedy, *Profiles in Courage*. Discussed in *New York Times*, 16 February 1964, section 7, p. 8.

18. United Press International and *American Heritage* Magazine, *Four Days: The Historical Record of President Kennedy's Death* (New York: UPI and American Heritage Publishing, 1964).

19. "The Presidency: Battle of the Book," *Time*, 23 December 1966, p. 15.

20. One spurned writer claimed the Kennedys were "trying to copyright the assassination." See Bishop, *Day Kennedy Was Shot*, p. xvi. The number of writers censored by the Kennedy family far exceeded those granted approval for pending manuscripts. It was claimed that the family tried to block former JFK confidant Paul B. Fay, Jr.'s book, *The Pleasure of His Company* (New York: Harper and Row, 1966). The pattern also persisted into the eighties, when

writer David Horowitz, who coauthored with Peter Collier *The Kennedys: An American Drama* (New York: Warner, 1984), maintained that the Kennedys exercised "totalitarian control" over their memories and canceled interviews with him at the last minute (quoted in "Re-evaluating the Kennedys," *U.S. News and World Report*, 4 May 1987, p. 68). Also see "Camelot Censured," *Newsweek*, 3 November 1966, pp. 65–66; and Logan, "Stained Glass Image," p. 6.

21. "Presidency: Battle of the Book," p. 15.

22. *New York Times*, 17 December 1966, p. 1, 23 January 1967, p. 1. See also "Camelot Censured"; and "Presidency: Battle of the Book." Ultimately this also detracted from Kennedy's memory. As one observer remarked, Kennedy was "overmemorialized in too short a time . . . the sudden folk hero has obscured the man" (Loudon Wainwright, "Atlantic City and a Memory," *Life*, 4 September 1967, p. 17).

23. Logan, "Stained Glass Image," p. 7. Logan discussed what he called a "style sheet" for historical material. Stylistic rules included the following: "don't call Bobby 'Bobby,' as everyone else does"; "pretend you have always called the President's wife 'Mrs. Kennedy' or 'Jacqueline,' not 'Jackie' as the whole world knows her"; "the President's father is not to be called 'Joe,' 'Old Joe,' or 'Big Joe.' Refer to him as Mr. Joseph P. Kennedy or 'the Ambassador'—and always respectfully" (p. 75).

24. One favored commemorative practice was the public exhibition of Kennedy's mementoes, such as his amateur attempts at painting or building model ships. See Jacqueline Kennedy, "These Are the Things I Hope Will Show How He Really Was," *Life*, 29 May 1964, pp. 32–38.

25. *New York Times*, 25 June 1970, p. 1. Other figures loyal to the official Kennedy memory made the same plea; see Theodore Sorensen in the *New York Times*, 22 November 1973, p. 37. Also see Barbara Gamarekian, "Hundreds Are in Capital for 25th Remembrance," *New York Times*, 22 November 1988, p. A24.

26. In 1964, certain reporters even marked the "six-month anniversary" of Kennedy's death, which ironically fell six days short of his birthdate. *New York Times*, 23 May 1964, p. 6. This was actually not surprising, for Kennedy's death was a bona fide news event by journalistic standards, while celebrating his birthday would have seemed like a public relations stunt. One news organization that addressed suggestions to commemorate Kennedy's birthday was *McCall's* magazine. It published a commemorative article by Theodore Sorensen under the simple title "May 29, 1967," in which Sorensen discussed possible gains from remembering Kennedy's birthday (Theodore Sorensen, "May 29, 1967," *McCall's*, June 1967, p. 59).

27. Schlesinger, *Thousand Days*; Theodore C. Sorensen, *Kennedy* (New York: Harper and Row, 1965).

28. In the summer of 1965, Sorensen's book was excerpted in *Look* and Schlesinger's in *Life*.

29. Carleton, "Kennedy in History." The justification went as follows:

"Carleton's qualifications for an 'early historical appraisal' of the Kennedy years are not only his stature as a political scientist but in the early 1940s . . . he had an opportunity to observe the Kennedy boys during their formative years" (p. 277).

30. Manchester, *Portrait of a President*, pp. 239–65.

31. H. Faber, *The Kennedy Years* (New York: Viking, 1964); Tom Wicker, *Kennedy Without Tears*; Sidey, *John F. Kennedy, President*. Pierre Salinger and Sander Vanocur's book, *A Tribute to John F. Kennedy* (New York: Dell, 1965), was discussed in the *New York Times*, 27 March 1964, p. 10.

32. "John F. Kennedy Memorial Album: His Life, His Words, His Deeds," special issue, *Life* (1964).

33. Review of *There Was a President*, *New York Times*, 16 January 1967, p. 39.

34. "Four Days in November," United Artists and United Press International (*New York Times*, 8 October 1964, p. 48).

35. Faber, *Kennedy Years*. The book was discussed in the *New York Times*, 28 August 1964, p. 27.

36. UPI, *Four Days*; discussed in *New York Times*, 16 February 1964, section 7, p. 8.

37. Associated Press, *The Torch Is Passed*. . . . (New York: Associated Press in association with Western Publishing, 1963).

38. One such book was Jim Bishop's *Day Kennedy Was Shot*, timed to coincide with the fifth anniversary of Kennedy's assassination. The book was billed as "the book that the former Mrs. John F. Kennedy urged Jim Bishop not to write" ("New Kennedy Book Set for Release," *New York Times*, 24 October 1968, p. 95).

39. "Camelot Revisited," *The Nation*, 19 November 1983, p. 483.

40. "Peephole Journalism," *Commonweal*, 3 September 1965, p. 613.

41. Meg Greenfield, "The Kiss and Tell Memoirs," *Reporter*, 30 November 1967, p. 15.

42. Jack Minnis and Staughton Lind, "Seeds of Doubt: Some Questions about the Assassination," *New Republic*, 21 December 1963, pp. 14–20.

43. Ford noted that Lane harassed the commission "by innuendo and inference." See Gerald Ford and John R. Stiles, *Portrait of the Assassin* (New York: Simon and Schuster, 1965).

44. Mark Lane, "A Defense Brief for Lee Harvey Oswald," *National Guardian*, 19 December 1963; rpt. in *The Assassinations: Dallas and Beyond*, ed. Peter Dale Scott, Paul L. Hoch, and Russell Stetler (New York: Vintage, 1976), pp. 49–52.

45. Harold Feldman, "Fifty-One Witnesses: The Grassy Knoll," *Minority of One*, March 1965, pp. 16–25.

46. *Warren Report*.

47. Michael L. Kurtz, *Crime of the Century: The Kennedy Assassination from a Historian's Perspective* (Knoxville: University of Tennessee Press, 1982), p. 26.

48. *Warren Report*. Novelist Don DeLillo likened the *Warren Report* to a novel "in which nothing is left out" (See Don DeLillo, "American Blood: A

Journey Through the Labyrinth of Dallas and JFK," *Rolling Stone,* 8 December 1983, p. 28); also see "JFK/MLK: Is There More to the Story?" *Senior Scholastic,* 18 November 1976, pp. 9–13, for a pedagogic version of the commission's activities; and Calvin Trillin, "The Buffs," *New Yorker,* 10 June 1967.

49. Thorough critiques of the *Warren Report* were provided by Edward J. Epstein's *Inquest: The Warren Commission and the Establishment of Truth* (New York: Viking, 1966), which focused on the workings of the commission, and Sylvia Meagher's *Accessories after the Fact* (New York: Bobbs-Merrill, 1967), which offered a point-by-point discussion of the report's failings.

50. CBS News showed one of its first specials on the assassination, "November 22 and the Warren Report," shortly after the commission made its findings public (27 October 1964). Both the *New York Times* and the *Washington Post* praised the commission on 29 September 1964.

51. David Welsh and William Turner, "In the Shadow of Dallas," *Ramparts,* 25 January 1969, p. 62. Also see *New York Times,* 23 September 1964, p. 20.

52. This included a summary report made available in both hardback and paperback by the U.S. Government Printing Office for $3.25 and $2.50 respectively (*New York Times,* 23 September 1964, p. 20).

53. The *Times's* soft-cover edition was cheaper than the official summary report, costing only one dollar (*New York Times,* 23 September 1964, p. 20).

54. *Warren Report* (New York: Associated Press, 1964). A cheaper hardcover edition of this report was made available to members of the Associated Press for one dollar (*New York Times,* 23 September 1964, p. 20). Interestingly, the pictures in question did not document the assassination itself, only the moments that led up to it, suggesting yet again professional journalists' failure to record the president's shooting.

55. *Warren Report* (Associated Press edition), p. 366.

56. Trillin, "Buffs," p. 43.

57. Examples included Dwight MacDonald, "Critique of the Warren Report," *Esquire,* March 1965, pp. 59–63; Sylvia Meagher, "Notes for a New Investigation," *Esquire,* December 1966, p. 211; "Kennedy Assassination: Question of a Second Investigation," *New Republic,* 12 November 1966, p. 8. The *Texas Observer* issued a number of articles in critique of the commission. See Ronnie Dugger, "November 22, 1963: The Case Is Not Closed," *Texas Observer,* 11 November 1966; pp. 1–2; Ronnie Dugger, "Batter Up," *Texas Observer,* 3 February 1967.

58. The quality of the enormous body of assassination literature was uneven. Some arguments were put forth with little reference to other works and little documentation; others were meticulously researched and documented. Among many others, a few frequently cited works included Harold Weisberg's implication of the Dallas police, *Whitewash: The Report on the Warren Report* (Hyattstown, Md., 1965); Penn Jones, Jr.'s *Forgive My Grief* (Midlothian, Tex.: Midlothian Mirror, 1966) about Texas right-wingers; and Thomas G. Buchanan's *Who Killed Kennedy?* (New York: Putnam, 1964), which implicated right-wing oil magnates.

59. Welsh and Turner, "In the Shadow of Dallas," p. 62; Sylvia Meagher, *Subject Index to the Warren Report and Hearings and Exhibits* (New York: Scarecrow, 1966).

60. Epstein, *Inquest*.

61. Epstein, *Inquest*; Meagher, *Accessories*; Mark Lane, *Rush to Judgment* (New York: Holt, Rinehart and Winston, 1966); Josiah Thompson, *Six Seconds in Dallas* (New York: Bernard Geis Associates, 1967).

62. "A Decade of Unanswered Questions," *Ramparts*, 12 December 1973, p. 43.

63. Roberts, *Truth about the Assassination*, p. 57.

64. Mark Lane, *A Citizen's Dissent* (New York: Holt, Rinehart and Winston, 1968), p. 11.

65. Quoted in Trillin, "Buffs," p. 41.

66. Lane, *Citizen's Dissent*, p. x.

67. Ibid., p. xi.

68. Ibid., pp. 253–54.

69. Ibid., p. 144.

70. See Anthony Summers, *Conspiracy* (New York: Paragon, 1980; rev. 1989), p. 31. In his autobiography (Rather with Herskowitz, *Camera Never Blinks*, pp. 133–34), Rather later explained his error by saying that

> I failed to mention the violent, backward reaction. This was, as some assassination buffs now argue, a major omission. But certainly not deliberate. At the risk of sounding too defensive, I challenge anyone to watch for the first time a twenty-two-second film of devastating impact, run several blocks, then describe what they had seen in its entirety. . . . I only know that I did it as well and as honestly as I could under the conditions.

71. Richard Goodwin, quoted in *New York Times*, 24 July 1966, p. 25.

72. Kurtz, *Crime of the Century*, p. 87. Kurtz provides a detailed analysis of the Clark Panel. Also see *1968 Panel Review of Photographs, X-Ray Films, Documents and Other Evidence Pertaining to the Fatal Wounding of President John F. Kennedy on November 22, 1963, in Dallas, Texas* (Washington, D.C.: National Archives, n.d.).

73. James Kirkwood, *American Grotesque: An Account of the Clay Shaw–Jim Garrison Affair in the City of New Orleans* (New York: Simon and Schuster, 1970). The case was largely derided in the media, particularly by Edward J. Epstein, "Garrison," *New Yorker*, 13 July 1968, pp. 35–81. Also see William Turner, "Assassinations: Epstein's Garrison," *Ramparts*, 7 September 1968, pp. 8, 12. In the late 1980s, Jim Garrison sought to publicize further his version of the case, in Jim Garrison, *On the Trail of the Assassins* (New York: Sheridan Square Press, 1988), and the book provided much of the foundation for a 1991 Warner Brothers movie by director Oliver Stone, *JFK*.

74. G. Robert Blakey and Richard N. Billings, *The Plot to Kill the President* (New York: New York Times Books, 1981), p. 43.

75. *New York Times*, 25 September 1966, section 4, p. 10.

76. "A Matter of Reasonable Doubt," *Life*, 25 November 1966, pp. 38–48. Some critics asserted that *Life* mishandled certain frames of the Zapruder film sequence, making it look as if the president fell forward instead of backward.

77. "A Primer of Assassination Theories," *Esquire*, December 1966, pp. 205–10.

78. The station was WNEW-TV, and the program was discussed in the *New York Times*, 15 November 1966, p. 1.

79. Salisbury claimed that the investigation never reached completion because he was sent to Hanoi. He did maintain, however, that nothing "undercut, contradicted or undermined in any fashion the basic conclusions of our original work or that of the Warren Commission." See Harrison E. Salisbury, *A Time of Change: A Reporter's Tale of Our Time* (New York: Harper and Row, 1988), pp. 71–72.

80. Jack Anderson, *Washington Post*, 3 March 1967.

81. Trillin, "Buffs"; Josiah Thompson, "The Crossfire That Killed Kennedy," *Saturday Evening Post*, 2 December 1967, pp. 27–31; John Kaplan, "The Assassins," *American Scholar* (Spring 1967), pp. 271–306.

82. See *New York Times*, 29 June 1967, p. 87, for a review of the first part of the series; also see "As We See It," *TV Guide*, 29 July 1967, p. 1.

83. *New York Times*, 25 June 1967.

84. CBS News press release, 29 June 1967, cited in Lane, *Citizen's Dissent*, p. 98.

85. "As We See It," p. 1. Also see "Warren Report," *TV Guide*, 24 June 1967, p. A29.

86. Interestingly, this was the very point of criticism leveled at journalists by some independent critics, who saw the journalists as not being sufficiently investigative in their efforts to reopen the assassination record. See Lane, *Citizen's Dissent*.

87. Trillin, "Buffs," p. 43.

88. Donner, "Assassination Circus," p. 660.

89. Roberts, *Truth about the Assassination*, p. 119. Interestingly, Roberts also contended that the reason the critics were so well received was because their books were reviewed by people little acquainted with the facts of the assassination. He said: "Where the newspaper had assigned journeyman reporters—many of them veterans of Dallas—to 'cover' the Warren Report, their book editors assigned literary critics—including some who had only a headline-readers' knowledge of the assassination—to review the books that appeared to destroy the Warren Report" (p. 118).

90. Brown, *JFK: History of an Image*, p. 66.

91. W. Shannon, in *New York Times*, 19 October 1971, p. 43.

92. Brown, *JFK: History of an Image*, p. 51.

93. Richard Boeth, "JFK: Visions and Revisions," *Newsweek*, 19 November 1973, p. 76.

94. Hamill, "JFK: The Real Thing," p. 46.

95. "Decade of Unanswered Questions," p. 43.

96. Michael Rossman, "The Wedding Within the War," cited in Stephens, *History of News*, p. 125.

97. Morley, "Camelot and Dallas," p. 646. On the flip side, increasingly prevalent discussions favoring conspiracy were labeled a "culture of narcissism" by Christopher Lasch in his book of that name (New York: W. W. Norton, 1979). Lasch based his observations on what he saw as a search for immediate political highs and a fascination with the sensational.

98. "Decade of Unanswered Questions," p. 44. As early as 1973, one writer juxtaposed the Kennedy assassination and the Nixon impeachment as "paraphrases of each other"—two examples of parricide—thereby suggesting a deep-seated need for documentary questioning (see Priscilla McMillan, "That Time We Huddled Together," *New York Times,* 22 November 1973, p. 37). McMillan, however, came under fire from certain independent critics, who maintained she had ties with U.S. intelligence that prejudiced her view of the Kennedy story. See Bernard Fensterwald, Jr., *Coincidence or Conspiracy?* (New York: Zebra Books, 1977). Also see Jerry Policoff, "The Media and the Murder of John Kennedy," *New Times,* 8 September 1975; rpt. in *Assassinations: Dallas and Beyond,* ed. Scott et al., pp. 262–70.

99. "Assassination—Behind Moves to Reopen JFK Case," *U.S. News and World Report,* 2 June 1975, p. 31.

100. Welsh and Turner, "In the Shadow of Dallas."

101. *Newsweek, Time,* and *U.S. News and World Report* all began to report about the critics during the mid 1970s.

102. Albert H. Newman, *The Assassination of John F. Kennedy* (New York: Clarkson N. Potter, 1970); Hugh C. McDonald, *Appointment in Dallas* (New York: Zebra Books, 1975); Weisberg, *Whitewash* and *Whitewash II: The FBI–Secret Service Cover-up* (Hyattstown, Md., 1966). There were other volumes in the *Whitewash* series.

103. *New York Times,* 10 November 1974, p. 107; also see *New York Times,* 3 February 1975, p. 14.

104. "Assassination: Behind Moves," p. 32.

105. Kurtz, *Crime of the Century,* p. 158.

106. "The Question That Won't Go Away," *Saturday Evening Post,* December 1975, pp. 38–39. Interestingly, the same article traced the magazine's efforts at reconsidering the assassination record, including editorials in both January and December of 1967 that called to reopen the case.

107. "Assassination: Behind Moves," p. 31.

108. Examples included Richard Condon, *Winter Kills* (New York: Dial, 1974); Mark Lane and Donald Freed, *Executive Action* (New York: Dell, 1973); Loren Singer, *The Parallax View* (Garden City, N.Y.: Doubleday, 1970). Film versions were made of *The Parallax View* and *Executive Action.*

109. Quoted in Trillin, "Buffs," p. 45.

110. *Report to the President by the Commission on CIA Activities Within the United States* (Washington, D.C.: U.S. Government Printing Office, 1975; New York: Manor Books, 1976). Discussed in Kurtz, *Crime of the Century,* p. 159.

111. *New York Times*, 15 May 1976, p. 13.

112. It was alleged that Exner had simultaneously been the mistress of two Mafia figures active in CIA plots against Fidel Castro—John Roselli and Sam Giancana (U.S. Congress, Select Committee to Study Governmental Operations with Respect to Intelligence Activities, *Alleged Assassination Plots Involving Foreign Leaders: An Interim Report* [Washington, D.C.: U.S. Government Printing Office, 20 November 1975], p. 129; cited in Brown, *JFK: History of an Image*, pp. 72–73). Also see "JFK and the Mobsters' Moll," *Time*, 29 December 1975, pp. 16–18; and "A Shadow over Camelot," *Newsweek*, 29 December 1975, pp. 14–16. In 1988, Exner admitted having had simultaneous affairs with Giancana and Kennedy, but she contended that she did so at Kennedy's request ("The Dark Side of Camelot," *People*, 29 February 1988, pp. 106–14].

113. These were thought to detail links between Lee Harvey Oswald and the FBI, which had not yet been made public. The fact that in 1977 the FBI issued its own assassination report in support of the lone-assassin theory suggested how out of step it was with the climate of opinion, which was moving steadily toward thoughts of conspiracy. See "The FBI's Report on JFK's Death," *Time*, 19 December 1977, p. 18.

114. Scott et al. (eds.), *Assassinations: Dallas and Beyond*, p. x.

115. Ibid., p. 8.

116. George Michael Evica, *And We Are All Mortal* (West Hartford, Conn.: University of Hartford Press, 1978), p. 205.

117. Policoff, "Media and Murder."

118. Evica, *And We Are All Mortal*, p. 212.

119. Daniel Schorr, *Clearing the Air* (Boston: Houghton Mifflin, 1977).

120. Walter Cronkite, "CBS Evening News," 25 April 1975. Also see *New York Times*, 26 April 1975, p. 12.

121. "Assassination: Behind Moves"; "The American Assassins," "CBS Evening News," 25–26 November 1975; "Assassination: An American Nightmare," "ABC Evening News," 14 November 1975; "JFK: The Truth Is Still at Large," *New Times*, 18 April 1975.

122. Geraldo Rivera, "Good Night, America," ABC News, 26 March 1975. Reviewed by the *New York Times*, 27 March 1975, p. 61.

123. Kurtz, *Crime of the Century*, p. 158.

124. David Halberstam, *The Best and the Brightest* (New York: Random House, 1972).

125. John Berendt, "Ten Years Later: A Look at the Record," *Esquire*, November 1973, p. 264.

126. Kurtz, *Crime of the Century*, p. vi.

127. Theodore White, "Camelot, Sad Camelot," p. 46.

128. The search for history's precise role within the assassination story also stirred interest in other potentially authoritative voices, such as that of fiction. The best example of the blurring of historical, journalistic, and fictional domains came from William Manchester's so-called "authorized" history of the assassination, *Death of a President*. Epstein lambasted it as a novel begun

as "Death of Lancer," contending that "far from being a detailed and objective chronicle of the assassination, it was a mythopoeic melodrama organized around the theme of struggle for power" (Epstein, *Between Fact and Fiction*, p. 124). It is telling that a similar discussion surrounded Oliver Stone's movie, *JFK*, in the nineties.

129. Morley, "Camelot and Dallas," p. 649. Tom Wicker stated in 1977 that "the notion of Camelot, always overblown and romanticized, has barely survived, if it has at all, allegations and disclosures about assassination plots and Mafia women, wiretaps and *Conversations with Kennedy*" (Wicker, "Kennedy Without End," p. 67).

130. Brown, *JFK: History of an Image*, p. 76.

131. Carl Oglesby, *The Yankee and Cowboy War* (New York: Berkley Medallion, 1976).

132. Peter Dale Scott, "From Dallas to Watergate—The Longest Cover-Up," *Ramparts*, 1973; rpt. in *Assassinations: Dallas and Beyond*, ed. Scott et al., pp. 357–74. Also see Peter Dale Scott, *Crime and Cover-Up* (Berkeley: Westworks, 1977).

133. Edward J. Epstein, *Legend: The Secret World of Lee Harvey Oswald* (New York: McGraw-Hill, 1978). Certain independent critics felt that this book caused Epstein to lose credibility because his treatment of the case drew too uncritically on intelligence sources.

134. Seth Kantor, *Who Was Jack Ruby?* (New York: Everest House, 1978).

135. Richardson Preyer, quoted in Blakey and Billings, *Plot to Kill*, p. 66.

136. *New York Times*, 18 November 1976, p. 17.

137. Kurtz, *Crime of the Century*, p. 160.

138. *The Final Assassinations Report* (New York: Bantam, 1979), p. 336.

139. Ibid., p. 104; also see *New York Times*, 31 December 1978, p. 1.

140. Discussed in *New York Times*, 15 July 1979, p. 1. For a thorough index of the House Committee Report, see Sylvia Meagher and Gary Owens, *Master Index to the J.F.K. Assassination Investigations* (Metuchen, N.J.: Scarecrow Press, 1980).

141. *Final Assassinations Report*, p. 104.

142. Ibid., introductory remarks.

143. Brown, *JFK: History of an Image*, p. 79.

144. Kurtz, *Crime of the Century*, pp. 186, 187.

145. Donner, "Assassination Circus," p. 654.

146. *Final Assassinations Report*, preface.

147. Summers, *Conspiracy*, p. 102.

148. Ibid., p. xxi.

149. Ibid., p. 473.

150. Blakey and Billings, *Plot to Kill*.

151. Josiah Thompson, quoted in "Who Shot President Kennedy?" "Nova," PBS, 15 November 1988.

8. Negotiating Memory: From 1980 to the Nineties

1. Hamill, "JFK: The Real Thing," p. 46.

2. *New York Times*, 23 November 1987, section 2, p. 10. This was somewhat revived during the following anniversary year, when estimates of the people in Dealey Plaza ranged from 400 (*New York Times*, 23 November 1988, p. A16) to 2,500 (*Washington Post*, 23 November 1988, p. A1). Regardless of the discrepancies, this showed an increased interest in the assassination during its twenty-fifth anniversary year.

3. Henry Allen, "JFK: The Man and the Maybes," *Washington Post*, 22 November 1988, p. E2.

4. Brown, *JFK: History of an Image*, p. 76.

5. This referred to a 1983 *Newsweek* poll, cited in Goldman, "Kennedy Remembered," p. 64.

6. William Manchester, *One Brief Shining Moment* (Boston: Little, Brown, 1983). Other examples here included Lowe, *Kennedy: A Time Remembered;* and Kunhardt, *Life in Camelot.*

7. Morley, "Camelot and Dallas," p. 649.

8. "Camelot Revisited," p. 483; "Camelot on Tape," *Time*, 4 July 1983, p. 122. Also see "In Camelot, They Taped a Lot," *Newsweek*, 15 February 1982, p. 29.

9. Goldman, "Kennedy Remembered," p. 63. Historians voiced a similar sentiment, traced in William E. Leuchtenburg, "John F. Kennedy, Twenty Years Later," *American Heritage Magazine*, December 1983, pp. 50–59.

10. Parmet, *JFK: The Presidency of John F. Kennedy.*

11. Wills, *Kennedy Imprisonment;* Collier and Horowitz, *Kennedys: An American Drama.*

12. Examples included "A Great President? Experts Size Up JFK," *U.S. News and World Report*, 21 November 1983, p. 51; Lance Morrow, "After 20 Years, the Question: How Good a President?" *Time*, 14 November 1983, p. 58.

13. *New York Times*, 17 February 1985, section 1, p. 51.

14. James Reston, Jr., *The Expectations of John Connally* (New York: Harper and Row, 1989); excerpted in Reston, "Was Connally the Real Target?" *Time*, 28 November 1988, pp. 30–41. Reston and Connally were also interviewed on ABC's "Nightline," 22 November 1988.

15. Books on organized crime included John H. Davis's *Mafia Kingfish: Carlos Marcello and the Assassination of John F. Kennedy* (New York: McGraw-Hill, 1988) and David E. Scheim's *Contract on America* (New York: Zebra Books, 1988). Also see "Did the Mob Kill JFK?" *Time*, 28 November 1988, pp. 42–44. In 1991, Mark Lane published *Plausible Denial* (New York: Thunder's Mouth Press), about CIA involvement. For a thorough discussion of the Warren Commission see Henry Hurt, *Reasonable Doubt* (New York: Henry Holt, 1985). See also Jim Marrs, *Crossfire: The Plot That Killed Kennedy* (New York: Carroll and Graf, 1989).

16. Don DeLillo, *Libra* (New York: Viking, 1988); the NBC series was discussed in Morley, "Camelot and Dallas," p. 649.

17. John Gregory Dunne, "Elephant Man" (review of Wills's *Kennedy Imprisonment*), *New York Review of Books*, 15 April 1982, p. 10.

18. Morley, "Camelot and Dallas," p. 649.

19. As Morley said: "The *Washington Post* said the truth would never be known. A *Los Angeles Times* reporter dared to conclude that the Warren Commission was right. *Newsweek* left the public misgivings about the government's version of events to an inarticulate barber in Iowa" (ibid.).

20. Lasch, "Life of Kennedy's Death," p. 32.

21. For a detailed discussion of this point, see Scott, "From Dallas to Watergate," p. 358.

22. James Reston, Jr., quoted in "25th Anniversary of JFK's Assassination," "Nightline," ABC News, 22 November 1988. To an extent this was foregrounded in the early years of retelling. Broadcaster Eric Sevareid, brought in to comment on a 1968 CBS report on the Warren Commission, was criticized because "as a witness, his credentials . . . seemed to consist entirely of his agreement to watch the CBS documentary" (Lane, *Citizen's Dissent*, p. 96). Yet for lack of a viable alternative, his secondary access, or access to the documentary efforts of others, was seen, at least by the network, as an acceptable form of investigation.

23. "Who Shot President Kennedy?" "Nova," PBS. This program was in effect an updated version of a highly acclaimed CBS special shown in 1967, in which Walter Cronkite discussed on-site acoustic tests. The fact that television took it upon itself to provide an overview of the different technologies, bodies of expertise, and evidence by which it was possible to differentially "read" Kennedy's death reflects the relevance of surrounding discourse about technology.

24. David S. Lifton, *Best Evidence* (New York: Carroll and Graf, 1988), introductory remarks.

25. Ibid.; Reston, *Expectations*; Summers, *Conspiracy*; Robert J. Groden and Harrison Livingstone, *High Treason* (New York: Conservatory Press, 1989).

26. Kurtz, *Crime of the Century*; Blakey and Billings, *Plot to Kill*.

27. Quoted in Summers, *Conspiracy*, p. xxiii.

28. See Parmet, *JFK: The Presidency of John F. Kennedy*; Wills, *Kennedy Imprisonment*; Collier and Horowitz, *Kennedys: An American Drama*.

29. Kurtz, *Crime of the Century*; Brown, *JFK: History of an Image*.

30. "Historians Lost in the Mists of Camelot," *Los Angeles Times*, 21 October 1988, p. I1.

31. For example, one book reviewing conspiracy theories was published by former reporter Jim Marrs (*Crossfire*); also see Summers, *Conspiracy*; Robert MacNeil, *The Way We Were* (New York: Carroll and Graf, 1988).

32. "Many Remember the Scene as It Was," *Washington Post*, 23 November 1988, p. A8.

33. MacNeil, *Way We Were*. Also see John B. Jovich (ed.), *Reflections on JFK's Assassination* (N.p.: Woodbine House, 1988).

34. Mary McGrory, "You Had to Be There to Know the Pain," *Washington Post*, 20 November 1983, p. F1.

35. Quoted in Donner, "Assassination Circus," p. 657.

36. "JFK," ABC News.

37. "Remembering JFK," "Good Morning, America," ABC News, 22 November 1983.

38. "JFK: A Time Remembered," Susskind Co. in association with Obenhaus Films, Inc., shown on PBS, 21 November 1988.

39. Examples included a 1964 documentary, "Four Days in November," United Artists and United Press International; and "Kennedy: One Year Later," KTRK-TV, Houston, 1964.

40. Examples included "Being with John F. Kennedy," Drew Associates in association with Golden West Television, 1983; and "America Remembers John F. Kennedy," Thomas F. Horton Associates, 1983.

41. These included "JFK: That Day in November," NBC News, 22 November 1988; *Week We Lost John F. Kennedy*, NBC News; "Four Days in November: The Assassination of President Kennedy," CBS News; "JFK Assassination: As It Happened," NBC News.

42. "Kennedy Remembered," "Action News: Channel Six Late Night News," Philadelphia, 22 November 1988; "25th Anniversary of JFK's Assassination," "Nightline," ABC News; "Assassination: Twenty-five Years Later," "CBS Evening News," eight-part series, CBS News, 14–23 November 1988.

43. Jack Anderson, in "Who Murdered JFK? American Exposé," Saban Productions, 2 November 1988; Geraldo Rivera, in "On Trial," London Weekend Television; "Remembering President John F. Kennedy," "Oprah Winfrey Show," 22 November 1988.

44. One predictable segment outlining the ties between John Kennedy and Marilyn Monroe was featured on "Entertainment Tonight" on the twenty-fifth anniversary of his assassination ("Where Were You When JFK Was Shot?" "Entertainment Tonight," 22 November 1988).

45. "TV Retells the Story of Slaying," *New York Times*, 23 November 1988, p. A16.

46. Morley, "Camelot and Dallas," p. 649.

47. Judd Rose, in "25th Anniversary of JFK's Assassination," "Nightline," ABC News.

48. Dan Rather, "CBS Evening News," CBS News, 22 November 1988.

49. Trillin, "Buffs," p. 65.

50. Hugh Sidey, "History on His Shoulder," *Time*, 8 November 1982, p. 26.

51. Theodore White, "Camelot, Sad Camelot," p. 47.

52. "Decade of Unanswered Questions," p. 43.

53. Mary McGrory, "And Did You Once See Kennedy Plain?" *America*, 18 September 1965, p. 279.

54. See, for example, George Lardner, Jr., "On the Set: Dallas in Wonderland," *Washington Post*, 19 May 1991, p. D1; Anthony Lewis, "J.F.K.," *New York Times*, 9 January 1992, p. A23; Kenneth Auchincloss, "Twisted History,"

Newsweek, 23 December 1991, pp. 46–49; Tom Wicker, "Does 'J.F.K.' Conspire Against Reason?" *New York Times*, 15 December 1991, section 2, pp. 1, 18.

55. DeLillo, "American Blood," p. 27.

56. P. E. Tillinghast, *The Specious Past* (Reading, Mass: Addison-Wesley, 1972), p. 171.

57. Lifton, *Best Evidence*, p. 9.

58. Greenfield, "Kiss and Tell Memoirs," p. 17.

59. Leuchtenburg, "John F. Kennedy, Twenty Years Later," p. 58.

60. "Did the Mob Kill JFK?" p. 42.

61. Goldman, "Kennedy Remembered," p. 62.

62. Jeff Greenfield, in "Remembering JFK," "Good Morning, America," ABC News.

63. "TV Retells the Story of Slaying," *New York Times*, 23 November 1988, p. A8; "CBS Replays November 22," *New York Times*, 17 November 1988, p. B3; "JFK and a Tribute to TV," *Washington Post*, 23 November 1988, p. A2; "TV: The Ghost of a President Past," *Wall Street Journal*, 7 November 1988, p. A12.

64. "TV Retells the Story of Slaying," p. A16. Even one historian began his assassination account with an introductory remark about television, which underscored the medium's centrality and vitality in perpetuating the story: "Television brought the assassination and its aftermath vividly into the national consciousness. In their finest hours, the electronic news media captured the events unfolding in Dallas and Washington and transmitted them instantaneously to the American people. Far more graphically and realistically than the printed page, the video screen depicted some of the most unforgettable scenes in recent history" (Kurtz, *Crime of the Century*, p. v).

65. Hugh Sidey, "A Shattering Afternoon in Dallas," *Time*, 28 November 1988, p. 45. Sidey's testimony underscored the fact that many journalists who promoted themselves as eyewitnesses were in effect only earwitnesses. A similar tension between earwitnesses and eyewitnesses at the time of Kennedy's death is discussed in chapters 4 and 5.

66. Tom Wicker, quoted in "JFK: A Time Remembered," Susskind.

67. MacNeil, *Way We Were*, p. 195; rpt. from Robert MacNeil, *The Right Place at the Right Time* (Boston: Little, Brown, 1982).

68. Nancy Dickerson, quoted in "JFK: A Time Remembered," Susskind.

69. Sander Vanocur, quoted ibid.

70. John Chancellor, *Week We Lost John F. Kennedy*, NBC News.

71. Jane Howard, "Do You Remember the Day JFK Died?" *Ladies Home Journal*, November 1983, p. 114.

72. Peter Jennings, in "Changing South," "ABC Nightly News," ABC News, 22 November 1988. Jennings also served as the narrator for the 1983 retrospective, "JFK" (ABC News).

73. Chuck Stone, quoted in "Kennedy Remembered," "Action News: Channel Six Late-Night News."

74. Malcolm Poindexter, in "John F. Kennedy Remembered," "KYW Eyewitness News."

75. Hugh Aynesworth, quoted in Nora Ephron, "Twelve Years on the Assassination Beat," *Esquire*, February 1976, p. 59.

76. Quoted in "Four Days in November: The Assassination of President Kennedy," CBS News.

77. "The Plot to Kill President Kennedy: From the De-classified Files," M. G. Hollo with Fox/Lorber Associates, Inc., 1983.

78. Leo Sauvage, "Oswald in Dallas: A Few Loose Ends," *Reporter*, 2 January 1964, p. 24.

79. "JFK: The Death and the Doubts," *Newsweek*, 5 December 1966, p. 26.

80. Ephron, "Twelve Years," p. 62.

81. Albert Newman, *Assassination of John F. Kennedy*, p. ix.

82. "JFK: The Death and the Doubts," p. 25. This was despite the wrath that *Life* magazine generated among certain independent critics over its publication of the Zapruder film sequence.

83. Geraldo Rivera, in "On Trial," London Weekend Television.

84. Salisbury, "Editor's View," p. 44.

85. Jack Anderson, in "Who Murdered JFK?" Saban Productions.

86. Walter Cronkite, in "Who Shot President Kennedy?" "Nova," PBS.

87. Mannes, "Long Vigil," p. 16.

88. Forrest Sawyer, in "25th Anniversary of JFK's Assassination," "Nightline," ABC News.

89. Wright, *In the New World*, p. 309.

90. Nicholas Lemann, "Growing Up with the Kennedy Myth: Not Quite Camelot," *Washington Post*, 20 November 1983, p. F1.

91. Michael Matza, "Five Still Probing the JFK Killing," *Philadelphia Inquirer*, 22 November 1988, p. 8E.

92. "The Men Who Killed Kennedy," "Investigative Reports," produced by Nigel Turner for Kurtis Productions; shown on Arts and Entertainment Network, 27 September 1991, 4 October 1991, 11 October 1991, 18 October 1991, and 25 October 1991.

9. The Authority of the Individual: Recollecting Through Celebrity

1. Leo Braudy, *The Frenzy of Renown* (New York: Oxford University Press, 1986), p. 592.

2. This had parallels in other eras. For example, during the 1940s, journalistic celebrity was defined through radio personalities like Edward Murrow and Howard K. Smith. Certain presentational formats have also traditionally spotlighted the news tellers alongside their news stories. The column, for example, let print journalists highlight themselves while relaying the news; the experience of many contemporary television anchorpersons is analogous. See Michael Baruch Grossman and Martha Joynt Kumar, *Portraying the Presidency* (Baltimore: Johns Hopkins University Press, 1981), p. 209. Thus in some

senses journalistic celebrity has been around for as long as journalism. Therefore, suggestions that television produced journalistic celebrity, due to the intensified focus on anchorpersons that satellite transmission and improved video equipment made possible, may be misplaced. They may derive more directly from the fact that television is the newest news medium; when that status changes, so will discussions of journalistic celebrity.

3. Schudson, "Politics of Narrative Form."

4. Daniel Boorstin, *The Image* (New York: Atheneum, 1962), p. 57.

5. Braudy, *Frenzy of Renown*, p. 10. Also see Richard Dyer, *Stars* (London: British Film Institute, 1978); John Rodden, *The Politics of Literary Reputation* (New York: Oxford University Press, 1989).

6. Broder, *Behind the Front Page*, p. 158.

7. Wright, *In the New World*, p. 34. Certain reporters utilized the celebrity status gained during the Kennedy reign, as in the publication of *Washington Post* editor Benjamin Bradlee's *Conversations with Kennedy*.

8. A flip side to constructions of celebrity was its pathology, exemplified by Oswald's statement to a Dallas police officer that "everybody will know who I am now" (quoted in Donner, "Assassination Circus," p. 656). Similarly, in reference to Oswald's mother, *Newsweek* said that "it was as if she had been waiting all her 56 years for this one floodlit moment of celebrity ("The Assassination: A Week in the Sun," *Newsweek*, 24 February 1964, p. 29).

9. Wills, *Kennedy Imprisonment*, p. 94.

10. I am here employing the idea of indicative and subjunctive dimensions of coverage in accordance not only with the terms' common meanings in grammar but also with the valences of meaning suggested by Victor Turner, *The Ritual Process*, and by French linguist Emile Beneviste. See Beneviste, *Problems in General Linguistics* (Coral Gables, Fla.: University of Miami Press, 1981).

11. Salisbury, *Time of Change*, p. 71.

12. Gay Talese, *The Kingdom and the Power* (New York: Laurel Books/Dell, 1986), p. 34.

13. Ibid., pp. 505, 36.

14. Ibid., p. 37.

15. Wicker, "Does 'J.F.K.' Conspire Against Reason?" p. 1.

16. Dan Rather, quoted in "JFK: A Time Remembered," Susskind.

17. Rather with Herskowitz, *Camera Never Blinks*, p. 122. A contrasting assessment of Rather's performance was offered in *The Rather Narrative*, which accused Rather of aiding the conspiracy through his "long history of inaccurate reporting of the circumstances of [the] assassination" (Monte Evans, *The Rather Narrative: Is Dan Rather the JFK Conspiracy's San Andreas Fault?* [Barrington, R.I.: Barbara Books, 1990], p. 194).

18. Gates, *Air Time*, p. 12.

19. *People*, 28 November 1988, p. 70. See also Barbie Zelizer, "What's Rather Public about Dan Rather: TV Journalism and the Emergence of Celebrity," *Journal of Popular Film and Television* 17(2) (Summer 1989), pp. 74–80, for a discussion of Dan Rather as a contemporary example of journalistic celebrity.

20. Gates, *Air Time*, p. 293.

21. The latter of these two activities possibly prompted a similar action by Dan Rather in October 1989, when he neglected to put on his suit jacket while anchoring CBS's breaking story about the San Francisco earthquake. Whether Rather's action was intentional or accidental, it seemed to suggest—to those who paid attention—the ultimate sacrifice to professionalism, the dedication to quickly conveying the late-breaking story.

22. "What JFK Meant to Us," special issue, *Newsweek*, 28 November 1983, p. 66.

23. Matusow, *Evening Stars*.

24. Joanna Elm, "From 'Good Evening, Everybody, Coast to Coast' to 'Courage,'" *TV Guide*, 6 May 1989, p. 31.

25. Gates, *Air Time*, p. 6.

26. Ibid., pp. 6–7, 1.

27. In the movie, Jacqueline Kennedy referred to White as "one of the friendlies."

28. Lance Morrow, "Of Myth and Memory," *Time*, 24 October 1988, p. 24.

29. Evan Thomas, "A Reporter in Search of History," *Time*, 26 May 1986, p. 62. The title was a play on White's book of the same name.

30. Gates, *Air Time*, p. 169.

31. *Broadcasting*, 2 December 1963, p. 46.

32. Ephron, "Twelve Years," p. 60.

33. Welsh and Turner, "In the Shadow of Dallas," p. 63.

34. His style was evidenced, in "On Trial," London Weekend Television.

35. "Reporter Engagé," *Newsweek*, 23 December 1963, p. 70.

36. Jack Anderson, in "Who Murdered JFK?" Saban Productions.

37. Robert MacNeil, in "Good Morning, America," ABC News, 22 November 1988.

38. Tom Wicker, in "JFK: A Time Remembered," Susskind.

39. Wills, *Kennedy Imprisonment*; Manchester, *One Brief Shining Moment*.

40. Greenfield, "Way Things Really Were," p. 98.

41. Included were "25 Years Later," special section, *U.S. News and World Report*, 24 October 1988, pp. 30–40; Goldman, "Kennedy Remembered"; "Ten Years Later: Where Were You?"; and Kunhardt, *Life in Camelot*.

42. This technique was favored by most popular media forums, notably *Esquire* ("Ten Years Later: Where Were You?") and *People* ("November 22, 1963: Where We Were," special section, 28 November 1988, pp. 54–70). Not surprisingly, these compilations also included the memories of journalists.

43. These included "25th Anniversary of JFK's Assassination," "Nightline," ABC News; "Who Shot President Kennedy?" "Nova," PBS; and "JFK Assassination: As It Happened," NBC News. The last was NBC's attempt to reproduce the exact coverage of twenty-five years earlier.

44. "The Warren Report," "CBS Evening News," CBS News, 25–29 June 1967; "Four Days in November: The Assassination of President Kennedy," CBS News; "Who Shot President Kennedy?" "Nova," PBS.

45. Gamarekian, "Hundreds Are in Capital," p. A24.

46. "JFK: A Time Remembered," Susskind.

47. *Broadcasting*, 2 December 1963, pp. 36–46.

48. "JFK Assassination: As It Happened," NBC News. "The club" of journalists who participated was also found in semireconstructed events associated with the assassination. For example, writer James Kirkwood discussed journalists covering the Garrison investigation of New Orleans businessman Clay Shaw in the following way: "The camaraderie of the [other reporters] was immediately evident. Most, if not all, had covered the preliminary hearing two years earlier and they were like war correspondents. The hearing had been their Korea and now they were once more gathering at the battleground for Vietnam. They were all seasoned journalist-reporters" (Kirkwood, *American Grotesque*, p. 78).

49. Tobin, "If You Can Keep Your Head," p. 54; *Editor and Publisher*, 7 December 1963, p. 44.

50. "James Reston," "ABC Evening News," ABC News, 31 July 1987.

51. *UPI Reporter*, 28 November 1963; UPI, *Four Days*.

52. Letter quoted in *Editor and Publisher*, 30 November 1963, p. 8.

53. Associated Press, *Torch Is Passed*.

54. "Reporters' Story."

55. Wicker, "That Day"; Wicker, "Reporter Must Trust His Instinct."

56. Wicker, "Reporter Must Trust His Instinct," p. 81.

57. Tom Wicker, "Kennedy Without Tears," *Esquire*, June 1964.

58. Berendt, "Ten Years Later," p. 263.

59. Wicker, *Kennedy Without Tears*; Wicker, "Kennedy Without Tears" (rpt., *Esquire*, October 1973).

60. Wicker, "Kennedy Without Tears" (rpt., *Esquire*, October 1973), p. 196.

61. Wicker, *Kennedy Without Tears*, p. 63.

62. Kunhardt, *Life in Camelot*, pp. 295–97.

63. Theodore White, "Camelot, Sad Camelot," pp. 46–47. Even publications not produced by Time-Life referenced "Theodore H. White's poignant 'Camelot' epilogue in *Life*" (A. William Bluem, "Looking Ahead: The Black Horse," *Television Quarterly* 3[1] [Winter 1964], p. 85).

64. The 1983 series was "The Kennedy Assassination: Myth and Reality," "CBS Evening News," CBS News, 7–9 November 1983; the 1988 series was "Assassination: Twenty-five Years Later," "CBS Evening News," CBS News; "Four Days in November: The Assassination of President Kennedy," CBS News.

65. Dan Rather, in "Four Days in November: The Assassination of President Kennedy," CBS News.

66. Sandy Grady, "JFK: A Look Back," *Philadelphia Daily News*, 22 November 1988, p. 5.

67. Some reporters were interviewed on the "Huntley-Brinkley Report" about what they had seen and heard. Chet Huntley and David Brinkley, "Huntley-Brinkley Report," NBC News, 22 November 1963.

68. Ike Pappas, in "On Trial," London Weekend Television.

69. "High Profile: Ike Pappas," *Philadelphia Inquirer Magazine,* 10 September 1989, p. 8. Pappas was described as having begun his career as "a UPI crime reporter at age 19 who eventually witnessed 'the crime of the century' while standing five feet from Jack Ruby when he shot Lee Harvey Oswald."

70. Sidey, "Shattering Afternoon," p. 45.

71. Dan Rather, in "Four Days in November: The Assassination of President Kennedy," CBS News.

72. Steve Bell, in "John F. Kennedy Remembered," "KYW Eyewitness News."

73. Wicker, "Kennedy Without End," p. 65.

74. Tom Wicker, "Lyndon Johnson vs. the Ghost of Jack Kennedy," *Esquire,* November 1965, p. 152. Wicker quoted four long paragraphs from the piece.

75. Braudy, *Frenzy of Renown,* p. 585.

10. The Authority of the Organization and Institution: Recollecting Through Professional Lore

1. A large body of literature exists on professionalism and journalistic practice, including Weaver and Wilhoit, *American Journalist;* and its precursor, Johnstone, Slawski, and Bowman, *News People.* Also see Becker et al., *Training and Hiring,* for an overview of journalistic professionalism.

2. The term, borrowed from folklore, connotes the ability of groups to consolidate themselves through narratives that relate the group's origin. A similar term, *constitutive narrative,* is proposed in Bellah et al., *Habits of the Heart.*

3. Greenfield, "Way Things Really Were," p. 98.

4. Barbara Walters, quoted in "Ten Years Later: Where Were You?" p. 136.

5. Gwenda Blair, *Almost Golden: Jessica Savitch and the Selling of Television News* (New York: Simon and Schuster, 1988), p. 71.

6. Rather with Herskowitz, *Camera Never Blinks,* p. 152.

7. Mention of technology has often accompanied discussions of journalistic professionalism. Journalistic training manuals, for instance, tend to provide sections on how to operate whatever technology is at hand in news work. For discussions about news and technology see, for example, Stephen Klaidman, *The Virtuous Journalist* (New York: Oxford University Press, 1987); and Goldstein, *News at Any Cost.*

8. See Wicker, "Reporter Must Trust His Instinct"; and Roberts, "Eyewitness in Dallas."

9. See chapter 5 for a discussion in detail.

10. Gabe Pressman, cited in Pressman, Shayon, and Schulman, "Responsible Reporter," p. 15.

11. Steve Bell, in "John F. Kennedy Remembered," "KYW Eyewitness News."

12. Salisbury, *Time of Change,* p. 70.

13. Ibid., p. 67.

14. Wicker, "Reporter Must Trust His Instinct," p. 81.

15. Wicker, "Lyndon Johnson," p. 152.

16. Bradlee, *Conversations with Kennedy*, p. 7.

17. "What's Fit to Print?" *Reporter*, 2 January 1964, p. 12; also see "Reporter Engagé," p. 70.

18. "Four Days in November: The Assassination of President Kennedy," CBS News.

19. Edwin Newman, in "JFK Assassination: As It Happened," NBC News.

20. See the discussion of synecdoche in chapter 3.

21. A similar point has recently been made about photographic authority. See Fred Ritchin, *In Our Own Image* (New York: Aperture Foundation, 1990).

22. "John F. Kennedy Memorial Edition," *Life*, Winter 1988; rpt. of December 1963 issue.

23. Kunhardt, *Life in Camelot*, p. 317.

24. "John F. Kennedy Memorial Edition."

25. Kunhardt, *Life in Camelot*, pp. 8, 13.

26. "Can You Believe That 20 Years Have Passed," *Forbes*, 5 December 1983, p. 26.

27. "Assassination: Twenty-five Years Later," "CBS Evening News," CBS News.

28. "JFK Assassination: As It Happened," NBC News; *Week We Lost John F. Kennedy*, NBC News. Some of the same footage was also shown as "Biography: The Age of Kennedy," NBC News, shown on Arts and Entertainment Network, 13 March 1989.

29. Gates, *Air Time*, pp. 1–13.

30. Blair, *Almost Golden*, p. 199.

31. See Matusow for a discussion of Kintner's exploits (*Evening Stars*, p. 76).

32. Perhaps in keeping with the fact that ABC's original coverage of the event was more problematic than that of the other two networks, assassination narratives were not featured as prominently within organizational histories of that news organization.

33. Edwin Newman, in "JFK Assassination: As It Happened," NBC News.

34. "The Assassination," p. 5.

35. Ed Cray, Jonathan Kotler, and Miles Beller (eds.), *American Datelines: One Hundred and Forty Major News Stories from Colonial Times to the Present* (New York: Facts on File, 1990). This collection reprinted Merriman Smith's account as it arrived over the UPI wire. See also Harold Hayes (ed.), *Smiling Through the Apocalypse: Esquire's History of the Sixties* (New York: McCall, 1969). *Ramparts's* example of muckraking reporting was Welsh and Turner, "In the Shadow of Dallas."

36. Larry Grove, "A City Is Tried and Convicted," *Dallas News* (March 1964); rpt. in *The Quill*, November 1987, pp. 53–55.

37. Barnouw, *Tube of Plenty*, pp. 332–40.

38. Norm Goldstein (ed.) and the Associated Press, *The History of Television* (New York: Portland House, 1991).

39. Matusow, *Evening Stars*, p. 107.

40. Ibid., p. 106.

41. "The Moments You Can Never Forget," *TV Guide*, 6 May 1989, p. 4.

42. "Four Days in November," CBS News.

43. Halberstam, *Powers That Be*.

44. Wright, *In the New World*, p. 71.

45. Robinson, "Reporting the Death," p. 8E.

46. Peter Kaplan and Paul Slansky, "Golden Moments," *Connoisseur*, September 1989, p. 136.

47. Kurtz, *Crime of the Century*, p. v.

48. Dan Rather, in "Four Days in November: The Assassination of President Kennedy," CBS News.

49. Quoted in Robinson, "Reporting the Death," p. 8E.

50. Ibid.

51. Dan Rather, in "Four Days in November: The Assassination of President Kennedy," CBS News.

52. "Icons: The Ten Greatest Images of Photojournalism," *Time*, special collector's edition, Fall 1989, p. 8.

53. "New Challenges: 1950–80," *Time*, special collector's edition, Fall 1989, p. 56.

54. Ibid.

55. See Greenberg and Parker, *Kennedy Assassination*.

56. Walter Cronkite, quoted in "Fifty Years of Television: A Golden Anniversary," CBS News, 26 November 1989.

57. Lance Morrow, "Imprisoning Time in a Rectangle," *Time*, special collector's edition, Fall 1989, p. 76.

11. The Authority of the Profession: Recollecting Through History

1. Richard A. Blake, "Two Moments of Grief," *America*, 24 November 1973, p. 402.

2. Murray G. Murphey, *Our Knowledge of the Historical Past* (Indianapolis: Bobbs-Merrill, 1973), p. 1.

3. See, for example, Daniel Boorstin, *Hidden History* (New York: Harper and Row, 1987). Also see Hayden White, "Value of Narrativity," and Kellner, *Language and Historical Representation*.

4. Michael H. Frisch, "The Memory of History," in *Presenting the Past*, ed. Susan Porter Benson et al. (Philadelphia: Temple University Press, 1986), p. 11. It is worthwhile mentioning that oral historians in effect use memory in much the same way that journalists do, suggesting that they offer a different form of recordkeeping than traditional historians.

5. Patrick H. Hutton, "Collective Memory and Collective Mentalities: The Halbwachs-Ariès Connection," *Historical Reflections* 2 (1988), p. 312. This is also discussed in Kammen, *Mystic Chords of Memory*.

6. Hutton, "Collective Memory," p. 317.

7. Leuchtenburg, "John F. Kennedy, Twenty Years Later," p. 58.

8. *Editor and Publisher*, 30 November 1963, p. 6.

9. "Assassination: History or Headlines?" *Newsweek*, 13 March 1967, p. 44.

10. One of the first examples was found in *Editor and Publisher* (30 November 1963, p. 67), but references to the assassination photographs were found over the entire time span of assassination narratives. Among the first of many discussions of films was Stolley, "Greatest Home Movie."

11. As with both photographs and films, claims to having made historic coverage were employed directly after the assassination (see, for example, *Broadcasting*, 2 December 1963).

12. Theodore White, *America in Search of Itself*, pp. 1–2.

13. William Manchester, *Portrait of a President* (Boston: Little, Brown, 1967 [1962]), p. x. Manchester went on to say that his book constituted journalism because it had been "written while moving along the advancing edge of the present. It is not definitive in any sense" (p. x).

14. Halberstam, *Powers That Be*, p. 229.

15. *Broadcasting*, 2 December 1963, p. 50.

16. *Editor and Publisher*, 30 November 1963, p. 67.

17. *Broadcasting*, 2 December 1963, p. 51.

18. "Shores Dimly Seen," *Progressive*, January 1964, p. 3.

19. "Plot to Kill President Kennedy," Hollo with Fox/Lorber.

20. Kenneth Auchincloss, "The Kennedy Years: What Endures?" *Newsweek*, 1 February 1971, p. 21.

21. Theodore White, "Camelot, Sad Camelot."

22. Norman Mailer, "Kennedy and After," *New York Review of Books*, 26 December 1963; rpt. in *Current*, January 1964, p. 14.

23. David Marannis, "In Dallas, the Lingering Trauma," *Washington Post*, 22 November 1988, p. E-1.

24. Talese, *Kingdom and Power*, p. 34.

25. Dallas Morning News, *November 22: The Day Remembered* (Dallas: Taylor Publishing, 1990).

26. Don DeLillo, "Matters of Fact and Fiction," *Rolling Stone*, 17 November 1988, p. 117.

27. For a discussion of Ariès, see Hutton, "Collective Memory." See also Fernand Braudel, *On History* (Chicago: University of Chicago Press, 1980); Pierre Nora, "Between Memory and History: Les lieux de mémoire," *Representations* (Spring 1989), p. 13.

28. See Hayden White, "Value of Narrativity"; Kellner, *Language and Historical Representation*. Also see Canary and Kozicki, *Writing of History*.

29. Halberstam, *Best and Brightest*.

30. Wills, *Kennedy Imprisonment*; John H. Davis, *The Kennedys* (New York: McGraw-Hill, 1984); Collier and Horowitz, *Kennedys: An American Drama*. Also see Manchester, *Portrait of a President*, pp. 239–66.

31. Parmet, *JFK: The Presidency of John F. Kennedy*, pp. 341–49.

32. Murphey, *Historical Past*, p. 11. Examples include Schlesinger, *Thou-*

sand Days; and Sorensen, *Kennedy.* Other examples include memoirs by Kennedy staff, such as Paul B. Fay, Jr., *The Pleasure of His Company* (New York: Harper and Row, 1966) and Frank Saunders, *Torn Lace Curtain* (New York: Holt, Rinehart and Winston, 1982). Still another alternative mode of historiography was represented by *American Heritage* magazine, which was praised for its successful application of photojournalism techniques to history. Like other forms of historiography, the magazine signified a mood of transition when it began to accommodate contemporary topics and abandoned the chronological emphasis of its predecessors. It was hailed as "the lively offspring of the marriage of history and journalism" and defined as "the newsmagazine of the past" (*History News* 13 [February 1957], p. 26; cited in Roy Rosenzweig, "Marketing the Past," in *Presenting the Past,* ed. Benson et al., pp. 32, 39, 44).

33. Initial disapproval came from McGrory, "And Did You Once See Kennedy Plain?"; Greenfield, "Kiss and Tell Memoirs"; and "Peephole Journalism." Additional disapproval was recently registered during the uproar over Oliver Stone's movie *JFK.* See, for example, Edwin M. Yoder, Jr., "With 'JFK,' Filmmaker Oliver Stone Shows He Isn't Up to the Job of Historian," *Philadelphia Inquirer,* 27 December 1991, p. A10; Tanya Barrientos, "'JFK' Film Has Students Talking About History," *Philadelphia Inquirer,* 24 January 1992, p. D1.

34. "Presidency: Battle of the Book," p. 18.

35. McGrory, "And Did You Once See Kennedy Plain?" p. 279.

36. Greenfield, "Kiss and Tell Memoirs." Greenfield held that the memoirs of Kennedy's administration suffered from the chroniclers' overindulgent attitude toward Kennedy.

37. Ibid., p. 15.

38. Ibid.

39. Raymond Moley, "Brief, Not a History," *Newsweek,* 20 December 1965, p. 108.

40. Logan, "Stained Glass Image," p. 75.

41. Ibid., p. 4.

42. Morley, "Camelot and Dallas," p. 649.

43. Sidey, *John F. Kennedy, President;* Fairlie, *Kennedy Promise;* Salinger, *With Kennedy;* Bradlee, *Conversations with Kennedy;* Theodore H. White, *In Search of History* (New York: Warner, 1978) and *America in Search of Itself.*

44. Talese, *Kingdom and Power,* p. 34.

45. *New York Times,* 29 August 1964, p. 46.

46. Bradlee, *Conversations with Kennedy,* p. 8.

47. Berendt, "Ten Years Later," p. 141.

48. Jack Anderson, in "Who Murdered JFK?" Saban Productions.

49. *Week We Lost John F. Kennedy,* NBC News.

50. Stone's claim to be a "cinematic historian" was made in Stephen Talbot, "60s Something," *Mother Jones,* March/April 1991, pp. 46–49. He is, said the article, "a de facto historian for a generation whose ideas and views are being increasingly shaped by movies and TV" (p. 49). Stone called for the turning

over of history to the people on the "Today Show" ("Who Killed JFK?" "Today Show," NBC News, 7 February 1992).

51. William Manchester, "No Evidence for a Conspiracy to Kill Kennedy," letter to the editor, *New York Times*, 5 February 1992, p. A22.

52. DeLillo, *Libra*, p. 301.

53. John Connally, quoted in "25th Anniversary of JFK's Assassination," "Nightline," ABC News.

54. Halberstam, *Powers That Be*, p. 568. Interestingly, similar claims were advanced about *American Heritage* magazine, which "because of its commitment to visualizing U.S. history" generated a different kind of historical documentation (Rosenzweig, "Marketing the Past," p. 39).

55. Eric Breitbart, "The Painted Mirror," in *Presenting the Past*, ed. Benson et al., p. 116.

56. Nora, "Between Memory and History," p. 13.

57. Breitbart, "Painted Mirror," p. 111.

58. Tillinghast, *Specious Past*, p. 171.

59. Steve Bell, in "Return to Camelot: Steve Bell and the JFK Years," Group W Television, 22 November 1988.

12. Conclusion: On the Establishment of Journalistic Authority

1. Morrow, "Of Myth and Memory," p. 22.

2. Hayden White, "'Figuring the Nature of the Times Deceased': Literary Theory and Historical Writing," in *The Future of Literary Theory*, ed. Ralph Cohen (New York: Routledge, 1989), p. 27.

3. Davis and Starn, "Introduction," p. 5.

4. See Carolyn Marvin, *When Old Technologies Were New* (New York: Oxford University Press, 1988), and Carolyn Marvin, "Experts, Black Boxes and Artifacts: News Categories in the Social History of Electric Media," in Brenda Dervin et al. (eds.), *Rethinking Communication*, Vol. 2: *Paradigm Exemplars* (London: Sage, 1989), pp. 188–98, for a discussion of how social exchange is shaped by new media.

5. See Barbie Zelizer, "CNN, the Gulf War, and Journalistic Practice," *Journal of Communication* 42(1), Winter 1992, pp. 68–81.

6. Michael Arlen, *The Living-Room War* (New York: Viking, 1969).

7. Davis and Starn, "Introduction," p. 2.

8. Peter C. Rollins makes a similar point about journalists and the Vietnam War. See Rollins, "The American War: Perceptions Through Literature, Film and Television," *American Quarterly* 3 (1984), pp. 419–32. The notion of archival memory is discussed in Nora, "Between Memory and History," p. 13. Also see Hayden White, "Figuring the Nature," p. 20.

9. Halbwachs, *Collective Memory*, p. 7.

10. Mary Douglas, *How Institutions Think* (Syracuse: Syracuse University Press, 1986), p. 70.

11. The idea of collective dignity is from in Barry Schwartz, Yael Zerubavel, and Bernice Barnett, "The Recovery of Masada: A Study in Collective Memory," *Sociological Quarterly* 2 (1986), p. 149.

12. Tuchman, *Making News*, pp. 59–63.

13. Halbwachs, *Collective Memory*, p. 86.

14. The term comes from Hayden White, "Figuring the Nature," p. 21.

15. Clifford Geertz, "Thick Description: Toward an Interpretive Theory of Culture," in *The Interpretation of Cultures* (New York: Basic Books, 1973), p. 5.

16. Lasch, "Life of Kennedy's Death."

Epilogue: Beyond Journalistic Authority to the Shaping of Collective Memory

1. Stone's film told the story of an unsuccessful attempt during the late 1960s by former New Orleans District Attorney Jim Garrison to prove conspiracy involvement in Kennedy's death. His claim—that the assassination could be laid to a parallel right-wing government motivated by a rising military-industrial complex—was not supported when brought to trial, and charges against the accused, local businessman Clay Shaw, were dismissed. The film was primarily based on three sources: Garrison, *On the Trail of the Assassins;* Marrs, *Crossfire;* and John Newman, *Kennedy and Vietnam* (New York: Warner, 1992). His selection of Garrison's book was in fact problematic, because years earlier critics had been divided in their appraisals of Garrison's investigation of Shaw. See Epstein, "Garrison"; William Turner, "Assassinations: Epstein's Garrison"; and Kirkwood, *American Grotesque.*

2. Talbot, "60s Something," p. 49.

3. Lardner, "On the Set," p. D1. Stone responded to Lardner in "Stone's 'JFK': A Higher Truth?" *Washington Post*, 2 June 1991, p. D3.

4. Jon Margolis, "JFK Movie and Book Attempt to Rewrite History," *Chicago Tribune*, 14 May 1991, p. 19; Richard Zoglin, "More Shots in Dealey Plaza," *Time*, 10 June 1991, pp. 64–66; Lardner, "On the Set," p. D1.

5. The publication *Lies of Our Times* devoted a large section to the issue of precensorship. See, for example, Carl Oglesby, "Who Killed JFK? The Media Whitewash," *Lies of Our Times*, September 1991, pp. 3–6; Zachary Sklar, "Time Magazine's Continuing Cover-Up," *Lies of Our Times*, September 1991, pp. 7–8; Herbert Schiller, "JFK: The Movie," *Lies of Our Times*, September 1991, pp. 6–7. More even-handed media views were laid out in Elaine Dutka, "Oliver Stone Fights Back," *Los Angeles Times*, 24 June 1991, pp. F1, F2; and Jay Carr, "Oliver Stone Defends His Take on 'JFK,'" *Boston Globe*, 11 August 1991, pp. 81, 84. Critics Harrison Livingstone and Harold Weisberg both attacked the film, with Weisberg calling it "a travesty," (quoted in Zoglin, "More Shots in Dealey Plaza," p. 64).

6. Arthur Schlesinger, Jr., "'JFK': Truth and Fiction," *Wall Street Journal*, 10 January 1992, p. A8.

7. Manchester, "No Evidence for a Conspiracy," p. A22.

8. Lewis, "J.F.K.," p. A23. Stone responded to Lewis's charges in "Warren Panel Findings Should Stir Outrage," letter to the editor, *New York Times*, 3 February 1992, p. A14.

9. Auchincloss, "Twisted History." Interestingly, *Newsweek*'s film critic praised the film, saying, "If history is a battlefield, 'JFK' has to be seen as a bold attempt to seize the turf for future debate." David Ansen, "A Trouble-maker for Our Times," *Newsweek*, 23 December 1991, p. 50.

10. Wicker, "Does 'J.F.K.' Conspire Against Reason?" pp. 1, 18. Wicker's longstanding presence in the assassination story is discussed in chapter 9.

11. Ibid., p. 18.

12. Ibid.

13. "JFK," "48 Hours," CBS News, 5 February 1992. These patterns of re-telling, exhibited by both Rather and CBS, have a long history, as discussed in chapter 9.

14. Bill Carter, "Rather Pulls CBS News Back to the Assassination," *New York Times*, 4 February 1992, p. C11. This was, in fact, not Rather's scoop but that of the lesser-known Eddie Barker. Chapter 3 discusses this case of omission as an example of narrative adjustment.

15. Ibid., p. C16.

16. Gail Shister, "Rather and JFK," *Philadelphia Inquirer*, 5 February 1992, pp. E1, E7.

17. Ibid., p. E1.

18. Rather, quoted in "JFK," "48 Hours."

19. Ibid.

20. Ibid.

21. Steve Bell, quoted in Gail Shister, "Steve Bell Discounts Assassination Theories," *Philadelphia Inquirer*, 10 January 1992, p. 6D. In the same article, Bell also recounted how "tough" it had been to cover Kennedy's death.

22. Lisa Grunwald, "Why We Still Care," *Life*, December 1991, pp. 35–46; Robert Sam Anson, "The Shooting of JFK," *Esquire*, November 1991, pp. 93–102, 174–176; Chris Heath, "Killer Instincts," *Details*, January 1992, pp. 60–65, 114.

23. "Oliver Stone's 'JFK,'" "Nightline," ABC News, 19 December 1991; also "The JFK Assassination Files," "Nightline," ABC News, 22 January 1992.

24. David Ehrenstein, "JFK—A New Low for Hollywood," *The Advocate*, 14 January 1992, pp. 78–81; G. Robert Blakey, quoted in "JFK: Fact or Fiction?" "Crossfire," CNN, 23 December 1991.

25. "Lyndon B. Johnson: JFK's Vice-President or Assassin?" "Geraldo," NBC, 23 December 1991; "The JFK Controversy," "Oprah Winfrey Show," ABC, 22 January 1992; "Director Oliver Stone on the JFK Assassination," "Larry King Live," CNN, 20 December 1991; "JFK's Assassination: The Continuing Controversy," "Larry King Live," CNN, 16 January 1992; "JFK," "The Ron Reagan Show," 19 November 1991. The PBS popular culture magazine,

"Edge," screened a spoof of the Stone movie in December 1991, claiming that "yet again Oliver Stone was trying to get the sixties right."

26. Robert Tanenbaum, former official with the House Select Committee on Assassinations, interviewed on "JFK: Fact or Fiction?" "Crossfire."

27. Quoted in Bernard Weinraub, "Substance and Style Criticized in 'J.F.K.,'" *New York Times*, 7 November 1991, p. C19.

28. Larry King, quoted in "Director Oliver Stone, "Larry King Live."

29. Quoted in "Lyndon B. Johnson," "Geraldo."

30. Robert Sam Anson, quoted in "JFK," "The Ron Reagan Show." As Anson said, "There has never been a systematic ongoing investigation by the press . . . And I think that's inexcusable on our part." When asked why the media had not produced its own Woodwards and Bernsteins for the assassination story, Anson said:

> this is an unbelievably complex story. The Warren Commission alone generated nearly a million pages of testimony and evidence. There are very few news organizations that have the resources to get through that morass. Secondly, there have—dealing with buffs and people who are interested in the assassination is not always easy. You hear some really wild theories. . . . And frankly, reporters, by and large, are middle class straight thinking people who've got their sources and they want to protect them, and when they run into a conspiracy, at least at the presidential level, they have an impossible time thinking about this.

31. Quoted in Carr, "Oliver Stone Defends His Take," p. 84.

32. Lardner, "On the Set," p. D4.

33. Yoder, "With 'JFK,' Stone Shows He Isn't Up to the Job," p. 10A.

34. "JFK's Assassination: The Continuing Controversy," "Larry King Live."

35. "Oliver Stone Address to National Press Club," C-Span, 15 January 1992.

36. Ibid.

37. "Director Oliver Stone," "Larry King Live." This disdain for journalists' role in the story was also upheld in the movie itself, which portrayed most journalists either as indifferent to the Garrison case or as blatantly obstructing it.

38. Ibid.

39. Shister, "Rather and JFK," p. E7.

40. "Who Killed JFK?" "Today Show." Stone made the same claim on "Oliver Stone's 'JFK,'" "Nightline." "If these critics feel so secure with their truth," he said. "why don't we let the American people see it. Let the files out . . . trust the American people with the truth and with their history."

41. Quoted in "Director Oliver Stone," "Larry King Live."

42. Talbot, "60s Something," p. 49.

43. Mark Rowland, "Stone Unturned," *American Film*, March 1991, pp. 41–43.

44. Wicker, "Does 'J.F.K.' Conspire Against Reason?"

45. Ellen Goodman, "The Problem With 'JFK' Is Facts," *Philadelphia Inquirer,* 4 January 1992, p. 7A.

46. Arlen Specter, "'JFK' the Film Mangles the Facts," *Philadelphia Inquirer,* 5 January 1992, p. 5C. Stone replied to Specter a week later ("Oliver Stone Replies to Sen. Specter," letter to the editor, *Philadelphia Inquirer,* 12 January 1992, p. 4C). Also see Katharine Seelye, "New Film Fires a Bullet at Specter's Re-election," *Philadelphia Inquirer,* 5 January 1992, pp. 1A, 8A.

47. Ron Rosenbaum, "Taking a Darker View," *Time,* 13 January 1992, pp. 38–40.

48. Clifford Krauss, "A Move to Unseal the Kennedy Files," *New York Times,* 22 January 1992, pp. A1, A14. Also see Larry Margasek, "Film Adds Pressure to Open JFK Files," *Philadelphia Inquirer,* 20 January 1992, p. D1.

49. Krauss, "A Move to Unseal the Kennedy Files." Also see Pete Yost, "Warren Panel Lawyers Ask Release of JFK Files," *Philadelphia Inquirer,* 31 January 1992, p. A17, and *New York Times,* 27 March 1992, p. A14.

50. "Get the Rest of the J.F.K. Story," editorial, *New York Times,* 16 January 1992, p. A22.

51. Robert Sam Anson, quoted in "JFK," "The Ron Reagan Show."

52. "Director Oliver Stone," "Larry King Live."

53. Stephen E. Ambrose, "Writers on the Grassy Knoll: A Reader's Guide," *New York Times Book Review,* 2 February 1992, pp. 1, 23–25.

54. Rosenbaum, "Taking a Darker View."

55. Assassination Symposium on John F. Kennedy, 14–15 November 1991, Dallas, Texas. In fact, the centrality of Stone's film to the critics' efforts was upheld at a final session of the conference, when critic Mark Lane castigated one journalist in the audience for "lying to the American people in an effort to destroy the film before it took place."

56. Ambrose, "Writers on the Grassy Knoll," p. 25.

57. Michael Isikoff, "'JFK' Is No Hit With the Archives," *Philadelphia Inquirer,* 22 January 1992, p. C9.

58. See, for example, "Readers Find Fault With Doubters of 'JFK,'" letters to the editor, *Philadelphia Inquirer,* 12 January 1992, p. 4C. Said one such letter: "The *Inquirer* editorial board repeatedly bashes any new evidence on the assassination, including the recent film 'JFK'. . . . Why is the press being so stupid?" See Richard Laverick, "Why So Reluctant?" letter to the editor, *Philadelphia Inquirer,* 12 January 1992, p. 4C. Also see "Letters," letters to the editor, *New York Times,* 5 January 1992, p. H4, which suggested a considerable degree of expertise. The readers' targets included the film, the mainstream media, the official investigatory agencies, and Senator Arlen Specter.

59. They included Garrison, *On the Trail of the Assassins;* Groden and Livingstone, *High Treason;* Marrs, *Crossfire;* and Lane, *Plausible Denial.*

60. "Who Killed JFK?" "Today Show."

61. Anson, "Shooting of JFK."

62. Shortly after the film opened, Encore Books arranged special areas with assassination-related literature.

63. Maralyn Lois Polak, "Mark Lane: Deep in His Plots," *Philadelphia Inquirer Magazine*, 19 January 1992, pp. 7–8. "Geraldo" featured interviews with critics Robert Groden, Jim Marrs, and a third theorist, Craig Zirbel. See "Lyndon B. Johnson: JFK's Vice-President or Assassin?" "Geraldo."

64. "Who Killed JFK?" "Today Show."

65. Sam Donaldson, "PrimeTime Live," special segment on the Kennedy assassination, ABC News, 16 January 1992.

66. Dan Rather, "CBS Evening News With Dan Rather," CBS News, 13 December 1991.

67. Yoder, "With 'JFK,' Stone Shows He Isn't Up to the Job," p. 10A.

68. Auchincloss, "Twisted History"; quoted in "PrimeTime Live," ABC News.

69. "Director Oliver Stone," "Larry King Live."

70. Goodman, "Problem with 'JFK' Is Facts," p. 7A.

71. "Get the Rest of the J.F.K. Story," p. A22.

72. Quoted in "Director Oliver Stone," "Larry King Live."

73. "PrimeTime Live," ABC News.

74. "JFK Assassination Files," "Nightline."

75. Quoted in "Director Oliver Stone," "Larry King Live."

76. Wicker, "Does 'J.F.K.' Conspire Against Reason?" p. 18.

77. Goodman, "Problem with 'JFK' Is Facts," p. 7A.

78. Dutka, "Oliver Stone Fights Back," p. F1.

79. Anson, "Shooting of JFK."

80. Examples of fictionalized sequences in retrospectives included "Who Murdered JFK?" "American Exposé" and "On Trial," London Weekend Television.

81. In Stone's case, these boundaries had earlier proved problematic when those claiming more expertise had accused him of historical inaccuracy for his filmic representations of the Vietnam War and the rock music industry. See "A True Story That's Not So True," *Insight*, 2 April 1990, p. 58; "The Eyes Have It," *Premiere*, July 1991, p. 14.

82. Quoted in "Who Killed JFK?" "Today Show." The claim was also made in "JFK," "48 Hours."

83. Kammen, *Mystic Chords of Memory*, pp. 667–668.

84. Ambrose, "Writers on the Grassy Knoll," p. 25.

Bibliography

References Related to Kennedy and the Kennedy Assassination
Books

American Society of Newspaper Editors. "Dallas Revisited." In *Problems of Journalism*. Proceedings of the 1964 Convention of the American Society of Newspaper Editors, 16–18 April 1964, pp. 22–49. Washington, D.C.: ASNE, 1964.

Associated Press. *The Torch Is Passed. . . .* New York: Associated Press in association with Western Publishing, 1963.

Belin, David W. *Final Disclosure.* New York: Macmillan, 1988.

Bird, S. Elizabeth. "Media and Folklore as Intertextual Communication Processes: John F. Kennedy and the Supermarket Tabloids." In *Communication Yearbook 10*, ed. Margaret McLaughlin, pp. 758–72. Newbury Park, Cal.: Sage, 1987.

Bishop, Jim. *The Day Kennedy Was Shot.* New York: Bantam, 1968.

Blair, Gwenda. *Almost Golden: Jessica Savitch and the Selling of Television News.* New York: Simon and Schuster, 1988.

Blakey, G. Robert, and Richard N. Billings. *The Plot to Kill the President.* New York: New York Times Books, 1981.

Bradlee, Benjamin. *Conversations with Kennedy.* New York: W. W. Norton, 1975.

Broder, David S. *Behind the Front Page.* New York: Touchstone, 1987.

Brown, Thomas. *JFK: History of an Image.* Bloomington: Indiana University Press, 1988.

Buchanan, Thomas G. *Who Killed Kennedy?* New York: Putnam, 1964.

Collier, Peter, and David Horowitz. *The Kennedys: An American Drama.* New York: Warner, 1984.

Condon, Richard. *Winter Kills.* New York: Dial, 1974.

Dallas Morning News. *November 22: The Day Remembered.* Dallas: Taylor Publishing, 1990.

Davis, John H. *The Kennedys.* New York: McGraw-Hill, 1984.

———. *Mafia Kingfish: Carlos Marcello and the Assassination of John F. Kennedy.* New York: McGraw-Hill, 1988.

DeLillo, Don. *Libra.* New York: Viking, 1988.

Dickstein, Morris. *Gates of Eden: American Culture in the Sixties.* New York: Penguin, 1989.

Epstein, Edward J. *Inquest: The Warren Commission and the Establishment of Truth.* New York: Viking, 1966.

———. *Legend: The Secret World of Lee Harvey Oswald.* New York: McGraw-Hill, 1978.

Evans, Monte. *The Rather Narrative: Is Dan Rather the JFK Conspiracy's San Andreas Fault?* Barrington, R.I.: Barbara Books, 1990.

Evica, George Michael. *And We Are All Mortal.* West Hartford, Conn.: University of Hartford Press, 1978.

Faber, H. *The Kennedy Years.* New York: Viking, 1964.

Fairlie, Henry. *The Kennedy Promise.* New York: Dell, 1972.

Fay, Paul B., Jr. *The Pleasure of His Company.* New York: Harper and Row, 1966.

Fensterwald, Bernard, Jr. *Coincidence or Conspiracy?* New York: Zebra Books, 1977.

Final Assassinations Report, The. New York: Bantam, 1979.

Ford, Gerald, and John R. Stiles. *Portrait of the Assassin.* New York: Simon and Schuster, 1965.

Garrison, Jim. *On the Trail of the Assassins.* New York: Sheridan Square Press, 1988.

Gitlin, Todd. *The Sixties: Years of Hope, Days of Rage.* New York: Bantam, 1987.

Greenberg, Bradley, and Edwin Parker (eds.). *The Kennedy Assassination and the American Public.* Palo Alto: Stanford University Press, 1965.

Groden, Robert J., and Harrison Livingstone. *High Treason.* New York: Conservatory Press, 1989.

Halberstam, David. *The Best and the Brightest.* New York: Random House, 1972.

———. "Introduction." In *The Kennedy Presidential Press Conferences,* pp. i–iv. New York: Earl M. Coleman Enterprises, 1978.

———. *The Powers That Be.* New York: Laurel Books, 1979.

Hayes, Harold (ed.). *Smiling Through the Apocalypse: Esquire's History of the Sixties.* New York: McCall, 1969.

Hurt, Harry. *Reasonable Doubt.* New York: Henry Holt, 1985.

Jameson, Fredric. "Periodizing the Sixties." In *The 60s Without Apology,* ed. Sohnya Sayres et al., pp. 178–209. Minneapolis: University of Minnesota Press in cooperation with *Social Text,* 1984.

Jones, Penn, Jr. *Forgive My Grief.* Midlothian, Tex.: Midlothian Mirror, 1966.

Jovich, John B. (ed.). *Reflections on JFK's Assassination.* N.p.: Woodbine House, 1988.

Kantor, Seth. *Who Was Jack Ruby?* New York: Everest House, 1978.

Kennedy, John F. *Why England Slept.* New York: Funk and Wagnalls, 1961 [1940].

———. *Profiles in Courage.* New York: Harper and Row, 1956.

Kirkwood, James. *American Grotesque: An Account of the Clay Shaw–Jim Garrison Affair in the City of New Orleans.* New York: Simon and Schuster, 1970.

Kunhardt, Philip B., Jr. (ed.). *Life in Camelot: The Kennedy Years.* New York: Time-Life Books, 1988.

Kurtz, Michael L. *Crime of the Century: The Kennedy Assassination from a Historian's Perspective.* Knoxville: University of Tennessee Press, 1982.

Lane, Mark. *Rush to Judgment.* New York: Holt, Rinehart and Winston, 1966.

———. *A Citizen's Dissent.* New York: Holt, Rinehart and Winston, 1968.

———. *Plausible Denial.* New York: Thunder's Mouth Press, 1991.

Lane, Mark, and Donald Freed. *Executive Action.* New York: Dell, 1973.

Lasky, Victor. *JFK: The Man and the Myth.* New York: Dell, 1977 [1963].

Lieberson, Goddard (ed.). *JFK: As We Remember Him.* New York: Atheneum, 1965.

Lifton, David S. *Best Evidence.* New York: Carroll and Graf, 1988.

Love, Ruth Leeds. "The Business of Television and the Black Weekend." In *The Kennedy Assassination and the American Public,* ed. Bradley Greenberg and Edwin Parker, pp. 73–86. Palo Alto: Stanford University Press, 1965.

Lowe, Jacques. *Kennedy: A Time Remembered.* New York: Quartet/Visual Arts, 1983.

Lower, Elmer. "A Television Network Gathers the News." In *The Kennedy Assassination and the American Public,* ed. Bradley Greenberg and Edwin Parker, pp. 67–72. Palo Alto: Stanford University Press, 1965.

McDonald, Hugh C. *Appointment in Dallas.* New York: Zebra Books, 1975.

MacNeil, Robert. *The Right Place at the Right Time.* Boston: Little, Brown, 1982.

——— (ed.). *The Way We Were.* New York: Carroll and Graf, 1988.

Manchester, William. *Portrait of a President.* Boston: Little, Brown, 1967 [1962].

———. *The Death of a President.* New York: Harper and Row, 1967.

———. *One Brief Shining Moment.* Boston: Little, Brown, 1983.

Marrs, Jim. *Crossfire: The Plot That Killed Kennedy.* New York: Carroll and Graf, 1989.

Mayo, John B. *Bulletin from Dallas.* New York: Exposition Press, 1967.

Meagher, Sylvia. *Subject Index to the Warren Report and Hearings and Exhibits.* New York: Scarecrow Press, 1966.

———. *Accessories after the Fact.* New York: Bobbs-Merrill, 1967.

Meagher, Sylvia, and Gary Owens. *Master Index to the J.F.K. Assassination Investigations.* Metuchen, N.J.: Scarecrow Press, 1980.

Newman, Albert H. *The Assassination of John F. Kennedy.* New York: Clarkson N. Potter, 1970.

Newman, John. *Kennedy and Vietnam.* New York: Warner, 1992.

Nielsen Co. *TV Responses to the Death of a President.* New York: Nielsen, 1963.

1968 Panel Review of Photographs, X-Ray Films, Documents and Other Evidence Pertaining to the Fatal Wounding of President John F. Kennedy on November 22, 1963, in Dallas, Texas. Washington, D.C.: National Archives, n.d.

O'Donnell, Kenneth P., and David F. Powers. *"Johnny, We Hardly Knew Ye."* Boston: Little, Brown, 1970.

Oglesby, Carl. *The Yankee and Cowboy War.* New York: Berkley Medallion, 1976.

Paper, Lewis. *The Promise and the Performance.* New York: Crown, 1975.

Parmet, Herbert S. *Jack: The Struggles of John F. Kennedy.* New York: Dial, 1980.

———. *JFK: The Presidency of John F. Kennedy*. New York: Penguin, 1983.

Pettit, Tom. "The Television Story in Dallas." In *The Kennedy Assassination and the American Public*, ed. Bradley Greenberg and Edwin Parker, pp. 61–66. Palo Alto: Stanford University Press, 1965.

Rather, Dan, with Mickey Herskowitz. *The Camera Never Blinks*. New York: Ballantine, 1977.

Report to the President by the Commission on CIA Activities Within the United States. Washington, D.C.: U.S. Government Printing Office, 1975; New York: Manor Books, 1976.

Reston, James, Jr. *The Expectations of John Connally*. New York: Harper and Row, 1989.

Rivers, William. "The Press and the Assassination." In *The Kennedy Assassination and the American Public*, ed. Bradley Greenberg and Edwin Parker, pp. 51–60. Palo Alto: Stanford University Press, 1965.

Roberts, Charles. *The Truth about the Assassination*. New York: Grosset and Dunlap, 1967.

———. "JFK and the Press." In *Ten Presidents and the Press*, ed. K. W. Thompson, pp. 63–77. Lanham, Md.: University Press of America, 1983.

Rovere, Richard. "Introduction." In *Inquest: The Warren Commission and the Establishment of Truth*, Edward J. Epstein, pp. ix–xiv. New York: Viking, 1966.

Salinger, Pierre. "Introduction." In *Kennedy and the Press*, H. W. Chase and A. H. Lerman, pp. ix–xi. New York: Thomas Y. Crowell, 1965.

———. *With Kennedy*. New York: Doubleday, 1966.

Salinger, Pierre, and Sander Vanocur (eds.). *A Tribute to John F. Kennedy*. New York: Dell, 1965.

Salisbury, Harrison E. "The Editor's View in New York." In *The Kennedy Assassination and the American Public*, ed. Bradley Greenberg and Edwin Parker, pp. 37–45. Palo Alto: Stanford University Press, 1965.

———. *A Time of Change: A Reporter's Tale of Our Time*. New York: Harper and Row, 1988.

Saunders, Paul. *Torn Lace Curtain*. New York: Holt, Rinehart and Winston, 1982.

Sayres, Sohnya, Anders Stephanson, Stanley Aronowitz, and Fredric Jameson (eds.). *The 60s Without Apology*. Minneapolis: University of Minnesota Press in cooperation with *Social Text*, 1984.

Schachtman, Tom. *Decade of Shocks: Dallas to Watergate 1963–74*. New York: Poseidon, 1983.

Scheim, David E. *Contract on America*. New York: Zebra Books, 1988.

Schlesinger, Arthur M., Jr. *A Thousand Days*. Boston: Houghton Mifflin, 1965.

Schorr, Daniel. *Clearing the Air*. Boston: Houghton Mifflin, 1977.

Schramm, Wilbur. "Communication in Crisis." In *The Kennedy Assassination and the American Public*, ed. Bradley Greenberg and Edwin Parker, pp. 1–25. Palo Alto: Stanford University Press, 1965.

Scott, Peter Dale. *Crime and Cover-Up*. Berkeley: Westworks,1977.

Scott, Peter Dale, Paul L. Hoch, and Russell Stetler (eds.). *The Assassinations: Dallas and Beyond*. New York: Vintage, 1976.

Sidey, Hugh. *John F. Kennedy, President*. New York: Atheneum, 1964.

Singer, Loren. *The Parallax View*. Garden City, N.Y.: Doubleday, 1970.

Sorensen, Theodore C. *Kennedy*. New York: Harper and Row, 1965.

———. *The Kennedy Legacy*. New York: Macmillan, 1969.

Stone, I. F. "The Rapid Deterioration in Our National Leadership." In *In a Time of Torment, 1961–67*, pp. 5–8. Boston: Little, Brown, 1967.

Summers, Anthony. *Conspiracy*. New York: Paragon, 1980; rev. ed., 1989.

Talese, Gay. *The Kingdom and the Power*. New York: Laurel Books/Dell, 1986.

Thompson, Josiah. *Six Seconds in Dallas*. New York: Bernard Geis Associates, 1967.

Thompson, K. W. (ed.). *Ten Presidents and the Press*. Lanham, Md.: University Press of America, 1983.

United Press International and *American Heritage* Magazine. *Four Days: The Historical Record of President Kennedy's Death*. New York: UPI and American Heritage Publishing, 1964.

U.S. Congress, Select Committee to Study Governmental Operations with Respect to Intelligence Activities. *Alleged Assassination Plots Involving Foreign Leaders: An Interim Report*. Washington, D.C.: U.S. Government Printing Office, 20 November 1975.

Warren Report. New York: Associated Press, 1964.

Warren Report: Report of the President's Commission on the Assassination of President John F. Kennedy. Washington, D.C.: U.S. Government Printing Office, 1964.

Watson, Mary Ann. *The Expanding Vista*. New York: Oxford University Press, 1990.

Weisberg, Harold. *Whitewash: The Report on the Warren Report*. Hyattstown, Md., 1965.

———. *Whitewash II: The FBI–Secret Service Cover-Up*. Hyattstown, Md., 1966.

White, Theodore H. *The Making of the President, 1960*. New York: Atheneum, 1961.

———. *In Search of History*. New York: Warner, 1978.

———. *America in Search of Itself*. New York: Warner, 1982.

Wicker, Tom. *Kennedy Without Tears*. New York: William Morrow, 1964.

———. *JFK and LBJ*. New York: William Morrow, 1968.

———. *On Press*. New York: Berkley, 1975.

Wills, Gary. *The Kennedy Imprisonment*. New York: Pocket Books, 1983.

Wright, Lawrence. *In the New World: Growing Up with America from the Sixties to the Eighties*. New York: Vintage, 1983.

Newspaper and Journal Articles

"'Accused' or 'Assassin.'" Editorial. *Editor and Publisher*, 14 December 1963, p. 6.

Allen, Henry. "JFK: The Man and the Maybes." *Washington Post*, 22 November 1988, p. E2.

Ambrose, Stephen E. "Writers on the Grassy Knoll: A Reader's Guide." *New York Times Book Review*, 2 February 1992, pp. 1, 23–25.

"And Then It Was November 22 Again." *Newsweek*, 30 November 1964, pp. 25–28.

Ansen, David. "A Troublemaker for Our Times." *Newsweek*, 23 December 1991, p. 50.

Anson, Robert Sam. "The Shooting of JFK." *Esquire*, November 1991, pp. 93–102, 174–176.

"Assassination, The." *Columbia Journalism Review* (Winter 1964), pp. 5–36.

"Assassination—Behind Moves to Reopen JFK Case." *U.S. News and World Report*, 2 June 1975, pp. 30–33.

"Assassination: History or Headlines?" *Newsweek*, 13 March 1967, pp. 44–47.

"Assassination of President Kennedy, The." *Life*, 29 November 1963, pp. 23–38.

"Assassination Story Raises Legal Snares." *Editor and Publisher*, 14 December 1963, p. 12.

"Assassination, The: A Week in the Sun." *Newsweek*, 24 February 1964, pp. 29–30.

Association for Education in Journalism. "Official Minutes of the 1964 Convention." *Journalism Quarterly* 42 (Winter 1965), pp. 149–64.

"As We See It." *TV Guide*, 29 July 1967, p. 1.

"At Issue: Judgment by Television." *Columbia Journalism Review* (Winter 1964), pp. 45–48.

Auchincloss, Kenneth. "The Kennedy Years: What Endures?" *Newsweek*, 1 February 1971, p. 21.

———. "Twisted History." *Newsweek*, 23 December 1991, pp. 46–49.

Bagdikian, Ben H. "The Assassin." *Saturday Evening Post*, 14 December 1963, pp. 22–27.

Banta, Thomas J. "The Kennedy Assassination: Early Thoughts and Emotions." *Public Opinion Quarterly* 28(2) (1964), pp. 216–24.

Barrientos, Tanya. "'JFK' Film Has Students Talking About History." *Philadelphia Inquirer*, 24 January 1992, pp. D1, D3.

Bell, Jack. "Eyewitnesses Describe Scene of Assassination." *New York Times*, 23 November 1963, p. 5.

Berendt, John. "Ten Years Later: A Look at the Record." *Esquire*, November 1973, pp. 140, 263–65.

"Birch View of JFK." *Newsweek*, 24 February 1964, pp. 29–30.

Blake, Richard A. "Two Moments of Grief." *America*, 24 November 1973, pp. 402–4.

Bluem, A. William. "Looking Ahead: The Black Horse." Editorial. *Television Quarterly* 3(1) (Winter 1964), pp. 84–87.

Boeth, Richard. "JFK: Visions and Revisions." *Newsweek*, 19 November 1973, pp. 76–78.

Boorstin, Daniel. "JFK: His Vision, Then and Now." *U.S. News and World Report*, 24 October 1988, pp. 30–31.

Brackman, Jacob. "The Sixties: Shock Waves from the Baby Boom." *Esquire*, June 1983, pp. 197–200; rpt. from *Esquire*, October 1968.

Branch, Taylor. "The Ben Bradlee Tapes: The Journalist as Flatterer." *Harper's*, October 1975, pp. 36–45.

Brucker, Herbert. "When the Press Shapes the News." *Saturday Review*, 11 January 1964, pp. 75–85.

Bruning, Fred. "The Grief Has Still Not Gone Away." *MacLean's*, 28 November 1988, p. 13.

"Camelot Censured." *Newsweek*, 3 November 1966, pp. 65–66.

"Camelot Revisited." Editorial. *The Nation*, 19 November 1983, pp. 483–84.

"Camelot on Tape." *Time*, 4 July 1983, p. 122.

"Can You Believe That 20 Years Have Passed." *Forbes*, 5 December 1983, p. 26.

Carleton, William G. "Kennedy in History: An Early Appraisal." *Antioch Review* 24 (Fall 1964), pp. 277–99.

Carr, Jay. "Oliver Stone Defends His Take on 'JFK.'" *Boston Globe*, 11 August 1991, pp. 81, 84.

Carter, Bill. "Rather Pulls CBS News Back to the Assassination." *New York Times*, 4 February 1992, pp. C11, C16.

Catledge, Turner. "Until Proven Guilty." Letter to the editor. *New York Times*, 27 November 1963, p. 36.

"CBS Replays November 22." *New York Times*, 17 November 1988, p. B3.

Commager, Henry Steele. "How Explain Our Illness?" *Washington Post*, 1 December 1963; rpt. as "The Pervasiveness of Violence," *Current*, January 1964, pp. 15–18.

"Comments on Coverage: 'Well Done.'" *Broadcasting*, 2 December 1963, p. 50.

"Cover Ups and Conspiracies: A Unique Investigation into the Dark Side of the Kennedy Legend." Special issue. *Revelations* 1 (Summer 1988).

"Dallas Rejoinder, The." *The Nation*, 25 May 1964, p. 519.

"Dark Side of Camelot, The." *People*, 29 February 1988, pp. 106–14.

"Day Kennedy Died, The." *Newsweek*, 2 December 1963, p. 21.

"Decade of Unanswered Questions, A." *Ramparts* 12 (December 1973), pp. 42–44.

DeLillo, Don. "American Blood: A Journey Through the Labyrinth of Dallas and JFK." *Rolling Stone*, 8 December 1983, pp. 21–28.

———. "Matters of Fact and Fiction." *Rolling Stone*, 17 November 1988, pp. 113–21.

"Did the Mob Kill JFK?" *Time*, 28 November 1988, p. 42.

Donner, Frank. "The Assassination Circus: Conspiracies Unlimited." *The Nation*, 22 December 1979, pp. 483, 654–660.

Dugger, Ronnie. "The Last Voyage of Mr. Kennedy." *Texas Observer*, 29 November 1963; rpt. in "The Reporters' Story," *Columbia Journalism Review* (Winter 1964), pp. 6–17.

———. "November 22, 1963: The Case Is Not Closed." *Texas Observer*, 11 November 1966, pp. 1–2.

———. "Batter Up." *Texas Observer*, 3 February 1967.

Dunne, John Gregory. "Elephant Man" (review of *Kennedy Imprisonment* by Gary Wills), *New York Review of Books*, 15 April 1982, p. 10.

Dutka, Elaine. "Oliver Stone Fights Back." *Los Angeles Times*, 24 June 1991, pp. F1, F12.

Ehrenstein, David. "JFK—A New Low for Hollywood." *The Advocate*, 14 January 1992, pp. 78–81.

Elfin, Mel. "Beyond the Generations." *U.S. News and World Report*, 24 October 1988, pp. 32–33.

Elm, Joanna. "From 'Good Evening, Everybody, Coast to Coast' to 'Courage.'" *TV Guide*, 6 May 1989, pp. 30–31.

Ephron, Nora. "Twelve Years on the Assassination Beat." *Esquire*, February 1976, pp. 58–62.

Epstein, Edward J. "Garrison." "A Reporter at Large" column. *The New Yorker*, 13 July 1968, pp. 35–81.

"Eyes Have It, The." *Premiere*, July 1991, p. 14.

Fairlie, Henry. "Camelot Revisited." *Harper's*, January 1973, pp. 67–78.

"FBI's Report on JFK's Death, The." *Time*, 19 December 1977, pp. 18–23.

Feldman, Harold. "Fifty-One Witnesses: The Grassy Knoll." *Minority of One*, March 1965, pp. 16–25.

Fensterwald, Bernard. "Ten Years Later: A Legacy of Suspicion." *Esquire*, November 1973, pp. 141–43.

Friedman, Rick. "Pictures of Assassination Fall to Amateurs on Street." *Editor and Publisher*, 30 November 1963, pp. 16–17, 67.

———. "The Weekly Editor: The Kennedy Story." *Editor and Publisher*, 7 December 1963, pp. 44–46.

Gamarekian, Barbara. "Hundreds Are in Capital for 25th Remembrance." *New York Times*, 22 November 1988, p. A24.

"Get the Rest of the J.F.K. Story." Editorial. *New York Times*, 16 January 1992, p. A22.

Goldman, Peter. "A Shadow over Camelot." *Newsweek*, 29 December 1975, pp. 14–16.

———. "Kennedy Remembered." *Newsweek*, 28 November 1983, pp. 60–66.

Goodman, Ellen. "The Problem with 'JFK' Is Facts." *Philadelphia Inquirer*, 4 January 1992, p. 7A.

Grady, Sandy. "JFK: A Look Back." *Philadelphia Daily News*, 22 November 1988, p. 5.

"Great President, A? Experts Size Up JFK." *U.S. News and World Report*, 21 November 1983, p. 51.

Greeley, Andrew M. "Leave John Kennedy in Peace." *Christian Century*, 21 November 1973, pp. 1147–51.

Greenfield, Meg. "The Kiss and Tell Memoirs." *The Reporter*, 30 November 1967, pp. 14–19.

———. "The Way Things Really Were." *Newsweek*, 28 November 1988, p. 98.

Griffin, Leland M. "When Dreams Collide: Rhetorical Trajectories in the Assassination of President Kennedy." *Quarterly Journal of Speech* 70(2) (May 1984), pp. 111–31.

Grove, Larry. "A City Is Tried and Convicted." *Dallas News*, March 1964; rpt. in *The Quill*, November 1987, pp. 53–55.

Grunwald, Lisa. "Why We Still Care." *Life*, December 1991, pp. 35–46.

Halberstam, David. "President Video." *Esquire*, June 1976, pp. 94–97.

Hamill, Pete. "JFK: The Real Thing." *New York Magazine*, 28 November 1988, pp. 44–51.

Hayden, Casey. "The Movement." *Witness* 2(2/3) (Summer/Fall 1988), pp. 244–48.

Heath, Chris. "Killer Instincts." *Details*, January 1992, pp. 60–65, 114.

Henry, William A., III. "The Meaning of TV." *Life*, March 1989, pp. 66–74.

"High Profile: Ike Pappas." *Philadelphia Inquirer Magazine*, 10 September 1989, p. 8.

Hinckle, Warren, III. "The Mystery of the Black Books." *Esquire*, April 1973, pp. 128–31.

"Historians Lost in the Mists of Camelot." *Los Angeles Times*, 21 October 1988, p. I1.

Horn, John. "Television: A Transformation." *Columbia Journalism Review* (Winter 1964), pp. 18–19.

Howard, Jane. "Do You Remember the Day JFK Died?" *Ladies Home Journal*, November 1983, p. 114.

"Icons: The Ten Greatest Images of Photojournalism." *Time*, special collector's edition, Fall 1989, pp. 4–10.

"I Just Heard Some Shots . . . Three Shots." *Editor and Publisher*, 30 November 1963, p. 14.

"In Camelot, They Taped a Lot." *Newsweek*, 15 February 1982, p. 29.

"International Press Institute Rejects Move to Admit Radio-TV Newsmen." *New York Times*, 8 June 1983, p. 52.

Isikoff, Michael. "'JFK' Is No Hit with the Archives." *Philadelphia Inquirer*, 22 January 1992, p. C9.

"JFK: The Death and the Doubts." *Newsweek*, 5 December 1966, pp. 25–29.

"JFK/MLK: Is There More to the Story?" *Senior Scholastic*, 18 November 1976, pp. 9–13.

"JFK and the Mobsters' Moll." *Time*, 29 December 1975, pp. 16–18.

"JFK: Reflections a Year Later." *Life*, 20 November 1964, p. 4.

"JFK: Ten Years Later." Special section. *The Christian Century*, 21 November 1973, pp. 1138–51.

"JFK and a Tribute to TV." *Washington Post*, 23 November 1988, p. A2.

"JFK: The Truth Is Still at Large." *New Times*, 18 April 1975.

"John Fitzgerald Kennedy." Special section. *Newsweek*, 2 December 1963, pp. 15–53.

"John F. Kennedy Memorial Album: His Life, His Words, His Deeds." Special issue. *Life*, 1964.

"John F. Kennedy Memorial Edition." *Life* (Winter 1988); rpt. of December 1963 issue.

Johnson, Gerald W. "Once Touched By Romance." *New Republic*, 7 December 1963; rpt. as "The Birth of a Myth," *Current*, January 1964, pp. 7–8.

Kaiser, Charles. "The Selling of a Conspiracy." *Rolling Stone*, 16 April 1981, p. 11.

Kaplan, John. "The Assassins." *American Scholar* (Spring 1967), pp. 271–306.

Kaplan, Peter, and Paul Slansky. "Golden Moments." *Connoisseur*, September 1989, pp. 135–38.

"Kennedy Assassination: Question of a Second Investigation." *New Republic*, 12 November 1966, p. 8.

Kennedy, Jacqueline. "These Are the Things I Hope Will Show How He Really Was." *Life*, 29 May 1964, pp. 32–38.

"Kennedy Retained Newsman's Outlook." *Editor and Publisher*, 30 November 1963, p. 65.

"Kennedy, Vietnam Topped '63 News." *New York Times*, 29 March 1964, p. 16.

Kopkind, Andrew. "JFK's Legacy." *The Nation*, 5 December 1988, p. 589.

Kraft, Joseph. "Portrait of a President." *Harper's,* January 1964, pp. 96–100.

Krauss, Clifford. "28 Years After Kennedy's Assassination, Conspiracy Theories Refuse to Die." *New York Times*, 5 January 1992, section 1, p. 18.

———. "A Move to Unseal the Kennedy Files." *New York Times*, 22 January 1992, pp. A1, A14.

Krock, Arthur. "Mr. Kennedy's Management of the News." *Fortune*, March 1963, pp. 82, 199–202.

Lane, Mark. "A Defense Brief for Lee Harvey Oswald." *National Guardian*, 19 December 1963; rpt. in *The Assassinations: Dallas and Beyond*, ed. Peter Dale Scott, Paul L. Hoch, and Russell Stetler, pp. 49–52 (New York: Vintage, 1976).

Lardner, George, Jr. "On the Set: Dallas in Wonderland." *Washington Post*, 19 May 1991, pp. D1, D4.

Lasch, Christopher. "The Life of Kennedy's Death." *Harper's*, October 1983, pp. 32–40.

Laverick, Richard. "Why So Reluctant?" Letter to the editor. *Philadelphia Inquirer*, 12 January 1992, p. 4C.

Lemann, Nicholas. "Growing Up with the Kennedy Myth: Not Quite Camelot." *Washington Post*, 20 November 1983, p. F1.

"Letters." Letters to the editor. *New York Times*, 5 January 1992, p. H4.

Leuchtenburg, William E. "John F. Kennedy, Twenty Years Later." *American Heritage Magazine*, December 1983, pp. 50–59.

Lewis, Anthony. "J.F.K." *New York Times*, 9 January 1992, p. A23.

"Life and Death of John F. Kennedy, The." *Current*, January 1964, pp. 6–45.

Logan, Andy. "JFK: The Stained Glass Image." *American Heritage Magazine*, August 1967, pp. 4–7, 75–78.

"Lone 'Pro' on Scene Where JFK Was Shot." *Editor and Publisher*, 7 December 1963, p. 11.

MacDonald, Dwight. "Critique of the Warren Report." *Esquire*, March 1965, pp. 59–63.

McGrory, Mary. "And Did You Once See Kennedy Plain?" *America*, 18 September 1965, p. 279.

———. "You Had to Be There to Know the Pain." *Washington Post*, 20 November 1983, p. F1.

McMillan, Priscilla. "That Time We Huddled Together." *New York Times*, 22 November 1973, p. 37.

"Magazines: Good and Bad." *Columbia Journalism Review* (Winter 1964), pp. 24–25.

Mailer, Norman. "Kennedy and After." *New York Review of Books*, 26 December 1963; rpt. in *Current*, January 1964, p. 14.

———. "Enter Prince Jack." *Esquire*, June 1983, pp. 204–8; excerpted from "Superman Comes to the Supermarket," *Esquire*, November 1960.

Manchester, William. "No Evidence for a Conspiracy to Kill Kennedy." Letter to the editor. *New York Times*, 5 February 1992, p. A22.

Mannes, Marya. "The Long Vigil." *The Reporter*, 19 December 1963, pp. 15–17.

"Many Remember the Scene as It Was." *Washington Post*, 23 November 1988, p. A8.

Marannis, David. "In Dallas, the Lingering Trauma." *Washington Post*, 22 November 1988, pp. E1–E2.

Margasek, Larry. "Film Adds Pressure to Open JFK Files." *Philadelphia Inquirer*, 20 January 1992, p. D1.

Margolis, Jon. "JFK Movie and Book Attempt to Rewrite History." *Chicago Tribune*, 14 May 1991, p. 19.

"Marxist Marine, The." *Newsweek*, 2 December 1963, p. 27.

"Matter of Reasonable Doubt, A." *Life*, 25 November 1966, pp. 38–48.

Matza, Michael. "Five Still Probing the JFK Killing." *Philadelphia Inquirer*, 22 November 1988, p. 8E.

Meagher, Sylvia. "Notes for a New Investigation." *Esquire*, December 1966, p. 211.

Minnis, Jack, and Staughton Lind. "Seeds of Doubt: Some Questions about the Assassination." *New Republic*, 21 December 1963, pp. 14–20.

Moley, Raymond. "Lasky's Estimate of JFK." *Newsweek*, 16 September 1963, p. 96.

———. "Brief, Not a History." *Newsweek*, 20 December 1965, p. 108.

"Moments You Can Never Forget, The." *TV Guide*, 6 May 1989, pp. 2–8.

Morley, Jefferson. "Camelot and Dallas: The Entangling Kennedy Myths." *The Nation*, 12 December 1988, pp. 646–49.

Morrow, Lance. "After 20 Years, the Question: How Good a President?" *Time*, 14 November 1983, p. 58.

———. "Of Myth and Memory." *Time*, 24 October 1988, p. 22.

———. "Imprisoning Time in a Rectangle." *Time*, special collector's edition, Fall 1989, p. 76.

Muggeridge, Malcolm. "Books" column. *Esquire*, October 1966, pp. 14–15.

Nestvold, Karl J. "Oregon Radio-TV Response to the Kennedy Assassination." *Journal of Broadcasting* 8(2) (Spring 1964), pp. 141–46.

"New Challenges: 1950–80." *Time*, special collector's edition, Fall 1989, pp. 56–64.

"New Kennedy Book Set for Release." *New York Times*, 24 October 1968, p. 95.

"News Managing Laid to Kennedy." *New York Times*, 25 February 1963, p. 5.

"News Media Act to Study Charges." *New York Times*, 9 October 1964, p. 21.

"Newspapers: Hunger for Print." *Columbia Journalism Review* (Winter 1964), pp. 20–23.

"November 22, 1963: Where We Were." Special section. *People*, 28 November 1988, pp. 54–70.

"Office Memo." *The Progressive*, January 1964, p. 1.

Oglesby, Carl. "Who Killed JFK? The Media Whitewash." *Lies of Our Times*, September 1991, pp. 3–6.

"Oswald Shooting a First in Television History." *Broadcasting*, 2 December 1963, p. 46.

"*Parade* Reprints Because of Death." *Editor and Publisher*, 30 November 1963, p. 73.

Payne, Darwin. "The Press Corps and the Kennedy Assassination." *Journalism Monographs* 15 (February 1970).

"Peephole Journalism." *Commonweal*, 3 September 1965, p. 613.

Polak, Maralyn Lois. "Mark Lane: Deep in His Plots." *Philadelphia Inquirer Magazine*, 19 January 1992, pp. 7–8.

Policoff, Jerry. "The Media and the Murder of John Kennedy." *New Times*, 8 September 1975; rpt. in *The Assassinations: Dallas and Beyond*, ed. Peter Dale Scott, Paul L. Hoch, and Russell Stetler, pp. 262–70 (New York: Vintage, 1976).

"Presidency, The: Battle of the Book." *Time*, 23 December 1966, pp. 15–18.

"President's Assassin Shot to Death." *New York Times*, 25 November 1963, p. 1.

Pressman, Gabe, Robert Lewis Shayon, and Robert Schulman. "The Responsible Reporter." *Television Quarterly* 3(2) (Spring 1964), pp. 6–27.

"Press, Radio and TV." *Editor and Publisher*, 30 November 1963, p. 6.

"Primer of Assassination Theories, A." *Esquire*, December 1966, pp. 205–10.

"Professionalism in News Photography." *The Quill*, November 1968, pp. 54–57.

"Question That Won't Go Away, The." *Saturday Evening Post*, December 1975, pp. 38–39.

Quindlen, Anna. "Life in the 30's." *New York Times*, 24 November 1988, p. C2.

"Radio-TV's Deportment." *Broadcasting*, 2 December 1963, p. 54.

"Readers Find Fault with Doubters of 'JFK.'" Letters to the editor. *Philadelphia Inquirer*, 12 January 1992, p. 4C.

"Re-evaluating the Kennedys." *U.S. News and World Report*, 4 May 1987, p. 68.

"Reporter Engagé." *Newsweek*, 23 December 1963, p. 70.

"Reporters' Story, The." *Columbia Journalism Review* (Winter 1964), pp. 6–17.

Reston, James. Jr. "Why America Weeps." *New York Times*, 23 November 1963, p. 1.

———. "What Was Killed Was Not Only the President But the Promise." *New York Times*, 15 November 1964, section 6, pp. 1, 7.

———. "Was Connally the Real Target?" *Time*, 28 November 1988, pp. 30–41.

Roberts, Charles. "Eyewitness in Dallas." *Newsweek*, 5 December 1966, pp. 26–28.

Robinson, Alan. "Reporting the Death of JFK." Associated Press dispatch printed in *Philadelphia Inquirer*, 22 November 1988, p. 8E.

Rosenbaum, Ron. "Taking a Darker View." *Time*, 13 January 1992, pp. 38–40.

Rowland, Mark. "Stone Unturned." *American Film*, March 1991, pp. 41–43.

Salinger, Pierre. "John Kennedy—Then and Now." *MacLean's*, 28 November 1983, pp. 18–30.

Sauvage, Leo. "Oswald in Dallas: A Few Loose Ends." *The Reporter*, 2 January 1964, pp. 24–26.

Schiller, Herbert. "JFK: The Movie." *Lies of Our Times*, September 1991, pp. 6–7.

Schlesinger, Arthur, Jr. "'JFK': Truth and Fiction." *Wall Street Journal*, 10 January 1992, p. A8.

Scott, Peter Dale. "From Dallas to Watergate—the Longest Cover-Up." *Ramparts*, 1973; rpt. in *The Assassinations: Dallas and Beyond*, ed. Peter Dale Scott, Paul L. Hoch, and Russell Stetler, pp. 357–74 (New York: Vintage, 1976).

Seelye, Katharine. "New Film Fires a Bullet at Specter's Re-election." *Philadelphia Inquirer*, 5 January 1992, pp. 1A, 8A.

Sgarlat, John P. "A Tragedy on TV—and the Tears of a Crestfallen Nation." *Philadelphia Daily News*, 22 November 1988, p. 35.

"Shadow over Camelot, A." *Newsweek*, 29 December 1975, pp. 14–16.

Shister, Gail. "Steve Bell Discounts Assassination Theories." *Philadelphia Inquirer*, 10 January 1992, p. 6D.

———. "Rather and JFK." *Philadelphia Inquirer*, 5 February 1992, pp. E1, E7.

"Shores Dimly Seen." *The Progressive*, January 1964, p. 3.

Sidey, Hugh. "History on His Shoulder." *Time*, 8 November 1982, p. 26.

———. "A Shattering Afternoon in Dallas." *Time*, 28 November 1988, p. 45.

"Sixties, The." Special double issue. *Witness* 2(2/3) (Summer/Fall 1988).

Sklar, Zachary. "Time Magazine's Continuing Cover-Up." *Lies of Our Times*, September 1991, pp. 7–8.

Smith, Merriman. "The Murder of the Young President." United Press International dispatch, 23 November 1963; rpt. in "The Reporters' Story," *Columbia Journalism Review* (Winter 1964), p. 7.

Sorensen, Theodore. "May 29, 1967." *McCall's*, June 1967, p. 59.

Spector, Arlen. "'JFK' the Film Mangles the Facts." *Philadelphia Inquirer*, 5 January 1992, p. 5C.

Stine, Peter. "Editor's Comment." *Witness* 2(2/3), special double issue on "The Sixties" (Summer/Fall 1988), pp. 9–11.

Stolley, Richard B. "The Greatest Home Movie Ever Made." *Esquire*, November 1973, pp. 133–35.

Stone, Oliver. "Stone's 'JFK': A Higher Truth?" *Washington Post*, 2 June 1991, p. D3.

———. "Oliver Stone's 'JFK.'" Letter to the editor. *Time*, 1 July 1991, p. 4.

———. "Oliver Stone Replies to Sen. Specter." Letter to the editor, *Philadelphia Inquirer*, 12 January 1992, p. 4C.

———. "Warren Panel Findings Should Stir Outrage." Letter to the editor. *New York Times*, 3 February 1992, p. A14.

Talbot, Stephen. "60s Something." *Mother Jones*, March/April 1991, pp. 46–49.

"Television's Fiftieth Anniversary." Special issue. *People*, Summer 1989.

"Ten Years Later: Where Were You?" *Esquire*, November 1973, pp. 136–37.

Thomas, Evan. "A Reporter in Search of History." *Time*, 26 May 1986, p. 62.

Thompson, Josiah. "The Crossfire That Killed Kennedy." *Saturday Evening Post*, 2 December 1967, pp. 27–31.

Tobin, Richard L. "If You Can Keep Your Head When All about You . . ." "Communications" column. *Saturday Review*, 14 December 1963, pp. 53–54.

Trillin, Calvin. "The Buffs." "A Reporter at Large" column. *The New Yorker*, 10 June 1967, pp. 41–71.

"True Story That's Not So True, A." *Insight*, 2 April 1990, p. 58.

Turner, William. "Assassinations: Epstein's Garrison." *Ramparts*, 7 September 1968, pp. 8, 12.

"TV: A Chapter of Honor." *New York Times*, 6 November 1963, p. 11.

"TV: The Ghost of a President Past." *Wall Street Journal*, 7 November 1988, p. A12.

"TV Retells the Story of Slaying." *New York Times*, 23 November 1988, p. A16.

"25 Years Later." Special section. *U.S. News and World Report*, 24 October 1988, pp. 30–40.

"Unresolved Issues." *Columbia Journalism Review* (Winter 1964), pp. 26–36.

Van der Karr, Richard K. "How Dallas TV Stations Covered Kennedy Shooting." *Journalism Quarterly* 42 (1965), pp. 646–47.

Vidal, Gore. "Camelot Recalled: Dynastic Ambitions." *Esquire*, June 1983, p. 210; excerpted from "The Holy Family," *Esquire*, April 1967.

Wainwright, Loudon. "Atlantic City and a Memory." *Life*, 4 September 1967, p. 17.

"Warren Report." *TV Guide*, 24 June 1967, p. A29.

"Washington Shoot-out, The." *The Quill*, May 1981, pp. 8–13.

Weinraub, Bernard. "Substance and Style Criticized in 'J.F.K.'" *New York Times*, 7 November 1991, pp. C19, C22.

Weisman, John. "An Oral History: Remembering JFK, Our First TV President." *TV Guide*, 19 November 1988, pp. 2–9.

Welsh, David, and William Turner. "In the Shadow of Dallas." *Ramparts*, 25 January 1969, pp. 61–71.

"What JFK Meant to Us." Special issue. *Newsweek*, 28 November 1983, pp. 3–91.

"What's Fit to Print." *The Reporter*, 2 January 1964, p. 12.

White, Theodore H. "Camelot, Sad Camelot." *Time*, 3 July 1978, pp. 46–48; excerpted from *In Search of History: A Personal Adventure* (New York: Warner, 1978).

Wicker, Tom. "Kennedy Is Killed by Sniper as He Rides in Car in Dallas." *New York Times*, 23 November 1963, p. 2.

————. "That Day in Dallas." *Times Talk* (*New York Times* internal publication), December 1963.

————. "A Reporter Must Trust His Instinct." *Saturday Review*, 11 January 1964, pp. 81–86.

————. "Lyndon Johnson vs. the Ghost of Jack Kennedy." *Esquire*, November 1965, pp. 87, 145–58.

————. "Kennedy Without Tears." *Esquire*, June 1964; rpt. in *Esquire*, October 1973, pp. 196–200.

————. "Kennedy Without End, Amen." *Esquire*, June 1977, pp. 65–69.

————. "Does 'J.F.K.' Conspire Against Reason?" *New York Times*, 15 December 1991, section 2, pp. 1, 18.

"World Listened and Watched, A." Special report. *Broadcasting*, 2 December 1963, pp. 36–58.

"Year after the Assassination, A: The U.S. Recalls John F. Kennedy." *Newsweek*, 30 November 1964, pp. 26–27.

Yoder, Edwin M., Jr. "With 'JFK,' Filmmaker Oliver Stone Shows He Isn't Up to the Job of Historian." *Philadelphia Inquirer*, 27 December 1991, p. 10A.

Yost, Pete. "Warren Panel Lawyers Ask Release of JFK Files." *Philadelphia Inquirer*, 31 January 1992, p. A17.

Zoglin, Richard. "More Shots in Dealey Plaza." *Time*, 10 June 1991, pp. 64–66.

Documentary Films, Videotapes, and Broadcast News Segments

"American Assassins, The." "CBS Evening News," CBS News, 25–26 November 1975.

"America Remembers John F. Kennedy." Narrator: Hal Holbrook. 100 min. Produced by Thomas F. Horton Associates, Inc.; shown on Arts and Entertainment Network, 1983.

"Assassination: An American Nightmare." "ABC Evening News," ABC News, 14 November 1975.

"Assassination: Twenty-five Years Later." Eight-part series. "CBS Evening News," CBS News, 14–23 November 1988.

"Being with John F. Kennedy." Narrator: Nancy Dickerson. 90 min. Produced by Robert Drew Associates, in association with Golden West Television; shown on Arts and Entertainment Network, 1983.

"Biography: The Age of Kennedy." Narrator: Peter Graves. 60 min. NBC News; shown on Arts and Entertainment Network, 13 March 1989. (Uses 1960s NBC News coverage, identical to that in "The Age of Kennedy: The Presidency," vol. 2 of *The Week We Lost Kennedy* [see below].)

"Changing South." "ABC Nightly News," ABC News, 22 November 1988.

"Director Oliver Stone on the JFK Assassination." "Larry King Live," CNN, 20 December 1991.

"Edge." PBS popular culture magazine. Segment spoofing Oliver Stone's *JFK*, PBS, 25 December 1991.

"Fifty Years of Television: A Golden Anniversary." CBS News, 26 November 1989.

"Four Dark Days, The: From Dallas to Arlington." Narrator: Charles Collingwood. 60 min. CBS News, 25 November 1963.

"Four Days in November." Narrator in-film: Richard Basehart. 150 min. Produced by David L. Wolper for United Artists and United Press International, originally shown 7 October 1964; reshown by Combined Broadcasting Corporation Channel 57, November 1988. (Uses 1963 news coverage from networks and local TV stations.)

"Four Days in November: The Assassination of President Kennedy." Narrator: Dan Rather. 120 min. CBS News, 17 November 1988. (Uses 1963 CBS News coverage.)

"Good Night, America." Narrator/anchor: Geraldo Rivera. ABC News, 26 March 1975.

"James Reston." "ABC Nightly News," ABC News, 31 July 1987.

"JFK." 120 min. Narrator: Peter Jennings. ABC News, 11 November 1983.

"JFK." "48 Hours." Narrator: Dan Rather. CBS News, 5 February 1992.

"JFK." "Ron Reagan Show," 19 November 1991.

"JFK Assassination: As It Happened." Narrator: Edwin Newman. 365 min. NBC News; shown on Arts and Entertainment Network, 22 November 1988. (Uses 1963 NBC News coverage.)

"JFK Assassination Files, The." Narrator/anchor: Ted Koppel. "Nightline," ABC News, 22 January 1992.

"JFK Controversy, The." "Oprah Winfrey Show," ABC, 22 January 1992.

"JFK: Fact or Fiction?" Anchors: Michael Kinsley and Robert Novak. "Crossfire," CNN, 23 December 1991.

"JFK: In His Own Words." 60 min. Kunhardt Productions, Inc.; shown by HBO, November 1988.

"JFK's Assassination: The Continuing Controversy." "Larry King Live," CNN, 16 January 1992.

"JFK: That Day in November." Narrator: Tom Brokaw. 60 min. NBC News, 22 November 1988.

"JFK: A Time Remembered." Narrator: Mark Obenhaus. 60 min. Produced by Susskind Company, in association with Obenhaus Films, Inc.; shown on PBS, 21 November 1988.

"John F. Kennedy Remembered." Narrator/anchor: Steve Bell. 10 min. Segment on "KYW Eyewitness News, Channel Three Eyewitness News Nightcast," Philadelphia, 22 November 1988.

"Kennedy Assassination, The: Myth and Reality." Series aired on "CBS Evening News," CBS News, 7–9 November 1983.

"Kennedy: One Year Later." 30 min. KTRK-TV, Houston, 1964.

"Kennedy Remembered." Anchor: Jim Gardner. 10 min. Segment on "Action News: Channel Six Late-Night News," Philadelphia, 22 November 1988.

"Kennedy v. Wallace: A Crisis Up Close." Narrator: David McCullough. 60 min. Produced by Drew Associates as film *Crisis: Behind a Presidential Commitment,* 1963; shown on "The American Experience," PBS, November 1988.

"Lyndon B. Johnson: JFK's Vice-President or Assassin?" "Geraldo," NBC, 23 December 1991.

"Men Who Killed Kennedy, The." "Investigative Reports," produced by Nigel Turner for Kurtis Productions; shown on Arts and Entertainment Network, 27 September 1991, 4 October 1991, 11 October 1991, 18 October 1991, and 25 October 1991.

"November 22 and the Warren Report." "CBS Evening News," CBS News, 27 October 1964.

"Oliver Stone Address to National Press Club." C-Span, 15 January 1992.

"Oliver Stone's 'JFK.'" Narrator/anchor: Forrest Sawyer. "Nightline," ABC News, 19 December 1991.

"On Trial: Lee Harvey Oswald." Narrator: Geraldo Rivera. 300 min. Simulation of trial of Lee Harvey Oswald, London Weekend Television, 1986; production of trial with Rivera inserts by Peter R. Marino for Tribune Entertainment Company; shown on Fox Network, 22–23 November 1988.

"Plot to Kill President Kennedy, The: From the De-classified Files." Narrator: Larry McCann. 60 min. Produced by M. G. Hollo with Fox/Lorber Associates, Inc.; shown on Arts and Entertainment Network, 1983.

"PrimeTime Live." Narrator: Sam Donaldson. Special segment on the Kennedy assassination, ABC News, 16 January 1992.

"Remembering JFK." Segment on "Good Morning, America," ABC News, 22 November 1983.

"Remembering President John F. Kennedy." "Oprah Winfrey Show," ABC, 22 November 1988.

"Return to Camelot: Steve Bell and the JFK Years." Narrator: Steve Bell. 30 min. Group W Television, Inc.; shown on KYW News, Philadelphia, 22 November 1988.

"25th Anniversary of JFK Assassination." Segment on "Good Morning, America," ABC News, 22 November 1988.

"25th Anniversary of JFK's Assassination." Narrator/anchor: Forrest Sawyer. 60 min. Special program of "Nightline," ABC News, 22 November 1988.

"Warren Report, The." Segment on "CBS Evening News," CBS News, 25–29 June 1967.

Week We Lost John F. Kennedy, The. Narrator: John Chancellor. Set of 3 video-tapes. NBC News, March 1989. Vol. 1, "The Age of Kennedy: The Early Years," 60 min., 1966, 1988; vol. 2, "The Age of Kennedy: The Presidency," 60 min., 1966, 1988; vol. 3, "The Death of a President," 120 min., 1963, 1988. (Uses 1963 NBC News coverage.)

"Where Were You When JFK Was Shot?" Segment on "Entertainment To-night," NBC, 22 November 1988.

"Who Killed JFK?" "Today Show," NBC News, 7 February 1992.

"Who Murdered JFK? American Exposé." Narrator: Jack Anderson. 120 min. Saban Productions; shown on the Discovery Channel, 2 November 1988.

"Who Shot President Kennedy?" Narrator: Walter Cronkite. 90 min. Special edition of "Nova"; shown on PBS, 15 November 1988.

Additional Historical, Critical, and Theoretical References

Abrahams, Roger. "Ordinary and Extraordinary Experience." In *The Anthropology of Experience*, ed. Victor Turner and Edward Bruner, pp. 45–72. Urbana: University of Illinois Press, 1986.

Arlen, Michael. *The Living-Room War.* New York: Viking, 1969.

Barnouw, Eric. *Tube of Plenty.* London: Oxford University Press, 1975.

Barthes, Roland. "Introduction to the Structural Analysis of Narratives." In *Image, Music, Text,* pp. 79–124. New York: Hill and Wang, 1977.

Bauman, Richard, and Roger Abrahams (eds.). *'And Other Neighborly Names.'* Austin: University of Texas Press, 1981.

Becker, Lee, et al. *The Training and Hiring of Journalists.* Norwood, N.J.: Ablex, 1987.

Bellah, Robert, R. Madsen, W. Sullivan, A. Swidler, and S. Tipton. *Habits of the Heart: Individualism and Commitment in American Life.* Berkeley: University of California Press, 1985.

Beneviste, Emile. *Problems in General Linguistics.* Coral Gables, Fla.: University of Miami Press, 1981.

Berger, Peter L. *Invitation to Sociology: A Humanistic Perspective.* New York: Anchor Press, 1963.

Berger, Peter L., and Thomas Luckmann. *The Social Construction of Reality.* New York: Anchor Press, 1967.

Blau, Peter, and M. Meyer. *Bureaucracy in Modern Society.* New York: Random House, 1956.

Boorstin, Daniel. *The Image.* New York: Atheneum, 1962.

———. *Hidden History.* New York: Harper and Row, 1987.

Bosk, Charles L. *Forgive and Remember.* Chicago: University of Chicago Press, 1979.

Braudel, Fernand. *On History.* Chicago: University of Chicago Press, 1980.

Braudy, Leo. *The Frenzy of Renown.* New York: Oxford University Press, 1986.

Breed, Warren. "Social Control in the Newsroom." *Social Forces* 33 (1955), pp. 326–35.

Breitbart, Eric. "The Painted Mirror." In *Presenting the Past*, ed. Susan Porter Benson et al., pp. 105–17. Philadelphia: Temple University Press, 1986.

Canary, Robert H., and Henry Kozicki (eds.). *The Writing of History*. Madison: University of Wisconsin Press, 1978.

Carey, James W. "A Cultural Approach to Communication." *Communication* 2 (1975), pp. 1–22.

———."The Dark Continent of American Journalism." In *Reading the News*, ed. R. K. Manoff and Michael Schudson, pp. 146–96. New York: Pantheon, 1986.

———. *Communication as Culture*. Boston: Unwin Hyman, 1989.

———, (ed.). *Media, Myths and Narratives*. Beverly Hills: Sage, 1988.

Carter, R. F., and Bradley Greenberg. "Newspapers or Television: Which Do You Believe?" *Journalism Quarterly* 42 (1965), pp. 22–34.

Cray, Ed, Jonathan Kotler, and Miles Beller (eds.). *American Datelines: One Hundred and Forty Major News Stories from Colonial Times to the Present*. New York: Facts on File, 1990.

Curran, James, Michael Gurevitch, and Janet Woollacott (eds.). *Mass Communication and Society*. Beverly Hills: Sage, 1977.

Darnton, Robert. "Writing News and Telling Stories." *Daedalus* 120(2) (Spring 1975), pp. 175–94.

Davis, Fred. *Yearning for Yesterday*. New York: Free Press, 1979.

Davis, Natalie Zemon, and Randolph Starn. "Introduction." *Representations* (Spring 1989), pp. 1–6.

Dayan, Daniel, and Elihu Katz. *Media Events: The Live Broadcasting of History*. Cambridge, Mass.: Harvard University Press, 1992.

Degh, Linda. "Folk Narrative." In *Folklore and Folklife*, ed. Richard M. Dorson, pp. 53–83. Chicago: University of Chicago Press, 1972.

Douglas, Mary. *How Institutions Think*. Syracuse: Syracuse University Press, 1986.

Dundes, Alan. "What Is Folklore?" In *The Study of Folklore*, pp. 1–3. Englewood Cliffs, N.J.: Prentice-Hall, 1965.

Durkheim, Emile. *The Elementary Forms of the Religious Life*. New York: Free Press, 1965 [1915].

Dyer, Richard. *Stars*. London: British Film Institute, 1978.

Eason, David. "On Journalistic Authority: The Janet Cooke Scandal." *Critical Studies in Mass Communication* 3 (1986), pp. 429–47.

Elliott, Philip. *Sociology of the Professions*. London: Macmillan, 1972.

Epstein, Edward J. *News from Nowhere*. New York: Vintage, 1974.

———. *Between Fact and Fiction: The Problem of Journalism*. New York: Vintage, 1975.

Fisher, Walter R. "Narration as a Human Communication Paradigm." *Communication Monographs* (March 1984), pp. 1–22.

Fishkin, Shelley. *From Fact to Fiction: Journalism and Imaginative Writing in America*. Baltimore: Johns Hopkins University Press, 1985.

Fishman, Mark. *Manufacturing the News*. Austin: University of Texas Press, 1980.

Fish, Stanley. *Is There a Text in This Class?* Cambridge, Mass.: Harvard University Press, 1980.

Fiske, John. *Television Culture*. London: Methuen, 1987.

Fowler, Roger. *Language in the News*. London: Routledge, 1991.

Friedson, Eliot. *Professional Powers*. Chicago: University of Chicago Press, 1986.

Frisch, Michael H. "The Memory of History." In *Presenting the Past*, ed. Susan Porter Benson et al., pp. 5–17. Philadelphia: Temple University Press, 1986.

Gallagher, Margaret. "Negotiation of Control in Media Organizations and Occupations." In *Culture, Society and the Media*, ed. Michael Gurevitch et al., pp. 151–73. London: Methuen, 1982.

Gans, Herbert. *Deciding What's News*. New York: Pantheon, 1979.

Gates, Gary Paul. *Air Time*. New York: Harper and Row, 1978.

Geertz, Clifford. "Thick Description: Toward an Interpretive Theory of Culture." In *The Interpretation of Cultures*, pp. 3–30. New York: Basic Books, 1973.

Gerbner, George. "Cultural Indicators: The Third Voice." In *Communications Technology and Social Policy: Understanding the New "Social Revolution,"* ed. George Gerbner, Larry Gross, and William Melody, pp. 555–72. New York: John Wiley, 1973.

Giddens, Anthony. *Central Problems in Social Theory*. Berkeley: University of California Press, 1979.

Gitlin, Todd. *The Whole World Is Watching*. Berkeley: University of California Press, 1980.

Glaser, Barney, and Anselm Strauss. *The Discovery of Grounded Theory*. New York: Aldine, 1967.

Glasgow University Media Group. *Bad News*. London: Routledge, 1976.

———. *More Bad News*. London: Routledge, 1980.

Goffman, Erving. *Forms of Talk*. Philadelphia: University of Pennsylvania Press, 1981.

Goldstein, Norm (ed.) and the Associated Press. *The History of Television*. New York: Portland House, 1991.

Goldstein, Tom. *The News at Any Cost*. New York: Simon and Schuster, 1985.

Grossman, Michael Baruch, and Martha Joynt Kumar. *Portraying the Presidency*. Baltimore: Johns Hopkins University Press, 1981.

Habermas, Jürgen. *The Theory of Communicative Action*, vol. 1. Boston: Beacon Press, 1981.

Halbwachs, Maurice. *The Collective Memory*. New York: Harper and Row, 1980; trans. of *La mémoire collective* (Paris: Presses Universitaires de France, 1950).

Hall, Stuart. "Culture, the Media and the Ideological Effect." In *Mass Communication and Society*, ed. James Curran, Michael Gurevitch, and Janet Woollacott, pp. 315–48. Beverly Hills: Sage, 1977.

Hall, Stuart, Dorothy Hobson, Andrew Lowe, and Paul Willis (eds.). *Culture, Media, Language*. London: Hutchinson, 1980.

Hartley, John. *Understanding News*. London: Methuen, 1982.

Hutton, Patrick H. "Collective Memory and Collective Mentalities: The Halbwachs-Ariès Connection." *Historical Reflections* 2 (1988), pp. 311–22.

Hymes, Dell. "Functions of Speech." In *Language in Education: Ethnolinguistic Essays*, pp. 1–18. Washington, D.C.: Center for Applied Linguistics, 1980.

Innis, Harold A. *Empire and Communications*. Toronto: University of Toronto Press, 1972.

Jamieson, Kathleen Hall. *Eloquence in an Electronic Age*. New York: Oxford University Press, 1988.

Janowitz, Morris. "Professional Models in Journalism: The Gatekeeper and the Advocate." *Journalism Quarterly* 52 (Winter 1975), pp. 618–26.

Johnson, Richard, G. McLennan, B. Schwartz, and D. Sutton (eds.). *Making Histories: Studies in History-Writing and Politics*. Minneapolis: University of Minnesota Press, 1982.

Johnson, Terence. *Professions and Power*. London: Macmillan, 1972.

Johnstone, J., E. Slawski, and W. Bowman. *The News People*. Urbana: University of Illinois Press, 1976.

Jones, Clement. *Mass Media Codes of Ethics and Councils*. New York: UNESCO, 1980.

Kammen, Michael. *Mystic Chords of Memory: The Transformation of Tradition in American Culture*. New York: Alfred A. Knopf, 1991.

Kellner, Hans. *Language and Historical Representation: Getting the Story Crooked*. Madison: University of Wisconsin Press, 1989.

Klaidman, Stephen. *The Virtuous Journalist*. New York: Oxford University Press, 1987.

Knapp, Stephen. "Collective Memory and the Actual Past." *Representations* (Spring 1989), pp. 123–49.

Knight, Graham, and Tony Dean. "Myth and the Structure of News." *Journal of Communication* 32(2) (Spring 1982), pp. 144–61.

Kress, Gunther, and Robert Hodge. *Language as Ideology*. London: Routledge and Kegan Paul, 1979.

Kristol, Irving. *Our Country and Our Culture*. New York: Orwell Press, 1983.

Kruger, Barbara, and Phil Mariani (eds.). *Remaking History*. Seattle: Bay Press, 1989.

Larson, Magali Sarfatti. *The Rise of Professionalism*. Berkeley: University of California Press, 1977.

Lasch, Christopher. *Culture of Narcissism*. New York: W. W. Norton, 1979.

Lévi-Strauss, Claude. *The Savage Mind*. Chicago: University of Chicago Press, 1966.

Lipsitz, George. *Time Passages*. Minneapolis: University of Minnesota Press, 1990.

Loftus, Elizabeth F. *Eyewitness Testimony*. Cambridge, Mass.: Harvard University Press, 1979.

Lowenthal, Ralph. *The Past Is a Foreign Country*. Cambridge, Mass.: Cambridge University Press, 1985.

Lucaites, John L., and Celeste Condit. "Reconstructing Narrative Theory: A Functional Perspective." *Journal of Communication* 35(4) (Autumn 1985), pp. 90–108.

McLuhan, Marshall. *Understanding Media*. London: Routledge and Kegan Paul, 1964.

Marvin, Carolyn. *When Old Technologies Were New*. New York: Oxford University Press, 1988.

————. "Experts, Black Boxes and Artifacts: New Categories in the Social History of Electric Media." In *Rethinking Communication*. Vol. 2: *Paradigm Exemplars*, pp. 188–98, ed. Brenda Dervin et al. London: Sage, 1989.

Matusow, Barbara. *The Evening Stars*. Boston: Houghton Mifflin, 1983.

Mead, G. H. *The Philosophy of the Present*. Chicago: University of Chicago Press, 1932.

"Memory and American History." Special issue. *Journal of American History* 75 (1989).

"Memory and Counter-Memory." Special issue. *Representations* (Spring 1989).

Middleton, David, and Derek Edwards (eds.). *Collective Remembering*. Beverly Hills: Sage, 1990.

Molotch, Harvey, and Marilyn Lester. "News as Purposive Behavior." *American Sociological Review* 39 (February 1974), pp. 101–12.

Moore, Wilbert. *The Professions: Roles and Rules*. New York: Russell Sage Foundation, 1970.

Moscovici, Serge. "The Phenomenon of Social Representations." In *Social Representations*, ed. Robert M. Farr and Serge Moscovici, pp. 3–69. Cambridge: Cambridge University Press, 1984.

Murphey, Murray G. *Our Knowledge of the Historical Past*. Indianapolis: Bobbs-Merrill, 1973.

Neisser, Ulric. "Snapshots or Benchmarks?" In *Memory Observed*, ed. Ulric Neisser, pp. 43–48. San Francisco: W. H. Freeman, 1982.

Nerone, John. "Professional History and Social Memory." *Communication* 11(2) (1989), pp. 89–104.

Nerone, John, and Ellen Wartella. "Introduction: Studying Social Memory." Special issue on "Social Memory." *Communication* 11(2) (1989), pp. 85–88.

"News as Social Narrative." Special issue. *Communication* 10(1) (1987).

Nora, Pierre. *Les lieux de mémoire*. Paris: Editions Gallimard, 1984– .

————. "Between Memory and History: *Les lieux de mémoire*." *Representations* (Spring 1989), pp. 7–25.

O'Brien, Dean. "The News as Environment." *Journalism Monographs* 85 (September 1983).

Park, Robert E. "News as a Form of Knowledge." *American Journal of Sociology* 45 (March 1940), pp. 669–86.

Rimmer, Tony, and David Weaver. "Different Questions, Different Answers: Media Use and Media Credibility." *Journalism Quarterly* 64 (Spring 1987), pp. 28–36.

Ritchin, Fred. *In Our Own Image.* New York: Aperture Foundation, 1990.

Rodden, John. *The Politics of Literary Reputation.* New York: Oxford University Press, 1989.

Roeh, Itzhak, Elihu Katz, Akiba A. Cohen, and Barbie Zelizer. *Almost Midnight: Reforming the Late-Night News.* Beverly Hills: Sage, 1980.

Rollins, Peter. "The American War: Perceptions Through Literature, Film and Television." *American Quarterly* 3 (1984), pp. 419–32.

Rosenzweig, Roy. "Marketing the Past." In *Presenting the Past*, pp. 21–49, ed. Susan Porter Benson et al. Philadelphia: Temple University Press, 1986.

Roshco, Bernard. *Newsmaking.* Chicago: University of Chicago Press, 1975.

Rubin, Bernard. *Questioning Media Ethics.* New York: Praeger, 1978.

Schiller, Dan. *Objectivity and the News.* Philadelphia: University of Pennsylvania Press, 1981.

Schmuhl, Robert. *The Responsibilities of Journalism.* Notre Dame, Ind.: University of Notre Dame Press, 1984.

Schudson, Michael. *Discovering the News.* New York: Basic Books, 1978.

———. "The Politics of Narrative Form: The Emergence of News Conventions in Print and Television." *Daedalus* 3(4) (Fall 1982), pp. 97–112.

———. "What Is a Reporter? The Private Face of Public Journalism." In *Media, Myths and Narratives*, ed. James W. Carey, pp. 228–45. Beverly Hills: Sage, 1988.

——— *Watergate in American Memory: How We Remember, Forget and Reconstruct the Past.* New York: Basic Books, in press.

Schwartz, Barry, Yael Zerubavel, and Bernice Barnett. "The Recovery of Masada: A Study in Collective Memory." *Sociological Quarterly* 2 (1986), pp. 147–64.

Shaw, Eugene. "Media Credibility: Taking the Measure of a Measure." *Journalism Quarterly* 50 (1973), pp. 306–11.

Simmel, George. *The Sociology of George Simmel.* New York: Free Press, 1950.

Smith, Barbara Herrnstein. *On the Margins of Discourse.* Chicago: University of Chicago Press, 1978.

"Social Memory." Special issue. *Communication* 11(2) (1989).

Stephens, Mitchell. *A History of News.* New York: Viking, 1988.

Sternsher, Bernard. *Consensus, Conflict and American Historians.* Bloomington: Indiana University Press, 1975.

Tillinghast, P. E. *The Specious Past.* Reading, Mass: Addison-Wesley, 1972.

Tuchman, Gaye. "Making News by Doing Work: Routinizing the Unexpected." *American Journal of Sociology* 79 (July 1973), pp. 110–31.

———. *Making News.* New York: Free Press, 1978.

————. "Professionalism as an Agent of Legitimation." *Journal of Communication* 28(2) (Spring 1978), pp. 106–13.

Tunstall, Jeremy. *Journalists at Work*. Beverly Hills: Sage, 1971.

Turner, Victor. *The Ritual Process*. Ithaca, N.Y.: Cornell University Press, 1969.

Turow, Joseph. "Cultural Argumentation Through the Mass Media: A Framework for Organizational Research." *Communication* 8 (1985), pp. 139–64.

Weaver, David, and G. Cleveland Wilhoit. *The American Journalist*. Bloomington: Indiana University Press, 1986.

Weber, Max. *Max Weber: Selections in Translation*. Cambridge: Cambridge University Press, 1978.

White, Hayden. "The Value of Narrativity in the Representation of Reality." In *On Narrative*, ed. W.J.T. Mitchell, pp. 1–23. Chicago: University of Chicago Press, 1980.

————. "Historical Pluralism." *Critical Inquiry* 12 (Spring 1986), pp. 480–93.

————. "'Figuring the Nature of the Times Deceased': Literary Theory and Historical Writing." In *The Future of Literary Theory*, ed. Ralph Cohen, pp. 19–43. New York: Routledge, 1989.

Wolfe, Tom. *The New Journalism*. New York: Harper and Row, 1973.

Wuthnow, Robert, James Davison Hunter, Albert Bergesen, and Edith Kurzweil. *Cultural Analysis*. London: Routledge and Kegan Paul, 1984.

Zelizer, Barbie. "'Saying' as Collective Practice: Quoting and Differential Address in the News." *Text* 9(4) (1989), pp. 369–88.

————. "What's Rather Public about Dan Rather: TV Journalism and the Emergence of Celebrity." *Journal of Popular Film and Television* 17(2) (Summer 1989), pp. 74–80.

————. *"Covering the Body": The Kennedy Assassination and the Establishment of Journalistic Authority*. Ph.D. dissertation. University of Pennsylvania, 1990.

————. "Achieving Journalistic Authority Through Narrative." *Critical Studies in Mass Communication* 7 (1990), pp. 366–76.

————. "Where Is the Author in American TV News? On the Construction and Presentation of Proximity, Authorship and Journalistic Authority." *Semiotica* 80(1/2) (1990), pp. 37–48.

————. "CNN, the Gulf War, and Journalistic Practice." *Journal of Communication* 42(1) (Winter 1992), pp. 68–81.

————. "From the Body *as* Evidence to the Body *of* Evidence." In *Bodylore*, ed. Katharine Young. American Folklore Society, and University of Tennessee Press, in press.

————. "The Making of a Journalistic Celebrity, 1963." In *American Heroes in a Media Age*, ed. Robert Cathcart and Susan Drucker. Norwood, N.J.: Ablex, in press.

Zerubavel, Eviatar. *Hidden Rhythms*. Berkeley: University of California Press, 1981.

Index